BREAKING OPEN
JAPAN

Smithsonian Books

Collins
An *Imprint of* HarperCollins*Publishers*

BREAKING OPEN

JAPAN

Commodore Perry,

Lord Abe, and

American Imperialism

in 1853

George Feifer

Photographs & illustrations appearing in the chapter headings of this book are courtesy of: Preface—Library of Congress; Ch. 1, 3, & 6—Nagasaki Prefectural Art Museum*; Ch. 2—Okinawa Prefectural Library; Ch. 4, 5, 10, 11 & 14—Reprinted from Francis L. Hawks, *Narrative of the Expedition of an American Squadron to the China Seas and Japan* (Washington, D.C.: Beverley Tucker, Senate Printer, 1856–57); Ch. 7 & 15—Honolulu Academy of Arts, Gift of Mrs. Walter F. Dillingham, 1960; Ch. 8, 13, & 19—Anne S. K. Brown Military Collection, Brown University; Ch. 9—Abe Family*; Ch. 12—U.S. Army Center of Military History; Ch. 16—Brooklyn Museum of Art; Ch. 17—Chicago Historical Society; Ch. 18—Naval Historical Foundation; Afterword—Newport Historical Society (Perry) & Fukuyama Castle Museum (Abe)*

* Special thanks to the Japan National Tourist Organization (www.japantravelinfo .com) for assisting in obtaining images from these sources.

HarperCollins books may be purchased for educational, business, or sales promotional use. For information please write: Special Markets Department, HarperCollins Publishers, 10 East 53rd Street, New York, NY 10022.

Published 2006 in the United States of America by Smithsonian Books in association with HarperCollins Publishers.

Designed by Cassandra Pappas
Maps by Nick Springer

The Library of Congress Cataloging-in-Publication Data has been applied for.

ISBN-10: 0-06-088432-0
ISBN-13: 978-0-06-088432-1

06 07 08 09 10 WBC/QW 10 9 8 7 6 5 4 3 2 1

for *Beautiful Barbara*

with gratitude to Professors
Fred Notehelfer, Miwa Kimitada, Kishida Shyu,
Matsumoto Kenichi, Steve Rabson, Takara Kurayoshi,
Teruya Yoshihiko, and Yamaguchi Eitetsu,

and to

Abe Masamichi, Kishaba Shizuo, and
Roxbury, Connecticut's Minor Memorial Library,

and with
loud thanks to talented, assiduous Rob Cowley

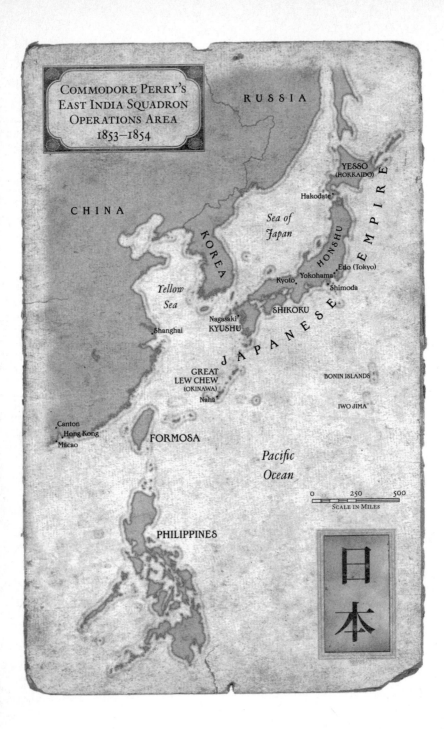

COMMODORE PERRY'S
EAST INDIA SQUADRON
OPERATIONS AREA
1853–1854

RUSSIA

CHINA

KOREA

Sea of
Japan

YESSO
(HOKKAIDO)

Hakodate

HONSHU

Edo (Tokyo)

Kyoto Yokohama
Shimoda

Yellow
Sea

Shanghai

Nagasaki
KYUSHU

SHIKOKU

JAPANESE EMPIRE

GREAT
LEW CHEW
(OKINAWA)

Naha

BONIN ISLANDS

IWO JIMA

Canton
Hong Kong
Macao

FORMOSA

Pacific
Ocean

0   250   500
SCALE IN MILES

PHILIPPINES

日
本

Edo.

Edo
Bay

Kanagawa

Yokohama

Area surveyed February – April 1854

"American Anchorage"

"Susquehanna Bay"

SARU SHIMA
("Perry Island")

Uraga

Kurihama

Area
Surveyed,
July 1853

Uraga Channel

CAPE SAGAMI

江戸湾

THE BLACK SHIPS IN
EDO (TOKYO) BAY
1853–1854

0   5   10
SCALE IN MILES

CONTENTS

PREFACE

American warship in Japanese Harbor, woodblock print

MAJOR HISTORICAL EVENTS NEED RETELLING every twenty-five years or so, an editor friend likes to say, usually without elaborating because he believes the reasons are self-evident. They were to me when he made them so. Even if fresh information about the events doesn't surface during those quarter centuries, younger generations view them with new attitudes, values, and general knowledge, especially about international conflicts. The cooling of passions and slackening of government spins enable more long-term consequences to emerge, including the un-intended ones. Later, I came across another way of saying that by Freder-ick Jackson Turner, an eminent historian of the American West: "Each age writes the history of the past anew with reference to the conditions upper-most in its own time."

Those observations much apply to the most important event in Japan's modern history. Commodore Matthew Calbraith Perry's opening of the long-isolated country caused much more conflict, if not armed, than most Americans suspect. And although Japan might seem to have less need of a new account because older ones proliferate there, their interpretations also changed with new eras, marked especially by gains in the self-esteem Perry damaged. America, by contrast—where all of two books about the seemingly remote event remain in print—has essentially assumed nothing new can be said about the gift to Japan, as it's overwhelmingly regarded, of Perry's expedition. Surely that's emblematic of our, generally speaking, costly lack of interest in history and popular ignorance of foreign percep-tions, although I was as ignorant as anyone about others' reaction to the 1853 mission before I stumbled upon hints of it.

Anyway, a good deal *is* new, even if also old as American history goes. Deeply moved by belief in their new republic's virtue and obligations, our great-great-grandfathers were resolved to bring freedom and democracy to a distant people whose inferiority they took for granted. Perry's unabash-edly imperialist vision was grounded in that certainty of our inherent good.

I SHOULD HAVE GUESSED the Commodore's heroic image never extended beyond America. Much of my adult life has been a lesson not to write about other people without trying to put myself in their shoes. Had I learned it, I might have known, for example, that whatever the feats and suffering of the Japanese and American forces during the Battle of Okinawa, about which I wrote a previous book, the struggle's most searing, longest-lasting aspect was the civilian tragedy. But I discovered that only when I visited the island, I thought mainly to see the lay of the battlefields. It took long, dismaying talks with civilian survivors to awaken me to what I'd have missed had I not seen their faces as their voices went directly into my ears and, yes, heart.

Okinawa was also where I heard my first hint of resentment of Perry. It was oblique because I'm American and Okinawans shy from offending; but the guarded dislike persisted when I prodded, and my navy years may have heightened my curiosity about the then minor mystery. What did the gentle islanders have against the Commodore of the mighty reputation? The answer was never stated outright, and Okinawan authorities continue to honor Perry despite his despicable behavior there.[1] Mainland Japanese sustain their substantial concealing and dissembling about him for somewhat different reasons, related, as the text will attempt to explain, to their proverbial and real discomfort in the presence of Westerners. However, I had great luck during my visits to Japan. A number of generous scholars, most of whom I'd traced from their writings or to whom I was introduced, dropped the psychological barriers and took me, I was convinced, into their confidence.

Their talk on their own patch, where they could be themselves, was what awakened me to how much Japanese views of Perry differ from conventional American wisdom and textbook explications. Mainland Japan also continues to honor Commodore Perry, but I believe the largest, most enduring consequence of his intrusion there is a predictable reaction to bullying. Where wouldn't inability to resist a diktat by military superiors cause anxiety and pain?

JAPANESE DOOMSAYERS' PREDICTION that submission to Perry would destroy their country's integrity and culture overstated the damage. Much push for progress, from personal to industrial, entered through the breach punched by the Commodore: good balm for the hurt. Women were permitted to climb Mount Fuji in 1860, seven years after his first landing. Some eight years later, men were given the right to choose their wives and occupations, and the first railroad, from Tokyo to Yokohama, began operating in 1872. Anyway, the opening was surely inevitable, soon to be forced by one country or another, in the same 1853 if a Russian squadron then headed for Japan with the same aim had succeeded.

But if the political, economic, and social consequences proved mixed, grave emotional ones underlay them. "For a century and a half now, America and Japan have formed one of the great and enduring alliances of modern times," a glittering Tokyo banquet was told in 2002, on the eve of the 150th anniversary of Perry's arrival. The usual Japanese reaction to such ignorance or insensitivity is silent resignation. That evening's luminaries masked their ridicule in order to spare not only the uncomprehending speaker, George W. Bush, but also the native guests, long practiced in bottling the anger that had been festering during the century and a half of the supposed alliance. Edwin O. Reischauer, a dean of American study of Japan and former ambassador to Tokyo, characterized the real relationship. "During the 20th century as a whole," Reischauer said a century after Perry's visit, "no country has more consistently regarded itself as in essential conflict with the United States than has Japan."

The South African writer Laurens van der Post thought he knew why: Europeans, with their "arrogant assumptions of superiority," had bent Asian "lives and spirits" to their inflexible will. Van der Post had good reason to reflect about that during World War II. Wasting away in a prisoner-of-war camp, he viewed the Japanese brutality as the proud people's delayed response to having been forced to live "a kind of tranced life" in the presence of Westerners who prevented them from being themselves. "In the open at last," their long-suppressed protest swept the normally disciplined people into "a chaotic mood of revenge."[2]

Did Perry's mission help ignite that appalling eruption? In 2003, Yokohama—into which Uraga, the Japanese town outside of which Perry's ships first anchored, had been incorporated—commemorated that 150th anniversary of their arrival. A Sunday parade charmed a forty-one-year-old American software engineer employed by a nearby U.S. naval base, but he had "no idea" what it was for. "Perry? He was an explorer, wasn't he? That's all I know."[3] Of course, he knew vastly more about December 7, 1941. Still living in infamy, the Pearl Harbor attack continued to prompt a Niagara of American memories on paper and celluloid, many in the tone of the commander of one of the demolished airfields: "To think that this bunch of little yellow bastards could do this to us when we all knew was that the United States was superior to Japan!" Still lacking any notion of why resentment had accumulated, the reaction of most Americans these sixty-five years later remains limited largely to outrage. The gaping perception gulf endures: in Japan, Pearl Harbor is scarcely mentioned and Perry's intrusion is treated as seminal. One of the most widely used high school textbooks devotes three lines to Pearl Harbor and three pages to the national metaphor of Perry's "Black Ships" and their seemingly black intent.

Of course, the disparate ratios are largely explained by whether the hit was to *us* or to *them*. Does a less subjective measurement exist? Four thousand Americans were killed or wounded at Pearl Harbor, most on the sunk or wrecked battleships, including the *Arizona*, where some thousand bodies remain unburied. However, America's rage and mobilization left it fundamentally unchanged, or maybe with an even fuller appreciation of itself. In Japan, the news of Perry's demands—which, in any case, the embarrassed government sought to conceal—spread more slowly without radio to broadcast it, but the shock was more severe and the country was soon hugely changed. The Black Ships' disruption of national thoughts and ways, perhaps the most traumatic to any culture ever, was followed by civil turmoil whose effect was incomparably greater and longer lasting than the damage of the 1941 sneak attack. And on some of it goes, including the comparison with the West that has dominated Japanese opinion of themselves ever since Perry.

More about Pearl Harbor's Perry connection follows, in its place in the narrative. Here I'll mention only that the attack had nearly universal support in Japan, despite, or because of, its potentially disastrous inferiority to the United States in size and wealth. The American power to intimidate and have its way had at last been challenged. A sense of everything having finally fallen into place uplifted the nation.

Some present-day students of the Japanese psyche attribute the joy to release from the pain of having been totally powerless to resist Perry. Throughout Japan's modern era that followed, people lived with "a sense of humiliation pushed somewhere deep in their mind": the undercurrent of a century of "continuous" affront, which Japanese also call their "hundred-year war" against Western imperialism. Determination to free themselves was what caused many Japanese to cheer themselves hoarse on that happiest of days in 1941 (December 8 in Japan).

> They felt the day of clearing their long-time grudges had finally arrived. The six months between this attack and the battle at Midway was the only time when they were happy, enjoying a relief from the sense of humiliation. And, this brief happiness was obtained in exchange for 3.1 million lives. It was a high price no matter how you cut it.[4]

That reading also misleads by ignoring Perry's positive contributions to Japan's development and oversimplifying its relationship to the U.S., which would have ups as well as downs, even intervals of apparent amity. Still, the Pearl Harbor news entered a distinguished novelist's room "like a shaft of light" and made him feel he was a new man, "cooled by the sacred breath of a deity [and] Japan had become a new country too."[5]

The jubilation uplifted even some whose knowledge of America's ten-to-one advantage in industrial strength warned them that the reckless, risk-all strike would prove extremely stupid, ending in *losing* all. They too cheered. "We'd done it at last; we'd landed a punch on those arrogant great powers Britain [whose Far Eastern Fleet was essentially destroyed three days after Pearl Harbor] and America, on those white fellows":

> All the feelings of inferiority of a colored people from a backward country towards white people from the developed world disappeared in that one blow. . . . Never in our history had we Japanese felt such pride in ourselves as a race as we did then.[6]

Until the Black Ships appeared, Japan considered America a lesser threat to its security than several European nations. Had the others succeeded, their demands might have been greater than Perry's. But the Lord of the Forbidden Interior, as some Japanese would call him, would be first to puncture their seclusion, and the past since then, to paraphrase William Faulkner, never died in their memory; their gall never passed.

A SMALL GLOSSARY of Japanese words and terms follows. Japanese names in the text are in their original order, family name first. Thus the chief protagonist of this story, Commodore Perry's opposite number in a way, is Abe Masahiro, Masahiro being his given name.

GLOSSARY

Bakufu: the Shogun's "tent" government; the national government; the shogunate

bakumatsu: the final years of the Tokugawa shogunate, ending in the Meiji Restoration of 1868

Edo: the Tokugawa Shoguns' capital city, renamed Tokyo in 1868

Edo Castle: the residence of the Shogun and center of his "tent government," or *bakufu*. Only some moats and ramparts survive from the very extensive complex of the mid-nineteenth century.

daimyo: literally "great name," the lord of a feudal domain, which he ruled with great latitude unless his decisions or actions provoked suspicions of disloyalty in Edo

Deshima Island: the dot of an artificial island just off Nagasaki, where the Dutch trading colony, or "factory," was confined

han: a fief of Japan's feudal clans, or a feudal domain, of which there were 260 when Perry landed

kaikoku: the national opening

Meiji Restoration: the name given to the events of 1868 that led to the "restoration" of the Emperor's power after the fall of the Tokugawa shogunate—specifically the Emperor Meiji ("enlightenment" or "age of brightness")—and to the great changes that are taken as the beginning of modern Japan

rangaku: "Dutch learning," based on materials imported by the Deshima colony. Scholars of Dutch studies were *rangakusha.*

ronin: masterless samurai

roju: an elder, one of the four or five highest-ranking posts in the shogunate. The term usually refers to the council as a whole.

sakoku: the seclusion policy, term used to connote Japan's national closing from roughly 1636 to 1853

Satsuma: the *han* of the Shimazu clan who occupied most of Kyushu, the southernmost of the main Japanese islands, closest to Okinawa, which it dominated

Shogun: short for *seii taishogun*, literally "commander in chief of the expeditionary forces against the barbarians," often shortened to "barbarian-subduing generalissimo." He was the head of the House of Tokugawa and ruler of feudal Japan's shogunate, or "tent government."

Tokugawa: the family of hereditary Shoguns who ruled Japan from 1603, when Tokugawa Ieyasu established the dynasty, to its collapse in 1867, fourteen years after Commodore Perry's first arrival

BREAKING OPEN
JAPAN

1

The Black Ships

A Black Ship in a woodblock print, ca. 1854

IN THE PREDAWN HOURS of July 14, 1853, the "Origin of the Sun," as Japan called itself, would have more honored the star for staying down. The darkness that hid the danger sustained the hope to which the secluded nation clung. Surely higher help would prevent the aliens from landing. Those "stupid and simple" people who came from the earth's "hindmost regions" were "incapable of doing good things," a prominent scholar had recently warned.

Some believed this last moment had been chosen for salvation. No one needed reminding that was when the previous rescue of rescues had come, heavenly protectors sending the Divine Winds that destroyed the foreign fleets of that living past. That was six centuries before, but its emotional significance remained largely intact. Since this was the land the divinities most cherished, their intervention by storm was logical and deserved.

A distinguished theologian had affirmed that law of the universe several decades earlier in this nineteenth century. "Ours is a splendid and blessed country, the Land of the Gods beyond doubt," he wrote with all the confidence of people who have visited no other. "Japanese differ completely from and are superior to the peoples of . . . all other countries in the world."

The superior people nevertheless trembled. "We're very, very afraid of foreign ships," the Shogun's most influential consort confided in 1846. "We have no idea what to do about them."

No idea, and the grave illness of the Shogun, the supreme military overlord, made the current emergency even more dire. As much as any one man—even the Shoguns themselves, when they were sound—could make the vital decisions for the labyrinthian government, responsibility had fallen to the invalid's Chief Senior Councilor, Abe Masahiro. Young as he was, Lord Abe had learned to negotiate the country's power mazes as well as anyone in living memory. The Councilor's mediating and manipulating skills well fit him to the complex domestic circumstances, and his training had been all the fuller for the Shogun's less-than-forceful leadership and protracted ailment. If this had been primarily a political matter, Abe might possibly have conceived rescue, despite feudal restraints on his freedom of action. But the struggle was almost entirely military, for which he was a sorry mismatch with the commander of the naval colossus confronting him from point-blank range. The mild-mannered lord was far from a military leader, and of a country that had become flabby for fighting, despite its reputation for the opposite.

Present events, the incapacitated Shogun is said to have despaired, were the most extraordinary since the beginning of heaven and earth. In distant Washington, which had sent the challenge, Secretary of State Daniel Webster pronounced it a "great national movement," one of the "most important ever." Not all Americans agreed. Some griped that it would be better to open America's West with good roads and services than to try to open Japan. The *Baltimore Sun* urged dumping the "humbug"; another newspaper disparaged the "romantic notion" that was of as much interest as a balloon soaring off "to one of the planets." While a senator denounced it as exercise for the bloated navy's unneeded ships, the *New York Times* warned that an armed force would probably "frighten the poor Japanese out of their . . . wits."[1] The fright, the paper predicted, might drive them to sign a treaty, but they will "feel at perfect liberty to violate [it] so soon as the vessels of war shall have been removed."

But many more Americans applauded the venture, even without swallowing Webster's "most important ever" hyperbole that had been adroitly aroused by Matthew Perry, the commander of the naval guns that were again becoming visible in July 14's approaching light.[2] It was hyperbole because bigger deals were happening elsewhere. Although Washington was here taking one of its earliest leads in world diplomacy, demonstrating a new willingness not to wait for European initiatives, it was only one of surging America's undertakings. A twentieth-century Tokyo scholar's view of the expedition as "a single step in the centuries-old march towards global colonial expansion"[3] rang of oversimplicity, but also of partial truth. The adventurous country that had recently completed its march to the Pacific was eagerly probing the opportunities beyond. And although the sparks it was winging toward Asia would soon dim at home, especially once obscured by the Civil War's flames, the conflagration they were about to light in Japan would continue blazing there, where the undertaking would be seen not as a new fling for American freedom and the happiness of prosperity, but as a terrible threat to security and independence.

From Edo Castle in particular, the seat of the Japanese government, the future wobbled. Of course Abe Masahiro betrayed no outward evidence of that. On the contrary, the cordial aristocrat radiated the serenity required of Japanese leaders. Slightly bulging his rich robes, the Chief Senior Councilor with the face a faithful retainer saw as "always lively, like spring" looked a little like a character from *The Tale of Genji*, the novel that describes court life and loves of the tenth and eleventh centuries. If he couldn't permit himself to tremble, his elegant nature rejected the swaggering affected by colleagues who wanted to attack the foreign squadron. Still, the government's de facto head had reason for profound anxiety, which would be the most enduring consequence of the impending clash of cultures and wills.[4]

At the moment, the dignitaries charged with preparing a satisfactory reply to Commodore Perry were producing mostly fury and confusion. Waiting in triple-tiered Edo Castle for developments beyond their control, some still hoped the foreigners would obey a command Abe had conveyed to them several days earlier: *"Leave immediately."* When the bluff fizzled, the tiny number who made Japan's political decisions could think of nothing else with which to counter the foreigners' threat.

Nor was heaven interceding. This time, the failure of miraculous salvation to materialize hardened the criticism of a handful of Japanese who had been chastising the government for inadequate preparation to defend their "little island with unprotected coasts," as one had recently written. "Only fools" would entrust a second rescue to heaven-sent wind that had destroyed the Mongol fleet.[5] But that rashness would earn the skeptic imprisonment, no doubt partly because he'd been right. Other critics were extremely few, even though no clouds were gathering to signal the arrival of fresh Divine Winds, *kamikaze*, that would blow away the new calamity. Nor were the gods otherwise intervening. In particular, the sun goddess Amaterasu, from whom the Emperor was believed to be directly descended, hadn't delayed the Earth's source of heat and light. Lustrous in that season, it rose on schedule and began burning off the haze over the normally placid bay.

THE BAY OF URAGA lies beside a town of the same name that controlled the entrance to far larger Edo—now Tokyo—Bay. Clutching an array of weapons and ceremonial colors, some five thousand warriors waited on the smaller bay's shore at dawn of that July 14. All were riveted by the source of their dread, now clearly discernible in the advancing morning light: four giant warships of America's East Asia Squadron.

Six days earlier, that bolt from the blue had sounded before it hit. Strange vibrations from across the waters off Honshu's Sagami Peninsula, where the squadron was making its way to Uraga, alarmed Japanese fishermen to the approach of something surely unnatural. Their astonishment swelled when the source of the throbbing was spied. The noisy monsters on the horizon were belching smoke. They were ablaze!

Shore-bound observers struggled to interpret more confounding evidence as it became visible. Two great frigates, with mysteriously churning paddle wheels, were making headway *against* the wind (each towing a sailing ship, the USS *Plymouth* and USS *Saratoga*). The beholders, none of whom had previously seen a steam-powered vessel, were dismayed even before making out their prodigious armament.[6] A handful of Japanese had previously caught sight of American whaling craft—a "staggeringly large apparition," one exclaimed, although it was far smaller than the fuming steamers now in sight. If the foreign whalers, displacing four or five times the largest native craft of 90-odd tons, were huge, the *Susquehanna*, Perry's recently launched 2,450-ton flagship, upped the multiple by another five times, making it more than *twenty* times larger. No one had imagined "veritable castles that moved freely on the water," as the magistrate of Uraga would call them.

Several "uncouth junks," as an American sailor saw Japanese fishing boats, hurried back to shore to sound an alarm, as if that weren't already being done on land. A man who ran up a mountain for a better look found an agitated crowd at the summit, trying to make sense of the distant fires until

> we found that what we'd taken for a conflagration on the sea was really black smoke rising out of [the ships'] smokestacks. When we came down, there was excitement all over town, and what with a report being dispatched to the government office at [the inland town of] Nirayama and special messengers being sent hurriedly up to Edo, there was a great uproar.[7]

A sentinel on Jogashima Island, just south of the peninsula, had also spotted the ships on the horizon. Soon looming "as large as mountains," they nevertheless moved "as swiftly as birds,"[8] their speed of eight or nine knots astounding defense personnel. Dashing up the Uraga Waterway, the ships ignored a large sign in French on a native boat: "Depart immediately and dare not anchor!"[9] Anchor is what they proceeded to do, obeying their commander's flag signal to form a line of battle outside the town and to conduct no communication whatever with the shore.

"ALL THE MESSENGERS SENT OUT from various lookout points are said to have arrived too late," a Japanese officer regretted. One of their dispatchers, a village magistrate, might have spoken for them all by describing himself as "filled with deep awe," no doubt more gripping because a folk song had long predicted an analogous catastrophe:

> Through a black night of cloud and rain,
> The Black Ship plies her way,
> An alien thing of evil mien,
> Across the waters gray.[10]

Although four ships rather than one had appeared, and in daylight rather than during a stormy night, the features by which all became instantly known—and would remain so, with the color's usual implication, to all schoolchildren since—were the black hulls and belching black smoke.* Lessons lingering from the Divine Winds' intervention deepened the distress. The foiled thirteenth-century threat had come in the form of two invasions by Kublai Khan, Emperor of China and of the Mongol empire. The grandson of the mighty conqueror Genghis Khan was seeking to further expand his vast dominion by subduing Japan and making it a tributary state—an ambition that figured in Europe's introduction to the country. When Marco Polo arrived in what's now called Beijing the following year, 1275, he heard excited talk in the Great Kublai Khan's court about beguiling islands located off China's east coast.[11] Marco Polo's was the West's first notice of Japan, under the name of Zipangu, otherwise spelled Chipangu and Jipango—"and what a very great Island it is!" he enthused. The first misinformation followed, featuring incredible riches, including an "endless" store of gold, "abundant beyond all measure." The Venetian explorer reported rumors that the Emperor's palace was "entirely roofed" with the precious metal, and its floors covered by slabs "a good two fingers thick"[12]—fantasies that would help lure Christopher Columbus from Spain two centuries later, in 1492.

Kublai Khan had sent ships transporting some 40,000 troops in 1274, but bad weather forced their withdrawal. Six years later, he made a second attempt, that one the largest invasion fleet hitherto assembled. Its 4,400 ships far surpassed the number in the Spanish Armada that would threaten

---

* They weren't, however, the *first* black ships, a label loosely applied to all Western ones because their hulls, unlike those from Asia, were painted black. The best known previous black vessels were large, highly profitable trading craft that annually plied between Nagasaki and Macao, a Portuguese colony on the Chinese coast more than 1,500 miles southwest.

England some three hundred years later, and their 140,000 or so warrior passengers matched it in might when they landed in 1281. The fierce attackers who shot their arrows twice as far as the defenders also employed novel explosives. Even more ruinous Mongol battle formations overpowered native samurai, whose honor required them to fight individually, in this case usually unto slaughter. But all that proved secondary, for confirmation was coming to the Japanese that what really mattered was spiritual strength, derived from their heavenly favor. After seven grueling weeks, when catastrophe seemed certain, the meteorological miracle literally saved the day. Hours after a massive appeal to Amaterasu, the Divine Winds smashed most of the invading fleet on coastal rocks, killing over 100,000 troops and giving victory to the worthy.

So taught the legend, which submerged examination of whether the Mongol attacks might have been beaten off without the aid of the hurricane or typhoon, as some recent research and even the earliest Japanese accounts seem to suggest.* Attributing the victory to gods committed to preserve sacred Japan was richer nourishment for the psyche. Their presumed intercession was a quintessential formative influence, becoming a leitmotif of many Japanese stories about the unique people's divine origins and favor. The country's fragmented state at the time—it was more a collection of warring principalities than a unified realm—further increased the importance of the *kamikaze* "proof" that prompted many to think of themselves as one people and nation for the first time. When Perry's squadron arrived, the belief had had more than two and a half centuries of isolation, equivalent to roughly thirteen generations, to harden into an article of faith.

THE BLACK SHIPS' AUDACITY mesmerized as much as their size. Apart from the rarest exceptions, no European had set foot in Japan for ages. Virtually all its people believed what they'd been taught to believe about the danger of contamination by lesser peoples. Although a few scholars, a larger number of merchants, and some feudal lords yearned for *more* contact with Westerners, the overwhelming majority wanted nothing less.

---

* The storms may have put the finishing touch on the crucial Mongol defeat, chiefly caused by Japanese defensive walls along the coast and by the Mongols' own failure to press advantages when they had them. See the description in *In Little Need of Divine Intervention*, a monograph by Tom Conlan of Bowdoin College, at www.einaudi.cornell.edu/eastasia/CEASbooks/item.asp?id=44.

Twenty-five years earlier, in 1818, a poet who was among a scattering that had laid eyes on Dutch ships described "huge cannon" relentlessly bellowing forth "their roar."

> The barbarian heart is hard to fathom; the [Japanese]
>   Throne ponders
> And dares not relax its armed defense.
> Alas, wretches, why come they to vex our anxious eyes,
> Pursuing countless miles in their greed. . . ?
> Crawling like gigantic ants after rancid meat.
> Do we not . . . trade our most lovely jewels for thorns?[13]

Japan wasn't *totally* sealed; neighboring Korea, which had closed its borders in an attempt to exclude almost all foreigners, was closer to a true "Hermit Kingdom," as it was called.[14] Chinese and Korean traders visited Japan regularly, and a few Western vessels—all Dutch—were actually permitted to land at Nagasaki, far south on the opposite coast from Edo, almost as distant from the capital as possible. Those sailing ships were bad enough, but these new black ones, whose brazen crews could now be seen preparing to launch boats for an actual landing, were of another order entirely, seen as a threat to the essence of Japanese society and culture. Many wondered whether their country would survive.

How could the American intention have been so misconstrued? The President who had dispatched the squadron was eager to assure Japan of its friendly intentions. "The constitution and laws of the United States," Millard Fillmore had written in a letter being prepared for delivery that very morning, "forbid all interference with the religious and political concerns of other nations." The essentially unmilitaristic Fillmore had "particularly charged" Commander Perry "to abstain from every act which could possibly disturb the tranquility" of the Japanese Emperor's dominion.

But such statements would have mystified rather than comforted the onlookers, or convinced them that American duplicity was as mighty as its warships—which, in turn, would have confounded all but a handful of the squadron's crews. Unaware of the Japanese abhorrence of dishonor, the thousand-odd Americans did know that their commander had instructed, in his rock-certain way, that they'd made their hard voyage in order to *protect* Japan. All also knew their own hearts were as free of political evil as the wholesome American spirit in general; that they were agents of *good*. "Truly, we may say that God has gone before and prepared our way among this [Japanese] people," rejoiced a missionary in China now serving as a translator for the expedition. "And I hope it is to be for their lasting benefit too."

Didn't Christianity extol peace on Earth? Wasn't that promise, as revolutionary in its time as the New World's great republic was now politically revolutionary, universal? Perry's crews in particular had no desire for conquest, let alone destruction; only for progress. Its great wheel, whose workings Americans had reason to believe they knew better than most, had to keep turning. A politically typical sailor who hoped blood wasn't about to be shed would write that "the sleeping empire"—"aloof from the world, shut in within itself, utterly severed from general world-consciousness"—would soon take advantage of brilliant opportunities, thanks to Perry's awakening.[15]

The crews' own heavenly inspiration blostered them as they made final preparations for the encounter on land. During their eight months at sea, their rest had come only on its day, which also imparted spiritual sustenance and strength. The Sunday worship of prayers, psalms, and sermons had been punctuated by a chorus of throaty song, accompanied by military bands on the larger ships:

> Before Jehovah's aweful throne
> Ye nations, bow with sacred joy

"Thus a small group of brave men congregate for an utterly simple service amid a wide ocean," observed an artist employed to capture images of the long voyage to little-known Asia. "They commend themselves to the protection of their Creator; the scene—gripping, stirring, profound in effect—must move the heart to reverence."[16]

The wide ocean was also deep with difficulties. The unreliability of early steam engines and difficulty of procuring coal had combined with oppressive heat and fickle winds to deal the ships many problems during their sailing and steaming more than halfway around the world—down the Atlantic, around the Cape of Good Hope, through the Indian Ocean to Singapore, Hong Kong, and Shanghai, and finally to here, via Okinawa, the main island of the Ryukyu Kingdom. The commander had taken uncommon pains to preserve his crews' physical welfare, but also worked them hard. Still, the reward was finally in sight. Of all the good the Americans wanted to share, their religion was highest. Before their departure, the Secretary of the Navy had reminded the squadron commander of a need to awaken the Japanese government to "its Christian obligation to join the family of Christendom." The prospect of participation in that enlightenment buoyed the weary seamen who were so far from home on that humid make-or-break morning for the difficult enterprise.

Some 400 men were making ready to serve in the landing party: a "formidable escort . . . all well armed and equipped," the commander would report. With his practical experience of designing and producing ordnance and of dealing with economically less developed peoples, the distinguished flag officer was helping cultivate the heavy reliance on massive advantage in weaponry and military materiel that would become an American trademark. Strong aversion to leaving anything to chance had prompted him to triple the watches during the days and nights at anchor off Uraga, convincing a veteran sailor that "a more vigilant watch has rarely been kept . . . than on board that fleet." Now the commander supervised the taking of, he specified, "every precaution" for the landing, including preparing the ships' guns to "send their balls and shells in showers upon all the line of Japanese troops which thronged at the shore, had they commenced hostilities" and placing howitzers in the landing boats "in readiness to be dispatched at a moment's notice" in case of any trouble.[17]

Lack of wind prevented the two sail-powered sloops of war from moving to positions commanding the site, but the frigates prepared to weigh anchor just before eight o'clock.

THE CONTRASTS BETWEEN the impatient young nation represented by the Black Ships and the ancient realm of their port of call would affect their new relationship more than the ten thousand miles separating them. "Poor, proud and afraid" Japan, a keen student of the country would reflect, was "about as different as a society can be from plebeian, acquisitive, overconfident America." Actually, Japan wasn't poor by Asian standards and even some Western ones. (Its extreme poverty in the natural resources needed for industry—apart from coal—would be discovered only when its industrialization began, in Perry's wake.) And although the great majority of Americans then were indeed plain and humble, that wasn't true of the squadron's ranking officers. Nor was their commander notably less proud than the samurai the commentator obviously had in mind. That mattered because Matthew Calbraith Perry's personality and attitudes stamped the mission hard, as his name would forever label it.

Perry hadn't sought the demanding assignment. The veteran of four-plus decades that had earned him enviable esteem but bad health and relatively limited means would have preferred the more prestigious command of the Mediterranean squadron, which would also have given him a little luxury after his trying foreign tours, the reward including the company of his devoted wife of 39 years. Still, it was his own cause he took up when he was appointed to lead the present operation. He'd been urging Washington to do something about Japan for years.[18]

Soon he was choosing close friends for his top subordinates and defining the mission even more than most captains set the tone of their ships—which was more, in turn, than in almost all land commands.[19] Even he, easily annoyed by restrictions on his judgment, was pleased with the authority and power entrusted to him by the Secretaries of State and the Navy, supported by the President. After he drafted their orders to him, a severe illness of the Secretary of State in particular ensured their approval virtually without change. In the end, his authority and license, he wrote a brother soon after his appointment in January 1852, "far exceed[ed] any that have hitherto been issued to any one [meaning any American]. No officer & perhaps no individual has before been entrusted with such extraordinary power." It was the power to treat not only with the Emperor of Japan "without limitation," but also "any other nations" with which the United States was not yet "in diplomatic intercourse—these extraordinary powers only admonish me to exercise still greater prudence & discretion."[20]

New self-confidence bolstered Perry's unwillingness to tolerate deviation from the orders he barked, which were said to drown out storms; not that he needed full volume on that climatically calm morning of July 14. He instructed his officers to don their dress uniforms for "the day appointed for my reception on shore." All hoped he'd select them for the landing party. Even the few who felt it was more accurate to call him despotic than self-confident acknowledged it was *his* venture in every way, unlikely to have been launched then or to have come that far without his combination of qualities.

So it would be right to consider the mission *his*, even if he didn't increasingly call it "my." The entire squadron saw the "big, dark, unsmiling man with a double chin that puffed over the gold of his high naval collar" as the "leader, inspirer, diplomat, treaty-maker," in the words of one of his clerks. The difficulty of communicating with Washington helped make him the mission's sole real arbiter of right and wrong.

And the two societies were indeed very different. Restrained by prototypes developed during some twenty-five centuries, Japan was a twenty-fifth the size of the sixty-four-year-old republic confronting it.* Since crowded countries tend to prize order and accord—which are also essential for cultivating rice—more than those blessed and burdened by wide-open spaces, the Japanese commitment to *wa* (harmony) may have been as "natural" as the American encouragement of individual ambition.[21] The notion that the general welfare is best assured by every individual being free to race off in his and her chosen direction would have contributed little to the harmony supposedly achieved by everyone knowing his and her place: Confucianism's bedrock.

Although Japanese devotion to the group is sometimes exaggerated and far from every American was a rugged individualist, majority inclinations differed correspondingly. While striving for advancement and acquisition stoked the American work ethic, the Japanese, resting in devotion to groups, placed high value on loyalty and obedience and usually disapproved of open pursuit of personal gain. Thus "The nail that sticks up will be hammered down," a proverbial warning against open display of individual aspiration and even opinion, as opposed to the encouragement of self-assertion in America's "The squeaking wheel gets the grease."

Mirroring and widening that contrast, American speech, even when hypocritical or mendacious, was unusually direct, while Japanese was full of euphemisms and silences. Explaining to Perry that Japanese people didn't come to the point as directly as Americans, one of Edo Castle's negotiators for the forthcoming treaty between the two countries would use an example of a gathering of men who wanted to visit the anchored American ships.

---

* The total land area was roughly one and a half times Britain's, but far less was useable. Mostly mountainous Japan's habitable 18 percent of its territory was roughly the size of the future state of Montana. Again, geography—now in a constricted territory as opposed to a frontier perceived as limitless—surely helped shape the very dissimilar philosophies and attitudes. They extended to the high Japanese value placed on remaining on the plot and in the house of their birth as opposed to the American tendency to pick up and move, with or without the family. If Japanese people believed they were essentially links in an unbroken flow of life, many Americans, having made a leap from the land of their roots, felt an urge to *keep going*.

One might start with a comment about the beauty of the morning, prompting a second to remark how pleasant the season was, and a third to observe that not a wave could be seen on the water. Only then might a fourth propose visiting the ships.

That circumspection would increase the difficulty of Lord Abe's attempts to deal with Commodore Perry's challenge, and so would the related Japanese reluctance to reveal the inner self. While many Americans felt virtually compelled to let intimate thoughts hang out, it was Japanese wisdom to conceal them, especially when they were prompted by disagreement with others. A very early European visitor found that extended even to trying to prevent others from *guessing* private emotions.[22] Few Western visitors, then or later, were adept at reading the body language and other nonverbal signals with which the Japanese often communicated. The hardiness of those tendencies showed itself in a twentieth-century anecdote. "You don't talk enough," says an American businessman disconcerted by a Japanese counterpart's long silences. "You talk too much," replies the latter.

In Perry's day too, Japanese might have added that Americans too openly strived for individual gain, in violation of the Confucian pattern of hierarchy that fixed people's stations and discouraged challenge to authority. That spurred the West, where myriad interests were pursuing the benefits of its recent industrial revolution, to become much more productive, especially of coal-fired manufactures. And for the moment, as with most in history, ascendancy was swinging hard toward the people with the greater material punch. "Young America, throbbing with expansive forces," cheered a recent immigrant now serving in Perry's squadron. A U.S. Senator's almost simultaneous declaration back in the thirty-one states was more pointed. "You may make as many treaties as you please to fetter the limbs of this giant republic, and she will burst them all from her, and her course will be onward to a limit which I will not venture to prescribe."[23]

Despite the exceptions among the roughly twenty-five million Japanese and slightly fewer Americans in 1853, the poet A. C. Benson's "strong beat the [Western] world's wild heart" while Japan stood "self-centred, mute, apart" expressed a general truth.[24] Even shared qualities encompassed profound differences. If Japanese and American certainty of being uniquely virtuous was no greater than the norm, both peoples were uncommonly loud about it, as if needing to prove something to themselves as well as to others. The Japanese took immense pride in alone being ruled by descendants of the sun goddess. A fourteenth-century declaration that "Nothing similar may be found in foreign lands. . . . That is why it is called the divine country" was still often proclaimed—and matched by Americans' belief in *their* singular place in the sun, fixed by a higher power that assigned *them* a unique mission to prosper and enlighten. With slight tweaking, Americans might have taken a nineteenth-century Japanese poem about "the sublime spirit of the universe" that "gathers pure over this Land of the Gods" for their own.★

But the composition of the peoples who felt so chosen—in the American case, also loved—was very different. In Japan, the melting pot "never needed to be turned on," as an historian put it, for the country's minorities were a relatively tiny percent of its population. At the same time, Americans, already of many ethnic kinds, thought of building the world's only universal nation. No doubt those divergences helped shape the qualities that distinguished Matthew Perry from Abe Masahiro. Of course circumstances too played a part in that difference, since Perry would be the imminent drama's powerful actor, while cautious Abe could only react. But the most crucial difference may have derived from something deeper. Although both peoples were indeed convinced they were favored by heaven, most Americans believed their ways should be exported. "American principles, American policies . . . are also the principles and policies of forward-looking men and women everywhere, of every modern nation of every enlightened community," President Woodrow Wilson would exult in 1917. "They are the principles of mankind, and must prevail." But while the notion bloomed that the entire human race was potentially American, most Japanese were convinced their unique blessings were for them alone.

AN OBSERVER WHO KNEW NOTHING about the contrasts would have seen hints of them in the bearing of those preparing to participate in the morning's confrontation: the exhilarated go-getters on the ships and the

---

★ "Divine Task!" exulted an American expansionist of Perry's day named William Gilpin. "Immortal mission! . . . Let every American heart . . . glow undimmed, and confide with religious faith in the sublime destiny of his well-loved country." Gilpin, a lawyer and newspaper editor who served with distinction in the Mexican War, believed America's role was to "change darkness into light and confirm the destiny of the human race." See footnote, p.186.

anxious watchers on land. One of the former called the undertaking "more than an expedition, it is an adventure"—and also, unapologetically, an "attack upon Japan."[25] During those previous nights when the ships rode at anchor with their tripled watches, an officer enjoyed the "marvelous" view of a shore ornamented by signal and sentry fires burning "everywhere on the hills." Often moving from place to place in the hamlets, villages, and forts that dotted the coast, the fires looked "like swarms of fireflies."[26] A bell's regular ringing during the nights also appealed to the crews. Its deep, rich tone interrupted sounds of frantic Japanese carpentry attempting to reinforce the defensive positions along the shore.

Even now, in the critical morning's waxing light, the visitors from the other side of the globe were confident enough to be enchanted by the "exceedingly picturesque and beautiful" shore and "fair, smiling landscape" toward which they were preparing to row. The bluffs were "lofty," the green was "brightest and freshest." A world traveler aboard the *Susquehanna* saw "the charming panorama" as far surpassing his expectation of Japanese scenery.

Commodore Perry was also moved by "deep ravines, green with rich verdure" that "opened into small expanses of alluvial land, washed by the water of the bay into the form of inlets bordered by villages." Cultivated fields and tufted woods embellished the handsome uplands too, "while far behind rose the mountains, height upon height."[27] Mount Fuji, the highest, was visible at a distance of some sixty miles. An early American visitor to the just-opened country would pronounce the "Matchless Mountain," still standing solitary and august in the distant plain from which it had sprung twenty-one centuries earlier, "the most beautiful sight in Japan" and "certainly one of the most beautiful in the world."[28] That morning, however, those who most cherished its sacred white cone could draw no comfort from the lofty guarantor of national pride and security: bound to the spectacle of the foreign ships, their backs faced inland.

Would the aliens really land? Would the gods permit them? No inhabitant of Japan then living or since born would forget how the country's opening, now about to begin after the prolonged effort to surpress even the thought, would happen. Few Americans of the time, not to mention later, would pause to consider the effect on a proud people jostled by force.

2

The Opening and the Closing

Western Ships in Okinawan Waters

J APAN'S FIRST WESTERN VISITORS arrived three centuries before Perry. The soundest of the several stories about them is that
they were Portuguese merchants bound for Macao on a Chinese junk
that put in at an island named Tanegashima, after a typhoon blew it off
course in 1542 or 1543.[1] Asian traders regularly landed on that island just
below Kyushu and some 150 miles south of Nagasaki, but no previous foreigners looked or smelled like the beefy Europeans who came ashore from
the junk. Nevertheless, officials greeted them cordially and the people

were eager to trade. Those arrivals and later ones moved freely about the country, whose closing wouldn't begin for almost seventy-five years.

Native fancy for Portuguese clothes and jewelry went beyond a frivolous craze when the Shogun tried on a few outfits and some of his retainers took to wearing Christian crosses. The Portuguese merchants did well, although potential Japanese customers showed little interest in the trinkets their fellows had been selling to less developed Asian peoples. But they were keen to learn about all things foreign—"very unlike the haughty Chinese," as a historian would put it[2]—and they appreciated the better goods, especially mechanical ones.

China's restrictions on foreign trade made Japan all the more attractive to Western merchants. Portuguese trading stations were followed by Spanish, then Dutch and English, all invited. Good money was made and trusting relationships established, even if some natives whispered that Westerners practiced black magic and both parties were more interested in the others' products than their thinking. Nevertheless, both were also generally content with the intercourse. Unusual as it was in Asia, some Japanese invited visitors home for eating, drinking, and passing an occasional night.

The trouble for Edo was that souls were also being corrupted. So it came to be seen before the end of the sixteenth century.

JAPAN HAD LONG BEEN OPEN TO, even hungry for, new ideas from abroad. The attribution of that appetite by some modern Japanese scholars to uncommon curiosity is a matter of opinion, but heavy borrowing from China several centuries earlier is fact.[3] Arriving in waves, Chinese culture washed in much of what would later be taken as the best of Japan's own intrinsic virtues.[4] (Its adept imitating and wholesale borrowing, including of the word *shogun*, prompted some Chinese to call Japan "Monkey Island.") Most of the ruling class was raised largely on Chinese thought, which included a certainty that Chinese civilization was superior to all others. Otherwise, inquisitive Japan accepted many beliefs from abroad.

Paradoxically or inevitably, the susceptibility to foreign influence would help stiffen later resolve to extirpate Western theology. But now the country was open to religious as well as other thought. Shintoism, the indigenous religion whose doctrine was largely about being at one with nature and whose bows to the Emperor came from belief that he was descended from the sun goddess, developed in the fourth century BCE. Later, Buddhism was borrowed from India—via China and Korea—and Confucianism came with the great influx of Chinese thought. Now it would be Christianity's turn to prosper. An estimated 150,000 people embraced the European faith during the forty years following its introduction, soon after the storm-lashed Chinese junk took refuge at Tanegashima. The two hundred churches that served that relatively large flock would double in number during the next few decades, partly because professing Western convictions was thought to enhance opportunities to connect with Western traders. Several of the feudal lords most eager for that trade ordered their subjects to be baptized.

The conversions were performed by Portuguese and, later, Spanish missionaries, chiefly Jesuit at the start. The first, an unusually energetic and resourceful priest named Francis Xavier, arrived in 1549, seven years after his pioneering countrymen. Like them, he found the Japanese, including peasants, impressively accomplished, with high intelligence and excellent manners. No doubt swayed by their wonderful openness to the true Catholic faith, one called them "superior not only to other Eastern peoples but also to Europeans as well." The converts, in turn, much admired the Jesuits' intelligence and courage.

They were extraordinarily successful, especially Father Xavier, who would be canonized some seventy years later. During that time of fervent devotion in the West—and of savage Catholic–Protestant rivalry to sustain the Reformation or repair what Catholics saw as its "ravages"—proselytizing was passionate, militant, and massive. Oda Nobunaga, Japan's most prominent leader, permitted the campaign, one of history's most ambitious; even favored it with generous concessions. Oda's successor, a great military commander named Toyotomi Hideyoshi, also sanctioned the conversions, and things continued going so well that the Society of Jesus was given responsibility for administrating Nagasaki from 1580 to 1587. In 1582, four Japanese Christian boys charmed European courts on their way to an audience with Pope Gregory XIII. Then Toyotomi ordered all missionaries expelled.

Christian arrogance figured in that abrupt reversal. For all of Francis Xavier's "apostolic greatness," in an admirer's phrase, he made no effort to understand the religions that were in place when he arrived. Even where they resembled his, the same admirer regretted, the soon-to-be saint saw them as Satan's work, to be "overthrown without compromise or sympathy."

Still, the Church rose and fell largely at the convenience of the Japanese rulers. Oda Nobunaga and Toyotomi Hideyoshi, whose struggles were partly against armed Buddhist monasteries and lay orders, used Christianity to help acquire the money (through trade) and weapons that enabled them to win their battles, but they and their successors had no reason to continue tolerating it after they'd triumphed. Their subsequent insecurity—the ultimate concern of all Japanese leaders then and later—became the primary cause of Christianity's setback. Predictably, Toyotomi thought less about God than about his possible rivals. He had never enjoyed more than shaky control of the country's feudal domains, especially in the southwest, where the Portuguese first landed and missionary work was most successful. Some of the domains whose loyalty he suspected had close ties with Jesuit leaders, and the profits of foreign trade strengthened them, too; those lords he regarded as potentially rebellious. He underlined his suspicion about threats to his position by having some foreign and Japanese Christians crucified.

But the movement was far from extinguished when Toyotomi died eleven years later. Conversions continued, partly because his expulsion order wasn't enforced. The ardent Church was even more encouraged by the attitudes of his eventual successor, a masterful warrior-statesman named Tokugawa Ieyasu. But although Tokugawa much fancied the benefits of foreign trade and was generally tolerant of the religion associated with it, he too began seeing danger in the Church, all the more because its influence remained greatest where opposition to him was strongest. That was still in the distant southwestern regions, centered by the excellent natural harbor of Nagasaki, which had become the Westerners' principal port.

Astute, farsighted Tokugawa, who had previously supported trips abroad for expanding Japanese knowledge and trade, was moved by more than paranoia. It was an article of faith among Europeans that trade would benefit Japan with new ideas in general and the right religious ones in particular: Christian, of course. Echoing the sixteenth-century Western confidence, Perry's missionary translator predicted that "With the [commercial] goods, the civilization and Christianity of foreign nations will extend."[5] More imaginative American religious leaders visualized merchants "opening a highway for the chariot of the Lord Jesus Christ."

Such chariots seemed ever less innocent to Tokugawa Ieyasu's entourage. In some ways, the charioteers were positively provocative. Although the Jesuits and others took pains to conceal their more audacious political and economic maneuvering, they felt no need to mask their certainty that their higher purpose of Christian triumph would be fulfilled. Even if that wasn't fully known in Edo, or not taken seriously, it swelled a growing sense of threat. "False religions delude the land with a ceaseless clamor," warned an outspoken feudal lord of the time. "I would strike the barbarian tribes, but the time comes not."[6]

If Western conspiracy couldn't be proved, its smell hung in the air—and was fanned by Buddhist officials who, with considerable justification, regarded the zealous missionaries as their enemies. It came partly from open flouting of the government's relatively mild attempts to regulate the missions and from its suspicion of Jesuit involvement in the foreign trade, some of whose profits went to support of their seminaries. Business scandals, alleged criminal connections, and court intrigues of lords known to be, or suspected of being, Christian were more alarming.[7] Soundings and surveys by European ships added additional whiffs of malicious intent, especially after an English pilot deepened the alarm by remarking that Europeans would have seen such actions as preparation for invasion.

Edo perceived a serious threat to the Japanese social order. Confucian doctrine, Toyotomi had written, established "our relationships between sovereign and minister, parent and child, and husband and wife." But Christian priests, in their "ignorance of right and wrong," were challenging the eternal truths with their "unreasonable and wanton doctrines." The Christian belief that spiritual authority, in the persons of bishops and priests, deserved higher obedience than secular, represented by the feudal lords, increased the government's insecurity. Its first concern was protecting its power; its first requirement was fealty. "In the final analysis, it was the conflict of loyalties"—to the Shogun or to a Christian God—"that sealed the fate of the missionaries."[8]

Japanese distrust of their purpose would never fully subside. One of the most effective ways to silence political enemies was to accuse them of Christian belief. In Perry's day, two centuries plus after the closing, a philosopher named Aizawa Seishisai warned that the militaristic West began subjugating others with commerce and probing for weakness. The barbarians "preach their alien religion to captivate the people's hearts," often with kindness. Once a shift of allegiance opens them to manipulation, traitors multiply and "nothing can be done to stop it."

The church-trade-war mixture that helped establish Western bases in Goa, Macao, and Malacca makes it harder to dismiss Japanese fifth-column suspicions about missionary activity in their homeland. But what real evidence, if any, supported it when the Church was flourishing under Tokugawa Ieyasu? The handsome profit generated by some foreign trade dragged a number of bishops into the way of the world. To enrich the Church and/or themselves, a few engaged in bribery and chicanery in collaboration with converted feudal lords. Some of it was in pursuit of ascendancy in the sporadically vicious conflicts—into which Tokugawa Ieyasu sometimes found himself drawn—between Jesuits and, later, the Franciscans, followed by Protestants who arrived in Dutch and English ships. Some skulduggery was committed in the name of God—a God whose servants, unlike those of the earlier adopted religions, took an active role in world affairs.

No stranger to stratagem and scheming, Tokugawa believed something much more ominous was afoot: that the arrival of the priests, as advisors warned, would soon be followed by that of the conquistadores. A Spanish sea captain's boast that it would happen in Japan as it had in the (conquered) Philippines hardly soothed that fear.* Nor did the fact that some Christian converts were among a group of lords who were seeking to overthrow him from their headquarters in heavily fortified Osaka Castle. For above all, it was fear of foreign military help for disloyal domains plotting revolt that prompted the Shogun and his heirs to think of closing the nation. The ruling Tokugawa house did not feel strong enough to tolerate that risk.

Osaka's open opposition to Tokugawa Ieyasu surfaced in 1613. During the same year, twenty-seven Japanese Christians in Edo, also acting openly, defied the prohibition against celebrating Mass. Tokugawa had them executed and proceeded to launch a vigorous campaign against the entire

---

* Some accounts attribute the very cautionary lesson, as the Japanese had to see it, to a Spanish pilot who showed a map of the world dotted with Spanish colonies as a warning not to mess with mighty Spain. But how, asked guards who had been sent to seize his ship, did Spain acquire so much territory abroad? The pilot reportedly answered that missionaries sent to countries marked for conquering induced people to embrace Christianity. "And when they have made considerable progress, troops are sent" to combine with them, making the rest doable with "not much trouble." John Roberson, *Japan: From Shogun to Sony* 1543–1984, p. 34.

movement. In 1615, members of the four nationalities that until then had enjoyed free movement were confined to designated areas. Dutch and English citizens were ordered not to leave the little port of Hirado, near Kyushu's easternmost tip. Portuguese and Spanish, offspring of the "southern barbarians," were required to stay within the city limits of nearby Nagasaki, which was much larger but nearly as far from Edo as possible. From there, far south on Kyushu's west coast, it took at least a week to travel the eight-hundred-odd miles overland to the capital on Honshu's east coast. Trouble could probably be stopped on the way.

TOKUGAWA BANNED "PERNICIOUS, most undesirable" Christianity and ordered the expulsion of all foreign priests, then numbering some one hundred and fifty. Trade, however, was something else. "As years and months pass," it could be carried on "in all sorts of articles," and those who didn't "disturb Buddhism" could continue to travel freely. But when his forces finally breached the walls of Osaka Castle in 1615 and found Jesuits within, Christians were among the thousands immediately executed. Nevertheless, the converts continued growing in number. Many were ministered to by priests who committed the "pious fraud" of pretending to leave the country as ordered but actually going into hiding. Others joined them from ships that were supposedly bearing them away forever, but who returned from boats once the ships were out of sight from the coast. The returnees succeeded in reestablishing themselves because the banning orders were again halfheartedly enforced until Tokugawa Ieyasu's death in 1616.

The relative laxness continued seven more years under his son, who closely followed Ieyasu's lead with respect to the Church, apart from ordering Japanese believers to renounce their faith or face death. But the persecution of priests, such as two decapitated in Nagasaki as a warning to others, remained selective, and the attraction of martyrdom, at least as powerful in Japan as elsewhere, sometimes produced a reverse effect. The Church's growing numbers and influence increasingly disturbed Edo Castle, which was ever more certain foreigners were using them as a wedge being driven into the land to prepare it for invasion. The crackdown began in earnest when Tokugawa Ieyasu's son stepped down in favor of *his* possibly pathological son, who initiated one of the fiercest religious persecutions until that time.

The third hereditary Tokugawa Shogun sanctioned the use of a variety of hideous tortures to force Christians to repudiate their faith. Some five hundred who refused were executed in 1623, the year he became Shogun, compared to sixteen Jesuit priests killed during his father's entire reign. The recantation campaign was particularly severe in and around Nagasaki, where the evangelical effort had been most successful, but it failed to have the effect Edo desired. Some officials attributed the Christians' capacity for enduring pain and suffering death to the alien religion, not the Japanese character. "In order to imitate Jesus Christ who died crucified between two thieves," wrote one, "the Christians glory in dying such a death, and for such a cause; hence they are a fanatical and pernicious sect, dangerous to the Empire."[9] Either way, the number of converts kept climbing toward a peak of some 750,000, roughly 10 percent of the population, reached during the following decade. Brave European priests kept arriving, although the English traders, having seen the writing on the wall, departed in the same 1623 and Spanish ones were expelled a year later.

Then came the decision that would drastically affect Japan's development during the coming centuries. It would account for the country's singular image, based on perceived fundamental differences from others—although some continental Asian kingdoms were similarly inclined to bar Westerners. That historic decision was the *sakoku*, a term later coined for the closing. Fearful of the remarkably persistent Christianity, the Shogun resolved to keep priests out once and for all by preventing the arrival of the vessels that brought them. Chinese ships could keep entering, since none had ever brought a priest. Dutch ships too because Holland was seen as an unassertive trading country that otherwise minded its own business; so far their ships had transported traders only, interested in commerce but not religion. However, all others were now banned. In particular, any Portuguese ship that entered a native port was to be destroyed.

The hardest hitting of five Exclusion Acts, as the *sakoku* decrees would later be known, were issued in 1636. Probably because the seclusion was originally from missionary activity rather than from the world, not all were clear about precisely what was and wasn't prohibited, including what people. Promulgated after other Westerners had already left the country, the edicts were originally intended to keep out the Catholic Portuguese. But time and interpretation extended them to all foreigners, apart from the Dutch, Chinese, and Koreans. Together the acts forbade Japanese, on pain of beheading, from leaving the country and, lest more alien ideas be imported, those who were abroad from returning.* The possibility of foreign travel was all but eliminated by prohibiting the building of vessels large enough to leave home waters. Persecution of scholars who'd worked with Western materials made some cautious about talking about foreign countries, not to mention talking to foreigners themselves.

Checks and patrols reinforced the edicts. Japanese seamen were outlawed from working on foreign ships, which many had been doing. No more than a handful of Westerners were permitted to remain in residence—on a dot of an island off Nagasaki.[10] Forbidden to visit anywhere else, they were also proscribed from learning the language, obtaining many kinds of information about the country, and acquiring maps. When an island resident did procure an important map almost two centuries later—a prize Perry would put to good use—he was expelled and the corpse of the Japanese supplier, who had died in prison, was beheaded.[11]

But Christianity's large beachhead still didn't shrink in numbers or influence. On the contrary, the new persecution further energized many believers. When thousands of peasants from the Shimabara Peninsula and nearby islands in Nagasaki Bay rebelled in 1637, the Christians among them, seemingly inured to adversity, carried crosses and laced their battle cries with calls to Jesus and Mary. That encouraged Edo to see the action as religious insurrection, even though many participants had other motives: the peninsula's lord had exploited his people, baptized and not, to an unusual degree. The rebels seized a castle and held out there, with their women and children, until their food and ammunition were exhausted almost four months later. The battle's final two days resulted in nearly 11,000 beheadings. Some 20,000 chose death by fire over surrender, and when shogunate forces finally broke through, they left but a hundred alive.

A new edict of the sadistic Shogun was displayed above the corpses of the dead, estimates of which ranged to 37,000:[12] So LONG AS THE SUN

---

* "No Japanese ship or boat whatever, nor any native of Japan, shall presume to go out of the country," read the pronouncement. "Whoso acts contrary to this shall die. . . . All Japanese who return from abroad shall be put to death." Katherine Plummer, *The Shogun's Reluctant Ambassadors*, p. 1.

SHALL WARM THE EARTH, LET NO CHRISTIAN BE SO BOLD AS TO COME TO JAPAN. Anyone who violated the command—be it the king of Spain, the Christian God, or "the Great God of all"—would "pay for it with his head."

That was the turning point. The grisly slaughter that crushed the Shimabara Revolt also ended the country's open Christian worship, and the few who would precariously sustain it in secret were likely to be tortured and executed if discovered. Many Westerners would soon know and care more about the religious persecution than anything else Japanese (although the killings and cruelties were a fraction of those committed in the previous centuries by Spanish conquistadores in South America). At the same time, apart from the torment of Christians, especially Catholics, substantial toleration continued, maybe more than in the West.[13]

Two years later, an influential tract boasted that foreign Christian barbarians who had come to make Japan "a domain of devils" by "spreading their cursed doctrine" and destroying "the Buddhas and the Gods" had been "exterminated, without being allowed to grasp an inch of our soil, to stand on a foot of our land."[14] The following year, fifty-seven (some said sixty-one) emissaries and sailors of a Portuguese ship sent to test the exclusion orders were beheaded, although the thirteen Chinese crew members were permitted to return to Macao. The Shogun then appointed a special board charged to fully liquidate Christianity. It and the seclusion, *sakoku*, were nearly complete in remarkably short order. (Samurai honor didn't shine during the process. Under pressure to renounce their new faith, the Christians among them were generally quicker to do so than peasants, artisans, and merchants, who were more willing to endure torture and death for it.)

Soon the frightened effort to preserve stability and Tokugawa rule was delivering bad with the good. Although isolation helped Japan enjoy centuries of peace while Europe and America waged their murderous internal and foreign wars, the isolation—from social, political, and humanistic as well as industrial and technological progress—commanded a heavy price. The Renaissance and Enlightenment that were enriching the West, if selectively, remained largely untasted.

Although those movements weren't totally unknown because the closing was never truly hermetic, the cardinal rule was that Westerners were *forbidden* to enter (and alien Asians' movements were closely supervised). That point is hard to belabor because it was so basic, fundamental, categorical, virtually unconditional. The Japanese rulers hoped it would also be immutable, and virtually all Westerners believed no change would take place unless they forced it.

3

The Initial Panic

Perry as a Buddhist devil, 1854

THE COMMERCIAL CENTER OF URAGA, outside which the Black Ships were anchored, performed maritime checks on local craft bound for Edo, since all shipping, even to and from domestic ports, required licenses. (Some captains caught transporting women during the vigilant searches were said to be beheaded.[1]) The collection of a hundred-odd wood and paper buildings was twenty-seven miles south of the virtually undefended capital, which Perry would soon find "quite certain . . . can be destroyed by a few steamers of very light draft, and carrying guns of the heaviest caliber."

Local people trembled without knowing such details. While most Americans with an interest in "Orientals" were convinced the "backward, treacherous and rapacious"[2] Japanese also excelled in cruelty, Japan's use of "barbarian" wasn't necessarily contemptuous. It had borrowed the term from China, where, as in ancient Greece, it could denote simply all who lived beyond the borders of their own (higher) civilization and "barbar"-ed: "babbled" in another tongue.[3] In that sense, "barbarians in far-off places" wasn't always a derogatory allusion to primitive tribes. However, dark overtones usually sounded to people convinced of their own uniqueness, more as in the Roman fear of enemies at the gate.

A government advisor saw foreign script, "confused and irregular, wriggling like snakes or larvae of mosquitoes," as symbolic of the difference between the depraved West and the elegant East. (The ugly letters also reminded him of worms, dog's teeth, slime lines left by snails, decaying skulls, and parched vipers' rotten bellies.) Most people who lived within the borders of the land favored by heaven and a divine Emperor did consider outsiders culturally and morally inferior. Some thought they were beasts that "merely look human"[4]—or not even that, as with the furry ones thought to live in trees. A prominent thinker of the time maintained that while his people, "down to the most humble," were descended from gods, Westerners were more like animals. The farmers and fishing people who comprised 80 or so percent of the population got their every impression of life abroad from folklore that had made Christians scary ever since the country's seventeenth-century closing (although contradictory tales told of divinities coming from across the seas). Luridly illustrated legends described demonlike monsters with bulbous or beaked noses and claws for hands. Thus popular denigrations such as "hairy foreigners" and "red-hairs" were sometimes used half jokingly, but more often than not by people who dreaded them as alien to the species as well as to Japan.

Those creatures killed animals—*animals!*—for food. When Perry would ask to buy sixty head of cattle for his squadron, puzzled native officials wondered what on earth he intended to do with them. The Commodore's reply—"Why, eat them of course"—prompted disgust. "We can never comply with your cruel wishes to kill and eat such animals."[5] (Never mind the Japanese slaughters of human beings, including Mongol survivors of Kublai Khan's invasion fleet destroyed by the Divine Winds and appalling numbers of domestic enemies during past civil wars.) Westerners were rumored to devour carcasses whole. Even if they left some larger bones unconsumed, the stench of the huge eaters of fatty meat deepened the prejudice, especially since they rarely washed their bodies, even after long sea voyages, whereas civilized people naturally enjoyed a daily hot soak.* Shocking behavior reinforced associations with the animals on which the hairy eaters fed. Failing to bow as well as to bathe, Westerners blustered and bragged. Spitting into handkerchiefs and stuffing the unsanitary-wetness back into their pockets, the strangers violated a hundred proprieties, often eating with their fingers and even expressing anger in public.

Once fearful suspicion replaced the original Japanese hospitality, other attributes of the crude visitors served to confirm prejudices. On the observation that Western footwear had wooden heels and a deduction that the wearers needed those novelties to prop themselves up, some Japanese posited that the alien feet had no heels of their own. (Winning battles with such defectives would be simple: tipping them over would leave them helpless on their backs.) Dutchmen were seen to have coarse skin, oversized noses, and bulging eyes, "really just like those of a dog," a scholar assured. Such evidence of inferiority served as confirmation of rumors that the red-hairs lifted their legs for urination. They were also said to use their canine-like penises as lasciviously as the dogs to whom they were believed related in that particular too.

Those lowbred beings, taught the standard explanation for the country's closing, had designs on Japan. Good people took the menace for granted. A noted political thinker and Tokugawa policy advisor named Shonan Yokoi alluded to it in an 1849 appeal to "Wipe out the beast-like barbarians of the world." Although Europeans had seemed the greater threat until recently, America's territorial and maritime expansion— knowledge of which had trickled in, despite the isolation—began shifting the focus even before the Black Ships arrived.

When they did, doom gripped most who heard of them "steam[ing] around the harbor displaying [their] marksmanship in artillery practice."[6]

---

* Most Europeans of the time believed bathing harmed health. The Japanese were convinced other Asians shared their disgust. A late-eighteenth-century woodcut has a Dutchman making love to a Burmese courtesan whose burning incense is clearly for combating his body odor. Many Japanese still recoil at Westerners' smell and harbor suspicions about their personal cleanliness. A rare written confirmation that they have "a strong body odor that is quite nauseating" came from an uncommonly candid, or undiplomatic, former diplomat named Kawasaki Ichiro, who wrote several popular books about his country in the 1960s and 1970s.

Whether or not the Commodore fired his cannon only in salute, as he'd maintain, few Japanese perceived the stunning salvos as such. On July 10, two days after the vessels were first spotted, an Edo physician recorded rumors "running wild" and agitation in "people high and low." The Americans' untroubled advance beyond a hidden sandbank that supposedly closed Edo Bay to all foreign vessels[7] was causing "great tumult in the whole court." A well-educated diarist noted a general feeling of "suddenly [being] thrown into the middle of a war," some fearing that bombardment would burn down the entire capital. An official notice prohibiting discussion of the foreign fleet kept it to a whisper for a day or so, but "people on the street began exchanging gossip in loud voices" from the evening of the tenth.[8] (Unable to suppress it, the government switched to assurance that Perry had come to offer tribute, which is how early paintings would depict him: a foreigner showing proper deference to Japanese officials.)

Some of the talk revealed ambivalence about the outside world. Intimidating as they were, the huge ships' builders and sailors obviously weren't "stupid and simple," as the scholar had assured seven years earlier. The volume of chatter increased the following day, when the summer sun seemed to speed a furious sprouting of rumors. The same diarist, who evidently practiced Western—then called "Dutch"—medicine to high society, including government officials, noted the exception he was making to his policy of not satisfying his patients' curiosity about the West because doing so would be a distraction from their treatment. In answer to their grim questions now, he sought to apprise them of Western power, with which he was acquainted because he also ran a highly unusual boarding school that made use of European materials. Why exactly had the Americans come? To see the Emperor? To lease a Japanese island? Other prospects were mortifying. Everyone with knowledge about the United States was hounded for information. By the evening of the first day, the "extremely grave" situation had deeply distressed even some in the Shogun's court who hadn't interrupted their ordinary routine when the news initially arrived. Meanwhile the price of rice soared and no fresh fish was delivered to the markets, presumably because fishermen didn't dare launch their boats, and the daimyo, baronlike lords of the country's feudal domains, were warned "to stand in readiness to meet an emergency." It was as if all Edo "was to be burnt to ashes this very moment."

Commoners . . . are evacuating the young and old of their family, and . . . their valuable possessions as well . . . and they themselves are planning to flee to the country as soon as fighting breaks out. . . . Government officials, whose state of consternation is indeed beyond description, seem to have been really awed by the military might of the formidable foreign fleet.

EDO'S ANXIETY HAD BEGUN FOUR DAYS EARLIER, when news of the first sighting of the Black Ships reached it and fear of imminent "invasion" raced from mouth to mouth. Another commentator painted the "popular commotion" as "beyond description."[9] In all directions, "mothers were seen flying with children in their arms, and men with mothers on their backs."

A third observer felt it was "like wartime."[10] Instructions were issued for lighting fires to "close the roads to Edo Castle and other crucial routes" on the sounding of a special alarm. Smaller beacon fires were already burning all along the coast, where soldiers with pikes and "rusty flintlocks" stood guard, some additionally armed with war fans bearing the emblem of the rising sun—all "inadequate," an Edo resident sadly observed. While officers frantically drilled green troops, seacoast inhabitants, some of whose houses had already been razed for frenzied construction of new fortifications, were pressed into service. And along the four-hundred-odd miles of the Tokaido, the state-of-the-art highway between Edo and the ancient capital of Kyoto, more "urgent messages follow[ed] one another" to the daimyo, all of whom had been issued defensive assignments.[11]

Back at Uraga, people were ordered to keep to their daily work, not succumb to panic. Fulfilling the first part would have been a trick in nearby villages whose every male from fifteen to sixty had been mobilized to "join the garrison forces as porters and laborers"[12] and whose fishermen were ordered to row private boats, all of which had been requisitioned. "Left in the country are only women and old people, who cannot till the farmland even if the family has any." For all their activity, the garrisons remained lean in equipment. Among the reinforcements rushed up were two cannon of just over one and a half pounds in shot, "quite a pitiful sight" to a demoralized official who guessed they were nearly useless compared to Perry's guns.

The capital's secondhand clothing stores displayed military items and coats of arms, while smiths worked overtime making swords, helmets, and armor, and weapons dealers sold their old stock for doubled prices. (Despite the fear, wags were already composing ditties mocking the country's weakness. Playing on words, one couplet stated armor suits were getting their summer airing "thanks to" or "in the shade of" a [supposedly inferior] foreign nation.) The diary-keeping physician with the uncommon knowledge of the West was among a tiny minority—composed mostly of intellectuals keen to learn, merchants eager to trade, and a handful of secret barterers with American whaling ships—who *welcomed* the intrusion at Uraga, if not the stampede it was causing. In his own "humble opinion," contact with foreigners would be "good medicine for the entire Japanese nation." That very rare view made him unlikely to have exaggerated the panic's scope and depth, which rose yet higher on July 14, the day Perry would come ashore from his anchorage. A general alarm was readied for sounding "at a moment's notice." The Black Ships' survey of the waters close to Edo spiked even greater fear by feeding a rumor that American soldiers had already landed and "moved around without being in the least molested." Some coastal defense units repeatedly requested permission to open fire on the Americans.

It was denied. Desperate as headquarters was to repel them, higher officials feared a wrong move would provoke an armed landing and occupation of critical territory. With the squadron's morning and evening cannon "salutes" widening anticipation of war, rumors, "gathering mass like a snowball," multiplied the Black Ships' number to eighty-six.[13] Still more people hauled their furniture and valuables this way and that, seeking safekeeping in houses of friends farther from where the foreigners would land and swelling a "wild rushing up and down the highway" to the hills. That and the other four excellent roads leading in and out of Edo were choked with pandemonium, while excitement "seethed like a cauldron" and Shinto priests prayed at shrines for "the sweeping away of the barbarians."

Rumors of an immediate action . . . added horror to the horror-stricken. The tramp of war-horses, the clatter of armed warriors, the noise of carts, the parade of firemen, the incessant tolling of bells, the shrieks of women, the cries of children, dinning all the streets of a city of more than a million souls, made confusion worse confounded.[14]

With the panic and chaos swelling in the heat, the "whole city" succumbed to "uproar."

THE AMERICANS CAUGHT GLIMPSES of Uraga's distress but knew nothing about Edo's. "Of all this," a sailor would write about the greater panic further north, "we were quite ignorant."[15] Perry in particular would have been happy to know about it but didn't, nor much else about the capital. For him, the densely populated metropolis of well over a million inhabitants might as well have been Atlantis. Actually, it was probably the world's second-largest city, after recently losing first place to London, hugely swelled by the Industrial Revolution's transformation of England. First or second, Edo was the highly urbanized, unusually lively home of a large slice of the twenty-five-odd million Japanese.

Spirited cultural pursuits, chiefly in literature, theater, fine arts, and a kind of gossipy block-print journalism—whose sellers read from the sheets on busy streets—enriched a wide variety of commerce and craft. Their flourishing was all the more remarkable for having quickly sprouted from virtually nothing. When Tokugawa Ieyasu, soon to found the great dynasty by which all Japan would be known for centuries, was designated Lord of the Kanto Plain in 1590, he chose a little fishing village for his base, partly for its distance from powerful rivals. The best the district could boast in structural achievement was a dilapidated castle near the settlement at the bay's innermost recess. But sweating, suffering peasants were commanded to build what would become the country's de facto capital from surrounding marshes and swamps. (Like St. Petersburg, which would rise in a similarly "artificial" way on similarly inhospitable grounds a century later, it would be subject to terribly destructive floods—and also, in Edo's case, fires.)

Now the sprawling city embraced former farmland and villages. Even without its beautiful parks and man-made rises for viewing Mount Fuji, the "broad, well-paved streets, handsome shops and the prosperous appearance" of the crowds would impress a British general visiting seven years later. The "admirable order and cleanliness" was even more striking because the officer had seen nothing comparable elsewhere in Asia.[16] The city could compete with Europe's most prominent, especially in lifestyle and spirit. "No less than Paris, the relentless energy of the people" shaped its growth, "changing Edo during the 17th and 18th centuries from Ieyasu's town into the merchants' city."[17]

For all the bustling of the merchant and pleasure quarters, it remained largely a government town, inhabited by thousands of officials in hundreds of positions in the *bakufu*, or Shogun's "tent government." The position of Edo Castle (then called Chiyoda Castle, for the name of the village where it stood), on a peninsula facing Edo Bay, enhanced the relative ease of defense that had originally attracted Tokugawa Ieyasu to the site. Started as a military bastion in that second half of the sixteenth century, when clan fighting rent the country, the complex was built in increasingly ambitious stages over some forty-two years, the majestic structures in their "richly-wooded, ornamented grounds" becoming one of Japan's great accomplishments. Their roof tiles, made of lead for protection against the elements, appeared white from a distance, prompting comparisons to snowcapped Mount Fuji.*

Protection against domestic enemies had prompted much greater thought and effort. The huge compound that also housed the higher offices of the Shogun's administration and his residence—consisting of his wife, children, concubines, and hundreds of personal attendants—was as close as possible to impregnable. A triple moat and the world's largest granite wall, ten miles long, guarded its grounds. Even the inner wall (which surrounds the present Imperial Palace grounds) was four miles long.

But as Plato observed, "when the mode of the music changes," city walls shake—even Edo's massive inner ones. At first, officials were dumb with alarm. But as "fresh messages" about the threat arrived, "one after the other," the great clans were ordered to keep strict watch on the seashore,

> as it was possible that these barbarian vessels . . . might proceed at once to acts of violence. The clans all declared their readiness, and proceeded at once to despatch troops to the posts assigned, to provide arms, and to hoist flags emblazoned with the crest of each noble house. It was a beautiful sight to see this firm attitude of defense.[18]

The historian who reported that went on to note that Shogun Tokugawa Ieyoshi was exceedingly troubled by the messages and "summoned all the

---

* Several disastrous fires in the 1860s destroyed the major buildings of the extraordinary architecture. Those that comprise today's Imperial Palace, built on the same grounds, are of modern construction.

officials to a council," but he failed to mention that the less-than-forceful leader took to his bed. Already ailing, he was stricken hard on the day after Perry anchored at Uraga, when Abe Masahiro could no longer delay informing him of the news, which caused him to tremble and, apparently, be stricken with fever.

Nothing had yet been reported to the Emperor in his Kyoto palace, where life continued unchanged in its detachment from political matters. The court's big event during the week of panic was the first celebration of Boys' Day by the baby Prince who would become the Emperor Meiji. The Divine Son of Heaven would know nothing at all about the terrible crisis, at least not officially, until the day *after* Perry's forthcoming presentation of President Fillmore's letter, when the *bakufu* would order the court informed. By that time, nothing remained to be discussed or decided, at least about how to respond to the Commodore's insistence that the Japanese accept that letter. For all his distress about the implications, the Emperor could now only hope and pray—the latter literally. He directed Kyoto's seven temples and seven shrines to pray for peace, for the imperial throne's continued long life, and for the people's tranquility.

But the throne's impotence was among the conditions that distressed segments of the population. Factions that had long wanted to restore some secular authority to the Emperor would use the shame of July 14 in their campaign to do that by discrediting the shogunate that would have suffered massive damage to its prestige by surrendering to Perry's demand.[19]

TOKUGAWA IEYOSHI'S CHIEF PHYSICIAN diagnosed heatstroke, but the usual countermeasures didn't work. Whatever the actual problem, the Shogun's retainers had little doubt the shock of hearing of the penetration by a squadron of huge warships severely worsened it. Oppressive July heat hardly helped. Despite all ministrations, now by a full team of physicians, the patient grew weaker, but he managed to convene his council in order to give its members his gloomy assessment that Perry's arrival constituted the most extraordinary event "since the beginning of heaven and earth."

The historian also didn't mention that firm, "beautiful" defense was exceptional, chiefly because centuries of peace had lulled most samurai into neglecting the rigorous necessaries. Before that, they'd been as fierce as any soldiers in the world—probably fiercer than many, thanks to their greater willingness to die for their lords. But few had donned their armor in years. Most ran "hither and thither" searching for it and for their rusty arms, with which they were now equally unfamiliar.

Abe Masahiro's major responsibility for coping with the samurai weakness came with his position as Chief Senior Councilor, the effective head of the *roju*. That "governing council" of four or five elders not being responsible to a parliament, he wasn't the equivalent of a nineteenth-century prime minister, and all the less because the *bakufu* had no real ministries, although it operated from offices and departments. Still, Abe did some of the things prime ministers do.

Exercise of such responsibility by a thirty-four-year-old wasn't as exceptional as it might seem. Skillful samurai had been assuming leadership roles at remarkably early ages for centuries. Unlikely as it would have been in other countries, Tokugawa Ieyasu, the dynasty's founder, took command of a guard detachment belonging to a daimyo, or feudal lord, at the age of ten. That armed force belonged to another family. Ieyasu, whose original surname was different, had been born heir to a small *han*, or domain, during a protracted period of ruinous civil wars, when daimyo with little trust in each other often took or exchanged hostages as insurance against sudden attack. Given for that purpose to a more powerful neighboring *han* when he was five, the boy was being led to his place of confinement when a still mightier daimyo kidnapped him along the way. Instead of killing him as threatened, however, the kidnapper exchanged him for a son of the original hostage taker, who arranged for the boy's good education in martial and civil arts.

Ten years after those unexceptional twists of the country's feudal struggles, Ieyasu, then fifteen, commanded the hostage taker's force in a successful battle against the area's most powerful daimyo, the son of the man who had kidnapped him when he was a hostage. The still boyish warrior was on his way to his central role in Japanese history.*

Abe Masahiro stood out even in that context of precocious feats. He was the youngest man ever to be appointed Chief Senior Councilor—in

---

* Even at that point, Tokugawa Ieyasu's route to the top would be anything but direct. Recognizing the kidnapper's son's potential for conquest, the ambitious young Ieyasu became *his* follower. He later proved his loyalty to him by ordering his own son to kill himself after he was (wrongly) accused of plotting against his leader. Those kinds of family connections and disconnections would persist over the centuries, compounding the complexity of political life that faced Abe Masahiro.

1845, when the twenty-six-year-old leapfrogged over the other senior councilors, all much older. But he was also much experienced by 1853, having been *roju shuseki* for eight tense years, during which time news that reached Edo through its narrow openings to the outside world made him all but certain ships too powerful to repel would arrive. That helped explain why the July 8 sighting of the Black Ships dismayed but didn't surprise him or the other senior councilors. In telling contrast to virtually all other Japanese, he'd *expected* Perry's arrival.

FOR YEARS, Abe and a few fellow realists had accepted, if never publicly acknowledged, that foreign economic and technological development was bound to end the seclusion. The proliferation of Western oceangoing vessels since Abe's birth in 1819 made all but certain that more and more would probe where they weren't wanted. Reports about recent events were more specific—in fact so on target that a man in the first Japanese boat to approach the Black Ships after they'd anchored off Uraga on July 8 immediately asked if they were American, "and by his manner of asking," one of the crew interpreted, "showed that our coming had been anticipated."[20]

During the seventy-five years before 1853, no fewer than seventy-two ships had entered Japanese waters (and another thirty-six approached Okinawa). Twenty-five, including the first of those seventy-two, were Russian and fifteen were British. One each came from France, Denmark, and Romania. The first of some twenty-seven to fly the Stars and Stripes—in 1791, sixty-two years before Perry—told local authorities it belonged to "Red Hairs from a Land called America"[21] who had been blown off course in the lucrative China trade. However, the captain probably landed intentionally, hoping to dispose of otter skins that hadn't sold in Canton. Although the effort failed because the Japanese didn't know what to do with furs, the ship's benign reception despite the *sakoku*, the national seclusion, was more significant.

It was also extended to the next eight American ships. Arriving between 1797 and 1807, they exchanged their ensigns for Dutch ones before approaching land because the Dutch East India Company that operated from the tiny island off Nagasaki (about which more very soon) had chartered them. The company took that precaution because it feared capture of its own vessels during that time of the French revolutionary wars, but more than trade accounted for the Americans' relatively cordial Japanese reception. When Edo learned the Dutch were sneaking U.S. vessels into Nagasaki, it demanded information about the country of origin, and the understandable Dutch inclination to make the intelligence attractive was furthered by Holland's support of the recent American revolution. The American crews of those eight ships were given more freedom to explore Nagasaki than Dutch sailors enjoyed because the New World's rebellion against oppressive England was known and appreciated.

Guards who accompanied them everywhere ensured it was far from full freedom, however, and it wasn't long before anxiety began eroding the hospitality. Early nineteenth-century America's surging strength and ambition that had sent so many voracious whaling ships near Japanese waters became even better known. That surfeit of American whalers, as the Japanese saw it, had all but erased the good feeling by the 1840s. The Opium War, news of which was conveyed by the Chinese and Korean ships that had never been excluded, was an even more chilling portent. Dutch traders provided additional information about the conflict in neighboring China, which came as a piercing alarm about Western appetite and power. Ten years later, the same traders warned the *roju* of more specific menace to its isolation. That was in 1852, just a year before it actually materialized in the form of Perry's East Asia Squadron.

THE HARASSED YET PRIVILEGED Dutch traders who delivered the disturbing reports lived in a compound called Deshima, which can be translated as "island in front of the town." The town was Kyushu's Nagasaki, whose location north of Tanegashima, the offshore island on which the first Portuguese visitors had landed, helped explain its emergence as the major Western outpost in Japan. That other compound where the Dutch were now confined was so much smaller that it barely deserved to be called anything so grand as an island. The traders' toehold there of about three acres, the size of a rural American house plot, was as slippery as it was small. As if to further demonstrate the precariousness of the Dutch footing, Deshima was a utilitarian contrivance rather than a natural geographical feature. The "fan without a handle," as a German medical officer employed there described the slightly curved rectangle of some two hundred by eighty yards, had been created by filling in a shallow area in the harbor and building walls just tall enough to keep out the sea.

The Dutch East India Company, which traded in spices, tea, silk, and other much-wanted commodities, was the largest of its kind and—in keeping with Holland's commercial lead over Britain at the time—more successful than the British East India Company, founded two years earlier, in 1600. The Dutch Factory, as its Japanese post was known,[22] was moved to Deshima in 1641, after the other Western colonies had left the country, voluntarily or otherwise, and after the slaughter of native Catholics who had mounted a rebellion tightened the seal on the national seclusion.[23] Even by a crowded country's standards, this crack in the Japanese wall was cramped, more by its constraints than by the warehouses and residences jammed onto the little patch. Chinese traders, who were confined to a designated quarter in Nagasaki, were much less restricted.

Deshima, with its vegetable garden and few farm animals, was no more than "a musket shot" from the city proper, but the narrow bridge linking them was heavily guarded to prevent unsanctioned crossings. Placards warned that the island's inhabitants weren't permitted to leave except when authorized, usually to visit Nagasaki's pleasure quarters. The only exceptions the other way were for courtesans and a few Japanese guests invited for holiday celebrations. Otherwise, island routine smacked of incarceration. The all-male residents, who never numbered more than twenty, lived under a kind of permanent compound arrest, and could be expelled for the slightest show of bad behavior or attitude. Despite their long-demonstrated lack of interest in proselytizing, they were constantly watched by resident guards and interpreters, reported on by guardians and informers, and "subjected to endless humiliations and indignities."[24] An account by a former resident—one that buttressed the American image of the Japanese people as "foul and fearful"—stressed that Western women were refused permission to reside on the island in order to increase dependence on "the least reputable females of Japan, who alone are suffered to . . . serve them," and were themselves subject to ugly persecution. All in all, it claimed, the poor Dutch were treated worse than European Jews during the Middle Ages.[25]

The insults were never grosser than during annual autumn visits of the Factory's chief agent to the Shogun in distant Edo. Homage was rendered in Edo Castle's Hall of a Hundred Mats, where, according to one of the German medical officers, the agent "crept forwards on his hands and feet, and falling on his knees bowed his head to the ground and retired again in absolute silence, crawling exactly like a crab." ("O Spring of Your Majesty!" wrote the haiku master Basho Matsuo. "Even a Dutch Captain is induced/To crawl before you.") To "amuse the court," as he was ordered to do, his entourage then had to "dance, jump, represent a drunken man, speak broken Japanese, paint, read Dutch, German, sing."[26]

Voluntary submission to such debasement would earn Perry's contempt of the colony for its "servile submission" to Japan's "capricious tyranny," and may have also strengthened Japanese conviction of Western moral inferiority. The Dutch "put up with being treated by our officials more as slaves than as free men," a twentieth-century writer would note. They would "meekly accept any affront, even from the prostitutes in the ports."[27]

Their willingness to be displayed "like Martians"[28] was part payment for their skillfully secured privilege of conducting their exclusive European trade. Two or three Dutch ships a year loaded with imports—later reduced to one (which didn't always arrive)—were permitted to land at Nagasaki after locking away their Bibles and every page of other Christian literature. (Mention of the hated religion was hunted even in the papers of incoming Chinese vessels.) At the same time, the profits from the cargoes were smaller than imagined. Japanese interest in Western goods was relatively weak, especially in comparison to those of China and Southeast Asia. (That, together with the growing anti-Western sentiment, had prompted the English to close their trading post in 1623.) Demand was also soft the other way around, Japan producing little of interest to the Europe and America that adored Chinese wares. The Canton trade was far more valuable than any in Japan, then or hoped-for.

Still, the Protestant Dutch persevered and their conditions improved. By the turn of the nineteenth century, their annual trips to the Shogun's court had been reduced to one every four years, and they'd been relieved of the worst of their humiliation there. Slight relaxation of their isolation at Deshima was equally encouraging. Philipp Franz von Siebold, a German physician who served on the island in the 1820s, would be imprisoned, then banished, for acquiring a map from a native astronomer—the rare treasure from the Dutch East India Company that Perry would buy when making his enterprising preparations for the mission. Before that, however, the Japanese so respected von Siebold for his skills as a naturalist as well as a physician that they permitted him to wander freely in Nagasaki, even to open a small school there.

What the *bakufu* didn't relax was a requirement that Deshima join the sanctioned Chinese and Korean traders in keeping them informed of developments in the outside world. Each ship that landed at Nagasaki was a source of eagerly sought news, which was formally presented in an obligatory annual report. After Nagasaki's brief placement under the jurisdiction of the Society of Jesus, the Tokugawas, in one of their earliest seclusion measures, took the Western-tainted city under their own direct rule, where it remained when Perry arrived. Thus the annual reports were delivered not to a local daimyo but to *bakufu* commissioners for faster forwarding to Edo.

The continued Dutch conveyance of cunning anti-Catholic tidings and rumors had helped them cling to their lone European outpost after the others were expelled in the seventeenth century. Their cultivation of skill in parsing what they passed to Edo during the following two centuries of their near monopoly on Western news was hardly surprising. The information that was partly intended to keep out their maritime competitors—and to fuel Japanese fear of the outside world—continued into the mid-nineteenth century, when the Dutch of course knew, even if Edo didn't, that their country had shrunk from its maritime prominence to a minor role. (That would dawn on Japan only after its opening, when students sent to Holland realized they'd been studying the wrong language and country.[29])

The Dutch also worried, if less anxiously than the Japanese, that stronger powers—most likely Russia, Britain, or America—would fairly soon end the seclusion one way or another, and with it their favored position. Before that happened, they wanted to secure that position by signing a trade pact with Edo.

That was among the reasons King William II of Holland wrote the Shogun in 1844 that Japan's future "causes us much anxiety" and offered "our good counsel" for "averting imminent disaster." The core of that counsel was a warning that "all sorts of vessels sailing in Japanese waters" would inevitably increase in number. "Distance," his majesty explained, "is being overcome by the invention of the steamship," making the shrinking of the world unstoppable. The King's letter, delivered by a warship dispatched to Nagasaki, connected the dots. "How easily might a quarrel occur" between the crews of the proliferating ships and "the inhabitants of Your Majesty's dominion. . . . A nation that tries to hold itself aloof . . . risks the enmity of others." Reminding the Shogun of the Opium War's "fatal" cost to China, whose resistance to European military power was "fruitless," King William advised that "wisdom directs" the softening of ancient laws when they "by strict construction, threaten the peace." The laws in need of softening were those severely limiting "exchange with foreign people . . . laid down by Your Majesty's enlightened predecessors."[30]

The warship waited and waited in Nagasaki for a reply, the long delay indicating that the shogunate's resolute words concealed anxious irresolution. Nine months passed before it was delivered. The Dutch suggestion, read a note signed by the members of the *roju* just after Abe Masahiro's appointment as its head, was entirely impossible. "Although this may appear discourteous, such is the strictness of the ancestral law that no other course is open to us." His Majesty was requested not to write again.

He didn't, but the governor of the Dutch East Indies sent a letter eight years later, after colleagues got wind of Perry's preparations for his expedition.[31] Appended to Deshima's obligatory 1852 report about world affairs, the governor's more specific warning should have been a bombshell. Citing "rife" rumors of a forthcoming dispatch of American ships to Japan, which had been conveyed by Dutch agents in Washington, he accurately predicted their purpose:

According to these rumors, an envoy will be sent . . . with a letter from the President to the Emperor of Japan. The envoy will also bring some [Japanese] castaways and ask that one or two Japanese ports be opened to trade, and that coaling conveniences be provided for steamships en route from California to China.

When the Black Ships entered Uraga Bay the following year, a rescued castaway was indeed aboard Perry's flagship, the *Susquehanna*. The panic caused by their arrival would leave his presence unnoticed and unmentioned (although he'd have a walk-on moment near the drama's very end).[32] But that would matter far less than the lack of notice and mention of the 1852 report of the talk about the probable imminent appearance of

American ships. Of course, the startling document was rushed to the Shogun—who, however, essentially ignored it. Tokugawa Ieyoshi's health was already weak enough to remove him from real direction of the *bakufu*, and he'd die of his ailment or shock too soon after Perry's arrival to experience great regret for failing to act on the Dutch warning. But when the lapse would become known, puzzlement and angst, then a full share of blame, would be directed to Abe Masahiro, who had been effectively in charge for years.

Meanwhile, Abe and the other members of the *roju* had even more reason not to be surprised by the news that was taking the rest of the country's breath away. If the 1852 warning hadn't been enough, the Viceroy of India repeated it in a letter received in Edo in August of the same year—three months before Perry's sailing from Norfolk. When knowledge of the later tip-off would leak in Japan, it would much sharpen criticism of the Chief Senior Councilor's indecisiveness. The embarrassing fact was that the *roju* had been forewarned—and even more clearly than by those predictions that insistent American ships would probably soon arrive. A detailed dispatch specifically about Perry's imminent approach was delivered in June 1853, more than five weeks before his anchoring off Uraga. Coming by fast junk from Okinawa, it reported that the squadron would soon depart from Naha, the island's principal port, for the final leg of its long voyage.

The grip of the news on the *roju*'s thoughts tightened even more because that handful had withheld it from everyone else. "The golden rule of the *bakufu* bureaucrats," observed the physician who recorded Edo's panic, "ran something like this: 'The more we keep the people in the dark, the better we can make them obey.' " The rulers' instinct for secrecy left them even more isolated. "Not only did they endeavor to prevent information from reaching the ear of outsiders," but their "addiction" often prompted them "to keep important government issues hidden from one another."[33] Thus Edo's prohibition of discussion of the squadron's arrival.

LORD ABE'S COLLUSION with the Shogun in ignoring the Dutch warning of 1852 weakened his position. His failure to strengthen the country's defenses significantly during his eight years as chief senior councilor weakened it even more. *Why* he'd failed was crucial.

Given the limitations of his office, his leadership may well have been as deft as anyone could have made it. If he couldn't pull a rabbit from his symbolic black cap with its dangle of ribbon, a token long worn by high officials, no one else was more likely to. Thirteen decades later, he'd be called "the last *Bakufu* leader to preserve—by his honesty and transparent reforming zeal—the illusion that the government he served was capable of leading Japan out of the diplomatic and military thicket in which it had become entangled."[34] That he would prove to be, but since the government *wasn't* capable, the operating word was *illusion*. The workings of *bakufu* rule—and, more significant, the nation's nature and condition—made adequate preparation all but impossible.

The fundamental problems in which feudal Japan was mired made it ill-equipped to tackle any new challenge. Its quasi-official Confucianism preached a need to know one's place and to worship authority while giving absolute loyalty and utterly devoted service. That helped reinforce the rote, severity, and excessive regulation that stiffened resistance to change. Although the strict class hierarchy was here and there giving way to commoners who were making good money, it still impeded development of talent. The political monopoly of the 6 or so percent of samurai at the top excluded or discouraged the best and brightest of the remaining 94 percent. To make that worse, the incompetence of the former may have exceeded the norm because so many had been languishing for so long. Perhaps ironically, that was partly thanks to the centuries of peace that inevitably bred strains of stagnation.

Much of the huge *bakufu* bureaucracy devoted excessive effort to preserving social and economic structures that grew increasingly divorced from the realities of commercial activity. The partial stagnation also nourished predictable stubbornness and corruption. Some samurai—the elite, it bears repeating, who alone could have a political voice—had begun questioning the ideology that served to keep so many incompetents in authoritative positions while failing to advance talented ones of lower rank. But on went the old, sometimes profligate ways—like the lavish processions, some of which stretched for kilometers, of daimyo traveling from their domains to Edo. And that expenditure was minor compared to maintaining a second home on the grounds of Edo Castle, required by laws mandating "alternate attendance" there. The system had been devised early during Tokugawa rule. Prominent daimyo—literally "great names"—had to spend every other year not in their home territory, where they might have plotted rebellion, but where the Shogun could keep an eye on them. Wives and children, who had to live *permanently* in Edo, were essentially hostages, and the draining of the lords' treasuries by obligating them to maintain two households was another way of diminishing the possibility of insurrection against the Shogun.

In short, late Tokugawa Japan was anything but congenial to the kind of progress most dear to New World go-getters. The social and cultural constraints on some forms of expression narrowed not only options, but also thought and imagination. Growing contradictions between real life and the Confucian model prescribed for it by the semiofficial national ideology increasingly alienated a slice of the well-educated populace. A dissident scholar—later called the "Japanese Benjamin Franklin," although his audience was minuscule—complained that the country persisted in slavishly copying discredited Chinese ways instead of advancing by adopting new ones.[35]

A dozen years before Perry, a translator of Dutch books, well oiled by alcohol, couldn't restrain himself from shouting *"Vrijheit!,"* "Liberty!"[36] (Seven years *after* 1853, a samurai group making a first visit to the United States, chiefly for acquiring enough technological savvy to help Japan fight back, would be shown some turbines. Yes, but we already know about those things, a nonconformist member objected. We have to learn about freedom, he said. No one has a concept of freedom.) The 99 or so percent of the people who had no voice in political matters scarcely even considered alternatives. With no public voice promoting anything like democracy or civil rights, the very rare mentions of their elements came closer to eccentricity than a trend. In that setting of Confucian worship of authority, the notion of rule by popular consent instead of secret, backroom decisions was embryonic. The mighty system, including the ordering of thought, devoted as much effort and energy to preserving itself as to advancing the general welfare. It had become a fortress against the new scientific and economic ideas that produced those huge oceangoing ships—the ones that couldn't be repelled much longer.

As for economic development, ignorance of the outside world joined the Confucian disdain for commerce in retarding it.[37] The isolation, although not total, all but guaranteed much misinterpretation in addition to massive blanks and blind spots. The entire country boasted not a single man, not to mention a woman, with a fluent command of a European language.[38]

Although that's less startling than it might seem because the same was essentially true the other way around, a much-admired twentieth-century Japanese author described the ignorance as "so profound" that even the Black Ships' rubbish was feared. Every carelessly discarded bottle that drifted ashore had to be reported. To take one home without doing so courted punishment. The authorities were convinced they were designed to harm, probably with poison. All doors and windows of the vacated house designated as the sole place of disposal were locked. "That was the way everything was. If a rattan chair swept off deck by a wind happened to wash ashore, it would be treated as a great mystery. A regular deck chair would be still another great mystery."

The economic constraints were particularly hard on the peasants, the 80-odd percent of the population that lacked even surnames until shortly before 1840. (The honor of having them was generally limited to the daimyo and other samurai.) In the grip of their lords, most scratched a living on their tiny, heavily taxed farms, sometimes rebelling when even scratching seemed impossible. Yes, peace and some kinds of security prevailed, but many officials apparently favored a motto likening peasants to sesame seeds: "the more you squeeze them, the more you can extract from them." No fewer than twenty-two serious famines, almost all caused or worsened by floods, fires, earthquakes, or other natural disasters, had occurred between 1690 and 1840.[39] Unrest and complaint were becoming almost commonplace. A shocked *bakufu* sentenced 562 people to execution for their part in an 1836 uprising. Although that was extreme, Osaka townspeople joined another one the following year—six years before Lord Abe's appointment to the *roju*—to protest Edo policies they claimed left them starving. The protest lasted only a day, but its impact added to a sense of tension and crisis.

Thus the country was in parlous shape. Late feudal Japan may well have endured "one of the most conscious attempts in history to freeze society in a rigid hierarchal mold," as E. Herbert Norman, a Canadian historian born in the country would write. But that diagnosis is incomplete because the attempt often failed; daily scrambles regularly broke the mold. Although most Americans may have pictured Japan as "a semi-civilized derelict . . . that might at any time succumb to the power willing to undertake the expense of conquering it,"[40] few Japanese would have agreed, even about the rigidity. Rules were bent to suit convenience, tension and crisis were rarely pervasive, and Tokugawa society—one of the "world's most advanced"[41]—was far from coming apart. On the contrary, it continued to flourish with great vitality, which is why emphasizing its defects creates a misleading image of a kind of dark age awaiting Western light. Ample as they were, none of those defects was as grave as the divide over slavery that threatened to sunder the United States.

Despite the many impediments to progress, especially the kinds most valued by Westerners, Japan was in many ways an *advanced* country, with a relatively prosperous and cultivated life. Although its industry lagged far behind European, it was self-supporting and self-sufficient. Saltwater fishing, progressive forest management, and inventions of a two-bladed plow, a spiked-wheel potato planter, and a weeding machine helped give it higher agricultural productivity than that of its Asian neighbors. Its literacy rate topped England's, and the country matched or bettered many other Western nations in education. In addition to better metallurgy that produced higher-quality swords and armor, a few other early technologies, such as for oil wells, were more efficient than those in the West. Some personal and social arrangements provided even greater advantages.

If cleanliness is next to godliness, the Christian missionaries' lamentation of Japan's failure to have embraced their true faith was misguided, since the country's inhabited areas were generally far cleaner than America's. It was freer of garbage in particular, partly because recycling had long been practiced. More modern sanitary engineering joined skillful medicine in helping prevent outbreaks of diseases, notably typhoid, that were then plaguing Europe. (Washington's sewage of the time accumulated on low ground or ran into the stinking Washington Canal from open sewers and ditches.) Roads and postal services were also superior,[42] invoices and checks were used in business, and more attractive and efficient shops, catering to a growing middle class, foreshadowed mass-market methods, including pre-pricing and -packaging, even point-of-purchase advertising. Fifty-three well-provisioned way stations served the Tokaido, that four-hundred-mile highway from Edo to Kyoto. A thriving packhorse industry made good use of it, and travelers consulted a forerunner of the Michelin guidebook to enlighten their sightseeing and find the best food.

As for the arts, they flowered intensely, at times brilliantly, despite the rigid Confucianism and bureaucratization—or partly in reaction to them. Western ideas trickling into Nagasaki from Deshima helped make the city an important cultural center, although outshone by Edo. The closed capital pulsed with creative energy, thanks to its relatively educated population eager to spend its leisure time and money on entertainment. Music, poetry, painting, theater (including for puppets), ceramics, and couture flourished so vigorously that their production and pursuit sometimes seemed feverish. Costumes and staging flaunted extravagance. Advanced reproduction techniques made available excellent prints, many of high artistic quality, to a relatively wide public. Pulp fiction was often shallow and clichéd, but it satisfied the national love of a good story, and the "alternate residence" requirement that prominent daimyo spend every other year in Edo had the unplanned effect of spreading culture deep into the provinces when the lords and their retinues returned home. "Even the most barbarous warlord desired the trappings of culture that would enable him to feel like a civilized man."[43]

Some of the literature and art frankly depicted the sensual side of city life. Writers of novels and sketches—a genre whose name, literally "spring books," has been translated as a cross between "love stories" and "sex books" because it "deal[t] freely with the amorous proclivities of both sexes"[44]—had abundant material from which to draw their stories. The richest source was the "Floating World" of the men and women who produced and enjoyed the various arts and entertainments.[45] Most worked and played in districts chockablock with theaters, geisha houses, sake shops, and teahouses—so-called "nightless cities" that advertised pleasure and liberally provided it. Most of the advertising was done in woodblocks, which developed into an art form of its own, some of it delightful. The mass-produced prints, in many colors since the mid-eighteenth century, were cheap enough to sell in great numbers. They depicted landscapes and a wide variety of street scenes portraying the life of peasants and laborers as well as the rich and famous, in addition to celebrating sexual beauty and vigor, including in explicit "spring pictures" that featured exaggerated images of the "jade stalk" and "jade gate."

(Nevertheless, the Japanese continued to avoid all hint of intimacy others might see, and would soon be shocked by the habits of visiting Americans, kissing first of all. The barbarian willingness to do that—to lick each other "like dogs," and in public!—would prompt amazement. And when a large delegation of samurai would visit the United States in 1860, seven years after Perry's first arrival in Edo Bay, couples behaving like "butterflies crazed by the sight of flowers," as one put it, would all but bowl them over. It was "simply insufferable to watch" men and women dancing together, especially since the women were shockingly "nude" from shoulders to arms.[46])

The artistic depiction of erotic pleasure—homosexual varieties too—would disturb early American visitors. In 1859, six years after Perry's first arrival, Francis Hall, an American journalist and businessman who long lived and worked in Japan when it remained largely sealed despite Perry's opening, visited a shop in Yokohama (into which Uraga had been incorporated). There he was shown books "full of vile pictures executed in the best style of Japanese art," he complained. (Attached poems, like one brushed onto a man's fan, reflected great interest in genitalia: "Its beak caught firmly in the clam's shell/The snipe cannot fly away/On an autumn evening.") The shop owner and his wife praised the beauty of the drawings, "apparently without a thought of anything low or degrading commensurate with the transaction." Hall correctly assumed he was the only person "whose modesty could have been possibly shocked."

> This is a fair sample of the blunted sense and degraded position of the Japanese as to the ordinary decencies of life. These books abound and are shamelessly exhibited. The official that comes into your house will pull perhaps an indecent print from his pocket.*

The Reverend Samuel Williams, Perry's disgusted translator, pronounced the Japanese people "a lewd people . . . the most lewd" of all the "heathen nations." Despite the near total absence of display of affection, let alone of erotic interest,

> modesty, judging from what we see, might be said to be unknown, for the women make no attempt to hide the bosom, and every step shows the leg above the knee; while the men generally go with the merest bit of rag, and that not always carefully put on. Naked men and women have both been seen in the streets, and uniformly resort to the same bath house, regardless of all decency.[47]

---

* Francis Hall, *Japan Through American Eyes*, p. 81. Hall wrote for Horace Greeley's *New York Tribune*. One of the earliest activities of the Japanese branch of the Woman's Christian Temperance Union would be to campaign for the abolishment of prostitution, into which many poor families sold their daughters. In 1871, the government, under Western prodding, attempted to ban the profession by passing legislation to emancipate prostitutes. It had minor effect.

TO SOME EXTENT, the enthusiasm for visual arts, theater-going, poetry reading, primping, drinking, gossiping, visiting geishas and courtesans, and devouring bawdy books and other bestsellers was an escape from, and rebellion against, the severe samurai codes, with their demand for service and frugality. The devotion to "fun," including enjoyment of good food, was a minor triumph of popular culture over the autocracy. But despite that, and the bawdiness of much of the literature, the Floating World, or world of pleasure, as it was also known, furthered enlightenment—even sophistication and refinement—much more than ignorance.

The written word commanded great importance. In one of the world's most literate nations, the ability to read and write was taken for granted in offices with serious responsibilities. And while that sometimes served to protect the status quo much cherished by those at the top, literacy also provided a channel for the personal and social improvement that was gaining momentum, whatever the semiofficial obstacles to reform. Predictably, it was the rich who most visited the Floating World and who had time— more and more of it—to enjoy books. And the rich were increasingly not the aristocrats but the merchants, together with farmers who were learning to convert their harvests into marketable products more sophisticated than unprocessed produce—for example, textiles instead of cotton. In theory, the merchants remained at the bottom of the class categories, with virtually no chance of jumping higher. But their increasingly progressive practices and growing stores of money were altering the rigid feudalism, slowly but relentlessly.

Still, those advances and achievements suggest no overall grade for social health or popular happiness. How did the people rate *their own* lives, consciously or otherwise? Difficult as it is to evaluate such an intangible, Japan of 1853 surely deserved a passing grade, at least when marked on a curve that includes the more ambitious but less secure Western nations. Although millions were dirt poor, like everywhere else, another haiku poet's image of the overall emotional atmosphere applied to other millions: "On a charcoal fire covered with ash/Simmered at last/Good things in a pot."

The good things much surprised the small corps of Westerners who actually lived there at more or less the relevant time. Well before that,

William Adams, who sailed to Japan in 1600 seeking trade and gold and would become the model for the English pilot in James Clavell's *Shogun*, believed there was "not a lande better governed in the worlde by civil pollecy." At the same time, Adams was shocked by, among other things, samurai mutilation of the corpses of crucified criminals left in the open—a practice from the time of the savage Onin War of 1467–1477, when slaughter of battle survivors was fairly routine. However, there were no battles and relatively very few criminals in the mid-nineteenth century. Among the boons found by one of the American aficionados of Japan who settled there after Perry's mission, a journalist named Lafcadio Hearn, was an extremely low crime rate and level of hostility. "I have lived in districts where no case of theft had occurred for hundreds of years," Hearn, who arrived in 1889, would exult, adding that "the people left their doors unfastened by night as well as by day." Instead of the "deceitful," "weak," and "semi-barbarous" people Perry saw—as he'd expected to see—the ardent Hearn observed a constant, almost universal "amenity, a tact, a good-nature such as he will elsewhere have met only in the friendship of exclusive clubs."[48]

Although Hearn's acclaim was excessive, others' almost matched it. A scholar named Noel Perrin collected praise from prominent Englishmen and Americans who resided in the country during the same twilight of Tokugawa feudalism.[49] Much of it seconded that of an 1804–1805 visitor to Nagasaki, who found "the people of distinction . . . uniformly polite and courteous." If not for their language and dress, "we might have supposed ourselves among the most polished Europeans."[50]

Five years after Perry's first arrival, an American consulate would open in the remote northern town of Shimoda.[51] An amiable young Dutchman named Henry Heusken was its first First Secretary, appointed partly for his ability to translate, since Dutch was still the Western language with which the Japanese were most familiar. After a year in the country, Heusken declared he'd "never been able to discern misery" there, and his solemn employer was scarcely less sweeping. That first American Consul General, a businessman and educator of considerable experience named Townsend Harris, stated in 1858 that Japan came closer to a "golden age of simplicity and honesty" than any other country he knew. The best evidence was its clean, well-fed, well-clad, and "happy-looking" people.

Britain's first Consul General there joined the little chorus two years later. Sir Rutherford Alcock saw "peace, plenty, apparent content, and a country more perfectly cultivated and kept . . . than can be matched even in England." An extended visit convinced another Englishman, Edward Barrington de Fonblanque, that the Western notion of civilizing Japan was invalid, since "civilization exists already." Nor, de Fonblanque said in 1861, could the West add to the country's happiness, "for a more contented people does not exist."

Heated praise of that kind is far from the last word about late Tokugawa well-being, partly because the sample is so small and is contradicted by other Westerners' impressions, partly because accurate readings of thoughts and moods were so difficult. Outside the Floating World, most Japanese exercised tight control of their feelings while continuing to honor humility, simplicity, frugality, and devotion to tradition. Expressing their resentments was even more shameful than revealing the quieter emotions they were skilled in concealing, especially from Westerners.

Besides, the fates of those particular admirers would soon belie their applause. Henry Heusken's declaration about the absence of misery would acquire a hollow ring four years later, when a super-nationalist enraged by the presence of foreigners in native cities assassinated the young secretary-translator at a time when furious military personnel were killing some in Tokyo too.

An alleged relationship with a native girl earned Consul General Townsend Harris extra hatred. The "Madame-Butterfly"–like story—most likely fabricated, but certainty of that will never be established—was that local lords compelled an uncommonly beautiful seventeen-year-old geisha or geisha-in-training to attend to the sexual needs of the fifty-three-year-old. (During the bachelor's three-year stint at that first consulate in Shimoda, another young woman was said to have been recruited for him and three more for secretary Heusken.) Although concern about the provenance of a skin disease from which she was suffering apparently moved Harris to dismiss her quickly, the tale of their contact, fabricated or not, disgraced the young beauty. Scorned as a foreigner's concubine, she ended some thirty years of torment by committing suicide, which novels and plays continue to uphold as classic self-sacrifice.[52] In addition, an annual memorial service is held at the river where the tragic victim of Harris, or of the antiforeigners who plotted his disgrace, drowned herself.

As for Sir Alcock, who celebrated Japan's "peace, plenty, [and] apparent content," a swordsman cut down his Japanese linguist outside the new British legation. Although failing to kill the consulate's other members because they mounted a spirited defense, angry samurai managed to scale a fence and butcher a gatekeeper and a groom.

However, that murderous resentment is also far from the last word, if only because it came in reaction to what was seen as Perry's aggression. And despite the bloody smearing of the enthusiasts' idyllic pictures of Japan, they broaden the one-dimensional image of its people as downtrodden and oppressed by a cruel dictatorship. The ardent Lafcadio Hearn argued that the 260 years of Tokugawa rule—"in no sense a reign of terror"—provided "a universal feeling of security." Although the country was "restrained, pruned, clipped in a thousand ways," it was also cultivated and refined. "The individual was bound more than ever by law and custom; but he was also protected; he could move without anxiety to the length of his chains."[53]

The image was broadened by Francis Hall, the astute American reporter offended by the art he considered obscene but nevertheless impressed by "so much of worldly peace and apparent content and . . . rustic happiness" he observed. Hall's remarkable journal recorded a wide variety of bads and goods, and his emotional antenna would be proved as keen as his eye. Although a late twentieth-century study put Japan's gross national product shortly after Perry at about a quarter of Britain's and just over a third of America's, the country fared far better when measured by quality-of-life indices of physical and mental well-being instead of the consumption of goods on which Western surveys focus. Despite a warning by the study's author that all such comparisons are subjective, since they must rest on amorphous cultural and even philosophical preferences, her conclusions were firm. She based them partly on such factors as sewage treatment, the availability of clean water, frequency of bathing, and agricultural productivity—all of which helped determine life expectancy, and in all of which Japan scored highly. Although, she wrote, most historians and economists share the persistent image of a backward country with a low standard of living, the scholars who study Japanese "lifestyles and material culture" disagree:

> Based on the evidence we have . . . it is hard to support the argument that [Japan's] people were living on average a lifestyle that compared negatively with that in the countries of the West. . . . Their physical

well-being can be compared with that of the most advanced industrial country in the West, England. . . . In . . . literacy, healthfulness of the housing, adequacy of the diet, and life expectancy, the Japanese were at a par with Westerners.[54]

However, the country's culture, achievements, and well-being, whatever they were, hardly mattered to the Perry mission or America at large because what did, overwhelmingly, was the critical inferiority in the industry driven by coal, that "great mineral agent of civilization," the industry that made guns. "Nothing counted more than American firepower," an historian would summarize. With all its pluses and minuses—the latter including relative stifling of modern thought—Japan's nature and condition in 1853 came down to the one measurement of its industrial lag that ordained the military one. The nation would devote much of the century following Perry's arrival to redressing it and acquiring the means for asserting "Never again!"

4

The Military Odds and Perils of Visiting

Uraga, 27 miles below Edo

WHILE THE JAPANESE WERE PANICKING, Americans were breathing easier: despite frantic reinforcement of the forts protecting Uraga's heights, their guns didn't fire. Three little shells—"to inquire after our health, or perhaps to consign us to perdition," an American sailor speculated—exploded "harmlessly astern," while spyglasses revealed that "not all the black muzzles frowning at us from their portholes were genuine." Some were wooden dummies, like the battery of a guard boat in Nagasaki harbor of which the sailor had heard. When the boat capsized in a squall, "various things went to the bottom, but most of her guns floated!"

Relieved crews applauded their surprising luck. Perry had reckoned that "every means, including force, would be devised by the Japanese (for they are a shrewd and cunning people) to get rid of the intruders." Although "intruders" revealed a grasp of his real role, he elaborated neither on why employment of force by the intruded-upon would derive from shrewdness or cunning, nor why his own determination to use it was more admirable. In any case, his prediction was shown to have erred from the first. On July 8, as the squadron was advancing toward Uraga Bay at anxious general quarters, a much-cheered officer found the reputedly formidable coastal forts "laughable." Japan's resources and military strength had been considered very impressive, a fellow officer would more soberly reflect. "Our experience has shown that both have been greatly exaggerated and overestimated."

A third officer who'd seen the squadron as more terrified than merely anxious celebrated that Japan's reputed fondness for war deserved no more worry than a churchyard's ghost, whose banishment required only bolder men than those who had earlier tried to puncture the country's seclusion: "us Yankees," he specified. When those bolder men began surveying local waters from the Black Ships' boats, their increasing confidence affronted the Japanese, who had strict orders from Edo to use no gunfire (and much vaguer ones to "settle the matter in a peaceable way"). An occupant of one of the boats responded to a Japanese officer's "get out of here" wave by putting some sand on his palm and making "a gesture of blowing it off with one breath," after which the American intruders "burst into laughter and left."

When another boat landed near a fortification the following day, Americans pointed their swords at a Japanese battery, "jeered at us, and were very overbearing." The battery's enraged commander rushed out, his spear pointed at the trespassers, who "laughed and clapped their hands. There have been reported numberless instances of insolence like this one."

Thus the fear of Perry's men that he was leading them into a trap that would end in death or the cages used for previous foreign visitors was evaporating. Hands adopted the term "dungaree forts" for the construction material employed: canvas rigged to deceive. (The Japanese apparently hadn't counted on the power of Western spyglasses.) The array of obsolete Japanese weapons interested the Americans "as a spectacle," an historian would note, but "it was evident that a broadside or two from their big guns would put an end to it."

Perry's study of Japan was largely responsible for the mission's remarkable success until now; but he was the least inclined to permit any partial achievement to lower his guard. His rank of commodore, then the American navy's highest,* made him a "titanic personage afloat or ashore." In addition to his sterling command qualities, his determination to maintain the vigilance of his ships was all the greater because they were nine fewer than Washington had originally promised him for the mission. His own renowned diligence gave him some comfort. At that critical hour, knowledge of the history of Japan's silent cannon might have provided more. The country's firearms had more than one story to tell, starting with a romance when Japanese warriors first made their acquaintance.

THE GUNS OF THE EARLIEST EUROPEAN VISITORS, the sixteenth-century Portuguese who landed on the island south of Nagasaki, prompted delight.[1] Their matchlock muskets, or arquebusses, were the first real ones—as opposed to a scattering of triggerless iron tubes with which a few Japanese had experimented—seen in the land.

That land could hardly be called a *country* as the word is now known. The Emperor had no army, virtually no power, and a life so prescribed that no feudal lord could visit him without permission. Since the twelfth century, authority issued far less from him than from the military overseer positioned to speak in his name: the Shogun, or supreme military leader. But even the Shoguns governed less authoritatively than their later reputations would suggest. The current one, in that sixteenth century, controlled only an area surrounding Kyoto, the city of the Emperor's residence, some three hundred miles from Edo, which hadn't yet been made the Tokugawa seat.

Those three centuries before Perry's arrival, the Japanese islands were a jumble of several hundred feudal domains. With few exceptions, the mostly independent *han* were ruled by largely sovereign masters called daimyo, who were more or less continuously plotting against one another when not actually battling for dominance. Relentless fighting preoccupied thought and prescribed behavior, the kaleidoscopic civil grappling involving nearly

---

* The grade of admiral would be established four years later. A commodore was usually a senior captain in command of a squadron of ships.

everyone and almost totally undermining central authority. "The dismal collapse of central government," Paul Varley would summarize in his *The Onin War*, led to "a century"—essentially the mid-fifteenth to the mid-sixteenth—"of near anarchy," further fractured by peasant uprisings. European barons and dukes of the Middle Ages, whom the lords of the *han* otherwise resembled in many ways, had never known quite such a free-for-all. Kyoto was repeatedly razed during that darkest period in Japanese history, and many other regions were devastated, together with their clans.

With a multitude of legions joining the hostilities, switching sides, dropping out, and returning to producing or becoming carnage, the daimyo and their retainers learned to trust neither their neighboring or distant counterparts. Whole regiments would sometimes desert to an enemy and be welcomed by him, but never accepted as reliable allies. Ceaseless conspiring for the mix-and-match scramble for survival and ascendancy made it highly imprudent to rely on any allegiance, which is why the forever insecure daimyo spent much of their time placing spies, in the persons of maids, advisors, and supposedly utterly loyal samurai, in the courts of their allies as well as their enemies.

Meanwhile, the combat in the field remained frequent and furious. Prodigious time and energy were devoted to preparing for the struggle, which lasted considerably longer than the parvenue American republic's full life span when Perry sailed from Norfolk. Many perceived it as endless, but end it finally did, thanks to shrewd and skillful scheming combined with stealthy posturing and negotiating. "Marriage politics" and, conversely, banishing enemies to remote regions helped forge crucial alliances. Above all, the prolonged achievement of supremacy took brilliant and brutal victories on battlefields that were left wet with blood, together with nearby villages where defeated warriors' relatives were also slain.

Because emergence from that ruinous time of troubles marked large social and economic steps forward, it remained at the roots of political arrangements and attitudes now, in Perry's summer of 1853. Not that Japan wasn't full of problems, some of which seemed beyond its creaky government's power to resolve. But since none was nearly so catastrophic as during the "age of the country at war," the present system's stock remained high in almost all eyes.

Peace in the land that had been splintered by strife and treachery helped the unified economy to soar. Castle towns much expanded, thanks especially to increasingly vigorous merchants who thrived despite their lowly official status. A middle class, although not so called, grew in numbers, wealth, and sophistication.

Three remarkable men were chiefly responsible for the healing unification. The first, Oda Nobunaga laid the groundwork by seizing Kyoto in 1568 and subjugating the *han* of central Japan. After his assassination, his most accomplished general, Toyotomi Hideyoshi—the military and political virtuoso who would first encourage and later attack Christianity—extended the territory under control to the remainder of the country. After his death, his place was very cleverly taken by yet another masterful leader, who, because he made use of the unified country's many advantages, was said to eat the cake Toyotomi had baked.

The third gifted commandant was the aforementioned Tokugawa Ieyasu, the son of a relatively minor lord. In 1600, he won a decisive battle, fought in driving rain at mountainous Sekigahara—probably the most important engagement in Japanese history because it enabled him to establish his dynasty. From then until 1867, when the dynasty would collapse—fourteen anything-but-coincidental years after the Black Ships' arrival—the great family was so important that the country would be known as "Tokugawa Japan." Now, as Perry was preparing to land, another Tokugawa—the twelfth in line since his ancestor had finally delivered national stability—resided in Edo Castle. He, Tokugawa Ieyoshi, ruled, if not forcefully, as the Shogun.

The Emperors' line (in contrast to those of regularly overthrown Chinese rulers) went even further back. Far further: the Emperors belonged to the longest continuous dynasty in world history, the whole of it believed to have descended from the sun goddess Amaterasu, who had been born from an eye of the ruler of the Plain of Heaven. However, the present one—shadowy Emperor Komei, the 121st in line—was no less ineffectual for his exalted lineage, except in rituals conducted inside the high walls of his inaccessible Kyoto castle. And the ineffective Shogun's grave illness that had recently shifted all real responsibility for decisions to Abe Masahiro made him not greatly more relevant on the hot July morning of 1853.

Perry couldn't be blamed for knowing none of that. The Japanese "are by no means communicative about themselves," he'd write with uncommon understatement about the country that had so long and rigorously isolated itself, adding that they alleged their laws forbade them to reveal to foreigners "anything relating to their country and its institutions, habits and customs." The rulers' devotion to secrecy on top of Western egocentrism left very few on other continents with more than guesses about the remote country's ways and thoughts. Early nineteenth-century Europe's most popular book about Japan described its religion as "gross heathenism and idolatry." Reversing the truth, it also stated that Japan traded with all nations except China and Holland.

The current *Encyclopaedia Britannica* offered only a pinch of garbled information about what others called the "mystery," "sealed book," and "vague and shadowy idea,"[2] of whose language no known Briton or American understood more than a few words. A crash course taken by Samuel Wells Williams, an American missionary in China whom Perry appointed as his interpreter, gave him but a sketchy grasp.[3] A hundred-and-thirty-odd years later, historian John Dower would call Japan's and America's conception of each other during World War II "a tapestry of truths, half-truths and empty spaces." In America's picture of the Japan of 1853, the empty spaces mightily prevailed, and its complex government was a blank.

The best books about Japan had been written by two Germans who'd served as physicians to the Dutch colony, the first late in the seventeenth century and the other, Philipp Franz von Siebold, for seven years during the 1820s. Although Perry would disparage von Siebold for "inordinate conceit" and decline to take the German on the expedition because he suspected he spied for Russia, the Commodore read his three volumes—unavailable to the general public because they were published in costly folios—with more care and broader interest than in the tides and currents off Japan. (For firsthand reports about maritime matters, he visited New Bedford, Massachusetts, to interview whaling captains.) But although his "master[ing]," as he allowed, of all the information books could provide further boosted his self-confidence, von Siebold's tributes to Japan's high cultural level left him unimpressed. He was aware that restrictions on the physician's movements and observations much limited his understanding, and that all knowledge of the country remained scant. While it was "not quite correct to say that the civilized world knows nothing of Japan," Perry acknowledged, "it may truly be asserted that what is known is very much less than what is unknown." Whether it was wise to mount the mission with such skimpy intelligence was a question rarely raised in the nineteenth century. The Commodore would never know the Emperor's name or where he lived, let alone his relationship to the Shogun. How the country he'd undertaken to improve was ruled—and how much it was changing on its own in response to domestic pressures—would forever remain beyond him.

JAPAN'S WAXING–WANING LOVE AFFAIR WITH GUNS also escaped mid-nineteenth-century Americans. Like the country's zigzags toward reforms without direct application of external force, it was counterintuitive to their assumptions. Image exerted its usual dominance, and the Western one of Japan suggested its backwardness in firearms was inevitable.

Far from it. Enthralled by the newfangled devices' ability to kill swiftly and from a relatively safe distance, mid-sixteenth-century Japanese warriors blazed away with their Portuguese prizes. A student's recent claim that within half a century "no soldier would venture into battle unless equipped with the most modern firearms"[4] probably overstates the fondness for them, and it may be an exaggeration to conclude, without specifying the method of counting, that by 1600, the Japanese owned "more and better guns than any country in the world." Still, the new gunsmiths— mostly former swordsmiths, the best of whom were probably the world's best—were crafting products as good or better than any European counterparts before the end of the century. Drawing on the country's highly developed preindustrial technology, they not merely copied Western models, but also made substantial improvements, such as adding an antiglow device to keep the matchlock's ignition invisible at night. Most were of splendid quality, like that of Japanese oceangoing ships before the country's closing prohibited their construction.

Some of the new weapons were used in a 1592 invasion of Korea. (The devastating onslaught was abandoned upon the death of Toyotomi Hideyoshi, but honored in Kyoto by a mound of the pickled ears and noses of some 40,000 Korean corpses.) The passion for firearms grew and grew—until early in the seventeenth century, when it began to fade. One explanation is that while any European nation that abandoned guns would have been quickly overrun by a neighbor, Japan's isolation—which also enabled it to maintain its seclusion—allowed it to take the risk. Besides, battlefield performance became less and less important once the Tokugawa dynasty was well established. By the time Perry arrived, Japan had been at peace for two and a half centuries, longer than a similar respite enjoyed by any other major nation. Peace helped to dull memory of the old bloodshed, and a growing sense of security nourished confidence that foreigners wouldn't invade because they perceived the country as too strong.

Other reasons were cultural. Decisive as bullets could be in crucial battles, vivid as were the demonstrations of swords' relative impotence against them, samurai warriors came to give more importance to traditional measurements of valor and honor.

During the first decades of guns' wide manufacture, they were used chiefly by peasant soldiers battling each other in their lords' unrelenting clashes. Their topknotted samurai betters generally stuck to their swords and rarely fell even when the occasional bullet was aimed at them: range was short and power often insufficient to penetrate their armor. But technology of course improved. In 1584, four decades after the arrival of the first Portuguese, military professionals were disturbed by the slaying of a mounted young lord preparing to lead his troops in a charge. The considerably more powerful and longer-range guns now in use were negating the elaborate samurai code of combat ethics, devised for swords. There was little skill and no honor in killing with the mechanical contraptions, which were also ugly, especially compared to the traditional sword's beauty. Yet a bullet from a "nobody," as Noel Perrin summarized, could now fell the greatest swordsman, thus deflating the value of "the samurai's chief art."

So the reaction was about class as much as about warfare. If some began despising the new weapons that reduced all combatants to the level of a peasant,* the larger cause was samurai reassertion of themselves, with their elaborate training in swordsmanship, as superiors in the social order. The great revulsion necessary for any extensive relinquishing of such proficient weapons had been accumulating from deep within the opinion makers' sense of themselves and their worth, and partly because the instruments were mechanical rather than works of craftsmanship, they could come to be seen as ultimately un-Japanese. More than that, the stark symbols of barbarian morals represented one side—Christianity and commerce were

---

* Use of the crossbow in Europe had encountered some of the same disapproval. In 1139, Pope Innocent II forbade its use by Christians against Christians because it was "deathly and hateful to God and unfit to be used among Christians."

the others—of what was in time considered an unholy trinity serving as the foundation of Western culture.

While building dikes against European mercantilism and aggrandizement, the Tokugawas carefully restricted guns' manufacture and use. As persecution of Christians began and weapons were taken from everyone but samurai, firearms in particular were declared contraband for private citizens. That wasn't disastrous for the smiths, most of whom returned to forging swords for the samurai, who still proudly wore them. However, the loss to traders from abandoning profitable routes into Southeast Asia and the Indian Ocean at roughly the same time was substantial. The reasons for retreating from the gun largely coincided with those for closing the previously hospitable maritime country.

Practical considerations also counted. Yes, Japan was now unified, but the power of some *han* remained strong, together with their penchant for scheming. The Tokugawas, whom history had taught to see the domains where most Westerners had lived as posing the greatest danger to their domination, took great pains to observe and constrain them. Why permit them to store guns?

But now the chief concern was the foreign menace rather than potential domestic rebellion, thanks to the attempts to breach the national seclusion. Were those attempts bad for the world? Did Edo's anxiety matter at all? After all, the foreign threat was partly to Japanese conceit, the leaders having long and diligently convinced themselves of their divinely ordained supremacy. Puncturing that pretension, as Perry was preparing to do, might well benefit the Japanese people. As noted, the threat could be seen as more to the status quo than to the general welfare. The Tokugawas' devotion to remaining in power was as strong as that of rulers elsewhere. Survival instinct fired much of their passionate resolve to exclude foreign thought and to control or suppress any of it that managed to sneak in through the barriers.

As true as that was, however, and as shaky as Japanese feudalism had become during recent decades of Western vessels breathing down its neck, the imperial powers' hunger to cut up nearby China for colonies and control made the threat larger and more terrible. For more than eight decades after James Watt's 1769 invention of the steam engine, the furnaces of the Industrial Revolution, firing ever hotter, had been producing new military might. The British victory in the Opium War, just eleven years before

Perry anchored at Uraga, was Asia's practical introduction to the phenomenon. The stunning news of China's defeat prompted an important advisor from the Mito domain—soon to figure prominently in Lord Abe's struggles—to warn the Shogun to "despise not" the war's lessons about modern weapons.

The 1842 rout by the Royal Navy and Marines led straight to the Chinese Empire's disintegration, foreigners extracting concession after concession in a process they called "slicing the melon." The Portuguese took Goa from India at about the same time as the British snatched Hong Kong. Japan's backwardness in the firearms that made possible those seizures in nearby Asia was due less to lack of mechanical ingenuity than to seeking security in seclusion more than in acquisition of weapons.

Perry's unawareness of Japan's former excellence in firearms manufacture can be assumed because he rarely restrained himself from logging his achievements, and left no record of having digested the curious history. More narrowly, he didn't know the cannon protecting Uraga were eight-pounders, the largest Japanese makers had come to believe could be safely cast. Nor did he know that most were a century or two old, and dangerous to their crews during their test firings. That happened only once every seven years, according a report by a Swedish botanist—one of the very few Westerners to glimpse Japan after its seventeenth-century closing to Westerners—some eighty years before Perry's arrival.

What the Commodore did know was that his cannon were vastly superior. Six years earlier, during the Mexican War, he'd won the relatively quick surrender of Vera Cruz by taking his flagship *Mississippi* in close and firing new explosive shells, whose range and power were considered phenomenal. The implication was understood even by those with little experience of how dominant were heavier guns in battle, or how the damage they caused soared in geometric proportion to their weight of shot. One of the artists the Commodore had hired to illustrate the mission—Wilhelm Heine, who enjoyed the nocturnal view of the "fireflies" on the shore—understood that at the worst, if hostilities did commence, "we could anchor beyond their range and at leisure bombard them with our sixty-eights"[5]—shorthand for sixty-eight-pounders, the main armament of the *Susquehanna*, Perry's flagship.

Although Western naval guns were now usually designated by the diameters of their barrels or shells, the consequences were the same, all the more because the newly rifled American cannon aimed much more precisely than the barrels that delivered old-fashioned balls. Shells weighing sixty-eight pounds could be a dozen times more damaging than the balls of the Japanese cannon guarding the mouth of Edo Bay, many of which fired only three-pounders. With a range almost four times longer—roughly three thousand meters compared to the eight hundred sometimes achieved by the Japanese cannon—they could wreak destruction on Japan's coastal cities with virtual impunity. (Ironically reporting a Washington correspondent's assurance that the Perry mission was merely for surveying Japan's coast and its shells would be used only as measuring instruments, the *New York Herald* said a Japanese foolish enough to "put his head in the way of these meteorological instruments" could blame no one but himself.[6]) Or they might starve Edo into submission by sinking the barges that delivered most of the capital's rice.

That was why Perry had always been intent on mounting the best guns on the largest squadron he could muster; maximum firepower was crucial to his plans. It was also why the silence of the coastal guns didn't really surprise him. Although unaware that Japan as a whole possessed no more than a few hundred small, mostly obsolete cannon, the commander had already satisfied himself that his squadron, manned by close to a thousand sailors and mounting some sixty-five modern guns,* constituted overwhelming superiority—display of which was also central to his strategy.

Experience had taught him to be forceful with foreigners even when he wasn't at war with them. Sent to help collect long-standing debts to American traders twenty-one years earlier, in 1832, he'd sailed his squadron into the Bay of Naples until the royal palace was within easy reach of his guns. Submission by the King of the Two Sicilies, who until then had stubbornly refused to consider the claims, prompted a very pleased Congress to allocate $1,500 to repay Master Commandant Perry for his personal expenses during the assignment. A recent biographer would conclude that he'd "never forget the importance of an intimidating naval presence in facilitating difficult negotiations."

A more recent Japanese rebuff to a colleague reinforced the lesson. In July 1846—seven years earlier almost to the day—another American

---

* Samuel Eliot Morison, *"Old Bruin,"* p. 356. The precise number of crew members and guns isn't known. On paper, it was 1,800 and 140, respectively, but the squadron was undermanned and some of its ships lacked their full complement of arms.

commodore had attempted the feat of opening the resolutely closed country: James Biddle, the commander of what was then called America's East India (rather than East Asia) Squadron, anchored a mile or so lower in the same Uraga Bay. President Andrew Jackson had instructed Biddle not to demand establishment of relations, as Perry was about to do; only to investigate whether Japan wanted them, and to avoid using force while doing so. Determined to demonstrate he'd come in friendship, the commander played the congenial guest by permitting boatloads of curious natives to inspect his two fine warships,[7] even though native officials—who nevertheless saw him as a menace—prohibited his crews from disembarking.

Biddle's gestures got him nowhere. He gave the President's letter to minor local officials—bad judgment Perry would make certain not to repeat—and after days of sterile talk with them, declared he expected a response to his proposals. At last a junk appeared carrying officers who requested Biddle to come aboard to receive the official reply. Overcoming his fear of lowering American prestige, the commander reluctantly agreed; but when he began climbing onto the junk from own ship's boat, a guard's block or shove sent him sprawling back. So went the American version that would be widely broadcast back home as the whole, insulting truth. In the Japanese version, the officers waited an hour for Biddle to change into his full dress uniform, after which his boat mistakenly approached one of the local patrol boats. "A guard pointed out the official junk, but the Commodore evidently misunderstood him and proceeded to step aboard the patrol-boat," whereupon another guard pushed him back and drew his sword.

Either way, a commoner's manhandling of a high officer produced shock waves in very hierarchical Japan, reinforcing the conviction of many that a little firmness could handle the Westerners despite their big guns. Very soon afterward, all interested Americans too learned about the grave affront—in Biddle's version only—and were little assuaged by Edo's profuse apologies and promise of severe punishment for the guard. The incident affected Japanese–American relations more than any larger issue.

Perry in particular shared Biddle's anger. Concern for the esteem due to his golden epaulets embroidered the Commodore's ardor for winning the young American republic international honor, making him extremely sensitive to slights. More to the point, he had reason to conclude the Japanese took Biddle's conciliatory approach—and his submission to their order to leave the country and never return—as indication of weakness. The better-prepared Perry would make no such mistake. In a sense, everything came down to a promise he liked to repeat: he would not be trifled with. His way would be "entirely contrary" to that of all who had previously undertaken the same exacting mission: "*To demand as a right* [italics added] and not to solicit as a favor those acts of courtesy which are due from one civilized nation to another; to allow none of those petty annoyances which have been unsparingly visited upon those who had preceded him."[8]

Together with that, underlying his strategy from the start of his planning, went reliance on displaying disdain for the "host" country's wishes. Again to his own satisfaction, Perry had made two crucial points during the tense but gratifying week since the squadron first sighted the Japanese mainland. With his weapons and stern resolution, the Commodore had made clear he'd no more be bound by Japanese customs and rules than be trifled with. Just as he'd demonstrably ignored the strict and severe forbiddance of the landing being prepared that morning of July 14, he'd performed many of his actions during the preceding week in Japanese waters to proclaim that his guide would be American rules, not Japanese. That was why he told Japanese officials he knew their laws perfectly well because he'd spent a year studying them, but that they didn't apply to him. It was also why he took pride in "purposely" violating their prohibitions— against surveying Uraga Bay, among other activities. His intention was to "alarm the authorities and induce them to give a more favorable answer to my demands."

Underlying that, in turn, was a deep distrust of his unwilling hosts. After completing the expedition, Perry would have some good things to say about them, including appreciation of their frankness, truthfulness, and hospitality "as private gentlemen." The craftsmen would win particular praise: "In the practical and mechanical arts, the Japanese show great dexterity; and when the rudeness of their tools and their imperfect knowledge of machinery are considered, the perfection of their manual skill appears marvellous." Those compliments, however, were scattered amid a general judgment of the Japanese people as "vindictive in character" and, crucially, "treacherous" and "deceitful."

The disparagement pained Samuel Wells Williams. Wondering why God had chosen such people to do His work, the missionary-translator confided to his diary that most of the squadron's officers spoke of "the whole race" of Japanese as "savages, liars, a pack of fools, poor devils." Not always; a few of the crew saw them as a nation of reporters and readers. But officers' quips that the natives were less than fully human undoubtedly revealed some of what they really felt. (Although the Japanese had similar suspicions about Westerners, their solution was to hide, not pounce.) The implied contradiction of thinking the natives they cursed worthy of making a treaty with evidently never struck Perry himself, who simultaneously derided them as "semi-barbarous" and "weak": "You have to deal with barbarians as barbarians."

Most relevantly, Perry found the functionaries, with whom he dealt almost exclusively, contemptible in their official capacities. "They lie and practice artifice to save themselves from condemnation by the higher powers," before whom they crouched in ways that would be torturous to Americans. If Japan weren't so distant, its government surely would long have been "treated as barbarians, or been compelled to respect these usages of civilized states *of which it receives the protection* [italics added]." His conclusion confirmed the assumption with which he'd begun, which was that Japanese were duplicitous almost by nature: "One would suppose that they consider it a compliment to be thought tricky and deceitful." The darkness he saw there, to borrow John Dower's observation of American views of Japan, was "opposed to [America's] own radiant light."

But that was part of the background. In the foreground was his intention to open the country with actions "for which the Japanese would not be prepared." The futile earlier missions had taught him a crucial lesson: he had to jolt the stubbornness out of people who failed to accept they must give way to the family of nations. Displaying his military might would "do more to command their fears . . . than all that the diplomatic missions have accomplished in the last one hundred years."[9] Among the other tactics that earned his self-admiration, he'd purposely ignore the "established rule of diplomacy."

WHAT POSSESSED WASHINGTON'S REPRESENTATIVE TO "demand as a right" acts of civilized courtesy while himself violating them by intentionally ignoring diplomatic rules? Virtually all Westerners were convinced their travelers and traders brought enlightenment to Asia. Official and unofficial communications about the expedition abounded in such phrases as "our duty," "higher civilization," "better life," "nobler principles," and "the blessings of modern thought and development." Twenty-first-century commentators might call that an early display of double-standard hubris, and the same Samuel Wells Williams, who, as Perry's translator, saw more of Japan than most other mission members, suggested something similar even then. Wells dismissed "our ostensible reasons" for "this great outlay and sending this powerful squadron" because he saw the "real" ones as "glorification of the Yankee nation, and food for praising ourselves." But Perry thought very differently, and he was moved by more than his considerable conceit. After his raising in the mainstream—or a little right of it, together with many other military officers—nothing seemed more right and proper to him than bringing civilization to (and establishing bases in) the benighted East. He was certain that his infractions of international rules would soon prove good for the Japanese.

The Commodore's attitudes were grounded in that all-but-universal Western assumption then that the West would inevitably conquer ideologically and spiritually because that was right and just. The racial hierarchy that reflected was self-evident to men of his station and lower. Supporting evidence was seen in the three categories into which the world's countries supposedly fell: civilized nation-states, half-civilized semistates, and even lesser bodies. Japan was in the second category, the United States *primus inter pares* of the first. Shortly before his death, the Commodore would predict his youthful homeland was destined, "at some indefinite time" after having attaining its full manhood, to fall into decline "by the consequences of its own vices and misdoings." But in the nineteenth century, America was "the great charity of God to the human race," as Ralph Waldo Emerson would put it thirty years later; it was the glorious "universal Yankee nation," Samuel Williams saw now. God ultimately ruled. The human species advanced, if unevenly, toward His design. Sooner or later, America's revolution—"in a great measure, the cause of all mankind," as Thomas Paine had put it in *Common Sense*—would become the world's.

Impatient to hasten the process, Perry knew the American empire would be a righteous one, conferring freedom, democracy, and prosperity to those it governed. Its ideas and power must spread across the Pacific until they "placed the Saxon race upon the eastern shores of Asia"—that is, the coasts of China and Japan, all the more because partially enlightened Japan needed a "higher civilization's" instruction, as the Reverend Williams saw it. Among the strongest, saddest proof of that was its refusal to adhere to what was considered a broad "law of nations" governing their behavior; even to discuss its obligations. Its own laws excluding foreigners were irrational, perverse, ridiculous, deeply self-damaging, and a negation of American values. It was "against nature" to prohibit international relations. Japan's isolation contravened "God's plan of bringing the nations of the earth to a knowledge of His truth." The existence of international law based on that premise—although not all its articles were written—was commonly accepted in the West. Japan denied it.

Another assumption moved Perry. As if intending to set a pattern, he believed he'd be welcomed as a liberator. The patriot who saw God's unique blessing of America as an obvious truth easily believed the Japanese "masses" would "connive" with him, defying their government that oppressed and indoctrinated with antiforeign prejudice.

As for the mission's practical aims, ostensibly the most urgent was stopping Japan's breeches of maritime customs and rules, which were more specific than the assumed universal law, although some were also unwritten. The outcast country's measures to protect its seclusion included repelling foreign vessels—with force, if considered necessary. Unarmed merchant and whaling ships had been fired upon when the guardians of the prohibited shores thought they approached too closely.

The whalers' catch was used to make the crude oil of the time, some of which lit the lamps of the then modern world. The American fleet soared in number after sperm whales, whose numbers had been much depleted elsewhere, were found off Japan's Pacific coast in 1820. That was five years before the discovery of oil in Pennsylvania, at a time when the huge appetite for whales made them, as a Japanese writer would venture, the "God of Marriage between Japan and the United States." When Perry sailed thirty-odd years later, hundreds of American whalers, manned by some twenty thousand crew members, made up the majority of the foreign ships working "on Japan," in the occupational lingo, meaning working the North Pacific, then the world's richest grounds. Nearly three hundred ships from a single New England port traversed the Bering Strait between the Pacific and Arctic oceans in 1848. (Confederate privateers would ravage the fleet at the end of the Civil War.) The return on investment could be huge. Six "greasy" (lucrative) runs to the rich grounds between 1841 and 1861 would net a three-hundred-ton bark named *Lagoda* an average profit of 98 percent.

The port was New Bedford, Massachusetts. It and others on mostly northeastern American coasts thrived, while the resentment of the Japanese industry, whose smaller boats couldn't compete, helped harden the attitude to foreigners. Despite the national seclusion, Japan had provided many foreign vessels with firewood, potable water, and foodstuffs, if in need—so long as they attempted nothing smacking of missionary activity. Japanese vigilance against commerce, as opposed to emergency provisioning, also continued. In 1824 alone, some three hundred Japanese, mostly fishermen, were imprisoned for surreptitious trading with half a dozen or so foreign ships that had annually approached one of the coasts. But growth of international commerce and advances in shipbuilding and ship handling were multiplying their number.

More and more veered into Japanese waters. Some British ships that ignored the prohibition and entered native ports were permitted to leave unmolested, sometimes with generous supplies of free provisions. In 1824, however, sailors of one of His Majesty's frigates fought with Nagasaki inhabitants, and its officers threatened force to demand supplies. A local magistrate complied, then committed suicide. Further convinced of a need to insulate the country from the outside world's discord and destructiveness, the Tokugawa government reacted the following year by issuing a severe "No Second Thought" edict, popularly known as "Shell and Repel." Prompted more by fear than hatred, it nevertheless changed the previous policy of destroying only the vessels that refused to answer questions about their complement and purpose. Now those venturing or straying too close to shore were to be fired on without hesitation, and any foreigners who landed "must be arrested or killed."

All Southern Barbarians and Westerners, not only the English, worship Christianity, that wicked cult prohibited in our land. Henceforth, whenever a foreign ship is sighted approaching any point on our coast, all persons on land should fire on and drive it off. . . . Never be caught off guard.

THE NEED FOR ALERTNESS was underlined in 1831, when an armed party from an Australian whaler stole supplies from a village whose inhabitants had fled. According to the ship's logbook, the crew torched the settlement after committing "Sackarlige by Robbing their temple." Coastal authorities were exhorted to be even more vigilant, and American ships were among those that suffered the consequences. Worse, their seamen seeking refuge after shipwreck on the country's rocky coasts were harshly mistreated. More than unfriendly, that was positively hostile—an expression of what was seen, in that middle of the nineteenth century, as Japan's barbarism.

Five years after Perry's arrival, an astute American preparing to settle in the newly opened country that had been "so long forbidden to strangers" described the "intolerant selfishness" that had inspired its seclusion. Its shores were "so inhospitable that the shipwrecked mariner escaped the sea only to find a more cruel fate on shore." Even Japanese who had left their homeland "could never return except to meet a certain death." But forbidding foreign travel and outlawing the building of ships capable of performing it—even beheading native violators of the seclusion laws— was one thing. Treating foreign castaways like "the most atrocious criminals," as put in the Navy Department's instructions to the Commodore, was another. A nation that did that must be considered mankind's "common enemy."

Recent incidents had heightened American outrage. When an 1846 gale sank the *Lawrence*, a whaler out of Poughkeepsie, New York, its captain was rumored to be killed. Although that would prove false, the seven survivors would testify that despite making clear that they'd been shipwrecked, they'd been "frequently struck" and insulted "in every way possible."

> They threatened to cut off our heads, because they thought we were English, whom they hate; but when we told them we were Americans, they said nothing more, except to ask of us what religion we were. Upon our telling them we worshipped [*sic*] God, and believed in Jesus Christ, they brought a cross bearing the image of our Saviour, and had we not tramped upon it at their request, they would have massacred us on the spot.

That was unlikely, despite their understandable fear; nor was their detention as atrocious as they painted it. Its eleven-month duration was caused less by intention than circumstance, albeit the kind to which rigid, frightened governments were often prey. Months passed while instructions from Edo were sought by local authorities in the Kurile Islands, where the survivors had eventually landed. Winter's approach led those authorities to consider their transport by sea to Nagasaki, where Japan still conducted its trickle of foreign intercourse, too dangerous.

Meanwhile, they were indeed treated as prisoners rather than victims of misfortune, but records of their captors and of the Deshima Dutch seem to document they were much less onerously abused than they'd assert, apart from the forced trampling of the cross. That abhorrence, hatched from Edo's dread of Christianity and supposedly required of all Nagasaki residents annually, had become an obligatory ritual. Otherwise, the Japanese intention to keep them carefully guarded but alive was clear from Abe Masahiro's instructions to administer medicine, in case of illness, "at once, regardless of whether or not they ask for it." Although one of the seven nevertheless died—of dysentery, the Japanese insisted, or maltreatment, according to his fellows—the survivors, when finally released, were given food for their outward voyage on a Dutch ship, whose captain was requested to ensure they would be well treated.

A worse case, probably the worst ever, began in Hokkaido two years later (shortly after the start of the gold rush to California and the outbreak of revolutionary movements in many European states, to put the incident in its Western contexts). Since the waters of mainland Japan's northernmost major island could be as dangerously stormy as rich in whales, castaways washed up on its coasts were no great surprise. But shocking harshness awaited the passengers of three small boats that landed in June 1848. They were fifteen crew members of the *Lagoda* whose whaling in the vicinity had earned the 98 percent average profit, but now, they explained, had foundered with the loss of twenty of their fellows.

The following month's arrival of James Biddle, Perry's less assertive predecessor, may have heightened Japanese suspicions that they were spies, but that was no excuse for the sailors' persecution. Imprisoned in filthy cages too short for standing erect and exposed to freezing cold in their rags, they were also insufficiently fed and, like earlier detainees, forced to trample on an image of the Virgin and Child. Ropes tied much too tightly gashed the skin of those placed in stocks. Shown the just-severed head of a Japanese prisoner while threatened with their own execution, the hapless men indeed seemed to have been treated like the Emperor's "worst enemies," as the acting Secretary of State put it in additional instructions to Perry, drafted by the Commodore himself.

Two or three of the fifteen died, one evidently of physical neglect, another by hanging himself. More than a year passed before the survivors were grudgingly delivered to an American corvette that had arrived to demand their return (which had been planned for the next Dutch ship scheduled to leave Nagasaki). American newspapers helped swell the numbers who knew little more about Japan than the cruelty they reported. Readers naturally detested the odious departures from civilized norms, the vicious violations of a cardinal provision of that vague but widely accepted law of nations. Decent people aided foreigners forced to land among them by storm or shipwreck instead of binding them to posts and beating them, another form of mistreating the *Lagoda* crew.

The real story, untold in America, was much more complicated, however. The New Bedford bark hadn't been shipwrecked, nor the crew "cast" anywhere; they'd jumped ship—apparently to escape *American* cruelty practiced there—and voluntarily rowed to shore, where their behavior helped bring their hardship on themselves. Whether or not their guards acted brutishly, the deserters were clearly a rough lot. They began by defying an order upon their landing to return to their boats and row off again with firewood and rice supplied by the authorities—who, however, later agreed that might be suicidal. The sailors' subsequent confinement, at first in a large house, became punitive after they displayed resistance, fought among themselves, and, despite promises to stop, made repeated attempts to escape, some temporarily successful. The proud but insecure Japanese leaders who wanted to manage foreign relations by forbidding them vacillated about what to do with the unwanted foreigners (whom the guards reported as looking "all alike," even though some were Hawaiian).

If only Westerners wouldn't come! If only they'd leave Japan's leaders, who wanted to manage foreign relations by forbidding them, alone in their insular feudalism. The uncertainty about the interlopers lurking beneath Edo's pretense of the opposite no doubt helped explain why the treatment of most visitors was less standard, and often much less severe, than the Western picture of it from the castaways' selective truth. At the same time, Perry's devotion to big guns was fed by a broader vision than his commitment to improve it. "We possess the power, why not use it?" he'd argued, shortly before taking command of the squadron. He was confident his modern guns would "command fears," which is why he was pleased to register it on the faces of Japanese fishermen manning their little boats, even when they "fancied themselves at a sufficiently safe distance."

Although even the Commodore's admirers saw him often behaving "as if suffering from permanent toothache," no sadistic impulse accompanied his conviction that higher powers promoting moral good ordained American expansion. His satisfaction in observing the Japanese fear derived not from a liking for domination for its own sake but for advancing his vision of the national interest. Power—especially naval power—was the name of the mid-nineteenth-century game. For this mission, surely to become the jewel in the crown of his career, his hazy image of Japan was no deterrent to his resolve to benefit humankind by spreading American sway. He was "serenely convinced," a scholar recently summarized, he was "bringing civilization to a benighted land that lived in flagrant violation of all norms of international society."[10]

5

The Commanding Commodore

A Matthew Brady photograph of Perry after the mission

PERRY'S NEARLY FORTY-FIVE YEARS of service, briefly interrupted to captain a merchant vessel, had earned him a place in naval history well before his appointment to lead the mission. Hard tours on ships supporting American settlements in Africa, confronting pirates in the Caribbean, and protecting American commerce in the Mediterranean preceded his command of the Gulf Squadron in the Mexican War, where he displayed his legendary courage under fire by leading his men into an enemy city as if, a fellow officer observed, he were taking a walk. His achievements on land were even more important because their contributions would be longer-lasting. Enlightened professionalism and rare persistence enabled him to overcome an obstacle course of technical and institutional barriers to improved naval recruitment, training, education, and thinking. He was instrumental in modernizing ordnance and a "single-handed" impetus in swinging the switch from cherished but outdated sail propulsion to steam.

Those accomplishments had put the Father of the Steam Navy high on the list of the navy's best, most farsighted officers, an assessment supported in their way by the mixed feelings of the men who served under him. "No one appreciates a joke less than he does," noted one of the squadron's better educated sailors.[1] He stayed true to his dour form while on the Japan expedition, and his officers kept their distance from him, knowing the danger of failing to. The "humorless, immensely vain" disciplinarian expected them to use any free moment they somehow had for improving their skills or enlarging their knowledge. An officer who ruminated about his commander's inability to smile—Lieutenant George Henry Preble, who was now serving him loyally and well—dryly observed that his crews ate little "bread of idleness."

The Commodore's precarious health might have been enough to keep him in the "perpetual frown" aptly suggested by the writer Peter Wiley. It had been seriously compromised in 1820, when the young officer was second in command of a corvette dispatched to West Africa. He believed the malaria to which he was exposed there caused permanent impairment, although its fever never struck him down. Rheumatism, contracted on a long, exhausting tour in the eastern Mediterranean, would also trouble him for the remainder of his life. A later tour in infested African waters and lands brought on another severe rheumatic attack, and a raging fever contracted near the end of the Mexican War left him so debilitated "as scarcely to permit me to attend to my duties."[2]

Similar symptoms struck during the present exhausting voyage, but although aches and pains sometimes kept him virtually immobilized in his cabin, the stubborn devotee of perpetual learning never failed to write in his journal and pursue a variety of concerns that little interested most naval officers: botany and other natural sciences, foreign languages, the history of the countries he visited, especially the classical roots of Mediterranean civilizations. His forceful, if often pontifical, writing belied his relatively elementary formal education. During the War of 1812, he taught himself Spanish and translated a book on Mediterranean hydrography, piloting, and navigation. One of the characteristically enlightened causes he championed was founding an American apprentice system, and later the forerunner of the naval academy.

The foresight that had energized his piloting of the navy's switch from sail to steam shaped other large objectives too. His command of USS *Fulton II*, the first steam American warship[3]—in 1838–1840, when he also organized the Naval Engineer Corps and the service's first gunnery school—was essentially for conducting revolutionary experiments. The problems arising from the conversion extended well beyond maritime propulsion. Perry saw the extremely difficult process in terms of a need to advance American interests and authority on the high seas and in the world. The challenge lay in attitudes even more than in engineering and mechanics: most other high officers knew nothing about steam or machinery and didn't want to know. Overcoming their dogged attachment to traditional canvas and yardarms required a crusade of enlightenment driven by statesmanly imagination and an end goal of power for the nation, not just power from boilers.

He was also unusually conscientious. At sea during this expedition, he'd retire to bed soon after dinner, awake near one o'clock in the morning, summon his amanuensis, and dictate thoughts and observations for that elaborate journal, which, like his writing in general, touched on a wide variety of subjects. His expansive curiosity and enduring drive for self-improvement fit the pattern of some of the Founding Fathers. When the ships were berthed or anchored, he sent his officers on exploring parties for gathering botanical and animal specimens and many other kinds of information.

He himself had what a contemporary called a "mania for collecting things," including seashells, fish skeletons, Japanese plants of every variety, umbrellas, even a piece of wood from one of the guard boats that had met the squadron. The Commodore believed a commander "ought to be behaving in the spirit of the age and according to Science; to observe, study, measure, count, estimate, sample, and record in the service of Knowledge and for the entertainment and instruction of all."[4] His exploring parties on this mission well represented the nineteenth-century urge to investigate scientific, political, and economic matters; and his hiring of a French chef (because the navy's cooks were incapable of pleasing foreign guests) and an

Italian bandmaster (because music was important to entertain foreigners as well as to sustain shipboard morale) was additional evidence of a broadness rare in military service of any time.

In short, Matthew Calbraith Perry was "a man of thought and a man of affairs: scholar, engineer, and officer converged with bluenose, missionary, and patriot"[5]—as close to a universal man as could be reasonably expected of anyone who'd spent a life in uniform. And despite his fragile health, he continued to radiate the categorical authority. In regarding "all under him as only means and agents for his purpose," Reverend Samuel Williams would suggest, the Commodore "perhaps too often disregarded the just wishes and opinions of others in comparatively trifling matters," but that must be "almost unavoidable in minds of strong fibre, trained during long years to command."[6]

HOW USEFUL WOULD Perry's categorical demand for obedience prove in the long run of a supposedly diplomatic assignment? (However, it was conducted without a proper diplomat and relied squarely on military supremacy. Perry much wanted it to be strictly naval, "untrammeled" by diplomats' "interference.") The same Samuel Wells Williams's first impression of the Commodore went directly to that question. Seeing pride and wrath in his new employer, he worried that Perry's recent exploits in the Mexican War might "strengthen his determination to drive by force matters which can be attained only by long and patient treating."[7] The Commodore's relentless scolding and failure to praise his subordinates' good work fit the pattern of the "predatory" mission to Japan, since he "cares no more for right, for consistency, for his country, than will advance his own aggrandizement and fame, and makes his ambition the test of all his conduct towards the Japanese."[8] The only honor that concerned Perry, Williams further complained, was his own. After a native boat's misunderstanding about a trifling matter put him "in high dudgeon," he'd order a hundred of his marines to land with two field pieces "in order to show the Japanese that he was not to be trifled with."[9] The haughty self-admirer accepted an apology in the end, but his behavior was hardly that of a diplomat.

However, precisely Perry's power to command made most Americans of the time regard him as the best man for the job. That quality, it should be remembered, derived as much from respect as from fear. The stern commander who seemed to embody his country's fighting spirit was known no less for his consistency and dependability than for his explosive temper. "So long as ye walked a chalk line there couldn't be a fairer man than the Commodore—but God help ye if ye slipped over that line!"[10]

The line extended to his solemn person. "Old Bruin," as he was sometimes called by seamen—most of them probably unaware the epithet had long been applied to commodores—was decidedly *not* known for gregariousness (although he liked his grog and freely partook of what the navy called the "flowing bowl"). Subordinate officers, not to mention enlisted men, knew not to be familiar with the old sea dog who took himself so seriously. Nor did his genius lie in easing up when more work lay ahead, especially now, when this assignment could be the jewel in the crown of his career. Bayard Taylor, a well-known travel writer whom he'd permitted to accompany the expedition, would tell of relentless training even during the last laps of the voyage to Japan: "the stiff drills required of the crew by their gravel-voiced commander; the daily calls to general quarters amid empty seas; the drum rolls and fife calls summoning all hands to run out guns, repel imaginary boarders, and rig pumps to douse hypothetical fires; the roar of topside commands over nonexistent battle smoke; and the bands ordered to play 'Yankee Doodle' after simulated victories over Oriental attackers who had not materialized."[11] Perry's zealous devotion to proficiency and the order necessary to achieve it was among the attributes that made him such an outstanding leader.

When he was a boy of six, his father, Captain Christopher Perry, was formally censured for having failed to maintain proper discipline on one of his ships. Whether or not the episode hung over Matthew like the shame of a family drunkard, his genes seemed to have equipped him with every means for never earning similar disrepute. A midshipman aboard twenty-seven-year-old Lieutenant Perry's first command, an efficiently performing but grumbling sloop of war, saw the central feature of the system to which his skipper was dedicated as "render[ing] everyone as uncomfortable as possible." Little comfort wasn't unusual in a nineteenth-century navy convinced that only fear prevented shipboard anarchy, but Perry's ships had less than most.

Rebukes of subordinates as he prowled the decks of his uncommonly tight ships had given him the "Old Bruin" tag, for the bear in the medieval "The History of Reynard the Fox." Some thought his thick black hair and eyebrows gave him the look rather of a shaggy dog, although "not the kind you'd ever pat." Either way, detection of an irregularity or a smudge of dirt would darken his face and produce long-remembered, sometimes profane tongue-lashings. Now fifty-nine, "Old Matt," as he was also known, wasn't *really* old, even by nineteenth-century measure, but his mien and manner had made him seem so even decades earlier, when his nicknames were coined.

Few who heard his growl or were lashed by the butt end of a rope in his hand[12] saw the tender side of him that emerged in his relationship with his family, especially his wife, a daughter of a prominent New York merchant, whom he'd married in 1814, after which he signed his frequent, devoted letters to her "Your affectionate husband." Before leaving Shanghai for the last legs of his just-completed visit to Japan—after almost four decades of marriage, that is—he cited a local resident who, after looking at photograph of her, called her " 'the most beautiful American female' he'd ever seen." Many officers *did* know that in the navy's "intensely political world," as a recent biographer put it, he was powerfully connected to trade, wealth, and social prominence through his siblings' marriages as well as his own.[13]

The Commodore no longer flogged. The navy had abolished that punishment in 1850, in response to public outcry roused largely by the publication of Richard Henry Dana Jr.'s *Two Years Before the Mast: A Personal Narrative of Life at Sea* and Herman Melville's *White-Jacket, or, The World in a Man-of-War* (a novel whose character of Captain Claret, a severe disciplinarian, may have been based partly on the Commodore). Before that, Perry believed he was restrained in his use of the brutal cat-o'-nine-tails, never allowing quick judgment, let alone anger, to influence his judicious decisions to resort to it—mostly for theft and abuse of alcohol, but also for lesser infractions, of which the navy's wretchedly paid sailors of the time committed many. Still, Old Bruin didn't join the efforts of other senior officers to reestablish flogging, relying instead partly on his mighty upbraiding to control rowdiness.

A subordinate on an earlier ship under executive officer Perry—whose duties included supervising the conduct of the crew—noted that "discipline, order & style" were carried to their "highest pitch," and that "the exec" was determined to punish all offenders to the fullest extent of the law. Kept hard at work "without the least interruption," the subordinate could "scarcely get my meals" during the course of his very long days. He was "never seated at the table more than two minutes" without the zealous exec giving him "some new order to execute."[14] The junior officers dropped their forks and dashed to carry out their orders. Lieutenant Preble summed that up too: "To hear was to obey."[15]

THE YOUNG MIDSHIPMAN had begun his service in a tight mix of naval and family affairs. At one point, seventeen close relatives served in, some people quipped, "Perry's navy."

His first shipboard tour, which began when he was fifteen, was on a schooner commanded by Lieutenant Oliver Hazard Perry, his elder brother, whose "We have met the enemy, and they are ours" would become an American echo of Caesar's *"Veni, vidi, vici."* Oliver Hazard's Lake Erie victory in the War of 1812 against the British would make him a hero while opening the young republic's westward thrust—a movement that would strengthen the push to open Japan decades later. Another Perry brother, then twelve years old, fought with the same Lake Erie squadron, while midshipman Matthew himself was serving on a warship that engaged a British frigate near Nantucket. All five brothers would eventually serve in the navy, and two of the three sisters would marry career naval officers. (The third never wed.) Although a Quaker, their father had fought in the Revolutionary War and went on to captain one of the new republic's frigates before his previously mentioned mild disgrace.[16] No wonder young Matthew loved watching ships coming and going to sea from Newport, Rhode Island, where he was raised.

A family story set in his early adolescence suggests a naval career wasn't inevitable, however. His dashing, adored elder brother Oliver, the future hero, was said to have told "Cal," as Matthew Calbraith's siblings then called him, to prepare for a life in commerce because he wasn't cut out for the navy. It was "the firebrands like father and me who win the gold braid and the glory"—whereas Cal was as "cautious as a cobbler and shy as a mouse."[17] It was only after the slight boy with the fondness for wandering in the harbor fought off two older, larger "wharf-rat" bullies armed with a club that his father and brother saw him as fit for a more manly calling than the paperwork for which his attention to detail had seemed to suit him.

His midshipman's appointment came in 1809, when he was fourteen. President Thomas Jefferson signed his commission, after which his commitment to enforcing rules and regulations, to control and more control, followed quickly. The notes he made for himself included a list of the qualities a first lieutenant needed for maintaining "perfect order and discipline." "Enforce obedience from Juniors" would remain a hallmark. His relentless persecution of bad habits kept his crews in consistently better shape than others, and not *all* his officers remained "half-frightened to death." But his healthy ships weren't happy ships.

None of that was remarkable in his hard navy, even less so because almost all his subordinates ended by admiring him, including those who enjoyed the luxury of looking back at the Japan expedition. What *was* remarkable was his accomplishments. Surely, Perry's inventive pains to improve his ships and men testified to his larger goals, almost always achieved to an enviable degree, and this mission might eclipse them all.

6

The Cracks in the
Double-Bolted Doors

Deshima Island in Nagasaki Bay

DO'S EFFORTS TO SEAL JAPAN from Western entry and influence continued throughout the first half of the nineteenth century. Some were clumsy and dangerous. Wishful thinking—*This will teach them to leave us alone*—left little room for considering how foreign seamen and governments might react when shells reinforced the snubs, as an American merchant ship named the *Morrison* was greeted in 1837.[1]

Forbidding Japanese from returning from abroad was cruelest to the victims of mishaps at sea, whose numbers were large enough for a word to be coined for their subsequent drifting. The fortunate ones who eventually reached a distant shore included sailors on a junk that had foundered while transporting rice to Edo in 1832. Carried across the North Pacific by the powerful Japan, or Black, Current, the hulk entered the Gulf of Alaska, then floated south, down North America's west coast. Three of the crew had survived seventeen excruciating months when they washed ashore, half alive, at Cape Flattery on the Olympic Peninsula, northwest of Seattle.

Enslaved by Macaw Indians, they were ransomed by workers of the Hudson's Bay Company, which sent them to London, then to the firm's Oregon headquarters, where they spent most of three more years between their odyssey and the *Morrison*'s departure for, it hoped, Edo.

The backers of the voyage, prominent New York merchants with a cargo of cotton and wool to export, also supported religious conversion, which Japan had forbidden for two centuries—at the terrible cost, missionaries anguished, of depriving the closed country and its member souls of Christian truth. "Who can withhold a tear," one of the *Morrison*'s missionary passengers would ask, "when he considers what Japan is, and what she might have been? Had pure Christianity been first introduced, the Gospel of the Redeemer might now perhaps be enjoyed not only in Japan but in China and throughout the eastern world."[2] "Pure Christianity" there meant Protestantism as opposed to the Catholicism of the sixteenth-century Portuguese and Spanish missionaries.

But if those motives were a familiar mix of creed and commerce, the *Morrison*'s principals were much more willing than Perry would be to appreciate the role of foreign "misconduct" in prompting Japan's closing. The previous year, the British *Quarterly Review* had suggested much needed to be done before Westerners would be able to approach Japanese coasts "in any other guise than that of invaders of an unoffending, we wish we could add unoffended, nation." The New York merchants saw the 1837 voyage as an opportunity for amends. Returning the three survivors of the junk that had landed at Cape Flattery would show the Japanese that some foreigners had good intentions. The "waifs" themselves, as Americans called them, yearned to be home, even though they informed the vessel's owners that death awaited anyone who tried to reenter after the most unintentional visit abroad.

The three were aboard—together with missionary Samuel Wells Williams, Perry's future translator—when the *Morrison* sailed from Macao in July. (Two had become what Williams would call "the first fruits of the church of Christ in Japan" by converting.) After a stop at the Kingdom of Okinawa, the ship proceeded toward Edo Bay. Hopes were raised by the sight of Mount Fuji and, unlikely as it might have seemed, cannon fire heard along the shore. Evidently eager enough for reunion with their kin to ignore the risk, the survivors assured the captain that was a signal to port officials; maybe even a welcoming salute. The following day, the vessel anchored off Kurihama, very near where Commodore Biddle's frigate and later the Black Ships would do the same. A bevy of visiting natives (including some women whose black-painted teeth startled the crew) minutely examined its fittings and spaces, although not the three returnees, who remained hidden. Hours later, a sudden shower of cannonballs substantially damaged the ship's deck and a gunwale. A hurriedly hoisted white flag seemed to intensify the barrage. Chased by guard boats, the unarmed *Morrison* retreated from the bay.

Stunned as they were, its officers were unwilling to abandon their mission. Navigating to the castaways' home island of Kyushu, the southernmost of the four major ones, they entered Kagoshima Bay and sent word ashore of their intention to return the waifs. Hopes again soared when fishermen and villagers warmly welcomed the announcement and the local governor sent even more heartening praise for the "benevolent foreigners" who "must be more than human."[3] But he was evidently overruled by a louder order rushed from Edo: the following day, another barrage of cannonballs was unleashed on the charitable visitors. The *Morrison* took some eighteen hours of it—the balls were very small—before sailing to sea.

An 1839 account of the misadventure—the first book about Japan published in America—said little about the reaction of the unreturned castaways, but they vividly revealed their feelings in letters to their families. Although resigned to the hardship of spending the rest of their lives in strange countries, the fishermen nevertheless described their grief—bigger than "the ocean, mountains, or anything"—when Japanese guns drove the *Morrison* from Kagoshima Bay. They composed their letters in Macao, to which the ship had then sailed. When the chief of the Dutch outpost on Deshima Island, who happened to be visiting Macao, returned to Nagasaki, he passed them to its magistrate.

A year later, Edo would learn the *Morrison* had been named for Robert Morrison, a celebrated missionary in China. Slim as it was, that connection to Christianity upped the suspicions about the ship's real intentions, especially since Robert Morrison was from England—which, before the arrival of Biddle and Perry, frightened the government more than America did. But a later letter alarmed Edo even more. In it, four of the seven nonreturnees, "moved by concern for their home country," predicted that after concluding its war with China, England intended to demand trade with Japan, and if Japan refuses, the English will take a closer look at the unlawfulness [of the Japanese] who earlier fired on the ship that brought back the castaways. Furthermore, according to what I have heard [from the Dutch] . . . once it finishes war with China, England will send warships to three places: Nagasaki, Satsuma, and Edo.[4]

THE SAMURAI SCHOLAR who reported that message was Sakuma Sho-zan, the man who, ten years later, would hear the Black Ships' band music as welcome evidence they were manned by human beings. (Climbing down from high ground above Uraga Bay, where he'd been observing the cause of the panic on shore, he then "frantically" drilled inexperienced troops.[5]) Sakuma was among the best of a small but important band who had been studying Western thought and ways, despite the many obstacles. The ambitious academic had shown great promise as a potential internationalist until switching to applied sciences, especially Western gunnery and tactics. In 1842, five years after the violence to the *Morrison*, he wrote "A Plan for Coastal Defense," a treatise dedicated to his lord, who'd been put in charge of that defense. The war between China and England to which he referred was the milestone that had moved him to concentrate on military science. It was turning "more and more unfavorable," and his treatise elaborated on its warning that Japan too might well be plunged into hostilities because the English doubtlessly "harbor[ed] sinister designs" on it too.[6] Although that may not have been worrying if Japan were certain to win, its present condition offered no such prospect. Sakuma therefore "humbly" implored the *bakufu* to "devote itself with all its power to solidifying military preparedness, thereby making the barbarian respect Japan . . . and letting the people live in peace."

The *bakufu* was the Japanese government—a military one weak in military affairs, it bears repeating. The conflict between England and China was the Opium War of 1839, the outcome of which had begun to alarm the relatively few Japanese who knew of it, Abe Masahiro prominent among them. Sakuma foreshadowed what would become Japan's foremost preoccupation during the coming century, even under relatively liberal governments: building military strength. His call to repel Western encroachment by acquiring Western technology—"so that Japan will remain unperturbed in case the worst should happen"—also anticipated the country's great contradiction: a drive to save its culture by copying an alien one.

Sakuma's appeal to acquire effective arms helped inspire renewed *bakufu* determination to parry penetration by unauthorized foreigners. The tiny circle of national decision-makers read his 1842 warning avidly:

> For hundreds of years, the barbarians have desired and resolved to subvert enemy nations through their occult religion and thus conquer the whole world. They will not be deterred by occasional acts of kindness or displays of force. When they wreak vengeance against us, they intimidate us into backing down; when they submit meekly before us, they lull us into a false sense of security.[7]

Many of the relatively few Japanese entitled to comment about national affairs shared that view. Since Westerners often used violence to extend their conquests, their advance men in the garb of traders and priests must be kept out, if necessary by force.

But what happened to those who purposely violated the proclamation that no Christian must come to Japan "so long as the sun shall warm the earth?" The fates of that handful of brave men told quite a different story because it was easier in Edo, as in other capitals, to talk big—in this case, big punishment—than risk applying it. The shogunate's uncertainty about what to do with the sprinkling of successful trespassers is almost as difficult to overstate as its mighty effort to keep them out. While American indignation about their treatment was building toward a crescendo, the old promise that any Christian bold enough to visit Japan would "pay for it with his head" was being honored more in the breach than the observance. Violators were punished, but mildly.

IN JULY 1848, while Perry's Mexican War feats were still being celebrated, a young visionary named Ranald MacDonald secretly made his way to Hokkaido, the northernmost of the four main Japanese islands whose waters attracted the flocks of whalers. MacDonald's origins may have accounted for his strength of character. His mother was a Native American princess, the daughter of a Chinook chief; his father, the much-respected Scottish chief trader of the Hudson's Bay Company in Oregon, whose British, French, Russian, and Hawaiian settlements gave it a touch of cosmopolitanism. Their adventurous son's curiosity and energy were among the traits that would prompt American sea captains and explorers to call him the "best man I ever knew."

Born in 1824, the impressionable "half-breed" impressed others with his purposefulness, even before his fascination with Japan began. Its principal stimulus was meeting the three castaways who spent time in the company's Oregon headquarters before seeking repatriation on the *Morrison*. Seeing a strong resemblance between the three and the Native Americans among whom he'd been raised, ten-year-old Ranald came to believe, singularly at the time, that his maternal ancestors originated in Japan. (Many present geographers rate the possibility as strong.[8]) After schooling made difficult by a prohibition of speaking French and Chinook, he submitted to distasteful work in a bank, then left to wander in America and sail to Europe. Years later, while still a youth, he resolved to visit what he'd call "our next neighbor" across the Pacific, perhaps to make his name and fortune if the country would open.

He signed on to a whaler heading from Sag Harbor, New York, for the bounty off Hokkaido. After very profitable hunting there, the captain begged him not to go through with an impossibly daring plan. Fully aware of the risk, MacDonald proceeded nevertheless. Other members of the crew wept as the twenty-four-year-old climbed into a tiny boat containing a few provisions and rowed toward a bantam island off northern Hokkaido (then called Ezo). A journalist would compare the solitary venture to riding a rocket to the moon, then a wild fantasy. Now the whaler sailed off into the fog, dipping its flag in salute.

MacDonald's disguise of his deliberate entry, suspicion of which had to be carefully avoided, tested his endurance as well as his courage. In order to pose as a shipwrecked sailor, he capsized his boat and lowered himself into the frigid water—in vain because the tiny island was uninhabited. Rowing back to sea and repeating the performance, he lost many of his provisions, including his pistols and some of the books he intended using to teach about the West. (When another foreign ship spied the little boat's rudder floating in the sea, Ranald's father was among those convinced the young man had drowned.) Eventually, however, the cold, wet "survivor" made the intended impression on tattered fishermen who inhabited a second island. Far from being hostile to the stranger, they bowed and bowed, then favored him with all the hospitality they could manage.

That may have said nothing about how Japan actually treated foreigners then because the fishermen were Ainu rather than Japanese. The indigenous Ainu, whose origins may have been European, had been essentially conquered by the Japanese in the sixteenth and seventeenth centuries[9] and treated very badly (if less so, all in all, than Native Americans by *their* conquerors). Still, the island's Japanese officials were also cordial, if more guarded than the other inhabitants. It was only when superiors arrived to take charge that the stranger's movements were restricted. He was incarcerated, at first in same house from which the *Lagoda* sailors had tried to escape just weeks before—but still treated with courtesy, even generosity.

He would remain ten months in Japan, until the corvette that had come for the *Lagoda* deserters fetched him away. Almost all that time was spent in confinement, chiefly in Nagasaki, to where he was conveyed by junk. It included some unhappy moments, as when he was made to kneel to high officials and was stared at like an animal during his land transport by palanquin. Protestant MacDonald was less angered than the American Catholics at being ordered to trod on an image of the "devil" outside the Nagasaki governor's residence, apparently the same little effigy of the Virgin and Child that the *Lagoda* men had been forced to desecrate. And although the supposedly symbolic act to which the Shogun and his officers attached so much importance again demonstrated the enduring Japanese hostility toward Christianity, MacDonald sensed no ill will toward him personally. Nor did he feel relief when he regained his freedom. On the contrary, he regretted having to leave the country.

His affection for its people grew and grew. He found them curious, gregarious, and amiable: "naturally chatty, always in a vein of good humor. . . . I never had a cross word with any of them."[10] Although government officials often displayed "markedly militaristic instincts," his treatment during most of his confinement in a small room on the grounds of a Buddhist temple was relatively generous. It came with four meals a day, use of a bathhouse, and long visits from native interpreters eager to exchange language lessons—some of whom would interpret during negotiations with Perry five years hence. Without knowing that many shipwrecked Russian mariners were well treated by the people of the north, or that a new 1842 decree had changed official policy toward foreign ships in general,[11] MacDonald concluded that the conventional wisdom about Japan's untrustworthiness and severity—which he'd been inclined to accept before making himself a test case—was much exaggerated.

Not beaten, let alone beheaded, he was even given sweetmeats. A governor promised better treatment if he was "good." "And I must say that whether or not I was 'good,' the Governor—good and kind soul!—kept his word to me to the letter and to the spirit." The prisoner's confiscated Bible was returned, and guards who saw its importance to him made a shelf for it (again showing the profound hostility was less to Christianity as a whole than to Roman Catholicism).* "Everyone was kind to me."

Shortly before he died in 1894, MacDonald wrote that he "never ceased to feel . . . ever grateful to my fellow men of Japan for their really generous treatment of me." After encountering many peoples during a lifetime of wandering the globe, "there are none to whom I feel more kindly—more grateful—than my old hosts of Japan; none whom I esteem more highly."[12]

The young man's "exemplary deportment," as a Japanese scholar would call it, surely helped prompt the generosity to him. Officials contrasted it with the "truly vulgar and rude" *Lagoda* seamen who caused "no end of trouble" during their simultaneous imprisonment in Nagasaki. No doubt growing fear of Western military power also contributed to MacDonald's kind treatment. The only certain answer to what accounted for the Japanese resignation to trespass is that paying with one's head for it was apparent bluff. Surely the two latest cases of contact—MacDonald and the *Lagoda* men—should have negated the Navy Department's talk of mankind's "common enemy" treating castaways like "the most atrocious criminals."

Edo believed it had a legal and moral right to confine violators of its laws, even shipwrecked sailors—to whom it was now actually according halfway humane treatment. American captives complained bitterly about, for example, the confining little palanquins used for their transportation.

---

* MacDonald had some sympathetic help from Moriyama Einosuki, an interpreter who would provide conciliatory initiative and wisdom during Perry's second visit to Japan. Asked whether he believed in a God in Heaven, the prisoner said he did—and, in answer to further questions, began elaborating about the Jesus Christ and Virgin Mary he loved from his raising as an Episcopalian until Moriyama cautiously interrupted. "That will do! That will do!" he whispered, then reported in his official translation that MacDonald said he "merely cultivate [*sic*] mind and will and reverence heaven in order to obtain clear understanding and to secure happiness."

But since Japanese prisoners had to walk, Edo saw provision of those cramped conveyances that tortured the larger-bodied Westerners as a positive indulgence. And while the Americans groaned about their cruelly inadequate rations, their captors considered them generous.

Other foreigners found fault with Japanese food. A member of a Tsarist mission that arrived soon after Perry would complain that the tiny native dinner portions "will not make a snack for a man with a good appetite."[13] Evidently unmoved by one of their folk sayings that "An uninvited guest is worse than a Tartar," Russians had relatively extensive experience of that because they were the first Europeans to probe closed Japan.[14] Imprisoned in Hokkaido with six of his crew in 1811–1813, a naval captain joined the chorus of protest about skimpy rations that may have satisfied Japanese appetites, but certainly not Russian. Nevertheless, the long-confined captain acknowledged that repeated Russian raids on minor Japanese islands had frightened his captors, whose harshness was motived by a hope of deterring more—and he too left Japan with much affection for its people. Although the Japanese had caused him and his men "much suffering," the captives also "experienced the generosity of a pacific people" who generally "acted from feelings of humanity." "This just and upright people must by no means be provoked," he warned in vain.[15]

RARELY DID CULTURAL CONDITIONING and the beholder's eye more determine what was considered standard or substandard, compassionate or punitive. The Japanese fed their American captives relatively choice rice and fish, which the latter detested and the American press featured in its stories about Japanese persecution. In 1852, when Perry was making final preparations for his mission, a prominent Washington paper published a long letter with multiple kinds of misinformation, including that Japanese children's first lesson in the nursery was "the art and grace of suicide."[16] Describing a Japanese "murder" that had never happened, a *New York Times* report in June of the same year also included a six-year-old account by a *Lawrence* survivor about having been "thrust into a prison cage similar to those in which wild beasts are kept for exhibition."

Happenstance further darkened the image. After the American corvette deposited Ranald MacDonald in Hong Kong, he sought new adventures rather than rest or fame. "I, a penniless waif on the ocean of life, took ship again before the mast," and ended, temporarily, in Australia.[17] Thus it was left to the angry *Lagoda* sailors to provide most of America's information about those two most recent cases of internment, and the public swallowed their predictably disparaging accounts with gusto. The influential *New York Herald* decried the "inhuman barbarity" practiced during the long course of an "ignominious and cruel imprisonment." The captain of the corvette that brought the survivors home agreed. In a report about "those unhappy mariners" that was sent to the Senate, the captain concluded by urging action, although not specifically military, to counter the "cruelty of the Japanese government. . . . The facts of that case are of a character to excite the indignation of the people of the United States." Although it would be better to work peacefully with Japan, if "they won't come to terms—make them." Their "unnatural system would . . . fall to pieces upon the slightest concussion."[18]

Moral indignation strengthened that notion, especially on the eve of Perry's departure, in speeches and editorials about the "barbarous" isolationists. "Japan has no right," declared the *New York Express*, "to bury her treasures behind her walls, and to imprison her people under cover of loathing and ignorant superstition." That was a fair example of profoundly ignorant commentators' misrepresentation, invention, and vilification. The *Express* went on to evoke a "*duty* [italics in the original]" by those who know Japan "*even better than she knows herself, to force upon her the dawning of a better day.*"

IF EDO HAD KNOWN how American pens were distorting the essentially unknown into the substantially monstrous, it might have applauded, for it was busy worsening its own image by painting its conduct as much fiercer than it was. The imprisoned Russian naval captain who expressed affection for Japan nevertheless lamented their tricks, one of which was to inform Russian authorities that he, the captain, was dead—at just the time when they, the captors, were actually taking "every precaution for the preservation of our health." Thus the *bakufu*'s resolve to scare off potential visitors served to anger and provoke—especially in pious America, with its heightened sense of moral obligation to combat evil.

School textbooks shared the press's liking for lurid copy about dangerous potential enemies, but gullible newspapers led in taking umbrage at
Edo's bluster and swagger. Leaping at every opportunity to run a shocking
new story or reprint an old one about Japanese evil, they excelled in reporting faulty intelligence. A *Morrison* officer reported that Japan was re-
gressing ever deeper into seclusion, and Perry apparently swallowed that
reversal of the truth more or less whole. Although the *Morrison*'s abuse had
taken place fourteen years before his mission, the officer was convinced
that Japanese intransigence was worse than ever. The implication that the
repugnant practices would continue forever unless retaliatory measures
were taken helped harden the Commodore's certainty that the offenders
deserved "signal punishment."

The reality was that cautious challenges to the seclusion orthodoxy
were being made from both the Japanese left and right, as it were. On the
left, they were propelled by intellectuals' appetite for Western learning,
the materials for which seeped in through the Dutch colony on Deshima.
The scholars engaged in it—very few in number but disproportionately
influential and eager for more contact with the world—had begun criticizing the government's crass attitude toward Japanese castaways. (An even
smaller number, who had challenged the seclusion policy several years earlier, faced repression, but it was temporary.) Even some adherents of continued isolation disapproved of its harsher tactics. They included the *roju*'s
foreign affairs supervisor, who feared the shelling of the *Morrison* would
serve as an excuse for invading Japan.* Also on the right, some nationalists
urged more contact with the West in order to copy its technology.

Even though Americans couldn't be expected to be abreast of such developments, it should have been clear that the seclusion policy had been
revised. Convincing evidence of better treatment of would-be visitors was
available.

In 1845, eight years after the *Morrison*'s chasing, the *Manhattan*, a whaler
also out of Sag Harbor, sought to return another group of Japanese castaways, this time numbering twenty-two. Near the coast, the ship transferred four to a little local craft, together with notice it intended to enter

---

* A few Westerners surmised that fear gripped Japan. "They now regard foreigners as ready to pounce
upon their country the moment it should be opened," an observer correctly summarized (Samuel Wells
Williams, *A Journal of the Perry Expedition to Japan*, p. iii). Still, Japanese views counted for little or
nothing among most Westerners.

Uraga Bay to deliver the remaining eighteen. Now the answer came not from cannon barrels but from an emissary from Edo with official permission. While ever-curious dignitaries climbed aboard the anchored vessel, the official presented a note of thanks from what the captain took to be the Emperor but was surely the Shogun—its content approved, like the permission, by Abe Masahiro as head of the *roju*.[19]

What had changed the shells to courteous words? Nothing less significant than repeal of the inglorious "No Second Thought" edict. A new one instructed that foreigners should "on no account" be permitted to land. On the contrary, they should be driven off with "such measures as may be necessary"—but only after having been helped, if they were in need:

> It is not thought fitting to drive away all foreign ships irrespective of their condition . . . after investigating the circumstances of each case, you should, when necessary, supply them with food and fuel and advise them to leave.[20]

The retraction had taken place in 1842, a year before Abe's appointment to the *roju*. It was an effort to avoid violence—specifically, retribution from nations angered by the previous policy, which it considerably altered, if not fully reversed.

The new decree reflected greater acceptance of reality. Much as Edo wanted never to accommodate the outside world, it accepted that it couldn't continue using drastic measures for that manifestly impossible goal. Fending off Westerners was one thing, provoking those with powerful fleets another. Fear of those fleets was strong enough to prompt a few feudal lords, *daimyo*, and experts in world developments to propose trade with the West, for the purpose of building defensive strength. Although that was too much for the *bakufu*, its "Order for the Provision of Fuel and Water"—actually a return to policy established in 1803, before the proliferation of Western ships in native waters—reflected a critical change. The 1842 directive sustained the prohibition of Japanese castaways from returning, except, now, in Dutch and Chinese vessels. Ships arriving with intention to force a change in the *sakoku*, or even to try to talk about it, would still be rebuffed, as would be done to Commodore Biddle, Perry's predecessor, in 1846. But that was hardly evidence of the "great barbarity" Americans convinced themselves they had to stop.

Three years after the *Manhattan*'s arrival, in 1848, the *bakufu* considered restoring 1825's severity. Abe Masahiro was opposed, partly because "At present, one can scarcely say our coastal defense preparations are fully completed. There would be occasions when enforcing the No Second Thought Edict would invite conflict, and in the event . . . the foreigners retaliated, it would be a hopeless contest, and there would be no worse disgrace for Japan. . . . When we can fight effectively, we shall revive the law. This matter is now under discussion." But Abe, a master of telling colleagues and critics what they wanted to hear, offered that explanation to one of the most effective proponents of keeping barbarians out: the lord of the Mito domain. The Chief Senior Councilor himself was unlikely to support use of force, even if enough could have been mustered. And even the many Japanese who were eager to fight resisted thinking about paying for the necessary modernizing.

Meanwhile, Japan's new willingness to succor shipwrecked foreigners and help them return home should have invalidated the U.S. Navy Department's stamp of mankind's "common enemy." The note of gratitude to the *Manhattan* came with generous provisions: wheat flour, hulled rye, polished rice, radishes, carrots, sweet potatoes, fish, fifty chickens, two octopuses, painted dishes and lacquer bowls, tea, two hundred bundles of firewood, more than five thousand gallons of water, and four large cedar poles to replace broken masts. Payment was refused. (A British frigate that had arrived in 1845 was given even more generous provisions, and permitted to land on a small island in order to make astronomical and magnetic observations.)

The following year, the New Bedford whaler *Trident* marooned three seamen on Sakhalin Island when it made a quick departure from there to avoid a sudden worsening of weather. The three were confined and closely questioned for no fewer than fifteen months, partly because the investigation was delayed by the death of the magistrate in charge. But while some Japanese suspected they'd purposely left their ship in order to survey the coast, honest officials questioned that suspicion and resisted all pressure to punish or convict. Before dying, the magistrate had advised Chief Senior Councilor Abe that imprisoning innocent foreigners might be "objectionable to other nations"; and the suspects were detained in the tolerably comfortable house where Ranald MacDonad had been held the previous year. (The magistrate's replacement elaborated that "even foreigners are not without human feeling.") The Americans were at last sent off toward home on a Dutch ship, to which gifts of food were sent for them.

Washington knew those encouraging developments but preferred not to mention them while lamenting the *Lagoda*, *Morrison*, and *Lawrence* abuses. Perry in particular was informed of Edo's policy change well before he departed on the mission—before he began planning it, in fact. *Manhattan*'s captain described the Japanese to him as "quiet and friendly and intelligent," and, more to the point, he felt his treatment reflected "the most distinguished civility and kindness."[21] Essentially ignoring that good news, the Commodore did nothing to ease the half-informed American indignation.

Not that the new policy prompted no opposition in Edo, nor that the old stiff arms had been replaced by open ones. Nor had the seclusion policy itself been repealed, as opposed to the drastic measures for enforcing it. The shogunate remained far from embracing the notion of a common humanity. Even as the changes of 1842 were being enacted, attempts were made—soon to be pressed by Abe—to improve coastal defense: an early manifestation of simultaneous stumbling toward opposite strategies. Meanwhile, the improved diplomacy remained less than satisfactory by any reasonable standard. The lofty note of gratitude delivered to the *Manhattan* included a command to never return. Although not repelled, the anchored ship was surrounded by guard boats, and its crew was warned that anyone who attempted to go ashore would be killed. When Commodore Biddle appeared the following year, no one informed him, during his days of waiting for negotiations, of the *Lawrence* sailors still incarcerated in Nagasaki. (A ship leaving from Deshima would return them quite soon after that.)

Such behavior was uncivil enough to merit vigorous protest, which is what the Secretary of State had instructed Perry to deliver. If, the Secretary added, "humane treatment" of American seamen weren't promised, the Commodore was to "change his tone" to inform the Japanese "in the most unequivocal terms" that Washington was determined to insist on it. But Perry would go far beyond that, taking the liberty of threatening the Japan that was no longer rejecting castaways.

A nation's heading at any given time may be as important as its starting point. If the heading is in a promising direction, it may be even *more* important for other nations not to do more harm than good. The treatment of their shipwreck victims was a critical consideration for mid-nineteenth-century Western nations. A critical measure of Japan, which also threw light on its larger problems with openness and tolerance, was how it was dealing with its previous failures. A fair reading of the American examples would have showed a government pointed, if unsteadily, toward civility. Having reached its lowest level with the cases cited above—the only significant ones—it began inching upward. Grudging as it was, the assistance to castaways was far from the old imprisonment, which itself had been less outrageous than it was painted.

Even American whalers, who fairly detested Japan's seclusion policy for depriving them of the emergency help that was taken for granted elsewhere, acknowledged that some essentials of humane behavior had been attained well before Perry set sail. Melville's term for the closing, coined in *Moby-Dick*, was "double-bolted" doors. But the great novel set in the arduous Japanese waters—published, it's worth repeating, two years before Perry's voyage—also granted that the country was "on the threshold" of becoming hospitable. So the objective of protecting American sailors contained an element of camouflage. Although it led the government's list, no doubt because it had the greatest public appeal, it was secondary in the mission's real motivation. A less high-minded lure from China was first.

7

The First Ultimatum

"A true image" of Commodore Perry of the "North American Republican State" in an 1854 woodblock print

BACK IN AMERICA, preoccupation with which new Western states would allow slavery kept interest in the expedition relatively scant. As the truce achieved by the Compromise of 1850 broke down, great anxiety gripped the otherwise booming country. Still, the descent toward the pre–Civil War violence of the following years, most notably the mayhem and murder of "Bleeding Kansas,"[1] dimmed neither the faith in American supremacy nor the conviction that one of the country's missions was to raise others' morality. The Secretary of the Navy's reminder to Perry of the need to awaken the Japanese government to "its Christian obligation to join the family of Christendom" made no mention of America's tenacious retention of slavery even after it had been renounced by supposedly less modern and virtuous European nations.

The Commodore was closer to the practice than most Northerners. When he rejoined the navy in 1819 after his three-year interlude in commercial shipping, his initial billet was as executive officer of a corvette that escorted American blacks to Liberia, where they hoped to establish a settlement. Returning to the abortive colony two years later in his first command, a sloop of war, he also discharged the gamier task of patrolling Africa's west coast for slave traders. His mettle as a line officer in those assignments won him a reputation as one of the navy's most promising young leaders, but although he condemned the treatment of American Indians, he was less troubled, at least in public, about the tortured slavery question.

The large role in the slave trade played by Rhode Island in general and Perry's hometown of Newport in particular may have hardened his attitudes. His family's Trinity Church, attended by summering rich Southerners, preached no condemnation. His larger environment taught that the institution was an acceptable, if disagreeable, reality, all the more because an elder brother had married into a family of veteran slave traders who still used that labor to run their Cuban plantations.[2]

In any case, the moral arguments of abolitionists made no dent in Perry's belief in his mission's higher purpose. Like the overwhelming majority of his fellows, the Commodore had a penchant for criticizing other societies while remaining silent about the flaws of his own. The notion of a Japanese squadron sailing into the Chesapeake Bay to demand cessation of slavery or of the obliterating of Native American culture would have seemed preposterous to him and virtually all other Americans.

But while the root cause of Japan's inability to repel Perry was its industrial lag, Lord Abe's subordinates and rivals didn't necessarily care. Some of the most vocal dismissed all arguments based on numbers, including those measuring weight, caliber, or range of shell; they believed the crucial determinant was spiritual, not material. Whatever Japan's weapons, its sacred place in the world and its indomitable spirit, *Yamato damashi*, would decide any conflict with others. Of course the barbarians would be defeated! Besides, what madness was it—or treachery—to succumb without a fight?

Other prominent daimyo and *bakufu* notables remained undecided—about Abe too. All acknowledged his remarkable sixth sense with people, sharpened by rare sensitivity and intuition. His ability to build consensus, based on a talent for sniffing out and accommodating interests when exposed to the slightest hint—often with no hint—was largely what had carried him so high so fast. But whether or not his failure to stiffen the coastal defenses during his years as Chief Senior Councilor had been unavoidable, critics thought he hadn't made the necessary effort.

Some would later say that the courteous and equivocating young lord mentally surrendered to Perry from the very beginning because he'd long been convinced of the need to open the country. A number of his aides indeed favored repeal of the *sakoku*, if only because not enough about the modern world could be learned from Holland via its toehold on Deshima Island. Foreign countries were advanced in everything from medicine to astronomy to firearms and navigation, one such advisor prodded Abe even before he joined the *roju*.

But contrary opinions about the seclusion prevailed. Assigned to a two-man team that dealt with foreign affairs when he was appointed to the *roju* in 1843, twenty-four-year-old Abe quickly took control, thanks partly to his older colleague's willingness to yield to his judgment, which was then hard-line. His initial reaction to the news of China's humiliation in the Opium War was to recommend reinforcement of coastal defenses.

Convinced that serious foreign intrusion was inevitable, Abe had spent years pressing for restoration of the 1825 edict and for better military preparedness in order to sustain the *sakoku*. But those years pulled him in other directions too, especially after his 1844 appointment to head the *roju*, which made him a target of many factions with competing agendas. Consistency "was not an easy virtue in those very difficult times," Peter Wiley would note. "Abe was a cautious man, though by necessity an indefatigable intriguer, whose concerns centered on maintaining the shogun's rule."[3] That put the Chief Senior Councilor in a kind of permanent balancing act of conciliating, compromising, and negotiating compensation.

The divergent tugs that opened him to a wider collection of arguments had the predictable effect of softening his hard line. With the financially strapped *bakufu*'s budget office demanding cuts, who would pay for the very expensive reinforcement of defenses? And what about permitting Okinawa to trade with France? The Satsuma *han* on Kyushu, the southernmost main Japanese island, wanted that rich opportunity for the Ryukyus it largely controlled, but couldn't openly propose the idea because some would see it as a trial balloon for eventual European trade with Japan itself.

Secretly supporting Satsuma, Abe also disappointed hardliners by order-ing the relatively friendly reception of *Manhattan* in 1845 and approving its request to return the twenty-two Japanese castaways.[4] To quote Wiley again, he was "beginning to move, albeit cautiously, in two directions at once."[5]

He did the same when attempting to deal with the growing number of Western ships that were trying to call. Some highly influential daimyo wanted to come to terms with the powerful foreigners while others—especially the lord of the Mito domain, his chief domestic adversary—urged the opposite. That formidable figure had sharply warned that ignoring the Opium War's lessons about modern weapons would spell the end of the Japan they all loved. Criticism from those who championed re-pelling intruders at all costs embarrassed Abe, especially since it was so blunt. At one point, the *roju* went so far as to arrest the outspokenly anti-foreign Mito lord, who would become a kind of nemesis. Resistance to his pressure served to nudge cagey Abe further toward the center—or, as his critics later claimed, to inaction.

The arrival of Commodore Biddle in 1846, with his cannon that ex-posed the full feebleness of the coastal defenses, shifted the Chief Senior Councilor back toward military concerns. Resuming his efforts to strengthen them and again raising the question of restoring the No Second Thought edict, Abe also proposed that Japan begin building its own warships. But the West was growing ever stronger. While the political right, as it were, kept urging repulsion of the Westerners, defense officials warned against provoking ever-stronger powers that might well invade, as Britain had done in China. Although seclusion was surely the best policy, granting some concessions now might ward off a need to make larger ones later, at the point of very big guns.

In the end, far less reinforcing was undertaken than had been prom-ised, and many faulted Abe for that. However real the obstacles and sound his excuses, he hadn't been decisive, nor about the 1852 Dutch report that America was preparing to send more ships—the accurate warning that, together with the hard news from Okinawa that Perry's ships were actu-ally on their way, explained the *roju*'s lack of surprise when the Black Ships arrived. But Abe's forewarning made things no easier for him, as a verse he composed indicated when the squadron appeared.

Day in and day out
I am full of anxiety
over the black shadow
Which the Black Ships
cast on our country's future.[6]

AS THE *SUSQUEHANNA* ROUNDED Cape Sagami and headed up the Uraga Channel on July 8, its pride, sense of unity, and expectation of reward contrasted sharply with the anxiety, contention, and blame-seeking pervading Edo. When the flagship approached within two miles of land, a dozen or more larger boats, unarmed but displaying big banners, pushed off in its direction. Perry knew enough about Japan to guess the meaning of their banners' message: to order him to leave. But his far faster ships easily left the chasers behind. It was only when they foiled the hidden sandbank believed shallow enough to prevent all foreign vessels from entering Edo Bay—although Perry was apparently unaware of it—and anchored off Uraga in the late afternoon that the two sides came eyeball to eyeball. Their first verbal exchange produced support for the Commodore's conviction of Japanese duplicity.

A new cluster of small boats propelled by what some Americans saw as strange boatmen made to surround the squadron. Among them were apparent guard boats (including at least one that flew no government flag because it had been dispatched with such haste that the crew forgot to raise it). Oars worked by "large, brawny fellows, within a hair's-breadth of being stark naked,"[7] made them remarkably swift, especially the larger craft that carried thirty-odd such muscular men. Their intention seemed to be to station themselves around the ships, but Perry thwarted that too. "The Commodore," he'd write about himself in his customary third person, "had fully determined beforehand" to permit no such Japanese move. Some of the boats tried to come alongside so their men could board by climbing over railings and up anchor chains. Armed with pikes, cutlasses, muskets, and pistols, Perry's sailors cut their towlines and "unceremoniously" cast them off.

That was in keeping with "the policy of the Commodore . . . to assume a resolute attitude toward the Japanese government"—and more. Also knowing the country's extreme attention to rank, he decided to "practice upon them" a little Yankee diplomacy as he elsewhere described it.[8] That meant making the strongest possible first impression not only of the squadron's power and resolve to act in accordance with American rather than Japanese law, but also of his own importance. Having determined to speak to no native unworthy of his own station and the mission's significance, he'd given orders "forbidding the admission of anyone on board any of the ships, excepting the flagship." As for *Susquehanna*, Perry continued, "only those who had business with me" would be admitted. To all lesser messengers, he would hold himself demonstrably aloof.

When the guard boat with the "Depart immediately and dare not anchor" banner in French approached the flagship, a shipboard interpreter—using Dutch, the best Japanese-American lingua franca—shouted down to the functionary ostensibly in charge of it that a high official was wanted, one able to deliver a letter to the Emperor. However, the Americans would answer none of the questions of the functionary, distinguished by an imposing black cloak and red helmet, about the squadron's armaments, intentions, and country of origin: standard inquiries from Japanese coastal authorities. They also ignored his insistence that Japanese officials be permitted to board *Susquehanna*. No, the flagship declared, that permission would be granted only to a very high official, such as the governor of Uraga. No, the red-helmeted officer replied in turn, the law prohibited the governor from doing that.

Another boat joined the first. A conference between their commanders resulted in a proposal that the first talk to an American of comparable rank to his own. But what *was* the rank of the man in the red helmet? Perry would say he identified himself as the vice-governor of Uraga, whereas an official Japanese report would state he instructed his interpreter to present him as Uraga's "Director of Receptions." On top of the already evident translation problems, especially on the American side (in those earliest exchanges, Samuel Williams couldn't make himself understood in Japanese), the gentlemanly official would demonstrate high skill in obfuscating. Whatever caused this misunderstanding, Edo would quickly "promote" him, using a system of honorary titles; but at the moment, he was no more than a police magistrate. Nevertheless, Perry, seeing in his impressive livery "a personage of distinction," permitted him to approach *Susquehanna*.

After being made to cool his heels for a time, the magistrate was granted permission to come aboard, where Perry delegated his aide to receive him. Again ignoring most questions about the squadron, the aide informed the magistrate that his commander had arrived with a letter from the American President to the Emperor, and wanted to meet "a dignitary of the highest rank" in order to make arrangements for its fitting presentation. The pretended or misperceived vice-governor replied that the ships must repair to distant Nagasaki because another Japanese law required all foreign business to be conducted only there. Perry answered—through his aide, while remaining unseen in his cabin—that he *would not* go to Nagasaki. Having chosen Uraga for its proximity to Edo, he expected proper reception of his letter there; and although his intentions were "perfectly friendly," he would "allow of no indignity."

Nor would he permit the guard boats to keep trying to surround his ships. Unless they were removed immediately, he'd "disperse them by force."

That prompted the magistrate to rise quickly and issue an order from the *Susquehanna*'s gangway. A few boats that didn't disperse immediately did so upon production of warning gestures by a well-armed American launch. The Commodore was gratified that "nothing more was seen of them near the ships" during the remainder of their stay.

Before departing, the magistrate stated he lacked the authority to deal with the president's letter but offered a hope for more information from an officer of higher rank who might appear the following day. But when he himself returned that evening, it was with the same questions about the squadron's mission, complement, and armament, and the same insistence that it repair to Nagasaki. Now Perry's aide threatened the unthinkable: *American* delivery of the letter to the Emperor if a Japanese high official didn't do it. The magistrate inspected some of the flagship's big guns, then went ashore again, from where bonfires could be seen and signals heard throughout the night, together with the tolling of the great bell with its impressively deep, rich tone. A spectacular comet, or meteor, appealed to the Americans even more. Appearing at midnight, it threw hours of spectral light on the ships from its blue and red fireball, lifting spirits with a promise of a favorable omen. Pray God, an officer responded, that no blood be shed in the attempt to help civilize the singular, half-barbarous people.

THE MORE ORDINARY LIGHT OF THE FOLLOWING DAY, July 9, revealed the beauty of the hills that impressed the Americans despite their concentration on their purpose. In very early morning, two large barges rowed alongside Perry's flagship to announce that one of the passengers, a man dressed in a rich silk robe embroidered with silver and gold, wanted to come aboard. An interpreter identified him as the person of highest authority in Uraga. Permission was granted, and high *Susquehanna* officers engaged the boarder in a conversation that was actually with the still-secluded Commodore. The concession to receive the richly dressed new petitioner had been granted because he was taken, as Perry would state, for Uraga's "governor and greatest functionary"—never mind that the previous day's red-helmeted one had also been heard to call himself that. Either way, the new official was another police magistrate, and his response, again couched in already repetitive reference to Japanese law, was the same: the President's letter must be taken to Nagasaki.

Perry upped his threat. In all his dealings with "these orientals," he'd explain, "it was part of the Commodore's deliberately formed plan . . . to consider carefully before he announced his resolution to do any act, but, having announced it, he soon taught them to know that he would do precisely what he said he would." What he *wouldn't* do now, or ever, was retreat to Nagasaki. While he remained unseen in his steamy cabin, his subordinates continued speaking for him, now with an ultimatum. If the Japanese persisted in refusing to receive the letter, the visitors would go ashore "in sufficient force" to deliver it themselves, "whatever the consequences."

Undertaking to communicate that notice to Edo, the new representative asked for patience, advising it would take four days to obtain a reply. *Three* days, Perry countered through his subordinates, adding that his ships could cover those twenty-seven miles north to Edo in just one. He'd expect a definite answer by July 12.

The officers who delivered the Commodore's instructions during the July 9 exchange were the *Susquehanna*'s captain, Perry's chief of staff, and, again, his aide. They were conveyed to the trio by another officer: his son. Twenty-eight-year-old Oliver Hazard Perry II was serving as his secretary (prompting resentment of favoritism among some other junior officers).

ALTHOUGH EDO CASTLE HAD A GOOD IDEA of the mission's purpose, the Uraga officials didn't. Their efforts to throw light on that matter of supreme concern to them had yielded only the information that the commander wanted to deliver a letter from the American President to the Emperor through a high dignitary. But why, the second day's functionary had inquired in another attempt, were four ships required to deliver a single letter? The reply—"out of respect for the Emperor"—only deepened the questioners' suspicion that the hugely armed American wanted much more than they said. But if the Japanese remained in the dark, so did almost all Americans, there and at home. "The real purpose of the expedition should be concealed from public view," Perry had written the Secretary of the Navy thirty months earlier. Oliver Hazard Perry II's recent movements might have provided a clue. The Commodore's third son had joined *Susquehanna* after serving in China, and the commercial connection between that country and Japan was no less accidental than the family bond on the flagship.

The father's sense of self was also relevant to that real purpose, especially since the Japanese perception of him would be crucial. Perry would repeatedly explain the need for making the strongest possible impression of his own importance. "The Commander . . . was well aware that the more exclusive he should make himself, and the more unyielding he might be in adhering to his declared intentions, the more respect those people of forms and ceremonies would be disposed to award him." *That* was his reason for so far remaining in his "splendid isolation." If not for the overriding national purpose, he'd have been "ashamed" to "assume a superiority," an expression of "contemptible pride," based on "mere official rank." Perish the thought that he was "too lofty to stoop to the level of men below him in station," including his Japanese "brethren in the common heritage of humanity . . . no man is more easily approached by his fellow-men, or assumes less on account of the honorable position he fills in the service of his country." In short, his whole show of "stately and dignified reserve" was only to advance the cause. Later meetings with the Japanese would, he promised, reveal his true nature, grounded in "perfect equity in all he asked or did."

The significance of his *real* true nature, which evidently included that ability to misrepresent it, was all the greater because he'd been given even more authority than ordinarily vested in naval commanders at sea, whose powers were already near sovereign. (Perry described his own as "far exceed[ing] any that have hitherto been issued to any one."[9]) Decades of lessons learned in performance of delicate and highly responsible duties had taught the assertive veteran of foreign wars, skirmishes, and intrigues the importance of maximizing freedom to act, and quickly. Ten years before, natives on the southern coast of the big African bulge toward the West had killed two crew members of an American merchant schooner. Before landing there from an earlier squadron he commanded, Perry formed thirteen boats, packed with sailors and marines, into a battle line that advanced toward the shore "with flags flying and muskets glittering," while he "underscored his rank and authority" with his best uniform and most formal manner."[10] After conducting an inquiry (and surviving a personal assault by a local chieftain), Perry decided the killings had been in self-defense, but his greater finding was probably confirmation of the importance of assuming a powerful pose for gaining dominance over far larger numbers.

However, his dealings with national leaders, chiefly of small African states, evidently developed little facility for introspection or for understanding a full range of adversaries. Perry's Japanese "brethren" would have been dumbfounded by his claim that his meetings with them were conducted "on terms of friendship and equality."

If no thicker than that of most movers and shakers, the lens of personal ambition through which the Commodore saw his vision of national good was evident in his reaction to his 1851 appointment to lead the mission. Although he'd championed its goals, the Secretary of the Navy's announcement at first disappointed him because he'd be replacing an officer junior to him: John Aulick, who had been charged with unethical conduct. Feeling a "strong disinclination" to be Captain Aulick's "mere relief or successor,"[11] he preferred command of the Mediterranean fleet that would do more to crown his career. Unless the newly formed East Asia Squadron were enough beefed up to "hold out a well-grounded hope of its conferring distinction upon its commander," going to Japan would represent a retreat.

But with great distinction now in view, together with Mount Fuji, the lifelong achiever had little trouble playing the part of a superior being, or cloaking what one of his clerks called the "attack upon Japan" in humanitarian purpose. That diminished neither his strategic wisdom nor his tactical skill, both grounded in anger at Japanese offense to foreigners—which he of course hadn't invented. Only extraordinary measures could penetrate the screens and veils of their seclusion.

THE JULY 9 OFFICIAL IN HIS LUXURIOUSLY embroidered silk robe was Kayama Eizaemon, an aide to one of Uraga's two genuine governors as well as a police magistrate. He was given to understand no further discussion would take place until delivery of Edo's answer. When Kayama disembarked, armed American boats resumed surveying the bay and harbor. Invasion-fearing Japanese who had taken copious notes about the ships' weaponry saw that activity as supremely ominous, but their protests that that too was illegal went in vain.

Despite the resentment of the mistreatment of shipwrecked American sailors, the leaders of previous American missions had counseled restraint in the hope of establishing long-term relations with the closed country. Captain Aulick, Perry's predecessor as the East Asia Squadron commander, had warned that the Japanese would "believe no friendly profession accompanied by so warlike a demonstration."[12] Perry's opposite calculation was that showing force was essential for establishing normal relations with Japan, even cultivating friendship. He didn't want to open fire if he didn't have to. "The question of landing by force was left to be decided by the development of succeeding events; it was, of course, the very last measure to be resorted to, and the last that was desired." But he vowed to disregard any native acts or threats that "in the least conflicted with [the Commodore's] own sense of what was due to the dignity of the American flag."[13] And since his approach rested on making the Japanese believe that only their submission would prevent him from taking the last resort, displaying his guns was key, all the more because he was convinced they had a healing, not scarring, effect on those at whom they were trained.

The surveying was interrupted the following day; it was a Sunday, and Perry believed his duty to educate his crews included strict observance of holy services. While leaving the conversion of souls entirely to others, he retained his absolute belief in the superiority of Christianity. That helped form his attitudes toward the Japanese, who weren't quite created in God's image. Whether or not he read the entire Bible on each of his cruises, as he claimed, he himself conducted divine services, as he called them, when no chaplain was available (although his unwillingness to keep his sailors on deck to hear others' sermons in biting cold distressed missionary-translator Williams).

But the worship of that Sunday, July 10, probably wasn't responsible for turning away a Japanese boat with several passengers of apparent high rank, who wanted to come aboard. The more important reason was the Commodore's persistence in his policy of talking with no one until an answer from Edo arrived.

Returning to the sounding and charting on the next day, July 11, Perry sent his boats farther up the bay, protecting them with the *Mississippi*. He was "satisfied that the very circumstance of approaching nearer to Edo with a powerful ship would alarm the authorities and induce them to give a more favorable answer to my demands, and so it happened."[14] His prediction of the reaction was spot on. Reports of the mighty frigate's nearness to the sanctum sanctorum so frightened Abe and other *roju* members waiting to be received by the ailing Shogun that they hurried off to learn more.[15] The threat also moved the Council to take a decision at last—to accept President Fillmore's letter as a "temporary expedient" because avoiding war was now the top priority—while the panicky inhabitants were making their spontaneous evacuation of the capital in fear it would momentarily be "burnt to ashes."

THE SQUADRON OFFICER who saw Japanese officials as "without exception . . . the most polite people on the face of the earth" and the highly observant expedition artist who called them "perfect gentlemen" had police magistrate Kayama Eizaemon first in mind. Perry himself would describe Kayama as "naturally genial," with enough "affection towards his American friends" to develop "such a yearning for them" that he would "not be able to restrain his tears on their departure" from Japan.[16] Kayama's dignified bearing, formed by natural self-confidence and grace, impressed all the American officers, none of whom apparently suspected the real cause of his tears. The essentially conservative magistrate who wanted to preserve Japan's isolation and who concealed his anger for the good of *his* cause was about to become a critical figure in the clash: the first real diplomat because both sides trusted him. In the end, he'd be less responsible than only Lord Abe and his chief negotiator for avoiding bloodshed. There was some irony in that because Kayama's police position also gave him military duties: when fishermen from Jogashima Island had rushed to report the sighting of the American squadron on July 8, he was at gunnery practice with his coastal defense unit. He saw the huge ships when they first appeared near Uraga on the same July 8, then close up the following day. Inspection of their guns left him, who was all too familiar with the woefully inferior Japanese ones, in no doubt about the outcome of any battle that might be fought.

True to his word, however, he, after disembarking from the *Susquehanna* on that morning of July 9, set out to convey to Edo Perry's warning about what would happen if the presidential letter weren't accepted. But before making a heavyhearted departure for the capital early that afternoon, he visited his immediate superior, one of Uraga's real governors.

Kayama's judgment that the American ultimatum he was about to convey was utterly serious deepened his distress. His observation of the flagship's personnel, he'd write in his report, showed that they intended to complete their mission whatever the cost, and were ready "for the worst to happen." He could conclude only that the matter would never be settled peacefully "unless our government would receive the letter as they desired."[17]

Was he right? Would Perry have used his guns? President Fillmore's affirmation, delivered during his first annual address to Congress that the United States "did not suffer hostile military expeditions . . . to invade the territory or provinces of a friendly nation" didn't necessarily rule out military action in Japan. For one thing, the President's declaration was intended to restrain not naval commanders but Southerners who were planning to invade Cuba and secure its incorporation into the Union as another slave state. For another, Japan was hardly a friendly nation. Still, the Commodore had reason to suspect the administration would be unhappy to learn he'd opened hostilities because Edo had been uncooperative; by inclination and language, the President and Secretary of State Daniel Webster strongly suggested they wanted no such thing. The Commodore's State Department instructions, largely drafted by himself, were to show an imposing display of power with which Japan would be severely chastised if it didn't satisfactorily respond, especially about the shipwrecked sailors. But he was also expected to be forbearing and conciliatory, using force as a last, *defensive* resort. Not even the President had the power to declare war, Perry's instructions reminded. That he'd already exceeded his orders in that respect during stops on the voyage from Norfolk, especially on Okinawa, wasn't proof he'd do it again because the potential consequences of war with Japan were far more serious than any from the liberties he'd taken with weaker peoples along the way.

Nevertheless, war was far from inconceivable. Perry's statement that succeeding events would determine whether or not he'd land by force suggested he hadn't yet decided. At that point, it was up to the Japanese to avoid it, and more than the Commodore's lusty ambition and resolve that what Japan "would not yield to national comity should be wrested from her by force" suggests the possibility was real. Although he'd later insist he would have resorted to force only if the Japanese government committed an insult or other wrong, "and, of course, was not contemplated," he warned the Japanese in writing that if President Fillmore's letter weren't received and duly replied to, he'd "consider his country insulted and will not hold himself reponsible for the consequences," "be the consequences what they might."[18]

But if how Perry would have reacted to nonacceptance of the letter will never be known for certain, the Japanese assumption was clear and virtually assured. Kayama in particular had no doubt the Americans would use force if they felt it necessary. The *Susquehanna*'s captain had told him personally that Perry would "consider his country insulted"—a word that rang loudly in Japanese ears—and "not hold himself accountable for the consequences" if the "friendly" letter in question weren't received and "duly replied to."[19] Kayama, profoundly impressed, was about to warn Edo about the danger of refusing to receive the letter right there at Uraga, where the Commodore insisted.

Convinced that military resistance would be disastrous, however, he also profoundly regretted the disgrace *to Japan*—"the immeasurable harm"[20] if the letter were accepted under threat. That was what he'd told the Governor before departing for Edo, and what the governor wrote in memos of his own for consideration by higher authority in the capital, adding a recommendation of what Kayama would call "a lenient policy" toward the Americans. Rushed there by boat in three hours, the magistrate delivered his messages to a second Uraga Governor, or commissioner, who was in residence near Edo Castle.

Kayama happened to be among the scattering of officials below the upper *bakufu* level who had heard, in his case roughly a year earlier, that Americans might be coming. "Deeply concerned" and afraid of "grave consequence[s]," as he'd describe himself, he had enough initiative to inquire about the rumors. Passed higher by his superior, his question eventually went all the way to Lord Abe, who confidentially confirmed the substance of the 1852 warning about Americans coming soon, but called it groundless. However, he showed the alarming Dutch report to his questioner, who told Kayama about it, also in confidence. The police magistrate, closer to ground level at a critical stretch of the coast, didn't share Abe's optimistic denial of any actual danger.

Now, in the office of the Uraga Governor resident in Edo, he wondered why the prescient Dutch warning had been dismissed. "How should we explain this wide difference between what we'd been confidentially instructed and what we were now witnessing?"[21] Instead of counseling caution about questioning higher authority, the Governor opened up to his likeable junior. He was unusually knowledgeable about Americans, thanks to dealings with them in 1849, when he'd been Governor of Nagasaki, where Ranald MacDonald and the rebellious *Lagoda* deserters were incarcerated until borne off by the corvette. Now he acknowledged to Kayama that Abe's dismissal had been disingenuous; the Chief Senior Councilor made serious future trouble for himself by doing essentially nothing about the warning, not even preparing contingency plans.

The revelation refilled Kayama's eyes with tears. The *bakufu*'s inordinate secrecy, he lamented, had left Japan terribly unprepared and unnecessarily weakened for any attempt to negotiate with Perry. Mistaken confidence that Westerners could never assemble enough force to threaten the country had further diminished its powers. No doubt Kayama overestimated the defensive buildup that could have been accomplished during that year of excessive secrecy, or perhaps during the eight years since Lord Abe became the *roju*'s senior member. Higher officials and prominent daimyo who were about to participate in the terrible "what now" decision would do the same. For now, however, the question was limited to whether or not to receive the letter at Uraga. Many could pretend there was time to debate the larger challenges because they weren't at immediate issue; no one knew what the American President might demand. Nevertheless, battle lines were already being drawn for the great clash about the seclusion as such and Japan's deeply troubling future.

Still with the Governor, Kayama continued to "deplore the policy of our highest authorities," who had kept the matter completely secret. In the early hours, his host asked him to stay the rest of the night, then return to Uraga the following day with the *roju*'s decision, which would have been taken at a conference of what Kayama called "the Court."

When the decision wasn't taken by three o'clock in the afternoon, the

Governor directed him to return to Uraga for other urgent business involving the Americans. A chief constable would deliver the government's orders the *next* day, Monday, July 11—which also proved overly optimistic because the conference dragged on until late in the day. The sixty-year-old Shogun was too ill to have participated in the crucial discussion, whose spirit is probably caught by another recent Japanese historical novel, based on original sources.[22]

That dramatization has Abe inviting a student of Western military forces—based on an actual magistrate of a large *han*—to participate. Before the expert can speak, however, a high official known to dislike Abe's way of seeking others' opinions before taking decisions urges that the meeting save its dignity by ordering the outsider to leave. Abe counters that this is no time to raise questions about title or position; anyway, the custom of not permitting lower-class people to speak at *roju* meetings is outdated. Since the issue of the moment is what force the squadron may use if the letter isn't accepted and no one knows more about American military strength relative to Japanese, he gives the expert his special permission to do so, openly and freely.

The expert produces the effect on which Abe counted by asking the participants to remember why Britain easily defeated China, with its vastly greater manpower, in the Opium War. It was because China had no navy; and neither does Japan. "Without a navy, there's no way to win a war." If the American guns fired in anger, Edo Castle would be ablaze in seconds.

The grim prognostication is an updated version of the Deshima Dutch answer to a question Edo put shortly after it learned of the Opium War's outcome. Why had the Chinese lost, since they were said to be brave enough? "Because bravery alone is not sufficient. . . . No outlandish power can compete with a European one, as can be seen by the great realm of China, which has been conquered by only four thousand men [sent in twenty British Warships]." The dramatization now has Abe guardedly reading facial expressions. "Does that mean we should accept their letter?" he asks—disingenuously, because he and several supporters have already answered the crucial question in the affirmative.

Seeking an answer, the discussion resumes the customary oblique language and maneuvering, most deftly by Abe. Acutely aware of his need to win support rather than alienate, he feints, zigzags, and avoids revealing his own opinion—which is opposite to his lofty words about the importance of preserving the country's fundamental rule of receiving foreign ships exclusively at Nagasaki—until he feels he can ask whether everyone agrees an exception is acceptable. But all members *don't* agree, and one warns they never will. In support of his own wish to accept the letter, another lord asks whether Tokugawa Ieyasu, the dynasty's politically skillful founder, would stick to the law and let the country die if he were alive. But despite the seemingly iron logic of Japan's helplessness, speakers go back and forth over the same repellent ground, to veiled but increasingly sharp personal attacks and attempts to win advantage in blame for the disgrace and a collateral struggle over who will succeed the failing Shogun.

Tempers flare. Members accuse one another of chicanery. None can look Abe in the eye when the talk returns to the abhorrent prospect of bowing to the Americans. Two highly influential persons, including the powerful Mito lord who is Abe's loudest critic, are absent, ostensibly because of illness, but probably because they're unwilling to defend their resolve to keep the barbarians out by force now that that spells suicide. Fanning himself, sustaining his utterly calm mien while gently restating that the immediate issue is the country's security, Abe calculates how best to play on the family and political ambitions of those jockeying for power. Finally, late on the second day, he feels he can say agreement to accept the letter has been reached, and he takes responsibility for what may follow.

Those were among the real meeting's elements, however they actually played out. Another matter was the critical near-terror raised by Perry's July 9 and 11 surveying of the waters near Edo. The recent historical novel goes on to imagine what happens immediately after the members part, starting with the Chief Senior Councilor informing Shogun Tokugawa Ieyoshi of the crucial decision. The Shogun is depicted as close to losing consciousness from his great pain. Asking Abe to lean closer, he says his Senior Chief Councilor isn't merely called a *hytotan-namazu*—literally a gourd-catfish, actually someone too evasive for others to divine his thinking. No, the young lord also actually looks like one; and the Shogun is glad of that because Abe, who now promises to remain a *hytotan-namazu* forever, can also be tough in his quiet way. The Shogun then confesses, presumably because he knows the frailty of Abe's health, that he feared his faithful official might die before he did, but now is happy to leave life in the presence of someone of whom he feels so proud. Even if Abe has become the leader in the worst of times, he, Tokugawa Ieyoshi, has no worry about Japan's future.

Although the real Shogun had reason to be proud of Abe, any confidence in the future would have been self-deception. Ieyoshi's death would follow in two weeks, and his successor would be a son too mentally defective to comprehend his position. Meanwhile, Edo remained "on the verge of pandemonium."[23]

8

The Fateful Landing

The American landing, July 14, 1853

PRESIDENT FILLMORE'S LETTER would be presented at Kurihama, a village that lay in a coastal niche slightly south of Uraga.
Lack of wind on the morning of July 14 kept Perry's sailing ships
where they were, but the steamers covered the two-plus miles smartly,
making the desired impression of power and skill on the Japanese spectators and prompting even an American to appreciate "how big, black and
sullen" the ships looked. "Masterful, accustomed to having their own way,
full of pent-up force!,"[1] they dropped their anchors a mile from shore at
about eight thirty. The sun's drying of the air revealed the final Japanese
preparations for the morning's function, which had produced steady hammering and a babble of laborers' voices throughout the night.

For show and for real, the commander covered the bay's every possible
source of fire with his heavy weapons. Neglecting "no precaution that the

leader of an armed mission in a strange country ought to take," a chronicler would write not long later, he cleared his decks for action, cannon slotted, ammunition and small arms arranged, a pain-killing tincture of opium readied for the possible wounded. In admiration of his own, Perry would record that his ships and "thoroughly drilled" crews were "in perfect readiness as in time of active war."

The sounding of general quarters increased the men's awareness that they might soon be in battle. Happy as Edo's submission to the ultimatum had made them, there was no guarantee it wasn't a trick to lure the landing party into a trap. Springs on the ships' anchor chains would enable quick maneuvering for firing full broadsides should that prove necessary. While the defenders on shore, "truly in amazement" from the huge steamers' neat handling, watched and waited, the sailors eyed the Japanese ships patrolling nearby—toylike by comparison, but numbering some two hundred.

Kurihama (very near the present giant American naval base at Yokosuka) hadn't been chosen without dispute or deviousness by Kayama Eizaemon. On the morning of July 12, Perry's stated last day for waiting for a reply, the magistrate's barge had come alongside *Susquehanna* with orders from Edo, passed through the Uraga governor in local residence. They were to "Accept the letter. Deal with the matter . . . so that our national honor won't be lost and no trouble will arise in the future." The considerable national honor already lost pained Kayama. The "no further trouble" pipe dream in Edo's orders surely caused more.

News that the letter would indeed be accepted had given the Americans "intense relief," and Perry was gratified enough to relent on some secondary matters involving the forthcoming ceremony, including whether the official to receive it would be sufficiently "august." In an imperious letter he intended sending if Edo's answer hadn't arrived on time—and which he insisted be forwarded to the Emperor even though it had—he specified that the officer must be "one of the highest . . . of the Empire of Japan." That was when Kayama, who was rowed back and forth to Uraga for further instructions as the negotiations progressed, had won his minor concessions. Although still an exclusionist at heart, he overcame enough of his distress at what was in store for Japan to again impress the Americans with what Perry would call his "gentlemanly aplomb" and "most polished . . . high breeding." (Although some Japanese officials also recognized Kayama's merit—including the resident Governor of Uraga, who would declare his diplomacy deserved high praise—the accomplished police magistrate would never receive full credit in his own country, perhaps because his achievements were in a losing cause.[2])

The largest of the minor concessions to him concerned the venue of the presentation. The Commodore wanted it to be more or less opposite where his ships had been anchored for days, at the Uraga shore his lookouts had been scrutinizing and his guns sweeping for accurate aim. However, he eventually accepted the argument that a proper reception would require a more spacious site. Kayama's deviousness was in professing ignorance of possible neighboring towns.

Thus preparations for the ceremony began in Kurihama six days after the Black Ships' first sighting, while panicked Edo's soldierly guard again doubled. Abe—more than ever the country's real ruler as the feeble Shogun further declined—confirmed with extreme sorrow the government's decision to abandon national policy in favor of negotiating with Perry. War with America wouldn't be "the best decision for our Empire," the *bakufu* explained.[3] Its determination to avoid shame and its capacity for illusion were large enough for it to conclude that patience and compromise were better "in order to make them leave soon and to reach a better solution later on."[4]

PERRY DONNED HIS FULL-DRESS uniform despite the heat and ordered a call to boats shortly after 9 a.m. Less than half an hour later, the two steamers launched the first of fifteen small craft carrying three-hundred-odd sailors and marines, including some forty musicians. Armed with pikes, muskets, pistols, and cutlasses, the force was commanded by a captain who'd served under Perry in the Mexican War. As the captain's boat approached a temporary jetty of bagged sand and straw, the Commodore, still on the *Susquehanna*, cocked his hat, "dazzling with gold braid," on his manly head before descending into his personal barge, riding alongside. His seclusion had earned much native curiosity as well as respect. Japanese eyes laid on him for the first time strained to read what they could from his appearance. The flagship's thirteen-gun salute as he was rowed toward the landing echoed hard off the hills and back to the little village.

The not-yet-scorching sun had turned the day clear and bright. The bay—which the ships would soon mark as "Reception Bay" on their charts—was glassy smooth, a sign to the Americans of Nature's continuing approval of their enterprise. Even without the fanfare, the setting, so far from home in several senses, would have moved them deeply. "The gleam of arms, the picturesque mingling of blue and white, in the uniforms, and the sparkling of the waves under the steady strokes of the oarsmen, combined to form a splendid picture, set off as it was by the background of rich green hills, and the long line of [Japanese] soldiery and banners on the beach."[5]

Still, the squadron remained fully alert to the peril that might befall it—"ten million men, brave, enterprising, ready, never conquered," an officer had written his wife several nights earlier, truth underlying his hefty numerical exaggeration; "It behooves us to be watchful." The once fierce samurais were a better show than a fighting force. Their spears, bows, and lacquered armor and shields were beautifully crafted but obsolete. Their muskets were ancient smoothbores, and artillery support consisted of "a few miserable fieldpieces"[6] with questionable ability to fire. Nevertheless, their mass of superb swords was graphic evidence that the need for vigilance was greater than ever. At the same time, however, the approaching culmination of this phase of the enterprise heightened American excitement and optimism. All felt that "if not an augury of the future and complete success of the Expedition, it was at least a commencement more auspicious than we had ventured to anticipate."[7]

The Commodore landed. The American drums rolled to his step. If he could be "pompous to the point of making his dignity ridiculous at times," as a biographer would write,[8] this wasn't one of them; not to that audience. Thoroughly self-assured, he was as imposing as any foreigner could have been. His poise, portly bearing, and commanding presence, as a clear-eyed young clerk saw those qualities, temporarily dispelled the big show's hint of *opéra bouffe*.* The marines presented arms, the bands struck up a stirring "Hail Columbia." To the Japanese, the precise, colorful spectacle had to be "outlandish and insolent," as one of Perry's artists, uncommonly interested in native reactions, noted. "How egregious we alien barbarians must have seemed."[9]

Still gaping in curiosity and aversion, native soldiers made no move to

---

* The show might have been titled *Berri*, as the Japanese called him. More than a few Americans would suggest that with his love for center stage, the Commodore would have made a good, old-fashioned actor if he hadn't chosen the navy.

object even when the landing party began behaving "just as if they'd been marching into an enemy territory," Kayama Eizaemon would record. Would their mighty naval guns now fire to open a surprise attack? Would the Americans slice off a piece of Japanese territory, as the British had done with Hong Kong? Unit commanders who knew China's fate yearned to strike first so as not to repeat the terrible mistake of not driving out the imperialists while there was still time.

That fist remained raised while the other Japanese hand was extended to the self-invited guests. Splendid-looking cavalry contingents reinforced long ranks of armor and ornamentation, supplemented by "brazen" (in American eyes) helmets, bearers of flamboyant pennants of the units' daimyo, archers with bows taller than themselves, spearmen with even longer pikes, swordsmen with perhaps the world's sharpest blades, artillery units and squads of handsomely uniformed musketeers: a small army that outnumbered the Americans by some twenty to one. Its line, Perry would note, "extended around the whole circuit of the beach, from the further extremity of the village to the abrupt acclivity of the hill . . . while an immense number of the soldiers thronged in."[10]

Now cheek to jowl with their ranks instead of training guns at them from the great ships, the landing party no longer saw the ominous five-thousand-odd defenders as sitting ducks. If Lord Abe's *roju* had ordered an attack instead of commanding them to hold their fire, they'd perhaps have been able to kill all three hundred Americans in, a sailor calculated, fifty minutes. Although the retaliation would surely have been massive and the eventual outcome of a war was in little doubt, any fighting that morning would probably have been disastrous to the mission. Perry knew that at least as well as anyone else in the squadron. "It must be confessed that, had such been the disposition of the Japanese, there would have been no difficulty, with their large force, in completely hemming in the Americans."[11] Thus the venture rested a little on bluff and a lot on bravery.

Both were now in full display. The resplendent Commodore passed between parallel lines of his officers and men, drawn up according to his own choreography. A corps of marines, "a fine athletic body of men"[12] in smartly plumed shakos and with white straps crossing their chests, led the way toward a nearby reception hall, source of the nighttime hammering. One of the bands and a contingent of sailors, their bayonets fixed, marched on the heels of the marines. Newly issued caps decorated with bands of stars and stripes in red, white, and blue complemented their white shirts and blue trousers.

Next came two ship's boys bearing Millard Fillmore's letter and the Commodore's letter of credence in the special presidential boxes. His ample self followed, escorted by his staff and other officers, while a carefully selected boatswain's mate bore his pennant on high. If not quite decked out "with every scrap of gold braid in his wardrobe," as one account would claim, he displayed a rare amount of it, together with his substantial collection of medals.

No Japanese had seen a black person before. A pair of very dark, unusually powerful stewards serving as Perry's bodyguards seemed to fascinate the startled onlookers more than the box containing the presidential letter. Armed to the teeth and bearing the American ensign, the stewards towered over the "more effeminate looking" natives, as Perry saw them. Another contingent of bluejackets and a second band closed the procession. So far, it had suffered nothing more damaging than angry looks from some of the Japanese troops—who, however, were simultaneously impressed by the precision of the American marching. Both sides maintained their admirable discipline.

But a suicidal attack might yet be unleashed. In the way of Japan's murderous, pre-Tokugawa civil wars, ten samurai were positioned to cut down Perry and his aides when they'd be most vulnerable, inside the hastily built reception hall. Hidden in a chamber beneath it, they waited for a signal from above to charge with their lethal swords.

THE HALL'S VISIBLE FEATURES included a pyramidal roof and two ancient brass cannon guarding its entrance. Inside, braziers burned despite the morning's heat, helping light a kind of canopied court carpeted in white. The Commodore entered with his suite. Having made clear "there was to be no discussion at this meeting,"[13] he meant to keep his stay brief.

Under the canopy, kneeling retainers flanked two elderly men, their luxurious silk gowns embroidered in silver and gold. Seated on camp stools rather than in the usual legs-under fashion, they rose to make "a grave and formal bow." Announced as princes, taken by Perry as "representatives of

the Emperor" (Kayama Eizaemon would soon address one as a "First Councilor of the Empire"), they were actually the Governor of Uraga and his
counterpart in Edo, the shogunate minister/magistrate/chief of police who
watched over that *han* from there. Neither uttered a word as the Commodore was shown an armchair upholstered in red. Kayama and his interpreters, still kneeling, would serve as what Perry would call masters of
ceremonies. After several moments of total silence, they introduced the
parties, then asked Perry if he was ready to deliver the letters.

The action turned as swift as it could, given the need to go around a
linguistic horn, as it were. The translation to and from English and Japanese through Dutch also blocked any trace of congeniality that might
otherwise have materialized. Perry beckoned to the boys, who "immediately obeyed his summons,"[14] to deliver the "magnificent" rosewood boxes
with solid gold hinges and locks in which the historic documents lay. The
folios inside, bound in blue silk velvet and with seals also of pure gold, had
cost the then vast sum of a thousand dollars each. The boys, selected for
their good looks, duly presented the "splendid specimens of American
workmanship," and, the two "stalwart," "jet-black" stewards removed the
scarlet cloths covering the boxes, opened them in silence, and displayed
the letters' writing and seals.

Perry's letter of credence, as it was called, attested to his "full power"
to confer and negotiate with Japanese representatives, and to sign conven-
tions and treaties about "all matters" that "may be interesting to the two
nations." President Fillmore's communication to "His Imperial Majesty,
the Emperor of Japan" was of course more important. The friendly assumption of its salutation—"GREAT AND GOOD FRIEND"—surely
puzzled the Japanese. The missive quickly went on to assure the monarch
about whom Washington knew virtually nothing—these papers would go
to Edo Castle, not to the shadowy near figurehead all but confined to his
Kyoto palace—that the President entertained "the kindest feelings toward
your majesty's person and government" and had "no other object" in sending Perry, identified as an American naval officer "of the highest rank,"
than to propose the United States and Japan should "live in friendship"
and enjoy commercial intercourse. "The Constitution and laws of the
United States forbid all interference with the religious or political concerns
of other nations. I have particularly charged Commodore Perry to abstain

from every act which could possibly disturb the tranquility of your imperial majesty's dominions."

Perry's virtually every act in Japan already having jolted its tranquility, that affirmation too would puzzle all its people who would learn of it. An uncommonly composed Edo resident was reported as saying it all sounded to him like "that savage is setting us up for something weird." But no evidence exists of hypocrisy on Millard Fillmore's part. A compromiser—or a jellyfish, his critics complained[15]—in the increasingly divisive struggle over slavery, he didn't oppose foreign expansion provided it was peaceful, but had sounded positively un-Perry-like three years earlier, in his first annual address to Congress: "We should act toward other nations as we wish them to act toward us. . . . Justice and conscience should form the rule of conduct between governments, instead of mere power, self-interest, or the desire of aggrandizement." His letter's reassuring tone and praise of Japan apparently weren't devious, even if he knew so little about it and his writing seemed intended for the slightly simpleminded:

> We know that the ancient laws of your imperial majesty's government do not allow of foreign trade, except with the Chinese and the Dutch; but as the state of the world changes and new governments are formed, it seems to be wise, from time to time, to make new laws. . . . If your imperial majesty were . . . to allow a free trade between the two countries it would be extremely beneficial to both. . . . If it does not prove as beneficial as was hoped, the ancient laws can be restored.

Not even the heated issue of castaway mistreatment had goaded the President to threaten reprisal. "It sometimes happens, in stormy weather, that one of our ships is wrecked on your imperial majesty's shores. In all such cases we ask, and expect, that our unfortunate people should be treated with kindness, and that their property should be protected, till we can send a vessel and bring them away. We are very much in earnest in this."

His fundamentally unaggressive message concluded with mention of having directed Perry "to beg your imperial majesty's acceptance of a few presents . . . intended as tokens of our sincere and respectful friendship. May the Almighty have your imperial majesty in His great and holy keeping." Repeating his contrived but innocuous camaraderie, he signed "Your good friend."

THREE COMMUNICATIONS FROM PERRY supplemented Fillmore's. One was a copy of his message of July 12 to the Emperor—the one he needn't have sent because Edo delivered its answer within the three days he'd demanded. The superfluous note expressed hope that "an early day" would be appointed for the business that was being conducted that very morning of the fourteenth. Another was a kind of commentary to President Fillmore's letter, emphasizing the points the Commodore considered most important. Although it closed with an expression of "the most profound respect for your imperial majesty," its tone was several cuts sharper than Fillmore's. Raising the shipwrecked sailors issue, it cited the *Morrison*, *Lagoda*, and *Lawrence* cases, and described the President as "surprised and grieved" to learn their crews had been treated "as if they were your worst enemies." The old hostility had better cease, Perry admonished, as if it hadn't largely already done so. The steamships of increasingly great America could, he exaggerated, reach Japan in eighteen or twenty days and would soon "cover" its seas.

Thus did Perry take it upon himself to turn Fillmore's more or less friendly proposal into intimidation, despite his orders requiring him to be "firm and decided" but also "courteous and conciliatory," submitting "with patience and forbearance" to acts of discourtesy from people "unfamiliar with our ways." The President had stressed that the end should be attained "not only with credit to the United States, but without wrong to Japan."[16]

Perry's stance made a predictably deeper impression on the Japanese than the President's milder one. However, his very brief third missive somewhat tempered the threat. That one informed the Emperor that the importance of the matters involved and time required for deliberating them had rendered him willing to wait for an answer to the presidential letter until the following spring, when he "confidently hopes that all matters will be amicably arranged, and to the satisfaction of the two nations."

If the Commodore's inclusion of the three communications in his official narrative of the expedition is evidence he took pride in their display of devotion to country, his failure to mention another one—indeed, his pains to hide it—strongly suggests the opposite. A much more hostile "fourth letter," issued before the Japanese capitulation about receiving Fillmore's—perhaps when Edo's attempts to give its answer through the Dutch or Chinese traders in Nagasaki heightened the Commodore's irritation—apparently strengthened Kayama's conviction that the Americans intended to complete their mission "whatever the cost."

American documents make no mention of the fourth statement, which went virtually unmentioned until recently. Whether it took the form of an actual letter in addition to oral communication will probably never be known, but there is little doubt it was delivered on July 12, one way or another; the lord of the Mito domain who'd long been critical of Abe Masahiro for neglecting national defense would also mention the flags—which he saw as threatening war—in a letter to the Chief Senior Councilor after Perry would have left Japan. Translator Samuel Wells Williams stated that the Japanese were "clearly informed of a white flag,"[17] although he evidently didn't know how serious their effect would be. Those mentions went all but unnoticed, but a fuller rendering of the message would be found in a local Japanese official's note to Edo about Perry's demands, published in 1910 and judged to have "high credibility." The official's required report to the capital recounted that the Commodore, going well beyond the language of the three open letters, denounced Japan in unmistakably bellicose terms. Its prohibition of trade was criminal: no less than "a sin [that] . . . couldn't be greater against divine principles."

The practical effect, and perhaps the purpose, was to underline Japan's impotence. If Edo should insist on keeping the country closed, a Japanese writer would interpret the note, the Americans would "correct that attitude, with military force if necessary." Although the natives were entitled to fight back, "victory," the Japanese official's report rendered Perry's words, "will naturally be ours."[18]

To drive the point home, two white flags accompanied the fourth letter. An explanation of how to use them was also included because their meaning was unknown in Japan. Perry advised that if it came to combat—which Japanese units would have no chance of winning—they should hoist the flags when they were ready to surrender, whereupon American fire would immediately cease. The initiative little accorded with Perry's orders that the mission, "necessarily of a pacific character," should use no force except in self-defense.

The Commodore may not have put such instructions on paper—or if he did, later concealed the evidence to keep Washington from finding his push for surrender had violated the spirit of his orders. Either way, sober Japanese scholars are convinced that white flags given by a force so superior in firepower was a challenge to fight. Some believe *Do what I say or I'll open fire* indicates Perry was seeking a reason to attack.★ But Edo's interpretation was the critical factor: The "insolence and audacity of the American envoy" (whose own country would believe he'd exercised admirable tact and restraint) was taken as "hard" evidence for its suspicion the expedition was ultimately an act of aggression.[19]

Although Perry was nowhere near so blunt in the Kurihama hall itself, his stance remained purposely threatening. Unable to threaten in return, the Japanese representatives did their best to remonstrate. The boldest attempt was incorporated in what Kayama called "an imperial receipt" he produced after the interpreters' descriptions of the American documents were conveyed to the two richly dressed officials, neither of whose lips had yet parted. Although promising delivery of President Fillmore's letter to the Emperor, the receipt repeated that it had been received in opposition to the Japanese law requiring foreign business to be conducted exclusively at Nagasaki. The exception, it explained, had been made in recognition of Perry's insistence that to agree to sail there would have been "insulting" to the American President. "As this is not a place wherein to negotiate with foreigners," the feeble protest concluded, "so neither can conferences nor entertainment be held. Therefore, as the letter has been received *you can depart* [italics added]."

That blend of empty command and bountiful hope was as strong as the Japanese could make it. The curt wording disguised Edo's surrender from

★ One such scholar who recently reexamined Perry's mission is convinced that knowledge of the white flags further increased the resentment of Admiral Yamamoto Isoruku, who devised and led the Pearl Harbor attack (Miwa Kamitada, *Kakusareta Perry no shiro hara [Perry's Hidden White Flags]*, pp. 239–43. See Chapter 18. Professor Miwa calls the use of the white flags "threat diplomacy."

A few Japanese doubters believe the report of Perry's instructions was written from hearsay, after he'd left Japan. As for Perry's failure to mention white flags in his accounts of the expedition—apart from use on survey boats—"in this bit of bravado he was probably acting beyond his instructions, and since it gives a rather different picture of his achievements than he might have wished, he quietly omitted" it. Marius Jansen, *The Making of Modern Japan*, p. 277. "One can only speculate that Perry chose not to . . . be portrayed as threatening the Japanese." Peter Wiley, *Yankees in the Land of the Gods*, p. 529.

neither party, both of which, after their thirty or so minutes together, prepared to part. Rather than awkwardness, Perry saw in the ceremony observance of "the greatest formality, though with the most perfect courtesy in every respect."[20] Knowledge of the depth of his hosts' apprehension and resentment would not have diminished his satisfaction.

9

The Ephemeral Respite

Lord Abe, Chief Senior Councilor

WEIGHING ANCHOR THREE DAYS LATER, at early light on July 17, the Black Ships alarmed onlookers unable to guess their intention. Were they leaving at last or would they mount an invasion despite the submission to them on the fourteenth? Perhaps the Americans' insistence on presenting their President's demands had been camouflage for winning not just concession but conquest. The one about humane treatment of shipwrecked sailors puzzled the Japanese because that's what they'd been giving the unfortunates since 1842. Was it subterfuge for something else Perry wanted: justification for aggression?[1]

If an attack was scheduled for that morning, the ships would go north toward the country's Edo jugular instead of departing south. That is to say, *again* go north, as they'd done those three days earlier, after the Kurihama meeting. The acceptance of the letters in the new hall had been followed by more silent moments. Perry broke them by declaring, through the interpreters, that he'd be leaving the country in two or three days—but would be back in April or May 1854, nine or ten months hence. His pointed mention of return prompted intense concern. Would it be with the same number of ships? Japanese officials asked, not yet having read his letter that mentioned a much larger force for his second visit. No, more of them, he answered; the present four were "only a portion of the squadron."

Closing the box into which the American communications had been placed, the master of ceremonies declared the proceedings closed. The Commodore followed his script for departing "with the same ceremony with which I had landed."[2] As he left the white-carpeted hall, the bow of the two dignitaries who'd presided without uttering a word was noticeably shallower than at his entrance.

The landing party returned to the little jetty, their bands supplementing "Hail Columbia" with "Yankee Doodle." The departure of its fifteen boats produced visible Japanese relief, but the comforting assumption that the worst was over would quickly prove premature. Still before noon, Perry reboarded his flagship and ordered the squadron under way. The conclusion of the note of receipt for Fillmore's letter—initially translated for him as "you will leave here" rather than "you can depart"—intensified his savoring of the Japanese longing for his exit. He decided on the opposite: to advance up the bay, toward Edo. Not merely higher up, but "so near to the capital and in waters hitherto unknown to foreigners" as to "produce a decided influence upon the pride and conceit of the government."[3] He'd again "show these princes how little I regarded their order for me to depart."

The new waters were indeed unknown to everyone but natives. The ships pushed ten miles higher than any previous foreign vessel had since the national closing. Their purpose was to survey the channel to Edo—despite "the protests of the authorities," Perry added with renewed satisfaction, "and under the very guns of their batteries."[4] Commanders of those batteries yearned to sink the boats that performed the surveying, but the

Americans demonstrated "how thoroughly each . . . was armed and ready for emergencies."[5] Regarding their exploration as preparation for invasion, local residents again panicked. The foreigners, some magistrates would lament, surveyed even entrance straits in Edo Bay that "we regard as the most important of our strategic areas." If they "conceive ill-will towards us and sail at once to the capital, bombarding it with heavy guns and destroying the city's dwellings by fire," they couldn't be stopped.[6]

While Edo Castle braced for the worst, Perry, still flush with victory, read the situation differently. Seeing his officers and men "in raptures with the *kindly disposition* [italics added] of the Japanese," he took additional pleasure in the "magnificent" bay, where "nothing could be more picturesque than the landscapes wherever the eye was directed." Highly cultivated land, "thrifty villages," and "rivulets flowing down the green slopes of the hills and calmly winding through the meadows combined to present a scene of beauty, abundance, and happiness which every one delighted to contemplate."[7]

The Commodore stopped for the night at what the visitors named "American Anchorage." Launching twelve boats again on the morning of July 15, he sent the *Mississippi* another ten miles closer to Edo in the afternoon. "Almost within gun-shot of their capital," he could see the city's outline six or seven miles farther north. With nothing to stop him, he "might have gone still higher but was apprehensive of causing too much alarm"★ and calculated he'd "done enough to work up the fears of the Emperor," so he ordered the ship to come around. Retreating farther south toward Uraga the next day, he stopped at what he called "Susquehanna Bay," near charming little "Perry Island," as named by a surveying party.[8]

By proving "the practicability of sailing even to the capital of Japan" and providing the information necessary for compiling charts, his probe of Edo Bay made him confident that the *Vermont*, a huge seventy-four-gun battleship he counted on joining the squadron before it returned the following spring, could navigate to the American Anchorage, "or even higher if necessary"—"higher" implying to Edo itself. And while teaching the

★ *Journal*, p. *101*. "Not more than four miles distant stood a tall white tower, resembling a light house. Three or four miles beyond . . . was a crowd of shipping, which was without doubt the anchorage of Sinagawa, the southern suburb of Edo. There was every probability that the *Mississippi* could have advanced to a point within cannon-shot of the city" (Bayard Taylor, *Perry's Bay*, p. 33).

Japanese "the folly of attempting to frighten away the Americans by bravado and sham exhibitions of force,"[9] it supported the Commodore's persistent striving "to impress the Japanese with a just idea" of America's "power and superiority."

Japanese officials then came aboard for a reception and exchange of gifts, both, the Commodore explained, for "exhibiting the disposition to conciliate" and expressing "a courteous desire" for the "mutual trade and commerce" that best secures and sustains "international good feeling and reciprocal interest."[10] His understanding of "reciprocal" was singular. Much as Perry would make of the Japanese representatives' liberal partaking of American drink[11] and of his own "most friendly disposition," resentment of his vaunted "power to compel" of course overshadowed their appreciation of the fleeting sociability.

The Commodore used his gifts to reinforce his political points. Although Japan, like China, had previously accepted them "as so many tributes to their superior power," he determined the present little ceremony should be considered "merely as a mutual interchange of friendly courtesy." He'd carefully selected his items, including American seeds and wine, to exceed the estimated value of those he'd receive, and registered full Japanese appreciation of his "friendly courtesy." After all, he had—when not ejecting or otherwise insulting native visitors—sanctioned several social meetings between his officers and Japanese officials, and was proud of his ships' hospitality, expressed in offerings of ham, biscuit, and plentiful draughts of whiskey. No wonder "the greatest harmony" prevailed on those occasions, their amiability enhanced by his resolve to be "ever studious of exhibiting the most friendly disposition in all his relations" with the authorities in order to display Americans' desire for "kindly intercourse."[12]

While no Japanese could have found those notions anything but fatuous or duplicitous, he, despite despising the officials for being inveterate liars, evidently took their feigned happiness as genuine. Perry saw men who'd "evinced a great anxiety" about his surveying and fairly pleaded for it to cease* nevertheless cherishing "a mutual friendliness" during the very

---

* "Upon the interpreter Tatznoske asserting that the Commodore had promised to leave the bay immediately on the reception of the President's letter by the princes, he was reminded that the Commodore only promised to leave the shore, but had distinctly stated that it was his intention to advance further up the bay with his ships" (*Narrative*, p. 266).

days of their humiliation. A sovereign people who'd been chastened by a gun-backed resolve never to be swayed from the cause of benefitting America—which the Commodore scarcely tired of attributing to himself—was supposedly simultaneously flattered by his demonstration of "international good feeling and reciprocal interest." People who'd seen him approach to just short of shelling distance of their essentially unde-fended capital were "remarkably genial" in his presence. That view of Japanese reacting in ways no American ever would may have been the starkest evidence of Perry's belief that they were inferior. "After express-ing in the most courteous terms their thanks for the treatment they had received, and their regret on leaving their American friends," the visiting officials "shook all the officers warmly by the hand, and went bowing and smiling over the side of the ship into their boat."[13]

SHORTLY AFTER THE SQUADRON got under way that July 17, dawn again pleased the Land of the Rising Sun. "To everyone's great relief,"[14] the ships headed south, easing the psychological siege hour by hour. There were even moments of rejoicing, some triggered by burning Perry's gifts, including a few for the Emperor, on Uraga's beach. (Some people feared the bottles and boxes carried a curse.[15]) Meanwhile, the Commodore, who be-lieved he'd won Japanese friendship, saw the morning's "great event" in his ships moving off in a stately line, a maritime feat that indeed again much impressed the throngs watching from shore.

Two days later, Edo ordered resumption of normal business and sub-stantial demobilization of defense units that had been deployed up and down the coast, but chiefly around Edo Bay. Platoons of porters hauling cannon along country roads leading to the capital continued raising village eyebrows for several days, but the "wild confusion" prompted by the squadron's nine-day presence subsided, together with the sense of urgency. "Whether they be samurai or commoners," confirmed the high-society physician who'd recorded the earlier panic, "all people seem to have heaved a great sigh of relief." Withdrawal of the threat *un*concentrated the mind of even some of the political leaders who knew accepting Fillmore's letter had been playing for time, since it postponed the harder decision of whether to bow to its terms.

But not the mind of Lord Abe, confronted with the very definition of a dilemma as "a conflict between equally undesirable alternatives." Commoners had been forbidden to travel to Uraga to view the Americans, but a million or more block-print news sheets from least five hundred producers ran stories about them, some with an instantly popular ditty that satirized the shogunate's surprise and terror.

> Amid everlasting peace,
> Awake from a long sleep,
> Jokisen tea,
> With merely four cups,
> Sleepless moments all night long

(Another translation: "What a joke, the steaming teapot/Fixed by America/Just four cups/And we never got another night's sleep.")

"Peace" was pronounced almost identically with its homophone "Pacific." The same with "cups" and "sails," and "tea" and the word for "steamship." Thus the four cups of Jokisen, an expensive tea of the time, referred to Perry's vessels, which, rather than caffeine, kept official Edo awake at night—no one more than Abe, although the ditty's final line about sleeplessness was a guess. In fact, insomnia on top of the young Chief Senior Councilor's stress, or the two together, began worsening his fragile health. After all, the barely concealed fun was being poked at not just *any* government, but the proud military *bakufu* of the "barbarian-quelling generalissimos." Acceptance of President Fillmore's letter had revealed its vulnerability to foreign pressure. Prestige and face had been lost. A prospect of more submission in the near future stared the nation in its face.

The Tokugawas, whom Abe loyally served, had always used their reputation for ensuring safety to help keep them in control. Now, however, the capital was gripped by ridicule of exposed government weakness together with rumors that the government *had actually known* American ships would soon be coming, yet failed to take the necessary defensive measures: the same lapse that had dismayed magistrate Kayama Eizaemon when Uraga's governor told him about it in confidence.[16] Two days after Perry's withdrawal, the elite physician, who still favored an injection of foreign influence, recorded rare disapproval of the *bakufu* for inadequate preparation to meet the emergency. Its "extravagant negligence" was "being severely criticized."[17]

Lord Abe had more than enough worries without the lose-lose bind into which Perry had put him. "To acknowledge incapacity to resist Occidental aggression would be to invite the ruin of the Tokugawa house; to resist, on the other hand, would be to invite destruction of the Empire."[18] The Hobson's choice generated much torment of its own. "Friction and conflict between advocates of these two diametrically opposed ways of thinking lay at the heart of the national turmoil."[19]

Both courses threatened national upheaval, perhaps even civil war, because not mere policy seemed at stake, but the core of Japanese values. Japan's rulers, still raised largely on Chinese philosophy, believed genuine civilization depended on maintaining Confucian rules and arrangements. Never mind that both were being altered and undermined by domestic developments, especially economic; foreign pressure was entirely different. Permitting barbarian values to corrupt native ones would be to abandon the highest human goals and achievements in favor of inferiority. Anyway, *Why submit without a struggle? Let's fight it out, and capitulate only if we're defeated.*

But the threat that colonial domination would follow such defeat doubled the foolhardiness of attempting military salvation with so inferior a force, which would be even worse than betraying Japan's sacred seclusion. No two alternatives seemed so opposite to one another than admitting and expelling the barbarians, seen by the holders of two opinions as callow capitulation or dumb obstinacy that would destroy the country. "All who attempted to . . . realize the best within themselves suffered those contradictions and shared in the agony of the times," a novelist would write.

ABE MAY HAVE WANTED TO OPEN the *roju* debate about whether to accept President Fillmore's letter to another outsider, this one of even lower social standing than the expert who starkly described Japan's military inferiority. The second person was a castaway who had been rescued by Americans after his ship had been wrecked. That description fit more people then than one would have imagined, especially in the early nineteenth century, after the start of the intense American whaling in the North Pacific. Among the drifters was a fourteen-year-old fisherman named Manjiro, which was his full appellation, Japanese of his class then having no surnames. After their boat went down in 1841, Manjiro and two fellow survivors endured a Robinson Crusoe–like six months on a deserted island before being spotted by an American whaler and brought back to New Bedford, from where the ship's affectionate captain took the likeable teenager to a nearby Massachusetts town and adopted him as John Mung. (When the family church suggested young Mung move to its segregated section for Negroes, the captain switched to a church where the son could continue sitting with his new parents and siblings.)

Adapting easily, the first Japanese to set fully legal foot on American soil became the first to be educated there, all the way through then relatively rarefied high school, where the eager learner excelled. Subsequent service on a whaling ship's three-year, around-the-world voyage testified to his competence and also displayed an internationalist sense that would become more important in Japan's reaction to Perry. Then, after a decade away from Japan, twenty-four-year-old Manjiro resolved to risk death by trying to return, partly to see his mother again, partly in hope of somehow helping to open the country. In 1851, he landed in the Ryukyu Islands from an American ship's small boat. Careful interrogation of him there led to permission to proceed to Japan and, after much further investigation, during which he was imprisoned but treated courteously, on to his home village. The sewing machine, camera, English books, and, most important, English language he brought with him were all new to the country. His limited punishment—confinement in the village, but with a life pension because the local lord felt his many years abroad would make rehabilitation difficult—again showed that the bite of Japan's seclusion laws had become less severe than their bark. When the daimyo appointed the returnee to lecture at the *han*'s school about his world travels, especially in America, the bite seemed to have become a nuzzle, at least there on the island of Shikoku.

Manjiro's next improbable destination was Edo, where he actually arrived two months after the *roju* conference had decided in favor of Perry. Still the knowledge of America for which he was valued was put to excellent use—largely by Abe, who had summoned him and was pleased by his lucid answers. Abe's call, delivered by local officials, included a request to "please tell Manjiro there's nothing to worry about," meaning he wouldn't be punished for coming to Edo, although some conservative *bakufu* functionaries wanted to do just that. (Now awarded the right to have a surname, he chose "Nakahama," after the name of his village. He was also given a title, which gave him the right to carry the two samurai swords.) Abe's purpose was again manifold. Eager to learn what he could about the curious country to which his had been forced to submit, he also wanted to use the pardoned criminal's knowledge to allay the fears and temper the zeal of nationalists who were eager to resist the insolent Black Ships.

No doubt thanks to his American experience, young Nakahama Manjiro was little intimidated by the high *bakufu* officials who questioned him. (People began calling him unique because "he talks to daimyo and to beggars" and conversed with the former as "human beings, just like himself" rather than flattering them.) Convinced that Japan's isolation was harmful, knowing how irrational and inhumane it appeared abroad, he revealed much they couldn't have imagined, in particular about American government, especially the practice of electing the President, who was obligated to govern under the rule of law.

His warm view of Americans, considerably prettified by gratitude and affection for the compassionate family that had adopted him, may have been even more influential. Manjiro professed to be astounded by the "extraordinary fuss" Japan made about Perry's squadron, which was "absolutely" composed not of warships but ships that "did surveying and things." Moreover, America was supposedly too busy developing its new self to scheme of taking advantage of others. "Born to be gentle," its "physically perfect and beautiful" people were "virtuous and generous and do no evil." Instead, they "hold loyalty and modesty in high esteem" and have a "happy intimacy at home" which has "nothing comparable in any other country."[20]

The idealization would lead the aforementioned Tokugawa Nariaki, lord of the Mito domain—who was about to become Lord Abe's chief domestic adversary—to suspect Manjiro of being an American spy. Nariaki's worry that he'd favor the Black Ship intruders would keep him from being used as an interpreter during Perry's second visit the following year, but his more important teaching and cultural interpreting would win American praise as invaluable. With some exaggeration of his own, a contemporary would claim he "contributed more than any other person to the opening of Japan." The former fisherman indeed served as an ambassador—under the circumstances, an extraordinary one—in 1853–1854. His assurance that upright, generous America had utterly no interest in invading or conquering would impress Tokugawa opinion makers enough to aid the cause of, essentially, submission to Perry, on which Abe had counted. The Chief Senior Councilor had to take advantage of every stratagem he could conceive because although his office could bestow great institutional authority, the position was also very insecure.

Abe's position in particular was heavily besieged and sometimes precarious, even though authority had been shifting from the weakening shoguns to their civil servants for decades. Reign by reign, depending on circumstances and personalities, the top post of Chief Senior Councilor had been growing in power and prestige, partly because the shoguns, although they still had to approve all important decisions, were increasingly remote. Living in Edo Castle's "quiet isolation" and

able to see their highest officials for brief consultations only, they were even further distanced from the daimyo (and from the affairs of their own huge Tokugawa *han*), as well as utterly divorced from the imperial court. But while the shoguns' contact with the outside world was primarily through their personal attendants and the ladies in their household,[21]

roju members could "operate outside the castle and the formal *bakufu* structure as well as within it."[22]

Naturally, the Council's powers, especially those of its Chief, expanded to fill the partial vacuum left by the near impossibility of direct rule by shoguns—and Abe's influence grew even stronger during Tokugawa Ieyoshi's lengthy infirmities. Nevertheless, those developments (some of which paralleled movements in feudal Europe) left Abe politically weaker than necessary to truly govern, and not only because his official powers weren't enlarged to match the much greater responsibilities that descended on him because Shogun Ieyoshi's son and successor, twenty-nine-year-old Tokugawa Iesada, was mentally unsound.* (News of Ieyoshi's death was kept secret for a time out of fear that the simpleminded thirteenth Tokugawa Shogun

---

* Nearly all the twenty-three children Tokugawa Ieyoshi sired with his wife and consorts died; the fourth child was among the few survivors. Although he, sickly Iesada, could read—and liked to see the world in the pages of the *London Illustrated News*, his ability to speak was severely limited. Rarely communicating to others except through his mother and nurse, the otherwise genial new Shogun was incapable of serious discussion or responsibility. He was a "half-wit who liked to cook beans for his retainers, play with his kittens, and chase his retainers, with a gun fitted with a bayonet; he . . . could neither produce an heir nor fully understand the implications of his position" (Peter Booth Wiley, *Yankees in the Land of the Gods*, p. 333).

would be useless in handling the Perry crises.) More than ever, Abe was the national leader, but without commensurate means to make policy.

ABE'S UPBRINGING—in a far southern *han* that is now essentially Hiroshima Prefecture—would inspire as much lore as Perry's, but it stressed markedly different qualities. One pretty story about his early years featured goldfish. "Gozo," as the privileged boy was called, apparently adored them, especially those in a pond of his father's senior officer. "If you like them so much," the officer was said to offer, "I'd love to give them to you. . . . But," he pressed after the boy's polite refusal, "they'll be happy to be taken care of by someone so thoughtful as you." Six-year-old Gozo, whose nickname suggested stored energy or will, continued to decline—for a typical reason, the officer suggested when reporting the incident to Masahiro's father: the fish were so happy swimming in their pond that the lad didn't have the heart to move them. But the faithful officer worried whether some shortcoming of his own contributed to the rejection of his offer.

Discussing the matter with his son, the father praised his kindness to the fish, but advised more thought about the officer's kindness to *him*. After all, subordinates were willing to give their lives for their lords—the brighter ones in order to win respect by doing things well, others out of simple obedience. "Do you think they'll die happily for you if you don't consider their wishes? What's more important for you, subordinates or goldfish?"

Gozo's reconsideration was described as brief. "Yes, I was thoughtless. I'll accept the goldfish with pleasure."

Days later, when the father asked the boy whether he'd thanked the officer, he learned Gozo had sent him a roll of rice paper and a box of sweets because he knew the man liked calligraphy more than sake. "Well done," said the father, happy with his son's handling of the little problem. "And never forget to be thoughtful."[23]

Abe's devotees believed that pastel-tinted episode revealed some of his salient qualities. He loved all manner of living things—birds even more than fish, but he was even more reluctant to make pets of them because a bird's death would bring greater sadness to its handlers. He cherished harmony. He listened carefully to advice and expressed gratitude for it, especially when it came from his father, whose good nature and intellectual vigor would remain powerful influences. Long remembering his words, the gentle son would indeed be admired for his thoughtfulness throughout his brief life.

His detractors, on the other hand, would have seen the story as betraying the principal weakness of the "ever-placating" seeker of consensus. It was a tendency to try too hard to accommodate and conciliate, to "bend to the political winds" too easily, as an American scholar would put it,[24] or to be waffling and wishy-washy, in his critics' sharper words. A novelized study published in 2002 depicts Abe showing a translation of the viceroy of India's 1852 warning that American ships would be coming soon to a high Nagasaki official. So what will you do? the official is pictured asking the Chief Senior Councilor. For now, Abe responds, he's thinking of seeking a wide variety of opinions—first of all his, the official's, so what does he think? The shocked official can scarcely believe his ears. Was the lord who was supposedly in charge actually seeking others' opinions instead of devising countermeasures?[25]

Other paternal words "engraved on [Abe's] heart" may have had additional bearing on his tendency to bend and conciliate. In 1826, when Gozo was eight years old his ailing father is thought to have called the youth to his bedside for some political talk. "When the majority goes to the right, look for a way to go to the left," the elder advised. "But if you take a wrong step, it will lead to vicious revolution. If that's what you're generating, it's far better to do nothing."[26]

Ferocious revolution would indeed threaten during Abe's critical years in power. Meanwhile, his traits began affecting Edo's policies a decade or so before Perry's arrival, when, as noted, Masahiro ("righteousness, generosity") was still remarkably young.

Political savvy may have entered the bloodline of "Abe," an ancient clan name, even earlier. Although his branch's *han* wasn't among the richest or most powerful, the family was one of the country's most politically distinguished, with a record of public service almost as long, proportionately, as the Perry family's in young America. Having allied themselves with the Tokugawas from near the very start of their rise to power and remained staunchly loyal ever since, the Abes supplied high government officers, including three members of the *roju*, for almost half the dynasty's reign of two centuries plus.

Among the three was Masahiro's father, a passionate scholar and artist with a keen practical curiosity about the world. Lord Abe Masakiyo's wide interests, which included astrology pursued in an observatory he had built for the purpose, prompted him to read about the West in books written by practitioners of "Dutch learning," based on materials imported by the Deshima Dutch. Unusually liberal and open-minded in the context of Japanese society, he was also devoted to his children's education. Masahiro stood out. "Even as a child, [he] was brilliant, dignified, and well mannered, seemingly conscious of his destiny."[27]

Family happenstance helped him reach it. His father died two years after advising him that doing nothing was better than helping create the conditions for violent revolution, to which he appended the assurance that the boy would work out the rest himself—a prescient prediction because Masahiro, who was preceded by five brothers, wasn't expected to succeed him as the lord of the domain. In fact, he was a more likely heir of a family that had adopted him for the purpose, a common practice. But his brothers, whose health was poor like his father's (bad omen for his own), recognized their youngest sibling as most capable of leading the family. The boy in whom the father had seen great things, which is surely why he offered his political coaching, became the daimyo of Fukuyama *han* at age eighteen.

Two years later, when thirty-six-year-old Captain Perry was helping modernize naval ordnance, the corpulent young Japanese patrician with the very fair skin, shiny eyes, and abundant ambition was appointed Superintendent of Shrines and Temples. Rendering distinguished service in that high office, the urbane personage and precocious administrator became known for his sound judgment; he was on his way to becoming considered, an American expert would declare, "the Tokugawa *bakufu*'s last great politician." Going further, a Japanese novelist would note that many deemed the "brilliant" practitioner of the art of *bakufu* maneuvering "the finest bureaucrat to appear" in its three hundred years.[28]

The dissenters include one of the country's most eminent historians, who, in 1929, called him a "common politician, nothing special." Other critics would contend that even if he was a master of *bakufu* tactics, precisely that cunning illustrated, or engendered, his deficiencies. Dealing with the Black Ships crisis required no mere politician, let alone a bureaucrat, but a charismatic leader who would inspire and command a decisive rebuff to the Americans, something never likely to emerge from the boy who loved goldfish. While fear reinforced the respect for tongue-lashing

Perry, the respect for Abe was bolstered by, again, the near opposite. Not that he couldn't dismiss and disapprove. Like centuries of Japanese leaders before him, he condemned immorality and criticized private as well as public extravagance—but tactfully. The regard for him grew partly from gratefulness for the unusual courtesy of a person of such high position, and appreciation of *his* appreciation of the arts (which included painting in the Western as well as the Japanese style). But the critics felt he was too forgiving and eager to make accommodation. Although his education, like that of all samurais, had of course included schooling in the military arts, especially use of the sword and archer's bow, he was too . . . soft.

The two camps agreed that the skillful conciliator with no known personal enemies, as opposed to political ones, was slow to anger. His concern for subordinates, even servants in the hotels where he stayed when traveling, was exceptional. (When his farmers petitioned the *roju* over his head about water rights for their rice, he made no fuss about, and sought no punishment for, that rare challenge from lowly peasants.) Even if permanent springtime didn't shine from his (roundish) face, as one of his retainers claimed, the Chief Senior Councilor's patience and instinct for compromise were remarkable in that strictly hierarchical time and place.

Other Abe qualities remain central for reckoning where Japan was headed before America shifted its development. One was his tolerance for unorthodox ideas. Not all minds were closed in the closed country. Together with a small but growing number of similarly well-educated thinkers and leaders, the gracious young lord was open to and curious about thoughts of the outside world.

Another openness was to advice from ordinary folk, even near strangers, like shopkeepers. No public voice then advocated democracy, in the sense of government of or even for the people—the great majority of whom didn't even have surnames, as noted.* Devotion to rule by the small samurai minority entitled to carry swords, supported by the attachment to the Confucian ideal of fixed stations with established roles, was all but universal.

---

* Matsumoto Kenichi, a prolific Japanese professor of history, estimates that roughly ten people out of every thousand in the average domain were able to offer their opinions to its daimyo. "The other 990 counted for nothing politically" (interview, November 14, 2003). There were, however, expressions of discontent. In the 1840s and early 1850s, unhappy samurai, especially those who lacked serious employment and more than subsistence income, had questioned not only the competence of *bakufu* officials, but also the status quo and its philosophy. What loyalty did a system deserve that kept amateurish men in power and failed to advance talented ones? That may well have helped prompt Abe's determination to open his own staff and the country's bureaucracy to talent.

Fathers passed official positions to their sons, who, however, were rarely permitted to rise higher even if they were outstanding. Despite exceptions and some bending to pressure for change, the structure of social-political rankings remained largely solid. The classes—samurai, peasant, artisan, merchant, whose hierarchy was supposedly of moral virtue as well as secular authority—were still formally distinct. (The untouchables below—tanners, gamblers, and executioners—were deemed unworthy of inclusion in a class, and the census didn't even count the beggars below *them* because they were considered beneath even that.) The categorization continued even as money's new ways of talking stretched the feudal bonds, making people's hereditary class slightly less decisive in shaping their lives.

Abe, however, widened "the circle of his confidential advisers to an extent never before seen in the *bakufu*" by consulting daimyo who took no formal part in national politics.[29] Also ignoring the canon that limited political advice to prominent samurai, he sought it from a wide variety of types. They included tradespeople and a nanny and tutor from his childhood, with whom he discussed political matters, although the tutor, now in his personal entourage, supposedly had no business contemplating state affairs because he was without title, position, or high education. No doubt that was in Abe's nature, which prompted surprise among servants because he was openly grateful and concerned about their well-being. A contemporary characterized the young lord as magnanimous and responsive to "the wishes of the people."[30] Dim as that concept was in terms of heeding popular will as opposed to seeking individual opinions, his inclination to listen to people of all walks of life—and address them with terms of respect, even when they protested they were undeserving—was distinctly rare in his class.

The probably even rarer practice of choosing officials for their merit, even when it violated custom, underlay Abe's gift for putting good men, including some of lower standing, in important places. Measured by probable effect on the future, willingness to disregard the hierarchy of birth-stamped status may have been the most promising of all his traits. Well before his *roju* appointment, the advice he sought from what can be called progressive thinkers included recommendations for widening the talent base. Dependence on the hereditary system, an Edo veteran was pictured as urging, would weaken the *bakufu*'s administration. But since an elective system was out of the question, a start should be made by choosing low-level officials and jury members from outside the usual candidate pool.

That "revolution," as its relatively few proponents thought of it, had barely begun. Even in Edo, not to mention the hinterland, where near total authority still rested in the local daimyo, the effects of Abe's inclination toward meritocracy remained extremely limited. Still, employing good men from outside the aristocracy fed a self-generating force of geometric possibilities: the more of them in responsible positions, the more they'd consult, swelling the country's impetus for change.

Abe's challenges to restrictive tradition reflected as well as advanced that impetus of the past half century or so, during which "the tenor of Japanese political thought [had] changed profoundly . . . the range of ideas and magnitude of schemes had grown exponentially."[31] But the arrival of the foreigners who demanded speedy transformation to *their* satisfaction disrupted the homegrown impetus for change generated by Japan's own needs. It also greatly strained the country's decision-making ways and means.

AN OLD POEM celebrated the "eight million deities/the ten million deities" who had "gathered in godly assembly" to proclaim the sun goddess Amaterasu ruler of the heavens. That number may have been an unconscious reflection of the intricacy of Japanese political life. The culture as a whole, with its amalgams of native customs and borrowings from abroad, could be perplexing. A close observer of the late Tokugawa period saw it as "peculiar to a degree for which there is perhaps no western parallel . . . a very bewilderment of complexity"[32] Fiction, family loyalty, and ability for political feinting wrapped its governing in additional layers of ambiguity, on top of which a cloak of secrecy remained in place. Everything about it, one of America's most perceptive interpreters would caution, presented an "immense difficulty [in] perceiving and comprehending" what lay beneath.

"Nothing is so difficult to understand in Japan as the peculiar complex character of its political institutions. . . ."[33] So declared another keen American observer a few years after Perry, when many forms remained the same while the country roiled with anger the Commodore helped unleash. Ryotaro Shiba, hailed in 1997 as the Japanese "narrative historian *par excellence*," wrote of the "confused struggle" of those who shared power in 1853. They shared it because of that partial fragmentation of political authority, despite the seventeenth-century unification that ended the disastrous civil wars. It was confused because ancient configurations and rituals shrouded its many sources that waxed and waned in strength and significance as alliances were made and broken. Complicated inheritance arrangements, including by adopted sons, also jumbled the mix. So did the ladies of the Shogun's household in the castle's Great Interior, some of whom exercised formidable influence, while Abe was kept at a distance.[34] Thus the political process, with its codes of behavior, secret cliques, networks of obligations, and other patterns woven by history, was a little like the circumlocutions of Japanese speech. Shrewd Abe used plenty of his own secrecy, together with the old *bakufu* standbys of lavishing awards on his loyal supporters and convincing opponents to retire because of "sickness." But his skill with such devices didn't keep the political process from exhausting him.

The easiest knot to untangle is the balance of power between the two leaders at the top. Although all ultimate subservience was supposedly to the quasi-divine Emperor, the reality had long been quite different. Dwelling as they did "above the clouds," the Emperors had had no military or economic power of their own for centuries. They were, as Ian Buruma has written, a little like Popes, whose blessings were used to legitimate the secular rulers.[35] The secular ruler with by far the most authority was of course the Shogun, who, if this needs repeating, ran the country supposedly like a generalissimo—on the advice, among other providers, of the *roju*, markedly more important since Tokugawa Ieyoshi's health began weakening in the 1840s.

Again, however, nothing in Japan was quite that simple. Abe's political dexterity diminished some of the long-standing tension between Edo Castle and the Court, but their relationship was hardly one of equals. The above-the-clouds dwellers of course also lived below them, specifically in the old capital of Kyoto, some two hundred fifty miles west of Edo. In virtual isolation there, speaking to few apart from the handful of noblemen who attended them, the shadowy personages performed their ancient ceremonies and courtesies. Ever since a Divine Son of Heaven named the first Shogun in the late twelfth century, he and his imperial descendants often didn't know about, let alone influence, the affairs of state. Without an independent source of revenue, they existed on stipends fixed by the shogunate (which sometimes sent agents to watch them along with the money). Some were so poor that they resorted to selling their autographs in order to survive. Money for coronations was often unavailable, in one case for twenty years; and, in at least one instance, money for burial too. The royal body lay in state until it began decomposing.

Still, the Tokugawas generally treated the Emperors with more consideration than previous Shoguns, and the latter weren't always mere figureheads. Although the pretense that the government was responsible to them for waging war and preserving peace was transparent, all power still *derived* from them, with their sole authority to confer the title that made the Shoguns the highest living *mortals*. Besides, calls for restoring their earthly authority had been sounding for some time. Although the voices weren't nearly organized or strong enough to constitute a movement, the extreme imbalance of power was becoming less so. The shock to the *bakufu*'s standing for failing to counter Perry fed the interest in returning the Shoguns to being no more than the Emperors' military retainers, as they supposedly began.

The Shoguns' relationship to those *below* them further complicated political life. Many supposedly "unshatterable" *bakufu* bureaucracies spent as much time competing with each other as they did administrating. Samurais not all being born equal, the rivalries were convoluted by a large array of grades, from the Shogun's direct retainers—six thousand-odd bannermen, *hatamoto*, who had vassals of their own—to *ronin*, or samurai unattached to a lord. But the greatest source of complication was the national structure. Law-abiding as it had been during the several centuries past, Japan wasn't fully one country, not "really unified."[36]

Not really unified? Despite foreigners' image of it as a tyranny? But some of the domains that had fought fiercely before Tokugawa Ieyasu established the dynasty and was appointed Shogun had never entirely lost their spirit of independence or instinct for aggrandizement. Dominant as they became, the Tokugawas shared authority with lesser houses. For all of Japanese feudalism's resemblance to medieval Europe's, nothing in Europe quite matched the calculating and maneuvering of the subordinate daimyo in their castles that still breathed intrigue, if not conspiracy. In fact, the principal cause of the welter of restraints on the latter was fear they'd use their still substantial powers to orchestrate revolt. If not for their potential for that, it's doubtful the Tokugawas would have devoted so much effort to cementing alliances with lesser lords.

Never-soothed anxiety about internal as well as external danger also explained thirteen shogunate rules, one of which was that no ship be launched or castle built or repaired without permission. The same for surveillance over marriages among other daimyo family members, control of which reduced the chances of their forging anti-Tokugawa alliances. More important, the lords and their key advisors were required to spend every other year in Edo, where their wives and heirs had to remain more or less full time. (The biannual processions to and from Edo of the daimyo and their often grand entourages provided the stimulus for building the country's impressive network of roads with their way stations that offered food, drink, entertainment, and, perhaps, reason to be called the first tourist traps.) The "alternate residence" requirement that kept a rotating half the lords in the capital, under the Shogun's eyes, amounted to a velvet hostage system, rendered no less effective by another fiction: that the compulsory visitors were supposedly guests.

At the same time, *bakufu* agents roamed the country, watching, questioning, and listening for signs of disaffection or dissent in the subsidiary courts while also keeping an eye on shogunate officials.[37] Some historians would argue that the need to guard against remarks that might cause arrest fortified the Japanese tendency to conceal emotion—to refrain from talking about feelings, especially critical ones.

No doubt the Tokugawas' desire for order helped explain the restrictions on "ordinary" people too, such as the documents required for travel by land as well as sea (although clever operators could wriggle here and there without them). Their desire for security may also have bolstered the devotion to the formally rigid social hierarchy. Donald Keene's "Everyone was quiet and obedient, and careful not to oppose those in power" suggests the mood, if not the literal truth.

Still, the country was far from the dictatorship that some American writers would call it. Almost all other constraints and restrictions were on the domains' external relationships, not their internal affairs; within their own *han*, the daimyo were largely free to rule as they pleased. Most had their own army, as well as administrative and fiscal policies with which the Shogun rarely interfered. A number used their own currency together with clan customs and rules. Some continued placing "spies" in their opposite numbers' courts, just as the *bakufu*, or "tent government," did on a larger scale. In short, they remained quasi-autonomous—or more than quasi in a few outlying ones that prudent shogunate officials entered only after requesting permission; some daimyo retained an independence "unthinkable in a fully centralized state."[38]

Governmental interference was almost always from local *han* officials rather than from Edo. The latter imposed no national system of taxation and did not attempt to establish a truly national system of law. (*Bakufu* courts could intervene only in cases involving residents of more than one *han*.) Nor was the Pax Tokugawa sustained by an army. In contrast to the popular Western image of a masterful dictatorship imposing severe regimentation on the people, the shogunate raised no national military force and never enjoyed absolute military supremacy, nor did it ever attempt to "exercise all the powers normally associated with full sovereignty."[39] Despite the proliferation of bureaucracies attempting to regulate one thing and another, the essentially haphazard tent government couldn't even discipline or punish with impunity.[40] Although Edo Castle had the ultimate right to confiscate domains, it had to carefully consider the lesser lords' reaction, all the more because they held the primary allegiance of most samurai.[41] Samurai serving their local *han*—to which the word *kuni*, "country," applied—kept the concept of the nation as a whole somewhat fuzzy.

The great knowledge, skill, and patience required to set national policy in such circumstances didn't complete the demands on Abe. When Perry arrived, *no fewer than two hundred sixty domains*—many very small, down to ten thousand souls, but some large, rich, and powerful—added complexity to the political play.[42] If reckoning with them weren't exacting enough, the degree of their independence and influence varied considerably, depending primarily on their role in the seventeenth-century struggle for national domination. Although history wasn't an infallible guide, how Tokugawa Ieyasu had obtained their fealty largely determined which of Edo's variety of intimidating and appeasing devices it now used to control them. That is to say, placement in the hierarchy of the two hundred sixty rested largely on when they'd joined the Tokugawas—meaning the ruling ones; the family had several branches. "The fortune of every house stemmed from its fate at Sekigahara,"[43] the battle fought in the driving rain in 1600, which was to have a decisive influence during the next two and a half centuries of Japanese history.

THREE CATEGORIES WERE MOST IMPORTANT. The ninety-eight
Outside Lords descended from those who'd submitted to Tokugawa Ieyasu
only after his military victories. The most powerful of them came from
western lands, especially the Nagasaki area, where Christianity had flourished and anti-Tokugawa opposition had been strongest. That explains the
prohibition of their becoming heirs to the Shogun except in rare circumstances.[44] The forty-five Inside Lords were the regime's most loyal supporters, responsible for providing the leaders of the *bakufu* government and
military. Closest to the main Tokugawa family—most prestigious, but not
necessarily most trusted—were the Three Families or Three Houses, one
of whose daimyo was Tokugawa Nariaki, the lord of the powerful Mito
domain, the Cassandra who'd warned about the Opium War, sharply criticizing the government for failing to strengthen the country's defenses.[45]
Nariaki *did* know what to do with intruding Western ships. In the same
1846 when the Shogun's consort lamented there were no ideas for dealing
with them, he proposed building warships, strengthening coastal defenses,
and "shooting every single one of them to death, thereby . . . maintaining
Tokugawa rule throughout the ages."

Highly patrician Tokugawa Nariaki had long been openly critical of
the *bakufu* for inadequate attention to military matters. Abe, who had already taken much disapproval from him, would now take considerably
more, as the outspoken leader lectured about the Black Ship menace. While
virtually everyone else expressed relief when they departed on July 17,
Nariaki regretted that the fuss the government made at the arrival of foreign ships led to nothing constructive after their departure—and saw the
instinctively compromising Abe as slippery as an eel.[46] That was true in
the sense that the Chief Senior Councilor's skill in reading signals from
hundreds of other players in the complex tangle didn't exempt him from
the need to be exceptionally careful and adroit when pulling his strings.
Taking great pains not to alienate other decision makers, he could reveal
no personal interest, let alone the "watch my smoke" hubris in which
Perry excelled.

The impossibility of arriving at a good solution however Abe negotiated between opposing opinions was already apparent. The stress of trying
became so intense so fast that he asked to resign shortly after Perry's

departure, confessing that "things are often out of my control. . . . I'm not good enough to be leader of the government."[47] But while that fed the talk about his indecisiveness, it was also a way of outplaying his critics. During that time of political battle, the distinctly unmilitary Abe was as strong— sensitive, acute, artful in maneuver—as anyone could be.

10

The Land of Constant Courtesy

The "Regent" of Lew Chew

PERRY'S WARNING BEFORE LEAVING JAPAN that he'd return with a larger force wasn't bluff. Mechanical, logistical, and bureaucratic problems had prevented most of his promised ships from sailing with him from the States or meeting him in China, but while he remained irritated by the squadron's "poor show" compared to the twelve or thirteen vessels Washington had originally planned for it, he felt confident more would arrive in time for his next visit, in the spring of 1854.

He was "glad to have a good excuse for consenting to wait" for a Japanese answer to President Fillmore's terms because he didn't want to remain anchored off Japan until his supplies ran out, especially since new stores and the expected additional ships were presumably waiting at convenient ports on the Asian mainland. After assembling his enlarged force there, he'd be prepared with the coal and provisions needed for remaining in Japan, "if it be necessary, an indefinite time to secure such concessions as I believe they will be constrained to make."[1]

When the squadron left Uraga Bay on July 17, the steam vessels again towed the sailing ones. One of the latter would soon separate and sail to China, where the others would rejoin it in several weeks. Meanwhile, the ships towered over a thousand-odd guard boats as they passed the feeble Japanese forts and Kurihama reception hall where the Commodore had savored his victory. It had been nine days since the first lookouts had spied the visitors on their way in. They were among the 99 percent of the Japanese people who were deeply happy to see them go.

Perry had his own reasons to be pleased. "The concession to the demands of the Commodore," he'd write about the acceptance of the American letters, "though great for the Japanese, was yet very far from all that was to be reasonably demanded on the score of the usual comity of nations." Edo's reply, "remarkable as it was for its breaking through the Japanese law of exclusion, was still marked with traces of their restrictive policy."[2] Even with his diminished force, however, Perry's brief visit had won more than he'd expected. He hadn't permitted himself to be shunted far from Edo. ("The Commander-in-chief will not go to Nagasaki, and will receive no communication through the Dutch or Chinese."[3]) He trumped the Japanese tactic of delaying until his supplies would have been exhausted. With his threat to blow out of the water all boats and barriers placed in his way, he was, as he wrote in another pointed letter addressed to the Emperor before he left, "successful in gaining several important advantages hitherto denied to all other nations excepting in a very limited degree to the Dutch and Chinese, and awarded even to them at the expense on their part of the most degrading concessions."[4]

His men were happy too. Although his conceit still troubled Samuel Wells Williams, the missionary to China now serving as his interpreter was impressed enough to assert that anyone who refused to recognize "the hand and blessing of God" in Perry's feat was "unwilling to recognize it anywhere or in anything." The much more secular travel writer Bayard Taylor celebrated the Commodore for having done more to pry Japan open in just a few days "than any other nation had been able to effect for the last two centuries." An officer who'd served under Perry during the Mexican War noted that ships "seemed to have a sense of importance because he was aboard." Now Taylor felt "honest pride and exultation" uplift the *Susquehanna*. The commander had already buried the *Baltimore Sun*'s prediction that the "humbug" mission was "sure to become a matter of ridicule at home and abroad."

But even if the winner were capable of relaxing, now wasn't the time. A storm blew up soon after the squadron lost sight of the mountains of Kyushu, the southernmost of Japan's four main islands. Perry called it a gale but it would now be classified as a typhoon, common in those waters, although the season usually started later, in early autumn. The seas that battered the ships also lashed the country of their destination, but that was nothing new there: typhoons were among the perennial scourges of Okinawa, an island that lay roughly four days' sailing south of Edo Bay. However, its eighty-thousand-odd people would have shuddered to know greater misfortune was returning in the person of Matthew Perry. The Commodore had visited the little kingdom three weeks earlier, the last stop on his voyage to the Japan he'd now just left. Knowing it would be reported to Edo, he planned it as a warning to the authorities there as well as a rehearsal for the crucial show for them.

THE FIRST VISIT had begun on May 26. With a brief break to inspect the even smaller Bonin Islands to the east,* it lasted more than a month. Of that stay on Okinawa, Perry wouldn't boast, as with his dealings with Edo, of having ignored the "established rule of diplomacy." On the contrary, he'd report himself having observed "the strictest rules of moral law." After compelling the natives to satisfy his demands, he rewrote history on the spot by imagining or dissembling that they appreciated American "lenity and humanity."

---

* The Bonin, or Ogasawara, Islands are also just north of Iwo Jima and the other Volcano Islands. As with Formosa and Okinawa, Perry would try to make them American protectorates, believing their colonization was inevitable as well as good. "We shall have foreign settlements even if they are not established by positive enactment," meaning official Washington acts based on declared policy (Ronald Spector, "The American Image of Southeast Asia, 1790–1865," p. 305). An American settlement on Formosa in particular would benefit all countries and "be looked upon with favor by the Chinese." Cited in Samuel Eliot Morison, *Old Bruin*, p. 425.

The geography that shaped the real history of Okinawa—the largest and by far the most prominent of the Loo-choos, which Perry spelled as the then more favored "Lew Chews"—took away as much as it gave. Its Chinese characters, literally "offshore rope" but sometimes translated as bubbles or jewels "floating in the sea," are pronounced "Ryukyus" in Japanese.[5] That difference bore on the curious sway exerted on the islands from both China and Japan. The competing countries held the inhabitants in dual dependence.

China had been first. From the fourteenth century or earlier, the kingdom had been a kind of client state of Peking, like those of many less developed peripheral peoples—then including the Japanese. Okinawan bows to the Chinese emperors were largely ritual. The "toy state," as the admirable historian George Kerr would call it, paid tribute but stayed independent. When Perry arrived in 1853, however, Japan exercised a tighter, harsher dominance than Peking had ever imposed, although China remained the cultural model and most valued trading partner.

The hidden Japanese control had begun with an invasion by a fierce force of an aggressive *han* that easily overcame the unmilitary islanders' feeble resistance. It took place in 1609, roughly a quarter century before Japan's closing.

The purpose of the aggression was relevant because it underscored important contrasts. Okinawans and Japanese were neither ethnically nor culturally one and the same, particularly in the former's dislike of the martial arms and ceremonial self-sacrifice that appealed to many of the latter.[6] Mongol forces ravaged the island to punish it for having refused to support one of the huge thirteenth-century invasions of Japan from which the Divine Winds supposedly saved that country. Some three hundred years later, near the end of the sixteenth century, Toyotomi Hideyoshi—the leader said to have baked the cake for the Tokugawas to eat—ordered the Ryukyus to contribute men and arms to an invasion of China he was planning.[7] But while the aggressor had changed, Okinawan distaste for military ventures hadn't. Shuri Castle—the Ryukyuan monarchs' hilltop residence—again demurred.

It didn't want to spoil its trade with Korea, through which the invaders planned to attack. It was even more reluctant to offend China, its conceited but relatively benign big brother. The King apologized to Toyotomi that great distance and paltry funds had kept his "small and humble island kingdom" from rendering him due reverence, but he hoped some gifts he was now sending would show his "sincerity and courtesy."

That didn't work, and Toyotomi's death was even worse for the island-ers. Probably misinformed about events in Japan, Shuri declined to send respects to the eventual winner of the struggle to succeed him: the same Tokugawa Ieyasu who founded the dynasty, proclaimed himself the first Shogun of that name,[8] and was the antecedent of the Tokugawas who still ruled in Perry's 1853.

Having fought with the losers in that savage struggle—a miscalcula-tion that almost resulted in confiscation of his domain—the powerful chief of Satsuma *han* in southernmost Japan licked his wounds and plotted how to prevent his downfall. It was Okinawans' bad luck that that remote, mountainous domain, then embracing most of Kyushu, was their closest Japanese neighbor. Its inhabitants outdid all others in martial spirit.

Eager to ingratiate himself with winner Tokugawa Ieyasu, whom he'd failed to support, Satsuma's daimyo requested his permission to punish Shuri for not having paid him proper respect. Happy to divert warlike Satsuma to a harmless enterprise at sea, in the opposite direction from himself, the new Shogun sanctioned the 1609 invasion. That devastating expedition, prompted by the Okinawan refusal to join big-power military conflicts, ended the Ryukyus' promising separate development. Now the two great Japanese feudal houses, the Tokugawas in Edo and southern Satsuma's Shimazu clan, essentially controlled the islands.

However, nothing of that scale was so simple, least of all in Japan. For one thing, the Shimazus and Tokugawas often remained at odds, conceal-ing and conspiring in the manner of Japanese feudal politics—and some-times using the Ryukyus in their jockeying for wealth and power. Satsuma's Shimazu daimyo had invaded as much in order to snatch Okinawa's mari-time trade as to ingratiate himself with Tokugawa Ieyasu. It was a tempt-ing prize. Liked and trusted, open to the world and at peace with their neighbors, Okinawans were the Venetians of East Asia, whose ships were welcomed in Java, Singapore, Taiwan, the Philippines, and the South Sea islands as well as in China, Japan, and the not-yet-sealed Korea. The prin-cipal port of Naha, which lay some four miles below the hilltop capital of Shuri, bustled with foreigners and their goods.[9]

At the same time, Japanese pirates who roamed Asian seas troubled Peking, as did increasing commercial competition from upstart Japan as a whole, especially after the early seventeenth-century consolidation of Tokugawa rule spurred its economic development. The Chinese rulers cut off direct mercantile exchange between the two countries, while trade with Okinawa continued. But if China learned of Satsuma's control of the island, it would surely close its ports to that trade too, a prospect that gave the Shimazus powerful incentive to keep their domination secret. The profits they now monopolized were large enough to fund the family's restoration from its near demise after backing the wrong horse in Japan's succession struggle. Determined to keep Peking ignorant of Okinawans' subservience to them, they concealed their fifty-odd agents, overseers, and vigilant watchdogs who enforced the secrecy from their Naha headquarters.

Japan's closure in 1636 further upped the stakes because a sneaky exception was made for the still nominally independent Kingdom of the Ryukyus. With the Japanese islands now cut off from all but a trickle of foreign trade, imported goods became increasingly scarce and desirable. That boosted Shimazu profits on wares that continued to be imported from the Okinawan loophole, from where Japanese goods could also be shipped to China. (The trade being not quite patriotic, however, the Shimazus and Tokugawas kept Japan's other daimyo, together with Peking, ignorant of it, while also concealing as much as possible from each other.) From the time of the national closing, the Shimazus took even greater pains to hide their control of their hapless semisubjects in the Ryukyus.

Specifically, they ordered Shuri Castle to maintain its fictitious independence so the profitable China trade would proceed undisturbed—while virtually nothing trickled down to the Okinawan traders themselves. Forced to fish, as a native scholar described the arrangement, the islanders were forbidden to eat the catch. Squeezing in other ways too, Satsuma turned Okinawa's Golden Age of the previous centuries to lead. New taxes reduced most of the population, farmers of tiny plots, to terrible poverty. Nothing moved the Shimazu lords, who controlled everything political and financial through the sharp eyes of their patrolling, tallying inspectors and watchdogs, to ease their exploitation.

The absence of arms—the island had no pistols, muskets, bows, or arrows, let alone cannon; not even daggers—astonished Westerners who had visited before Perry. They didn't know the Satsuma overlords permitted none.* In Okinawa's quite distant past, before its first lasting dynasty was established in the thirteenth century, warlords had battled one another much as in Japan, if less fiercely. Some weapons were used in the fourteenth century too, but a fifteenth-century "Sword Edict" banned them, and the peace and relative prosperity until the disastrous 1609 invasion nourished a propensity for harmony. An eighteenth-century Chinese emissary found Okinawans extremely poor but unfailingly gracious, as another Chinese name for the island suggested: Shurei no kuni, "the Nation of Constant Courtesy" (or "Propriety"). When Perry arrived, they were among the world's least militaristic peoples, with a tradition of singing in their fields as well as at their convivial festivals. Good nature, tolerance, and a kind of tenderness seemed to soften the air.

Not closed like Japan, the little nation remained courteous despite Satsuma's control and the natives' wish for foreigners not to linger long enough to worsen their lot yet more by discovering their oppression. The appealing impressions made on calling Western ships couldn't be fully trusted because visitors of no more than a week or so were likely to idealize natives they hardly knew. Nevertheless, some were seasoned travelers, and their nearly unanimous praise for Okinawans' "singular humanity" and eagerness to please was enthusiastic enough to lend some weight to their opinions. "Nothing can exceed the honesty of these good and kindhearted people," a shipwrecked sailor enthused.

A surgeon on a British ship registered a "deep and lasting impression" of native kindness and hospitality. Another voyager lauded Okinawans' "dignity of manners, superior advancement in the arts, and general intelligence." The writer Ivan Goncharov—now secretary to a Russian Admiral who'd long campaigned to open Japan and was trying to beat Perry to it in 1853[10]—was skeptical when their frigate stopped at Okinawa, but soon found the inhabitants "all exuded such a feeling of peace, simplicity, honest labor and plenty that it seemed to me . . . a longed-for haven. . . . What a place, what people!"[11]

---

* Scythes were very occasionally used as weapons, as well as hairpins borrowed from well-groomed women. And karate—originally borrowed from China, like many aspects of Okinawan culture—was much cultivated. Some secretly trained in that art of unarmed self-defense for what they hoped would be a new means of resistance—which, however, proved useless against their oppressors' swords and armor.

Samuel Wells Williams's opposite impression was that Okinawans were "more wretched" than any people he'd previously encountered. Man, he explained, quickly and surely deteriorates in an isolated little community where "every member is compelled to labor for a bare living," and no means were available to support "government, education, or even religion, or an elementary civilization." However, that was in contrast to a "care and neatness" Bayard Taylor, the more experienced traveler, had "never seen surpassed" and Williams's own regret, elsewhere, that only the inhabitants' spiritual shortcomings kept the "exceedingly pretty" and "charming" landscape from perfection.[12]

Of course there was a full share of problems. The kings maintained Shuri Castle, an imitation of China's elaborate court, on the backs of a truly impoverished peasantry, and the fear of Satsuma punishment may have been more responsible than kind hearts for the gentleness. Surely the hospitality was heightened by eagerness for ships to provision themselves quickly—often with gifts from meager native stores—and sail off, without discovering the secret of their semicaptivity. Whatever that added to the qualities that endeared the islanders to their visitors, however, the cordiality was rooted in a culture formed much earlier.

The friendliness to foreigners, perhaps explained by Okinawans' racially mixed origins, was real as well as legendary. Women enjoyed status and authority. Despite the hardship of the overwhelming majority's farming life, essential decency and tolerance prevailed, together with much more relaxed social ways than in Japan. On his first visit en route to Uraga, Perry appreciated the pastoral delights, if not the people's good nature. If anything, he was more taken by the appearance of "this beautiful island" than he would be by Japan's verdure. "It would be difficult for you to imagine [its] beauties with respect to the charming scenery and the marvelous perfection of cultivation," he'd write. Bayard Taylor agreed: the island, "one of the most beautiful in the world . . . charmed us like a glimpse of paradise."[13]

The day after the squadron arrived on that first visit, gifts of pigs, a bullock, a goat, poultry, fish, fresh vegetables, fruit, and cakes—"all the good things"[14]—were delivered to the anchored ships. The Commodore permitted the *Susquehanna* to take them aboard but "thought it politic to remain in my cabin."

NO DOUBT MOST AMERICANS of the time would have had a hard time understanding the squeeze on the Ryukyus, even if they'd known about it. One jaw of the pliers was still Peking, the other Satsuma's daimyo, supported by the Shogun in Edo, both of whom sought to preserve the appearance of fealty to China. Perry's homework had given him vague knowledge of Japan's hidden dominance; at least he suspected *something* subjected the islanders, whose "worst vices are probably the result, in great measure, of the wretched system of government under which they live."

Upon the squadron's first arrival off Naha, his keen instinct focused on some junks headed north. He was right to surmise they were hurrying to inform Japanese authorities—first (although he didn't know this detail) the Shimazu daimyo, whose castle was in Kagoshima, Kyushu's largest city.[15] "The probabilities . . . are all on the side of the dependence, more or less absolute, of Lew Chew on Japan, and probably, also, of some qualified subordination to China."

A rare and singularly obstinate resident Westerner named Bernard Bettelheim helped him reach those conclusions. Dr. Bettelheim would assure him Japan maintained a hidden garrison on Okinawa, making it virtually integral with the closed country of Perry's ultimate interest. Of course, the information available to Perry from Bettelheim and others was very limited. The Commodore would never find proof of the Shimazu yoke. His officers' observations were further narrowed by their frequent denigration of the native culture as well as by the pained Okinawan secrecy. Perry in particular quickly concluded the people were deeply flawed by dishonesty.

While among them, however, he would exercise his intellectual, especially scientific, curiosity. Ordering studies and dispatching exploring parties, he made a typically conscientious attempt to learn their politics, social structure, and even spiritual inclinations, as well as the island's topography, vegetation, agriculture, and geology. Geology took pride of place, for coal was a holy grail that pointed to the mission's primary motivation—in that sense, the real one, although still disguised. (Searching for the fuel the new steamships consumed with a ravenous appetite was of particular interest to the *Susquehanna*'s chaplain, who led one of the exploring parties.) At the same time, the Commodore remained his driven, haughty self. When the authorities sought to wriggle from *his* new squeeze on the kingdom, his opinion of them swung toward contempt.

Never forgetting that his rank merited esteem or that he was America's representative—and to what he and his peers considered a manifestly lesser people—he was genuinely distressed by failure to obey on the part of those benighted islanders, with their odious shams. "These misgoverned people . . . have doubtless been taught from infancy . . . to practice duplicity and lying as necessary parts of an accomplished education and altogether essential to advancement in office."[16]

In the end, however, what Perry knew and didn't know mattered less than what he wanted. Overriding everything else, the Commodore's determination to make use of Okinawa left little room for sympathy for their mistreatment by the Japanese. On the contrary, his suspicions hardened his own mistreatment of them. His chief concern about their predicament was how to use it to his advantage.

What *did* he want from Okinawa? As suggested, coal, in pursuit of which he'd devote much of the squadron's time and energy while there. Implicit in that was a port that would service American ships and exhibit gratitude for the privilege. *More* than that, he sought a full American outpost, under his own control. And most immediately, a cowed Shuri to use as a warning to Edo.

The Commodore's first move revealed that his talent for frightening by dealing insults was as abundant as for displaying pomp. He ordered the food given as a welcome gift removed, together with the officials who'd brought it. Although he'd soon explain that he wanted to pay for his provisions, he very well knew, and desired, the effect his rebuff would produce. Meanwhile, "the Commodore," practicing for his upcoming Uraga performance, "remained secluded in solitary dignity, in his own cabin."

Some of his time there was surely used to prepare what he'd call his benefits to Okinawa, which wasn't necessarily hypocritical. Utter inability to put himself in others' shoes reinforced his confidence in the high morality of his pursuits.

PERRY'S "SOLITARY DIGNITY" didn't quite set the tone of the first formal encounter between Americans and Okinawans. It turned darker when he emerged from his cabin and upped his incivility to intimidation.

His term for it, flourished with as much self-satisfaction as anywhere in his accounts, was "a little Yankee diplomacy"[17]—needed, he'd explain, because his perception was that Okinawan duplicity exceeded the full store of it employed by Asians generally. The "eminently shrewd" people, "unsurpassed . . . in chicanery and treachery," were devoted to "shams and devices," seeped in "cunning and falsehood. . . . It was as if deceit was so much a part of [the authorities'] nature that they practiced it for its own sake alone."[18] But "the Commodore was not to be balked of his purpose"[19] by any of it. He'd confront the Oriental wickedness with his own transparent honesty and fairness—and he was right about some crucial matters. The first was the gift of food to welcome his ships.

Pliable and meek as Okinawans had become—from necessity as well as choice—they were no paragons of virtue. As with most peoples of most times, oppression tended to rouse their less attractive qualities. Even if their traditional hospitality would have prompted them to send provisions on their own initiative, a Japanese agent, the chief Satsuma overseer, had ordered those for the squadron. That was one of the ways in which Shuri was indeed working hard to fool Perry. A Satsuma manual for dealing with foreigners when they couldn't be shooed away provided replies for parrying likely questions, on the order of what the island produced and how it was ruled. Callers who wanted to stay for a few days and explore were assured "our poor little island off in this corner of the sea" wasn't worth their time or effort: "Please supply your vessel from what we're honored to give you, although our few presents are contemptible and beneath notice, and sail on to your far more important pursuits."[20]

Shuri may have resorted to camouflage even if its Satsuma superintendents hadn't ordered it. Despite Okinawans' inherent friendliness, the Western colonial powers' exploitation of China had prompted concern about protecting the island. But the primary reason was control by the Satsuma agents intent on protecting the overseas trade. Foreigners were buttered up to help sustain Shuri's masquerade of deference to Peking rather than to the real bosses in Kagoshima. Later during Perry's stay, officials would assure him that it had been Okinawa's great pride "to be ranked as one of the outer dependencies of China" ever since the Ming dynasty.[21]

Shuri's anxious secrecy would increase the Commodore's reliance on his own abundant suspicions and the more informed but even sourer ones of Bernard Bettelheim, the island's singular, and now sole (except for his family), Western resident.[22] Unhappy Dr. Bettelheim had been struggling there for almost eight years when Perry landed, a span that seemed even longer to the natives than to the forty-three-year-old physician himself.

Peter Wiley's otherwise apt description of the "strange character on a stranger mission" may reverse the order of magnitude: Bettelheim himself was probably stranger than his mission to minister medically and spiritually. The Anglican missionary had received his first religious training— rabbinical—in his native Hungary, where he'd been born to a prominent Jewish family. Medical studies and service in the Egyptian navy and Turkish army followed; then his conversion, which began when he met Church of England priests in Turkey, where he was studying Arabic, one of a dozen-odd languages he'd master with greater or lesser proficiency. Baptized after their love of Jesus overwhelmed him, he proceeded to study theology in London, where a meeting with the celebrated Dr. David Livingstone, Scottish minister and explorer of Africa, sparked his own ardor for missionary work. England's disapproving Jews took the brunt of his first go at it, after which he pushed on to Okinawa.

Denied permission to practice medicine there when he arrived in 1846, the missionary bribed members of his ship's crew to help smuggle him ashore, together with his wife and children. He wangled leave to stay a single night, then refused to depart on thousands of next mornings. When the thorn in Okinawans' side had become more a poisoned dart, their perplexity turned to despair. During his years on the island, which would be biblical in mutual suffering as well as in number, he and they lived in a state of what Samuel Wells Williams would call "undisguised hostility." The scores of men assigned to watch his enlarging family were a costly burden for the government. A guard station was erected near Gokoku-ji, its personnel ordered to accompany Bettelheim wherever he went.[23]

Gokoku-ji was an ancient Buddhist temple that overlooked Naha harbor. That was where the authorities had permitted him to stay for the requested single night, chiefly out of pity for his children and wife, for whose privacy its priests withdrew. When they returned to pray, Dr. Bettelheim accused them of wanting to ogle her and was amused by their taking him seriously enough to again depart. Ignoring Shuri's protests that the temple was for all Okinawans' worship, the squatter refused to surrender the premises for those same eight years. He threw out its "heathen" furniture, boarded up its entrances, and chalked up his denial of access to that place of "idolatry" as an early victory for Christianity.

It would be his biggest. Otherwise, "four-eyed doggy man," as he came to be called for his large dogs and spectacles that were novel to the natives, managed only to invade houses to shout God's word and to throw stones at those that succeeded in barring him. Although he eventually provided some medical service during outbreaks of smallpox, his main activities were bellowing outdoor sermons in hope someone would understand enough of his fractured Okinawan to heed his feverish words or breaking into town meetings before guards threw him out. But his converts were few—in fact, probably one in number: a loner who was banished from Naha and died in countryside exile—or, Bettelheim improbably claimed, was martyred when officials had him beaten to death.

The zealot himself remained alive, but his war with the authorities turned him ever weirder. While he raved against Satan's agents who thwarted his godly work, the island's tolerant culture increased the ineptness of attempts to remove the dart. Although China and Japan had resorted to violence against detested missionaries, Okinawans limited themselves to occasional slight manhandling and restricting his choice of food. (When he and his wife were forbidden to shop, merchants sent him their worst produce.) Even though they used sticks and stones but once during his years of provocations and threats, following a particularly wild challenge by him, their wish for his departure or death no doubt worsened his insomnia. He became "more than a little mad."[24]

Most of his threats promised retaliation from the Western ships sailing in nearby waters. A later British vessel indeed bore a warning, which Bettelheim himself had prodded by appealing to the Foreign Office for protection. Slight improvement in his treatment following the ship's notification of Shuri that his continued persecution would bring down force upon the island swelled his delight at the arrival of Perry, another foreigner. The Commodore's powerful manner reaffirmed his persuasion that "there is no way of aiding Loochoo and Japan better than by forcing upon them a foreign population." Perry was "so unmistakable an answer to our repeated and anxious prayer for Japan that I offered to serve him as a son serves a father."[25] From the "throne" of his flagship, the magisterial "autocrat" on his "glorious mission" would overcome Okinawan "chicanery and diplomatic treachery."

For his part, Perry, wary of "those contemptible acts of stupid folly . . . sometimes exhibited by foolhardy religionists in foreign countries,"[26] was initially cautious about Bettelheim. "The missionary, however meritorious he might be, seemed to promise but little for the extension of Christianity in the island."[27] Other American officers quickly grew even more leery of the self-pitying complainer whose opinions changed "like a weathercock," in one description.[28] George Henry Preble considered him "about the worst" person to enlighten about Okinawans because his evident despisal of them left him with less knowledge after his years' residence than some would acquire in months. "He will not allow them the commonest virtues and attributes all they do to deceit and hypocrisy." But the Commodore would rely on Bettelheim's intelligence because its confirmation of what he wanted to hear enabled him to justify his severity.

SOON AFTER THE SHIPS ANCHORED outside Naha on May 26, Okinawan officials paid their brief visit to deliver greetings and compliments together with the spurned provisions, then inquire about the visit's purpose and the squadron's needs. "Scarcely," Perry would note, had the officials obeyed his order to disembark when a small boat bearing Bettelheim, "almost beside himself with joy,"[29] hurried to the flagship.

The kindred political souls talked for hours in the captain's cabin and resumed at breakfast the following morning. On the day after that, May 28, the excited doctor sent his new "father" a long letter, the first of many that rarely failed to remind how scurrilous the natives were. That morning too, a more substantial boat, although still quite ordinary, approached the *Susquehanna*. America's thoroughly undiplomatic relations with the Kingdom of Ryukyus were about to begin.

No king would participate. The throne was empty, Peking not yet having invested the boy who would become monarch. With the dowager queen reportedly too ill to substitute, it was left to the regent to deal with Perry. He, the new boat's primary passenger, was a frail man with a long white beard and what struck one of Perry's men as "the most dignified demeanor." But while the Commodore himself would write of the regent's "imperturbable gravity," the courtly elder was soon profoundly perturbed by Perry's intention to call on Shuri Castle. A fellow American saw the regent turn grave enough to be "going to an execution."

11

The Mouse in the Eagle's Talons

Perry at Shuri Castle's Gate of Courtesy

PERRY'S DETERMINATION TO VISIT SHURI Castle shocked Okinawans because they feared Satsuma's oppression would worsen if Westerners learned of it. With great courtesy, the regent implored the Commodore not to make his call, or to do it at an official reception hall rather than the castle. Pleased by the great alarm the squadron had raised when it entered the harbor and no more interested in the stark evidence that he wasn't welcome at the royal palace than in Okinawa's customs and laws, Perry countered that he expected a reception worthy of his rank. Entreaties by what he recognized as the "half-stupefied" regent went in vain.

In 1895, one Basil Hall Chamberlain would cite Perry's visit as the sole foreign one that unfavorably impressed the islanders. (That wasn't entirely true: the British warship *Phaeton*, whose armed sailors had forced their way into Shuri Castle in 1808, of course made a terrible impression.) Chamberlain wrote that the "blustering" Commodore's

> haughty and masterful conduct . . . his violent threats, and contemptuous disregard for international law and courtesy, renders it scant matter of surprise that even Lucuhan patience should have been exhausted, and that the islanders should have resorted to deceit, which is the only weapon the weak have . . . against the strong.[1]

Although learned Chamberlain was then among the most important scholars of Japan,[2] his admiration for Okinawans—especially "their gentleness of spirit and manner, their yielding and submissive disposition, their hospitality and kindness, their aversion to violence and crime"—may have prejudiced him against Perry. He also had an ax to grind. He was a grandson of Basil Hall, an English captain whose picture of Okinawans after an 1816 visit as "an honest, peaceful, unassuming people, with neither money nor arms, kindly, hospitable and without guile" was as enthusiastic as any Western praise. Perry, however, became convinced that either Captain Hall had been mistaken or Okinawans had drastically changed during the thirty-seven intervening years since he'd supposedly seen a people who were "docile, tractable and honest, scrupulously obedient to their rulers and their laws. . . ." The Commodore's officers who'd expected to find the "beautiful" traits depicted by Captain Hall were "gradually and painfully undeceived."

Perry wasn't the only skeptic about the legendary Okinawan character that was said to match the island's beauty. Previous Western visitors of some duration, as opposed to those who came and quickly went, had complained about secrecy and fabrication. Most were treated to a litany of excuses about the "remote, impoverished little nation" not deserving the honor of foreign interest; the visitors should therefore provision themselves and quickly leave. Boilerplate hastily tweaked for Perry—Okinawa supposedly had "no official residences, markets or shops" and "no envoy from a foreign country" had ever entered into the palace—informed that the forced British entry to the same palace in 1808 had frightened everyone, "from the young prince and the Queen Dowager down to the lowest officers and people," who barely managed to keep "body and soul together." The adolescent monarch's mother was "dangerously ill even to this day," which was among the reasons why Perry's intention "troubled and grieved" all the country's officers:

> They urgently beg of your excellency . . . that you will take the case of the queen dowager and her severe indisposition into your favorable consideration, and cease from going into the palace. . . . If you deem it necessary to make this compliment, please go to the residence of the prince, there to make your respects in person.

AS THEIR INDEPENDENCE ERODED, Okinawans cherished Shuri Castle ever more. The thirteenth-century repository of the now fragile national identity reflected some of the differences between Okinawa and Japan. Smaller and more delicate than the seats of many Japanese *han*, it wasn't a real stronghold despite its massive stone walls. The inscription on a sixteenth-century bell set the nonviolent tone: *A BELL . . . WILL ECHO FAR AND WIDE LIKE A PEAL OF THUNDER BUT WITH UTMOST PURITY. AND EVIL MEN, HEARING THE BELL, WILL BE SAVED.* The squadron officer who saw the hilltop complex as a kind of mini-Acropolis without the marble caught some of its spirit. Most of all, the three hundred-odd acres with their serene pathways seeming to water the ancient vegetation were remarkable for their fusion of natural and man-made beauty. Other Asian castles were grander, but this one's scenes and setting formed a unique ensemble, the glory of the views—both the Pacific Ocean and East China Sea were visible—enhancing human-scale grace.

Perry had chosen June 6 for his self-invitation. No pleading or protest could change it. "The Commodore had power to carry out his determination, and the regent deemed it most prudent to concur, with the semblance of politeness, in that which he could not prevent."[3]

Despite fine weather, the procession didn't get an early start because Perry wouldn't "deprive my men even of a single breakfast" for the sake of the "Loochooan mandarins."[4] But he did don his full-dress uniform: "It was a matter of policy to make a show of it, hence some extra pains were taken to offer an imposing spectacle."[5] When the landing party was ashore, a sedan chair he'd ordered built for the occasion bore him up the lovely winding roads from the port toward the castle. "I cannot conceive of a more beautiful pageant," he'd enthuse. Eight Chinese coolies provided the locomotion; the *Mississippi*'s band supplied the "cheerful" music.

No Okinawans were cheered. The beautiful pageant included two field guns primped with American flags and drawn by forty-eight sailors in addition to two companies of marines in *their* full-dress uniforms—a total of some three hundred men, naturally seen by most natives as armed invaders. Their "terrified air" showed "how scared they were."[6]

A pagoda-like "Gate of Courtesy" marked the entrance to the castle grounds. Meeting the American detachment there, the regent implored Perry to visit his quarters instead. Ignoring him, the Commodore resumed his march, now to the closed gates of the palace itself, where another assertion of his muscle was required to intimidate "these foolish people" who were so "desirous . . . of denying to me the honor . . . of the principal entrance to the palace."[7] The principal entrance having been duly unlocked, in he strode to the band's "Hail Columbia." Then "the Commodore was conducted, as a mark of honor and respect due to his rank,"[8] into a courtyard.

No reception was waiting. The young prince and his mother, the dowager queen—who had been "so pathetically represented as being sick,"[9] scoffed Perry—were nowhere to be seen. But tea was served, together with gingerbread the Commodore found "very tough." He noticed his hosts were "not quite at their ease" but would profess ignorance as to why. An hour or so of painful silences punctuated by short, stiff exchanges followed, until all repaired to the regent's nearby mansion, where a meal *was* waiting. Lubricated by sake and courteous toasts, the conversation became easier, although Perry's interpreter detected a "wishing us away" in the Okinawan faces. The Commodore himself was delighted that the regent's interpreter knew some American history, and had even heard of George Washington. "Where is it that the honored name of the Father of our country, this man . . . whose peerless purity is the proud heritage of a common humanity the world over, has not reached?"[10]

But Perry's gratification dissolved into boredom. To show respect for and to try to placate him, the regent had laid on a banquet of an exceptional twenty-four courses of delicacies. To the distress of some in the American party, the guest of honor left abruptly after twelve.[11] Back at the port in early afternoon, he was pleased to find his sailors eager to learn "whether due honor had been shown to the United States in the person of the 'Old Commodore.'" His positive answer, together with satisfaction with having wielded "moral influence" up in Shuri, capped the day's "pleasure" and "success." The moral influence came from his "steadfast adherence to his avowed purposes."

So it went throughout that first visit. Perry waved his big stick partly to warn Edo he'd tolerate no rebuff like the one given Commodore Biddle in Uraga Bay six years earlier. "Every day," he'd assert about the four-odd weeks of his stay, "points out the importance and the positive necessity of bringing the government of Japan to some sort of reason, and the least objectionable course will be to establish an influence which they cannot prevent, here at the very door of the empire."[12] And if Japan somehow managed to repel his forthcoming visit, he could use Okinawa as a fallback base for recovering and regrouping.

Stressing that the Commodore struck no one with his stick, his admirers would loudly praise his restraint. Much as Okinawa shone in his strategic eye, he would take no slice of it; only frighten, cow, and exact. He forced a breach of the native tradition of supplying visiting ships without charge. The armed parties he sent ashore ignored all expressions of anxiety and objection to their exploration. Officers instructed to secure housing forced open locked gates and took possession of what turned out to be a schoolhouse. (When all attempts to repossess it failed, Okinawans brought fruits and vegetables for the squadron squatters.) Several other buildings were commandeered, together with land for raising cattle on the grounds of Gokoku-ji temple.[13] Emissaries bearing special food for the Commodore were treated with "utmost rudeness,"[14] while he displayed his overwhelming weaponry in maneuvers on ship and shore. At the same time, he was writing the Secretary of the Navy about his "considerable progress in calming [Okinawan] fears and conciliating their friendship," adding that he'd remain only long enough to "establish a good understanding with these people," partly so that news of "our friendly demonstration towards the Lewchewans" would precede him to Japan.

The islanders breathed easier when that first visit ended on July 2. The *Supply* remained at Naha to sustain a small American outpost there and to keep an eye on the natives while the rest of the squadron departed for the harder challenge in Japan.

AFTER ITS NINE DAYS IN JAPAN and a week returning to Okinawa, the squadron approached the island on July 24. "The Commodore had no time to spare," so he'd determined to make his second visit short. "Upon the Commodore's arrival at Lew Chew he lost no time in advancing the chief purpose of his visit, and prepared at once to enter negotiations with the authorities for obtaining from them further relaxations in their laws respecting strangers." He would never understand why his first stop, enriched by what he'd call "the blandishments of their courteous visitors,"[15] had been an ordeal for the inhabitants. To start the second round of courtesies, he assured the regent he wished "to continue on the most friendly terms" with the authorities. Squadron officers noted that although his achievement in Japan rarely eased his near permanent frown, it had given him confidence of enjoying similar success in "gaining additional concessions from the Lew Chewans," which he hastened to announce: rental of a house; use of another building for storing coal; an end to the provocative surveillance ashore and the "shunning" of his men; the "fly[ing] from us as if we were their greatest enemies," especially by native women and children.

With a mere week to work with, Perry indeed lost no time putting his demands to the mayor of Naha. The building for storing six hundred tons of coal would be constructed if nothing appropriate were available, then also rented, like the wanted house. If the army of "spies" didn't cease accompanying Americans ashore, "serious consequences," perhaps including "bloodshed," would follow. (Also disturbed by the "pestilence" of Okinawans who "surrounded" him, Bayard Taylor was far less angered because he and his party were nevertheless "treated with the greatest respect" during their extensive exploration of the island.[16]) Any disturbance would "be the fault of the Lew Chewans, who have no right to set spies upon American citizens who may be pursuing their own lawful business."

Again laying power on the line, the Commodore instructed that "It will be wise, therefore, for the Lew Chewans to abrogate those laws and customs which are not suited to the present age, and which they have no power to enforce, and by a persistence in which they will surely involve themselves in trouble. . . . *The authorities had better come to an understanding at once* [italics added]" that Naha would be a place of rendezvous, "probably for years." A written message to the regent also repeated the warning about "the system of espionage"—in his new use of the word, meaning Okinawan surveillance of their own territory—which Perry would "take the necessary steps to stop" if it continued during his next visit.

> It is repugnant to the American character to submit to such a course of inhospitable discourtesy, and though the citizens of the United States, when abroad, *are always regardful of, and obedient to, the laws of the countries in which they may happen to be* [italics added], provided they are founded upon international courtesy, yet they never can admit of the propriety or justice of those of Lew Chew, which bear so injuriously upon the rights and comforts of strangers resorting to the island with *the most friendly and peaceful intentions* [italics added].

Meanwhile, Naha's mayor, upon receiving what a member of Perry's party would call his "threatening expostulation," replied that only the regent could make the necessary decisions. It wouldn't be the regent with "the most dignified demeanor" who had met the squadron during its first visit. The new one was a member of the same family as his predecessor, although the Americans didn't know that, nor why the old one with the more impressive bearing had been replaced, or what had happened to him. The rumors were ominous. He'd resigned or been replaced under duress. He'd been exiled to one of the small Ryukyu islands. Having displeased the "spies"—here implying the concealed Satsuma agents—he'd been forced to kill himself. Actually, he'd been quietly removed, with no further punishment, by direction of those Japanese overlords unhappy with his inability to prevent Perry's penetration of the castle.

His younger replacement would fare no better. The "remarkably grave and taciturn" official promised replies on July 28, three days after the squadron's return. At a dinner that evening in a Naha building for receptions, Perry, even blunter than before, directed him to get to business before enjoying the refreshment prepared for him. An officer he'd appointed to work on the task at hand lied that Japan had received the squadron "in a very friendly manner." Americans were "persons of few words, but they always meant what they said." The Commodore expected compliance with his "reasonable and proper" demands.[17]

Giving assurances that the necessary replies would come very soon, the regent succeeded in starting the meal. Perry didn't hide his displeasure as it progressed—until the eighth course, when the regent indeed produced an official document. Beginning with polished evasiveness, it added complaints about Bettelheim, including the loss of proper use of the temple, on whose grounds the cattle were now grazing. Erecting a building for storing coal would be another great burden, and as for the market, the regent couldn't order shop owners to trade if they chose not to. But the officers who followed the Americans—not spies but guides and protectors from annoyance by the people—would no longer do so.

Perry, his face as dark as the veteran scowler could make it, directed the translator to return the document to the regent. It was "not at all satisfactory." He was asking Okinawa for no more than what other countries accorded America, including China and, soon, Japan. Repeating his conditions, he rose to leave, cutting short the regent's attempt to make another reply. "The Commodore reiterated what he had previously said, that all his demands were plain and simple, and ought to be granted without hesitation . . . and if they persisted in following up with spies hereafter he would not be answerable for the consequences."[18]

Although the regent was "ever ready with a thousand crooked arguments for not giving a direct answer to a direct demand," Perry granted him time for further thought—until noon of the following day. If, the Commodore declared, he did not receive a satisfactory answer to everything by then, he'd "land two hundred men, march to Shuri, and take possession of the palace there." (His instructions from Secretary of State Edward Everett—the successor to Daniel Webster, who had died a month before Perry sailed from Norfolk—had been to "pursue the most friendly and conciliatory course" on Okinawa. "Make no use of force, except in the last resort for defense if attacked, and for self-preservation.")

Topping all previous threats, that once again terrified the Okinawans, especially after they thought they saw dreaded evidence that it was about to be carried out. The sedan in which the Commodore had been lofted to Shuri Castle during his first visit was left at the temple. Now some islanders observed a squadron carpenter repairing it—for a second menacing procession, they assumed. "Their frightened imaginations," Perry would congratulate himself, "no doubt fancied the Commodore borne in his car of state . . . as a triumphant victor within the walls of their capital."[19]

The fortuity of the broken chair, he supposed, helped the regent come to his senses, although his own decisiveness had been paramount. "The

Commodore . . . was not to be balked of his purpose by any of the shams and devises of Lew Chew policy." He would not allow himself "to be diverted from a broad, honest course of fair dealing, into any of the bye-ways of the oriental hide-and-seek diplomacy." Therefore, the need for violent measures was "never seriously contemplated by the Commodore, as it was rightly judged that a resolute attitude would answer all the purpose of a blow."

The effect of the proxy blow pleased him all the more because it made occupation of the castle unnecessary. Settlement of the matter without it, entirely on his terms, no doubt reinforced his high estimation of the fear of force for dealing with Asians.

Not that all "pertinaciously insinuated" objections ceased. Okinawans, playing their only card, had become peerless procrastinators. Naha's mayor, who announced the kingdom's capitulation at ten o'clock the following morning, warned that people would steal from a coal depot if typhoons didn't blow it away. Surprisingly, however, preparations for its construction had already begun, and the Americans were invited to a bazaar to be held three days hence. Many attended, and although most of the lacquerware, straw sandals, cottons, silks, and bits of silver were disappointing, the principle wasn't. "This dealing with foreigners was the first authorized, and was in direct opposition to a fundamental law of the island, the abrogation of which cannot but result in the greatest advantage to the people of Lew Chew."[20] Meanwhile, the Commodore's resolve had been so effective that the depot had already been framed and reared. More than that, "friendly interest and good feeling" were abroad between the Americans and the islanders, "who were daily becoming more cordial."

Departing from Okinawa, the Commodore concluded that the natives' deportment had much improved because they recognized their attempts to deceive him had been "so much labor lost." Again, however, his satisfaction with himself wasn't fully shared. Translator Samuel Wells Williams—whose final judgment of Perry would be quite positive—felt much as he did during the squadron's first visit. "It was a struggle between weakness and might, and the islanders must go to the wall."[21]

Before leaving on August 1, Perry had warned he'd return in several months. Meanwhile, the *Plymouth* would remain because he "conceiv[ed] it to be of the highest importance" that one of his ships "be stationed almost constantly at Lew Chew"[22] (from where it would visit the Bonin and

Coffin islands, which he also coveted).[23] He instructed *Plymouth*'s captain to maintain "conciliatory but firm" relations with the natives, always bearing himself in a way that would prove Americans' desire to "cultivate their friendship and secure their confidence."

PERRY WOULD INDEED RETURN TO NAHA—in January 1854, on his way back to Edo Bay. He'd stop there a fourth time too, after that second visit to Japan. Later, he'd call the Ryukyu Islands "as pleasant . . . as any in the world" and praise the "industrious and inoffensive" natives for some personal virtues, including their rigorous cleanliness, which was in sharp contrast to what he'd seen in China. But charitable moments were few during the course of his third and fourth visits themselves, when things went even worse for the Okinawans.

When the nine ships of the third had assembled at Naha, Perry, "judging it politic" to accustom Okinawans to American visits to Shuri Castle in order to "weaken the very strong opposition they at first evinced" to that cordiality, ordered preparation of another "courtesy call" there. The dismayed new regent tried to shunt him to a reception elsewhere. That evasiveness and "crooked policy of deceit," which the Okinawans should by now have known wouldn't work, angered the Commodore. He'd passed off marine displays during the previous visit as practice for New Year's Eve, perhaps in belief that patent falsehood would increase their power to intimidate. Now he ordered a company of them to "exercise" by marching to the castle grounds.

Their arrival at the gate brought the former regent scurrying there in fright. The armed warriors told him their commander's visit was imminent, whatever the objections. Through the detachment, the Commodore "simply replied that . . . I would receive no excuses or equivocations." After the powerless Okinawans again succumbed, the procession to the castle was a quieter rendition of his grand first procession the previous June. Squadron bands played. A spit-and-polish military guard accompanied the sedan chair, again shouldered by eight, that bore Perry along the winding paths with the magnificent trees. "Accordingly all things were arranged as I desired, the visit was made, and every mark of respect manifested by the regent."

A banquet was given in the dwelling of the regent, whose sole success was again sparing the Dowager Queen and Prince from attendance. Treatment of the men Perry had left behind during his absence satisfied him that Okinawan behavior had further improved. Fairly priced supplies had been made available to them, women no longer fled from their appearance at markets, and the general tendency to "avoid a more friendly intercourse" was slowly diminishing. But the Commodore's new forcing of Shuri to honor its obligation to receive Americans didn't erase his anger.

He had evidence Okinawans used Japanese coins, although not in sight of Americans. Eager to donate some to the U.S. Mint, he proposed an exchange with American currency. But the regent claimed no coins were to be had because all were owned by Japanese residents who didn't want to part with them; Okinawans themselves relied on barter. While Perry's "pique" struck interpreter Williams as that of "a disappointed child" unable to obtain something on which he'd set his heart, the Commodore saw something very different at stake: one failure to "carry a point with these people" would lead to others. Thwarting an Okinawan attempt to return his American money, he warned the regent his coins must be waiting upon his return from his second trip to Japan, when he hoped to acquire something far more important too.

IT WASN'T FOR LACK OF PERRY'S urging that another half century would pass before America, exhilarated by victory in the "splendid little war" with Spain, would acquire its first full colonies. The Commodore's months in the Far East made it clearer than ever to him some should be established there now. "It is self-evident," he prophesied, "that the course of coming events will ere long make it necessary for the United States to extend its territorial jurisdiction beyond the limits of the western continent."

"Territorial jurisdiction" meant protecting American "rights" with some kind of land control. His responsibility for making far-reaching decisions of great national importance had helped grow his strategic vision even bigger and bolder, and the apparent payoff of his gumption during his first visits to Okinawa had convinced him that more could be won: the island should be made an American protectorate. During his six-month absence from there, he'd written Washington that "it would be a merit to extend over it the vivifying influence and protection of a government like our own." He did not "hesitate to recommend . . . continuing the influence which I have already acquired over the authorities and people of the beautiful island of Lew Chew."

That was no one-off on his part. During the Mexican War, he'd pressed for American colonization of the Isthmus of Tehuantepec, which links the country to Central America—and sometimes also for Central America itself. Soon he'd urge making Formosa too an American protectorate.[24] And upon returning to America later in 1854, he'd recommend opening Vietnam by "sufficient force to resist and prevent insult and to command respect and as a consequence secure the friendship of these singular people." Perry's understanding that the appetite for Asian trade would sooner or later prompt political and probably military assertion reflected greater realism than others' claims that America's exclusive interest in commercial and humanitarian activity made it neither militaristic nor imperialistic. He'd argue it was idle to suppose that because previous U.S. policy had been to avoid "by all means possible" all connection with other nations' political acts "we can always escape from the responsibilities which our growing wealth and power must inevitably fasten upon us":

> We cannot expect to be free from the ambitious longings of increased power which are the natural concomitants of national success. . . . The day will arrive and at no distant period when political events and the unanimous and urgent appeals of our commercial men will make it obligatory on the United States . . . to extend the advantages of our national friendship and protection as well to Japan as to the other powers little known by Western nations. I may refer to Siam, Cambodia, Cochin China [now central Vietnam] and parts of Borneo and Sumatra.[25]

But for now his plans focused on the Ryukyus, and he outlined them in two winter letters to Washington: "I assume the responsibility of urging the expediency of establishing a foothold in this quarter of the globe as a measure of positive necessity to the sustaining of our maritime rights"— another clue to one of his deepest interests—"in the east"; and "It is important that I should have instructions to act promptly, for it is not impossible that some other power, less scrupulous, may slip in and seize upon the advantages which would justly belong to us."

He specified the less scrupulous powers as Russia, France, and England.

Although much of the New World tended to see the Old as morally corrupt, Perry's passion to seize the advantages that "justly" should have been American further set him apart from almost all his fellow squadron commanders, who obeyed the Navy Department's frequent reminders that the United States, in contrast to those colonial powers, sought only commercial relationships with other states.[26] Still, the carve-'em-up colonialist spirit of the time gave him good reason to worry about those European empires that seemed eager to claim all the rich prizes of trade, influence, and prestige for themselves. Britain, whose naval power he especially resented, had an unfortunate head start in acquiring Far Eastern bases. And now the Russian squadron about which Perry knew—although not that it too would soon visit Okinawa—increased his concern about St. Petersburg's designs on Japan.[27] That was no doubt on his mind when he again departed for Edo Bay on February 7, four days after the regent's banquet-on-command. Pending Washington's reaction to his proposal for establishing the foothold in the Ryukyus, he continued holding them under "limited authority." It would be exercised by seventeen armed men, including two officers, who would remain in Naha while he was again in Japan, from where he'd detach a supply ship from his force and send it to join them.

WASHINGTON'S RESPONSE WAS QUICK and negative. America had changed significantly since Perry left it the year before, and not only because Millard Fillmore, the Commodore's ultimate sponsor, was no longer President. Even if his successor had taken the same interest in the mission, the country's increasing preoccupation with the slavery issue that threatened its destruction would no doubt have diverted his attention. The new President, Franklin Pierce, commended Perry's patriotism but dismissed his Ryukyus proposal. Without more urgent and potent reasons, he didn't want to "retain possession" of a distant island without congressional authorization. The expense of maintaining the necessary force would be too great and, the Secretary of the Navy particularized, it would be "rather mortifying" if the seized territory would ever have to be surrendered.

Without mentioning the rejection of his recommendation, Perry's account of the expedition would indirectly deny he'd made it. "It was not proposed by the Commodore to take Lew Chew, or claim it as a territory conquered by, and belonging to, the United States, nor to molest or interfere in any way with the authorities or people of the island, or to use any force, except in self defense." Since no American had seen a single Okinawan fire-arm or useable sword, it wasn't surprising that defense against what was never specified. At the same time, the Commodore explained Washington's reluctance in a way that might justify his expansive intention. America, he claimed, already possessed "all necessary influence" in the Ryukyus. He held to his notion that the influence had been "acquired by *kindness and non-interference with the laws and customs of the island* [italics added]"—and he'd have the last word. When he'd return for his fourth visit, on his way home from the second to Japan, he'd continue to dictate terms even while following his orders not to officially place the Ryukyus under American authority.

Meanwhile, his pride in none of his sailors molesting any Okinawan would run aground, as so often when womenless men more or less occupy foreign lands. While the Commodore was conducting his final negotiations with Lord Abe's representatives south of Edo, some of those he'd left on the island were cursed and targeted. The weapons were stones intended to hit them or come close enough to make a point—or nothing of the kind because they'd been thrown by children in careless play. Later, however, a crewman on the supply ship he sent from Edo Bay apparently produced a knife to threaten a butcher in a Naha market, although those circum-stances too would never be established with certainty. A magistrate would testify the knife appeared when the butcher protested the sailor's failure to pay for some meat. He and two mates were clearly well oiled. One was clubbed in an ensuing scuffle, but the beaten man's shipmates, the Com-modore would find, felt he got "no more than his deserts."

Perry would also conclude those "minor matters" would have gone no farther if not for what followed the market commotion. One of the tipsy trio went on to rape a young woman in her house. A crowd drawn by her screams chased him away. Seeking escape in a small boat in the harbor, he stumbled—or was hit by one of the stones his pursuers had been throw-ing, or maybe a stick—and drowned in the water, if the stick or stones, or a beating by the raped woman's son, hadn't killed him first.

Upon his arrival, Perry demanded an investigation, Concerned about the security of foreigners "who might chance to visit the island," he landed another detachment of marines. In the end, however, the Commodore would again judge that the behavior of the assaulter had provoked the Oki-nawans, even if his death wasn't legally deserved.

He also saw to other matters, such as obtaining Shuri's assurance it would carefully maintain the coal shed he'd compelled it to build, together with any deposit "the United States might wish to make there" in the future. Meanwhile, it was time for that last word of his. "There remained . . . one important piece of business yet to be done. This was the making of a compact or treaty between our government and that of Lew Chew." With the principal overt justification for cowing Shuri gone because Edo had already agreed, in principle, to the terms of President Fillmore's letter, why was a treaty necessary? Because the mission's purpose had always been larger than opening Japan.

The cynical Shimazu lord whose 1609 invasion ended Okinawa's independence and prosperity forced it to bear responsibility for its own pitiless persecution. After three years of imprisonment in Japan, the Ryukyuan king pledged to recognize an imagined "ancient" dependency on cruel Satsuma, to which he swore eternal obedience by himself and his heirs. The present Okinawan authorities differed in that they swallowed their extreme reluctance and submitted to Perry's humiliating compact far more quickly and with much less trauma than their predecessors. Whereas the seventeenth-century victors beheaded a royal advisor who refused to sign the documents, Perry merely landed another "small escort" of his howitzer-armed marines to convert 1854's royal advisors who had refused, protesting American practices during their virtual occupation of the island and trying to insert that the present document was "drawn and signed under compulsion."

Writing for publication later, the Commodore, evidently unaware of the irony, would urge the United States and Europe to "protect these and other defenseless communities, in remote parts of the world" from "acts of injustice and outrage" committed by visiting ships. Promising relief for the inhabitants of "an island beautiful beyond description" who were "trodden to the earth" by their Japanese rulers, he included among his selling points for establishing American control "amelioration of the condition of the natives," for which the "patience of kind and honorable measures toward them" would help. "Hence it will be politic and just to continue to these people the protection which I shall give them so long as I have the power and the countenance of American authority."

He'd indeed help near the end of his final visit. One of his ships would bear Bernard Bettelheim from the island after the missionary had had *his* last word about Okinawans—that they were "all liars"—and preaching a final sermon that likened Perry's mission to Jesus Christ's. (Removed at last, the thorn would spend his final years in America as a Presbyterian minister, military surgeon, lecturer about Okinawa, drugstore owner, and fund-raiser for himself.) However, the Commodore's compact was more of the same, further oppressing rather than protecting. Its seven substantive paragraphs were entirely and exclusively about what "Lew Chew" would be required to provide the United States, from "great courtesy and friendship" to any visiting citizens to skilled pilots searching the horizon for American ships they'd hasten to guide safely to a permanent place of anchorage of Naha. On shore, Americans "shall be at liberty to ramble where they please, without hindrance." Illegal acts by passengers and crew would be punished, but by the ships' captains.

Some of the spirit of Perry's proposed occupation of the Ryukyus—"justified," he believed, "by the strictest rules of moral law" and the "laws of stern necessity"—was thus enacted. An embarrassed *Mississippi* clerk said America's "commodorial gentry" had played "fantastic tricks" on a people "whose forts are disarmed; among whom not one offensive weapon was noticed after months of intercourse." The Okinawans signed like "a mouse in the talons of the eagle." The clerk (who would rise to admiral) wanted to alert Washington to that, but virtually no one cared, then or later. With Perry's praise of his own intentions sounding so good, few Americans in or out of government would ever learn of the treaty's bludgeoning terms.

A hundred thirty-three years later, after virtually every Okinawan cultural asset had been destroyed during World War II, dogged effort by a few patriots finally shamed a reluctant United States Naval Academy into returning a bell that had rung in the Gokoku-ji temple where Bernard Bettelheim squatted. The embattled missionary wanted it gone, and when it was, he "rejoiced," in his own description, at the disfigurement, at "seeing a heathen temple breaking up. . . . So let thy enemies perish, O Lord." It was Perry who made off with the lovely artifact, at Bettelheim's urging and evidently unaware of the additional irony in its inscription: "May the sound of this bell . . . enable the King and his subjects to live so virtuously that barbarians will find no occasion to invade the Kingdom." Soon translator Williams saw the Commodore more interested in its procurement than in even proper settlement of the case of his sailor's death. Perry indeed got his way again, but not when he returned home. He'd wanted his Okinawan trophy to sing his own praises, Samuel Williams thought; actually to cap the Washington Monument, which was under construction when he left on the mission but whose completion would be delayed for decades by political intrigues and the Civil War. Meanwhile, his widow would donate the unappreciated antiquity to the Naval Academy in 1859, after which it would be rung when Navy won the annual Army–Navy football game and occasionally hammered by bowling pins swung by midshipmen celebrating something else. In the interim, it remained in Perry's private possession, in violation of the rules for disposal of gifts received during the expedition.

How the Commodore actually obtained the Gokoku-ji bell may also never be known. The "not discreditable specimen of foundry work" was "a present from the regent,"[28] he'd report, adding that the "poor Lew Chewans" were delighted to learn it would be "acceptable" to contribute to the monument honoring the leader of the republic whose virtues inspired good men everywhere. Was the revered symbol that had been cast for a king in the fifteenth century, when the toy kingdom was in its Golden Age, exchanged for a cotton gin and butter churn, as some natives rumored? Did the Satusma overseers whom Perry detested insist it be "donated" in order to speed his departure from the island? No Okinawan historian supports his assertion that the bell was donated to the people of the United States. Whatever pressure was exerted to part Okinawans from their priceless treasure, its loss—or theft, as some call it★—was another blow, even if assuaged by knowledge that it signaled Perry's final visit was indeed coming to an end. "Farewell to the Loo-Chooans," a sailor jotted in his diary, "as much, no doubt to their delight as our own."

★ A crew member's mention of "a stone. . . . procured for the Washington monument" leaves the interpretation of *how* open. J. Willet Spalding, *The Japan Expedition*, p. 343. If it *was* stolen, it set a precedent for 1945, when American soldiers, from generals to privates, would loot a substantial number of the few cultural assets not destroyed in the Battle of Okinawa.

12

The Heart of the Matter

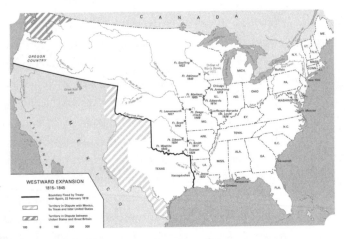

Map of U.S. Western expansion, circa 1853

MOSCOW'S COLD WAR DESCRIPTION of Matthew Perry a century later as a gun-toting capitalist who wanted to "convert Japan into an American colony" wasn't invented from nothing, although "outpost" instead of "colony" would have made it less propagandistic. When the squadron departed from Naha on August 1, 1853, the Commodore was following the money to his next destination. Americans' primary interest in the Land of the Rising Sun, John Curtis Perry would write, "was largely extrinsic: it lay athwart the major future route to China."[1] The mission's primary purpose was improving that route, a reflection of the New World valuing Niphon, as some then called Japan, less for itself than as a lead to bigger things. Hong Kong, that next destination after Perry's second visit to Okinawa, beckoned with more than stores for replenishing his supplies and facilities for giving his ships and crews much-needed rehabilitation.

Despite the distances involved, the China trade had been anything but peripheral to the American economy from the moment the colonies' independence from Britain lifted their prohibition from pursuing commerce east of the Cape of Good Hope. The revolutionary republic was still taking its baby steps when the first American ship, a heavily laden *Empress of China*, arrived in New York from Canton two years later. "Perhaps no species of traffic has promised more lucrative advantages," predicted the journal *American Museum* in 1784. With diligence, industriousness, and avoidance of "the voluptuous enjoyments of the tropical islands which lie in their way . . . there is no doubt but large fortunes may be made in this traffic" across the Pacific.[2]

Fortunes indeed. Gold hadn't yet been discovered in California, but the first American to behold the West Coast, recognizing its plentiful supply of excellent furs as another form of it, bartered with Indian hunters for sea otter pelts. Soon "black gold" skins bought cheaply in the Northwest were being resold for many times more in China or exchanged for native goods that fetched high prices back in America. (John Jacob Astor of New York, the future Prince of the China Trade, was among the entrepreneurs who got in early.) One ship netted a return of some $53,000—a huge sum in 1798—on a $7,000 investment. It wasn't long before only trade with Britain surpassed trade with Canton.

Return cargos bulged the holds of the sleek clippers of Perry's day with teas, silks, porcelains, elegant furnishings, and objets d'art: "musts" for style-conscious Americans, especially in the Northeast, where chinoiserie was high fashion. (Tons of ginseng were also imported for men hoping to restore their powers.) While an optimistic journal predicted that an opened Japan would produce $200 million in trade, the American Commissioner in China declared—while Perry was in Shanghai, preparing for the final leg of his voyage to Uraga—that "the advantages now actually enjoyed" there, in China, beat anything hoped for in Niphon. China trade profits indeed made even the whaling industry's seem piddling. What Perry most wanted from Japan was ways to increase that revenue: use of its ports and coal for steamships coming and going from China.

An amalgam of circumstances, perceptions, and national attitudes further nourished the drive to expand the China trade—and, in the Commodore's case, to exercise American power and influence everywhere in East Asia. During the decade before his departure, the country had, in Peter

Wiley's summary, "vanquished Mexico, doubled its size, become a continental power, taken the China trade from England, projected its naval power into the Pacific, and proclaimed the superiority of its democratic way of life."[3] All that was done with little change in America's essential image of itself as living its own hard but wholesome life down on the farm. For hadn't the country been founded in deep suspicion of militarism and resolution to avoid foreign entanglements? Weren't the people who'd won their independence from an empire run from London intent on minding their own business (and why shouldn't they when their economy was growing faster than almost any other in the world?). "We continue to think of ourselves as a kind of great, peaceful Switzerland, whereas we are in fact a great, expanding world power," Walter Lippmann would write. "Our imperialism is more or less unconscious."[4]

More so because it was also largely unplanned (even though George Washington called America "a rising empire" in 1783, and Thomas Jefferson hailed the "empire of liberty" twenty-six years later.) It began with the accident—unless one believed, as many Americans did, it was God's purposeful handiwork—of the geography that enabled the great expansion on terra firma that preceded the thrust overseas. New World immigrants were powerfully enticed by what they saw as an essentially uninhabited landmass, millions of Native Americans being dismissed as mere obstacles. Before them lay "a boundless continent," wrote Alexis de Tocqueville, author of the seminal *Democracy in America*, published in 1835 and 1840. "Millions of men are marching at once toward the same horizon. . . . Fortune has been promised to them somewhere in the West, and to the West they go to find it." De Tocqueville's observations of splendid ports, shipwrights, and ship handling that were helping charge the former underpopulated colonies with mercantile and industrial self-assertion led him to predict the movement wouldn't be limited to land. Americans were "destined by nature to be a great maritime people. . . . They will become, like the English, the commercial agents of a great portion of the world."

Despite mockery by many of Europe's well born, the American hunger for territory, influence, and money was no uglier or more sinister than that of the nineteenth-century European powers. Military acquisition drove the economy of prideful Britain, whose behavior during the Opium Wars made Perry's almost angelic by comparison. A Société de Géographie president would soon outline the vision of much of midcentury France by declaring that "a country has no lasting value except by force of expansion." And an explorer of Siberia's Amur River—an obstacle on Russia's route to Japan—revealed a good deal about Tsarist ambition when he assured his military superiors that his research would "camouflage the political goals of the expedition" and discourage interference by adversaries.

What distinguished American expansionism was the dynamism of a people composed principally of Europe's formerly uneducated poor and their offspring. The new nation's political and social structures may have contributed as much to what Walt Whitman described as "Yankeedoodledom" charging ahead with the "resistless energy of a sixty-five-hundred-thousand-horsepower steam engine" as the empty spaces sounding the call of the frontier. Freedom was anything but a cliché, especially to those liberated from their motherlands' much tighter rein on self-assertion and self-development. In contrast with the old countries, the new one could seem created by and for ordinary folk, in whose lives its government, wanted for helping release enterprise rather than restrain it or harmonize society, interfered vastly less. Low taxation, laissez-faire, and embrace of initiative had replaced regulation and honor-thy-betters restraint. Americans were also largely free of guilds, orders, and social and familial hierarchies—of almost all holdovers of feudalism—that had kept most of their ancestors in their subservient places. Of course they strived and scrambled; something was much more likely to come of it, especially in the 1830s and 1840s, when the economy was growing faster than ever.

Happy migrants' attainment of the Pacific Ocean failed to cool American restlessness or ambition. "By our recent acquisitions in the Pacific," Secretary of the Treasury Robert Walker celebrated in 1848, "Asia has suddenly become our neighbor, with a placid intervening ocean inviting our steamships upon the track of a commerce greater than that of all Europe combined."

The British opening of Shanghai to trade and an 1844 treaty that gave American merchants essentially the same rights increased interest in Asia yet more. New England clipper ships, the world's fastest wooden vessels, helped win domination of the China trade from Britain even before settlement of the West Coast, with California's springboard harbors, neared Chinese ports by some 2,500 miles. Washington's view of the Pacific as "the seat of an immense and lucrative commerce" made Japan appear ever bigger in sights focused on China. "The same law of civilization that has compelled the red men . . . to retire before the superior hardihood of our pioneers" will make the Japanese abandon their "cruelty," a popular magazine urged in 1852, when Perry was preparing his mission. Another magazine stated in the same year that Japan's opening was "demanded by reason, civilization, progress and religion"—much the same imperatives that were seen as having enabled the United States to complete its coast-to-coast expansion and begin surveying for the transcontinental railroad that would soon seal it.

In the same vein, Senator Thomas Hart Benton urged that "the apparition of the Caucasian race rising upon the Yellow race" must reanimate torpid Asia, after which "the intellectual superiority of the White race will do the rest." A New York congressman whose 1845 oratory helped convince the administration to send Perry's predecessor, Commodore Biddle, to Japan predicted that "another year will not elapse before the American people will be able to rejoice in the knowledge that the Star Spangled Banner is recognized as ample passport and protection" for his enterprising countrymen eager to further expand American commerce. The *Presbyterian Review* felt the time had come "in the providence of God" for Japan to be opened by force if it didn't submit voluntarily, and the *New York Herald* editorialized that it was "our Manifest Destiny to implant ourselves in Asia."* John O'Sullivan earned a special place among the givers of confidence in American goodness because he coined "Manifest Destiny" in an article published eight years before Perry sailed. The term expressed the country's need and right "to overspread the continent allotted by Providence for the free development of our yearly multiplying millions."†

The overspreading would be beautiful. "It is our unparalleled glory," O'Sullivan extolled, that America had "no reminiscences of battle fields, but in defense of humanity, of the oppressed of all nations, of the rights of con-

---

* A few years later, an Illinois senator would conclude a report about the West's importance by quoting a land speculator and visionary expansionist named William Gilpin. Gilpin declared the American people's *"untransacted* destiny" was to "subdue the continent—to rush over this vast field to the Pacific ocean—to animate the many hundred millions of its people and to cheer them upward—to set the principle of self-government at work . . . to establish a new order in human affairs—to set free the enslaved . . . to confirm the destiny of the human race. . . . Divine Task! Immortal mission! . . . Let every American heart . . . glow undimmed, and confide with religious faith in the sublime destiny of his well-loved country." Cited in Henry F. Graff (ed.), *Bluejackets with Perry in Japan,* p. 55.

† O'Sullivan exulted that America's birth had launched "a new history" that "connects us with the future only." The infant country stood alone in "the entire development of the natural rights of man, in moral, political, and national life. . . . Who, then, can doubt that our country is destined to be *the great nation* [italics in original] of futurity?"

science, the rights of personal enfranchisement." And heaven's allotment to the United States shouldn't be limited to "the continent;" its mission to sow "freedom of conscience, freedom of person, freedom of trade and business pursuits, universality of freedom and equality" didn't stop at its coasts.*

O'Sullivan's confirmation that the Almighty had placed the United States above, and made it a model for, all other countries affirmed that Americans (with the calm confidence of a Christian holding four aces, as Mark Twain would later remark) had "God-given rights" to spread their new political institutions and their commerce across the continent, then into others, uplifting benighted Asians, among others. "When half the naked millions of Asia shall attain Christianity and with it all the new wants which the necessary change in their social condition will produce, the soil of our country will be scarcely adequate to supply them."[5]

The sense of youth and freedom from European corruption that excited the American republic also swelled its conviction of virtue. Among many otherwise more moderate voices cheering Manifest Destiny, John Quincy Adams declared in 1846 that the people's new "spirit of aggrandizement" would "hereafter characterize their history." In the inaugural address of Franklin Pierce, who succeeded Millard Fillmore, the new president declared on March 4, 1853—as Perry was roughly midway from Norfolk to Japan—that no "timid forebodings of evil from expansion" would restrain the country.

Americans' individual mixtures of religious, commercial, and patriotic priorities usually included humanistic ones, too: most who thought about it were genuinely convinced Japan would benefit from being lifted into the family of trading nations. "Free trade," wrote Samuel Wells Williams, "begets a free interchange of thought"—which was as important to some as "Where the flag and the leger go, the Book must also go." Besides, the republican form of government *obviously* enabled more people to enjoy more happiness than all despotisms, especially feudal ones. Thus Manifest Destiny's tide "swept in a great wave across the Pacific and lapped on Oriental shores."[6]

---

* The rhetoric would disturb one of Perry's sailors. "The great misfortune attending the propagation of civilization and Christianity among heathens," the young midshipman would observe, was the kind of foreigner with whom those heathens first came in contact. They were men moved "only by motives of gain, irrespective of the method by which it is obtained." John G. Sproston, *A Private Journal of John Glendy Sproston*, p. ix.

A reviewer of Perry's forthcoming book about the mission would note that he and it exhibited Manifest Destiny's "compelling influence" on American foreign policy. Lapping hard on him in his vanguard position, it propelled him on his particular current of expansionism. His motives were mixed, like everyone else's. His patriotism was broader than strictly military or geopolitical. Knowing his cherished coast-to-coast country now offered the shortest route between Europe and Asia and eager for it to become a "highway for the world," he suggested calling it "The Middle Kingdom," as China had long labeled itself. He also had reason to attach special importance to winning commercial advantage.

Although the Commodore was the mission's moving spirit, many considered Aaron Haight Palmer its father. A powerful New York businessman with an early grasp of public relations, Palmer, as the head of a lobby for international trade, had repeatedly urged President Fillmore and Secretary of State Webster—veteran Whigs who were supported by and furthered the interests of the large merchant firms that handled much of America's international trade—to do whatever it took to establish relations with Japan. Denouncing the "barbarous and outrageous treatment of shipwrecked Americans," he campaigned for opening "that empire to our commerce." The "isolated and mysterious" land "will be compelled, by force of circumstances, to succumb to the progressive commercial spirit of the age; and the Japanese Islands will eventually become in the east what the British Islands are in the west." For anyone who didn't understand that "force of circumstances" should include military force, Palmer spelled it out. If the Shogun failed to comply with "so reasonable and just a request," Washington would be justified in taking such measures as humanity and the national honor would require "to enforce its immediate and effectual observance by the imperial and provincial authorities of Japan. A strict blockade of Edo Bay and port of Matsumae, in southern Hokkaido, for which two frigates are amply adequate, would soon compel that imperious Government to accede to our demands."[7]

THAT APPEAL OF 1849 came when the post–Mexican War economy was growing ever more rapidly. The discovery of California gold a year earlier "offered further stimulation and encouraged still more daring projects." Adventurers launched private military actions in lower California, northern

Mexico, and Nicaragua; "even the Sandwich [Hawaiian] Islands were threatened."[8] Meanwhile, American capture of virtually the entire fur trade with China dealt Great Britain a rare loss to a maritime rival.

Perry had already made an important contribution to the American ascendency. Realizing the vital importance of market knowledge and convinced that fast mail service across the Pacific would make it possible to deliver news from China before it could reach Britain, he'd begun campaigning in the 1830s to match London's subsidizing of mail carriers. Shortly after the Mexican War, the Commodore was appointed to the new position of General Superintendent of Mail Steamers, with responsibility for overseeing construction of new vessels that would carry government mail. At a time when better ships were faster ships, clippers had demonstrated a new superiority of American shipbuilding, able to beat the British in bringing goods as well as intelligence from China. Further sharpening the rivalry, steam propulsion also upped the importance of Japan. A steamship from a West Coast port could make the voyage to Canton or Shanghai in weeks instead of the five or six months New England sailing vessels required to round the African horn.[9]

That was where Japan came in. Its many reputed excellent harbors lay on the fastest run between California and China, the great-circle route that was also safer and more comfortable than the foggy, icy northern variants. The captain of the corvette that had fetched the angry *Lagoda* sailors from Nagasaki[10] made a point of that when emphasizing that the country was "directly on the line from San Francisco to Shanghai."

Besides, Japan had coal, precious coal: "the dearest mineral of the 19th century," Russians professed as commercial competition heated the passion for the precursor of oil. No steamship could carry enough on a voyage of any length to leave room for much cargo. Most burned roughly a ton an hour—warships slightly more; for example, the *Mississippi* consumed twenty-six tons a day. Secretary of State Webster had made procurement of Japanese coal the mission's primary goal. Then the Commodore's long voyage east, with its coaling stops whose rendezvous arrangements—not to mention the loading—required great effort, had convinced him more than ever of the vital importance of coaling stations to his vision of American prominence in Asia and bigger profits in New York.

His research had established that Japan's supply was plentiful. "They have no want of coals in Japan," he quoted Engelbert Kaempfer, one of

Deshima Island's German physicians.[11] Thus the pointed mention in President Fillmore's letter that had been delivered in Kurihama on July 14: "Commodore Perry is also directed by me to represent to your imperial majesty that we understand there is a great abundance of coal . . . in the Empire of Japan. Our steamships, in crossing the great ocean, burn a great deal of coal and it is not convenient to bring it all the way from America." Secretary Webster's declaration that God had placed the Japanese supply where He did "for the benefit of the human family"[12] wasn't appended.

THE SINGLE INTERRUPTION in Perry's naval service had come in 1816–1819, after budget cutbacks following the War of 1812 slimmed junior officers' prospects for promotion. The highly regarded lieutenant obtained a "honeymoon" furlough, moved to New York, and shifted to commercial pursuits, including captaining merchant ships for John Slidell, a prosperous merchant and banker as well as a shipowner, who profited from expanded European trade that also followed the war's end.

The work put young Perry on his way to joining the substantial naval brass of the day that was intimately connected to mercantile families. In time, virtually all of his closest friends and supporters would be from the great houses that were making fortunes in the China trade. One of his daughters would marry August Belmont Sr., whose enormous wealth from business and membership in New York's highest society made him "King of Fifth Avenue." (New York's Belmont Racetrack and the Belmont Stakes, one of the Triple Crown races, are named after him, while in Newport, Rhode Island, one of the sumptuous "cottages" was built by Oliver Hazard Perry Belmont, the son of the "King" and of Perry's daughter, together with his wife Alva Vanderbilt, previously married to William K. Vanderbilt.) Young Lieutenant Perry himself was already in bed with allied interests. John Slidell was his father-in-law. From the time he went to work for him, "his thought," an admiring biographer has written, "and most of his major efforts, seem to have been centered on the value of the navy not alone as a weapon of war, but as the spearhead of American commerce."[13]

Apart from the very occasional quiet commission, there was nothing underhanded about Perry's commercial connections.[14] On the contrary, he took pride in having "devoted a whole life" to the interests of "the mercantile community," as he'd exaggerate after the mission.[15] That devotion made his contribution to early American imperialism anything but accidental. With his fervent commitment to securing overseas influence and bases, Perry foreshadowed Alfred T. Mahan, author of the hugely influential *The Influence of Sea Power upon History, 1660–1783* (1890), and champion of pursuing the national welfare by applying that power abroad. "Our people," the Commodore declared while assembling the mission's ships and supplies, "must naturally be drawn into the contest for empire, whether for good or for evil."

13

The Tortured Reckoning

Black Ship fact and fiction in a blockprint news sheet

ORD ABE BELIED AN OLD SAMURAI PROVERB that "to know and to act are one and the same." Together with the political complexity and his father's increasingly relevant warning that a wrong step might lead to vicious revolution, a personal setback may have slowed his reactions. He'd married when he was twenty and his bride, a daughter of a prominent daimyo related to the Tokugawas, was sixteen. His devotion to her, undiminished by the union's customary arranged nature or his eye for other women, was bolstered by the loss of three newly born children.[1] Rather than exercise his right to divorce beautiful but frail Kinko for her failure to deliver a healthy male heir, he tried to cheer her. A story had him open a screen of their house on the grounds of Edo Castle to some hydrangeas whose color had been deepened by rain.

"They're more beautiful on rainy days than fine ones, just like you."

"That's just flattery."

"No, it's what I see."

Uncommonly caring during Kinko's decline, he expressed his affection in a series of poems and, it was said, brushed a comment onto a portrait of her he commissioned during her last year, 1852, which was also his last of pre-Perry calm: "I remember you morning and night. To never forget, I gaze at your likeness." Thanking her husband for their happy life together, Kinko urged him not to visit again because his burdens were heavy enough without adding hers. Further moved by the genuine feeling animating that expression of otherwise ceremonial modesty, he told her not to worry, "being with you is my happiest moment." Women having no place in public life, Edo Castle did nothing to mark her death, at age thirty, but everyone knew Abe was stricken.[2]

To relieve his sorrow and the strains of his office, he visited his still-handsome mother just outside the capital. Riding his horse was of course better for him than consuming more sake, but he did that too. Although the Black Ships hadn't roused him to anger or defiant patriotism, his knowledge of the Opium War made Perry's guns trouble him even more than it did many others. The haunting of Japan's decision makers by the crippling of China came from more than the evidence of Westerners regarding Asians as merely a great reservoir of supply and demand. They had reason to fear catastrophe when Perry returned, as he almost certainly would.

Fourteen years earlier, in 1839, the Opium War had barely begun when the *bakufu* ordered the Deshima Dutch to submit a report about it. The first Chinese description reached Nagasaki in 1844, a year after twenty-two-year-old Abe's appointment to the *roju*, to which the document was quickly forwarded. By the time he was promoted to *roju shuseki*, nervous censors had rushed more accounts to Edo Castle as soon as they arrived. Within a few years, Edo had circulated a half dozen or so to prominent daimyo, whose scribes responded to the considerable interest in foreign news by brushing additional copies. A few even went on sale.[3]

The Chinese accounts prompted exceptional anxiety. Their ancient weapons scarcely troubled the British warships that ranged the coast, destroying forts and landing steamrolling marines almost at will. What had their Emperor done to provoke their devastating firepower? The East India Company, which enjoyed quasi-governmental authority in British eyes and law, was engaged in what some saw even then as a vast criminal enterprise: growing opium in India and shipping large quantities to China, where it generated great misery. Those who "smuggle opium to seduce the Chinese people," the Imperial Commissioner would vainly write Queen Victoria, "are not tolerated by the laws of heaven and are unanimously hated by human beings. How can you bear to" sell harmful products "in order to fulfill your insatiable desire?"[4]

In 1836, three years before the war's outbreak, twelve million or so people—1 percent of the population, but up to 90 percent of some coastal provinces—were addicted. At that point, Peking made the trade legally as well as ethically criminal, as it was in England; but generous bribes kept the parlors proliferating. The profits made on addicts, larger than from any other trade, reinforced a stout pillar of the British Empire.

Then a rare incorruptible official appointed commissioner in Canton turned back some English vessels—which promptly called for British warships. After the Emperor refused to pay compensation for a large quantity of the ruinous drug the official had burned, the British authorities who represented, then supplanted, the opium's outraged owners objected in the name of the sanctity of property and the importance of free trade for bettering lives throughout the world. A decade later, on the eve of Perry's voyage, the *New York Times* described the "full benefit" of the progress Britain bestowed on China. For every missionary admitted under the terms of the Treaty of Nanking, the ignominious agreement it had been forced to sign in 1842, "a million dollars worth of opium" was introduced. "And for every soul reclaimed by the devoted missionary effort, tens of thousands have been lost through the effects of that frightful poison."

A dissident Englishman resident in China considered the slave trade "merciful" by comparison. "The opium seller slays the body after he has corrupted, degraded and annihilated the moral being of unhappy sinners, while every hour is bringing new victims to a Moloch which knows no satiety." Perry's contrary view, expressed near the end of his life, would be that the war "greatly" benefitted China, even if he couldn't approve of its cause;[5] it had opened the country wide to Western influence and the bestowal of more benefits. But while the rights and wrongs were utterly clear to a few conscience-stricken Westerners, Japanese who knew about the war were much more worried about the military implications of the quick British victory against the China that they had considered the world's preeminent power.[6] Everything looked very different after elimination of the measure of protection afforded by the old assumptions about China's strength.

Soon anxious Japanese writers were analyzing the war that had enfeebled and demoralized their neighbor. One said explicitly that he was holding the result "as a mirror" to the vulnerable Land of the Gods.[7] "This concerns a foreign country," urged another, "but I think it should provide a good warning for us."[8] A third cited a Chinese saying that they wouldn't be robbed by foreigners because their countries were supposedly separated by the equivalent of sixty thousand miles. "But the Chinese do not know that foreigners have made their beds on the waves and that their colonies are very near . . . they do not realize that armored ships are like mountains and that Chinese traitors are as multitudinous as flies."[9] Nor did the worried writers, in turn, know how justified their darkest suspicions would prove. Evidently not satisfied by the huge advantages just wrung from China, the governor of Hong Kong drafted a secret strategy for extracting the same from Japan.[10] Approved by the Foreign Office in 1845, the plan wasn't carried out only because sufficient naval force then happened to be unavailable.

Even without knowing how close British guns came to firing at Japan, its students of foreign affairs were shaken. If China, long seen as the world's mightiest nation, had been so easily forced to do the Westerners' bidding, what was in store for tiny Japan, which was even more vulnerable to naval attack? What chance did it have of resisting the even bigger American guns? When Abe Masahiro finally ordered acceptance of President Fillmore's letter, he wrote in his instructions to the Uraga magistrate that Japan's fate might well be like China's if it didn't submit.

JAPAN'S DISADVANTAGE WAS AS MUCH human as material. Even with their inferior weapons, the half a million or so adult males of the samurai class, which comprised roughly 6 percent of the population, could have mounted a powerful force if they'd been in fighting condition; but very few were. Only the politicians who were urging that the Americans be taught a lesson no matter what managed to ignore their decline as warriors. The centuries of peace during which most engaged in nothing more military than increasingly desultory training and suppressing occasional peasant revolts dulled more than their combat edge.

That wasn't necessarily harmful. Release from their old burdens facilitated more of the learning prescribed by the Confucian ideal of the complete man as a scholar-warrior, highly educated as well as proficient in arms. Some samurai vigorously pursued the knowledge needed for leading in peace as well as war—excellent preparation, although no one then knew it, for when the country would join the world and embrace capitalism. "To these men and to their successors, Japan was to owe much for her rapid rise from mediaeval obscurity to Great-Power status,"[11] to be announced by its stunning success using modern weaponry against Korea and China in 1895 (the Sino-Japanese War) and Russia in 1905 (the Russo-Japanese War).

But not all cocks of the walk were up to retraining. Many lived precariously on their sole source of support: rice subsidies. After the strapped government trimmed them, morale descended together with their sinking income and prospects. Forbidden to engage in trade—although some did, on the sly—more and more became *ronin*, samurai unattached to a lord; a variety that would play a large role in dismantling the shogunate. Tens of thousands of elitist reactionaries had become poor in spirit as well as pocket, turning all the more arrogant because they had little sense of accomplishment to sustain their pride.[12]

A good number sought solace in hedonism that was opposite to the samurai ideal of self-abnegating devotion to duty. In 1816, a social critic recalled the reaction of Tokugawa Ieyasu when a samurai retainer appeared before him in a shirt of luxurious silk: an indulgence so soon after the end of the bloody civil wars that the angered dynasty's founder drew his sword and expelled the dandy[13]—whereas even some low-ranking samurai now sported the same silk. Although a proportion of the best and brightest of the class helped administer *bakufu* departments, more and more worked but sporadically. Otherwise, they gossiped, read novels—and, when the means were available, went out on the town, often to the "The Floating World's" districts of restaurants, theaters, and teahouses. "All they talk about," complained a scholar of the Mito domain whose lord was challenging Abe, "is women, eating and drinking, actors and dramatic productions, gardening and floral arrangements, bird-catching and fishing."[14] "Their military skills have disappeared," a harsher critic charged. "Seven or eight out of ten of them are as weak as women."

Some took up farming, supposedly reserved for the class below them. Others sank into despised commerce—or became self-perpetuating little big shots with no productive function. Abhorrent as it was to traditionalists, that might have been tolerable for a country not under threat. The drift from obsolescent priorities was part of a potentially profound social rearrangement that had started, despite the Confucian prescription for everyone knowing his place and staying there. But the *roju* in general and Lord Abe in particular no longer had the luxury of waiting for the changes to proceed at their own pace, in response to internal needs. What now mattered about the samurai decline was that the ever smaller number practiced in their art narrowed the options of reaction to the Black Ships. The bragging about their ferocity and valor that rose in rough proportion to their slide in skill would make things harder for Abe by spinning pretense that Perry could be defied.

INABILITY TO FORGE CONSENSUS in the *roju* further disheartened the Chief Senior Councilor. The small feat of securing agreement to accept President Fillmore's letter had revealed seemingly irreparable divides in members' fundamental attitudes as well as tactical preferences. Besides, the public mocking of the *roju*'s timidness tended to focus on Abe. His weaving, flattering, and bending in order to avoid giving offense prompted increasingly open criticism, and his solicitation of potential opponents' opinions was disparaged, although he did that partly to sap resentment and anger before they spread. The no longer quite-so-young prodigy became deeply discouraged.

It was to his unusually competent retainers, chosen with his keen eye for merit, that he confided he wanted to resign because he wasn't good enough to lead the government, couldn't keep things under control. Well aware that no replacement of comparable ability was available, they pleaded that his departure would cause the country more suffering because the *bakufu* without him would surely go into steep decline, while he'd appear to have shirked his duty. Resuming it, he soon won a minor victory: the appointment of someone he'd recommended as the government's defense advisor.

The appointee was his most vocal critic, the daimyo of the Mito domain some seventy-five miles from Edo who'd long been railing about failure to strengthen defenses, spiritual as well as material, against all barbarians. Tokugawa Nariaki's importance, second only to Abe's own, was unique in living memory. Not since the establishment of the Tokugawa dynasty had someone not directly serving Edo Castle exercised so much influence.

Like the Shogun, Nariaki was a descendant of Tokugawa Ieyasu, the dynasty's founder. (Thirteen years hence, Nariaki's son would become the last Shogun and remain in the position during the shogunate's frenzied final years while his father's philosophy would continue fueling the rise of Japanese nationalism.) The ambition of the "Deputy Shogun," as Nariaki was occasionally called, matched his prestige as a member of one of the Three Families closest to the ruling Tokugawa clan—so lofty a member that he, as an exception to the "alternate residence" required of the important daimyo, was permitted full-time residence in Edo.

The prestige was sustained by culture and scholarship as well as the eminence and respect that came from the Mito domain's critical military role in the dynasty's establishment. In the seventeenth century, it founded a school for compiling an official, hundred-volume history of Japan, among other purposes. The Mito School was the intellectual home of Sakuma Shozan, the young scholar who had appealed for the acquisition of Western military technology in 1842,[15] and of Aizawa Seishisai, whose even more influential (although unpublished) 1825 *New Proposals*, or *New Theses*, applauded the "Shell and Repel" edict of the same year.

Aizawa's essay was the source of the statement that "stupid and simple" Americans were "incapable of doing good things" because, it explained, their land occupied "the hindmost region of the earth"—in contrast to Divine Japan, whose "Imperial Throne" had been occupied by the heirs of the Great Sun . . . "without change from time immemorial." It followed that Japan was "situated at the top of the earth," making it the "standard for the nations of the world," on all of which it cast its light. But the West threatened nevertheless, Aizawa warned. Its alien barbarians, the world's "lowly organs of the legs and feet," were "dashing about across the seas, trampling other countries underfoot, and daring, with their squinting eyes and limping feet, to override the noble nations." Yes, they were inviting their own downfall, but not necessarily immediately. "Unless great men appear who rally to the assistance of Heaven, the whole natural order will fall victim to the predatory barbarians."[16]

Aizawa's call to smash those barbarians "whenever they came in sight" specified the damage they'd cause: foreign trade would harm the economy, foreign influence would undermine morale, only stiffer defense could build national strength. As a whole, the Mito School championed native traditions (never mind that many had been imported from China) for developing the nation. While most scholars engaged in *rangaku*—"Dutch learning," based on materials imported by the Deshima colony—looked outward to the world, Mito people looked inward. Not that the Mito domain, which had also built an early school for samurai children and created the country's first public garden, ignored literature or the other arts. But a nineteenth-century slogan that "Civil and Military [arts] Go Together" was coined in response to the ever-growing number of encroaching foreigners, and the savants occupied themselves more and more with appeals to increase military strength for repelling them.

As for Tokugawa Nariaki, intellectuals held him in high esteem, partly because many illustrious ones had contributed to that first official history. He also became senior to Abe in formal personal status as well as in age when he succeeded to the powerful domain's leadership in 1829. Fifty-three years old in 1853, he was no figurehead, although his elegant voice and appearance would have made him a good one. If he lacked anything in brains, his spirit and ability to organize a strong staff made up for it—together with the perspicacity of his wife, a princess of impeccable ancient heritage. Although her looks were also much admired, Nariaki had the wisdom to say that "beauty fades but intelligence is irreplaceable."[17]

Moved by curiosity about the arts and sciences that bore resemblance to that of Abe's father, he engaged in a wide variety of pursuits, from theatrical to metallurgic. He cast his own cannon with a primitive blast furnace that melted down temple bells, and urged using copper to make more weapons instead of exporting the ore. He studied literature—and, above all, military subjects.[18] Deeply committed to the old samurai code, he pushed the Mito domain toward reform and renewed dedication to frugality and other traditional virtues, largely in a belief that the foreign threat would have been less perilous without domestic demoralization and decay. Among his other appeals to patriotism, he urged suspension of the trade with the Dutch, which gave Japan only "useless luxury goods." His trust in protecting the country by revitalizing samurai elan suggests that even he, whose warnings made him the Churchill of his day, *under*estimated the danger and the military gap, at least for the present. Since, he argued, England's Industrial Revolution had started a mere half century or so ago, Japan was only a little late. "If we start right in, there's no reason why we shouldn't be able to catch up."[19]

Why the appointment of such an accomplished major figure as the government's defense advisor would have been opposed instead of quickly ratified provides a glimpse into the labyrinth of Tokugawa politics. Why it was a victory for Abe does the same for his skillful treatment of his sternest public opponent. Nariaki's determination to reverse the *bakufu*'s flabbiness made him harshly critical of the Chief Senior Councilor, but the latter needed allies for girding to meet the threat from abroad, and Nariaki's impatient calls to reinforce the military were therefore a useful stimulant for sluggish and do-nothing *bakufu* officials. From Abe's point of view, no contradiction between opening the country, *kaikoku*, and defending it was involved because they were two different things. Even if *kaikoku* was inevitable, it should be accomplished in Japanese ways, in keeping with Japanese wants. Preventive measures *had* to be taken against foreign pressure or domination.

Eight years earlier, very soon after being appointed Chief Senior Councilor, he'd established a new office of coastal defense, a nascent ministry combined with some of the functions of a foreign office. Appointing himself its head, he began pressing for improvement of fortifications, badly needed after at least a century and a half of neglect. Some construction was started, but government officials who were lazy or loathe to develop "cowardly" cannon (as opposed to manly swords) resisted it. Most of all, the new works were slowed by inadequate funding, the *bakufu* being "as short of money as it was of true political wisdom."[20] While cultural life flourished, the strapped national government as well as the coastal daimyo who lived beyond their means were trying to cut spending, not increase it. Wanting to keep the financial squeeze as little known as possible, Abe backed down, or accepted reality, by letting things slide again.

He quietly transferred a Uraga official who'd told him how little progress had been made, even knowing perfectly well that his largely cosmetic effort left the defenses "ludicrously inadequate." Visiting a site, the Mito scholar Sakuma Shozan struck his chest and wept. A need to do much better gave Abe common cause with Nariaki, despite their differences. More than that, the Chief Senior Councilor wanted the influential Mito lord on his side. The rub was another major political issue: the sentiment expressed in Aizawa's 1825 reference to the "Imperial Throne" so long occupied by the heirs of the sun goddess. Scholars from the school that had produced the country's first official history wanted some real authority—although not yet governmental function—restored to what they believed was its legitimate source, the Kyoto court. But elevation of loyalty to someone other than the Shogun—even to the Emperor, as in this case—was a serious challenge to the shogunate.

Courteous Abe himself was partly responsible for the court's growing self-assertion. When it first expressed open concern about the increasing appearances of foreign ships—in 1846, the year of Commodore Biddle's visit—the Chief Senior Councilor might easily have dismissed Kyoto's inquiry as none of its business. Instead, the inveterate seeker of harmony tacitly acknowledged its right by taking the initiative to keep the court informed of foreign and defense developments. But now the threat to Edo Castle's prerogatives was gaining momentum. A few critics were charging the Tokugawas, at least implicitly, with centuries of usurping the devotion owed to the throne.

Philosophical and historical circles had long vented quiet discontent with the Emperors' relegation to a strictly ceremonial role, shorn even of the courtesy of consultation; but the shogunate's provision of stability and relative prosperity kept it at less than a simmer. But now the doubt eating into the government's prestige from its hesitant response to Perry marginally increased the possibility of restoring some of the authority emperors had exercised before shoguns governed. Renewed interest in the indigenous Shinto religion that exalted Japan for having first been ruled by an Emperor descended from a deity also grew, with the implication that Japan was unique and must be protected from corruption by lesser peoples.

Like all stances in every country, the antiforeigner one, with its xenophobic and obscurantist currents, had always served domestic politics as well as foreign policy. The Mito scholar who'd decried the "loathsome western barbarians" who were "scurrying impudently across the Four Seas, trampling other nations underfoot" did so partly in order to criticize the *bakufu*. That radical position of the 1820s was now becoming slightly more mainstream, as more and more people said or thought the supposedly "barbarian-subduing" government was incompetent. Look how it dithered when barbarians actually trod the country's sacred soil! The fledgling protest pinned hopes on Tokugawa Nariaki because he'd supported the pro-throne cause for years, despite his family tie to the Shogun, not the Emperor.[21] Linking it to maintaining the other most important form of traditional purity—keeping the country foreigner free—he used both in an effort to acquire more authority of his own.

As noted, the Mito lord wasn't opposed to *everything* foreign. Like Aizawa, he wanted to copy Western military technology while continuing to exclude Westerners themselves. The mission slogan of the academy he'd founded for the study and adoption of scientific discoveries would become a mantra for opponents of both foreigners and the shogunate: "Revere the Emperor, Repel the Barbarian." The first part was anathema to the *bakufu*, which had lost its resolute aura. The *bakumatsu*—the "end of the shogunate"—had begun, although the term hadn't yet been coined.

That wasn't the only snag in the government's relations with the "meddlesome" Nariaki. His disapproval of military weakness rankled. He called for the closing of the Dutch and Chinese colonies in Nagasaki and for cancelling visits from Korean ambassadors to prevent Westerners from disguising themselves as members of their retinues and stealing state secrets. Less paranoically, he denounced the retreat from the "Shell and Repel" policy as "extremely regrettable." Foreign vessels should be informed that "even castaways should not be received." And Abe should have replied in Japanese, not Chinese, to the Dutch king's letter counseling greater openness.[22] Weary of that plainspoken—some thought treasonable—criticism, the *bakufu* took the unusual step of removing Nariaki as the Mito daimyo in 1844 and placing him under a kind of house arrest. That punishment, which aggravated the extended Tokugawa family's most dangerous quarrel in a century, came just after Abe's appointment to the *roju*. He signed the humiliating order, but rescinded it soon after acquiring sufficient power in the council, extolling Nariaki in the process: "From the beginning of his administration, [the Mito lord] made special efforts to nourish his fief, reformed ostentatious manners, and thoroughly invigorated study of the civil and military arts. . . . For years, he has labored mightily on defense against foreigners and has prepared coastal defenses on his lands."[23]

More than that, Abe, alone among the *roju*'s members, began seeking his counsel, and the 1846 visit of Commodore Biddle furthered strengthened their ties, prompting some to say Abe was acting on the theory that great skill could put even a poisonous plant to medicinal use. His letters to the Mito lord were conciliatory and respectful (in contrast to Nariaki's characteristically brusque replies). Knowing that "the way to a man's heart is through his son," Abe also courted Nariaki with adroit family politics for advancing the prospects of the latter's son to succeed the present Shogun—which would enable the ambitious father to wield even greater influence. And several years after the "house arrest," four before Perry's arrival, he made him an advisor for maritime defense. Once the Black Ships had anchored, Abe, with his great need of allies as he sought to deal with them, hit his stride with his artful courting of the Mito lord.

However, some *roju* members remained uneasy about Nariaki, who hadn't abandoned what they saw as his destructive indignation about the country's decline. In addition to that aspersion on the *bakufu*, his men had demolished more than two hundred Buddhist temples, ostensibly in order to melt down their bells for recasting into weapons, but probably also in keeping with Nariaki's suppression of Buddhist activity in favor of the more nationalistic, potentially militaristic Shintoism. Abe's victory lay in overcoming the *bakufu*'s suspicion of him. Although he'd previously sought to keep the daimyo divided and weak, he now felt the much more pressing foreign issue required a united front, or at least the appearance of it.

Forging the desired harmony would require all his skill. If "every responsible Japanese official knew in his heart that Japan was powerless,"[24] that hardly settled the issue. As it would be with their descendants in 1941–1945, many angry samurai cared less about bad military odds than about honor. Convinced that defying Perry and destroying his ships would demonstrate "our martial vigor to the whole world," they wanted "all foolish talk of peace" forbidden. The extremists, as they'd later be called, felt that to go down fighting would be far better than to surrender.

The Mito lord's stirring calls for a military buildup to repel the predatory foreigners fortified antiforeign sentiment and raised the tensions straining the *bakufu* higher than they'd been since its founding. Personalities too sometimes threatened rupture. As Conrad Totman has written, cautious Abe "evidently saw no mortal weakness in the [existing] political order"— the shogunate he served—and "preferred to avoid unrest and to resolve conflicts by compromise." Unequivocal Nariaki, who saw Japanese society "in a state of advanced decay," found "policy compromise abhorrent," especially while foreign domination threatened.[25] To stop it, he sometimes resorted to intense intriguing against Abe as well as his policies.

Nevertheless, the Chief Senior Councilor sustained their dialogue and continued seeking what he called Nariaki's "enlightened strategy," for which he'd ridden to his residence when the news of Perry's arrival reached Edo Castle. Abe acted from more than his instinct for compromise and old determination not to provoke the powerful voice of opposition. With a country to be saved from suicidal obstinance, there was an urgent need to convert the elite—great numbers of whom knew virtually nothing about anything foreign—to an accommodation to reality.

SO MANY SO DISLIKED or detested the accommodation that Abe did something unprecedented. Until now, his idiosyncratic listening to ordinary folks' opinions had been almost entirely a personal matter, only loosely related to his official life. As far back as anyone could remember, all major state decisions had been made by consensus among members of the *roju*, with no other participation. Four years earlier, Abe had asked the lords of coastal domains whether the 1842 policy of giving aid to needy foreign ships should be scrapped in favor of restoring the 1825 order to fire at sight. But that was a stratagem partly for keeping everyone happy, one of the tendencies that earned him the criticism for being indecisive. Widening the tiny circle of the makers of state decisions was on very few minds, let alone official agendas.

Two weeks after Perry's departure, however, he took his exceptional venture in that direction. It wasn't for introducing the "unheard-of concept"[26] of participatory government but for soliciting the help he needed. Hoping the *roju* would speak with a unified voice, he "heard only cacophony"—and now the danger of fatal discord as well. His radical new move wasn't to advance Japan from its sometimes suffocating elitism but to cover himself by trying to spread the ignominy of reversing age-old policy, which is another way of saying it was less in response to any democratic instinct than to Perry's force. But England's King John didn't sign the Magna Carta to which some attribute the beginnings of his country's democracy because he wanted to make a statement about human rights, nor did he have the slightest interest in commoners' liberties. Few large steps toward democratic government had been taken anywhere else except under external pressure.

Abe's extraordinary gamble in early August 1853 was to organize a kind of referendum among a thousand-odd important persons. The deep resentment of the implication of Fillmore's message—and of Perry's two additions that sharpened it, topped by what many saw as his warmonger-ing white flags—was a given. But maybe the occasional praise for Perry's restraint from firing and the continued hope that Americans would prove less rapacious than the British would offer some leeway for maneuver. Hoping for that, the Chief Senior Councilor sent copies of the translation of the presidential letter to the daimyo, Confucian scholars, high *bakufu* officials, and even the imperial court: a who's who of the feudal system. What did *they* think about the demands? Should the country open itself or remain closed? Do not, he instructed, feel restricted by the old precedents. Even opinions that might offend the authorities should be expressed with-out hesitation.

Surely his acuity and experience warned him of the danger he was courting. Further undermining the shogunate's claim to wisdom and cred-ibility, the request for advice exposed its policies to discussion and criti-cism. However, the alternative of great loss of face by submission to Perry without outside support might be worse for the government.

The support proved to be weak. Most of the Confucian scholars urged driving off the Americans without making any concessions to them. The previously shackled court agreed. The Emperor's advice was to "Strengthen the coastal defenses."[27] Never mind that he and his advisors had scarcely ventured beyond his palace walls in the old capital of Kyoto, let alone crossed the Kamo River in the city center, to a place where they could conceivably have encountered a barbarian. Wanting protection for his line of nineteen centuries, His Majesty reasoned that a million samurai would make the country safe for two more thousand years of reign by the sun goddess's descendants. His reply to Abe, with its implication that he should be obeyed as in the very old days, revealed that the Chief Senior Council-or's unusual consultation of the Emperor had encouraged him and his supporters. While he had no pretension to resume direct rule, his expres-sion of concern for the country's safety, talk of which spread quickly and far, inched the shogunate-court balance of allegiance farther toward the latter.

Little good news came with the other replies, of which Abe would re-ceive almost eight hundred over the coming months. Most fell into three main categories, one of which advised keeping the Commodore "hanging on" long enough to acquire the means for resisting his demands. Estimates of the time required for implementing that "neutral strategy," or dilatory policy, ranged from five to ten years. Far-fetched as it was to imagine the Americans could be put off that long, Abe would now return to, and much expand, plans for improving Japanese defenses—more, some believed, for waking up those who knew virtually nothing about the outside world to the power of the West than for repelling Perry, which he considered impossible. According to that view, evading foreign and civil strife—for which he had to cautiously persuade the daimyo—remained his first priority. In any case, construction began, after so much talk, for enlarging forts and building new ones; and while some three hundred thousand alarmed patriots made their way to Edo and a smaller number to Kyoto, cannon were cast from monastery bells and rich families' donations of other metal objects.[28]

Another proposed solution might have seemed opposite because it advocated concession. The second group's major spokesman was the daimyo of a substantial *han* some two hundred miles southwest of Edo and not far from Kyoto. The emergence in that role of wealthy Ii Naosuke—one of the forty-five Inside Lords who served as direct retainers of the main Tokugawa house—was surprising, especially since the Black Ships' arrival had sent him hurrying to defend Edo Bay. (The prominent Ii clan was among the most loyal of those most trusted Inside Lords, who resented Abe's consultation with daimyo of lesser prominence and prestige.) That and Ii's urging to strengthen military forces seemed to place him with the exclusionists—of foreigners, of course. But he soon began recommending acceptance of some of Washington's demands, arguing that opening trade would constitute less a radical break from traditional policy than restoration of the older one that had been abandoned when the country was closed. "We must revive the licensed trading vessels that existed [in the early seventeenth century], ordering the rich merchants . . . to take shares in the enterprise."[29] However, the crucial reason wasn't precedent but the inability of "mere maintenance of the old seclusion laws" to ensure the country's safety and tranquility "in the present crisis."

Supporting that opinion, other daimyo would propose limits on trade, such as restricting it to Nagasaki, to Americans and Russians (who had requested it as far back as 1804), to a period of five or six years—and permitting the Americans to use a deserted island as a coaling station but providing no coal because the British, Russians, and French would also demand it.

However, Ii talked loudest for those willing to concede some privileges. A few years hence, he and Tokugawa Nariaki would be battling over a successor to the retarded and childless Shogun Iesada, whose life was expected to be short, with Nariaki championing his own son Keiki and Ii favoring a less antiforeign contender. Now they argued about the crisis.

Not that their long-term aims were opposed. A small minority accepted there was no alternative to opening the country. Some even wanted to scrap most things old in favor of Western science and civilization, but even they hated the prospect of bowing to foreigners while doing it. As for Ii, he explained that one of the purposes of trade would be to "buy time for a future confrontation with the Americans."

All factions were disturbed by the lack of a navy. Ii proposed building powerful warships disguised as merchant vessels for the "secret purpose of training" a proper seaborne force. If the program began immediately, "clever and quick-witted" Japanese would prove equal to Americans and Russians, who, he understood, acquired navigational skills only recently.[30] Dutch mariners would have to be temporarily employed while native crew members studied navigation, ship handling, and modern gunnery—all that would enable Japan to "sail the oceans freely and gain direct knowledge of conditions abroad. . . . Forestalling the foreigners in this way, I believe, is the best method of ensuring that the *bakufu* will at some future time find opportunity to reimpose its ban and forbid foreigners to come to Japan."[31]

That the chief advocate of trade saw opening the country as a tactic in a struggle whose ultimate purpose would be closing it again as quickly as possible testified as strongly as anything to the scope of antiforeign feeling. Other replies to Abe from non saber-rattlers showed that the national crisis was "more serious than any we have faced since the dawn of our history." President's Fillmore's letter, said one, "makes a number of impossible requests." Some of its passages, "such as those in which he threatens the use of force . . . and refers to our national laws as an unenlightened form of government," were "truly outrageous and show the utmost contempt for our country." They make it "absolutely essential, I believe, for us to . . . [completely destroy] his ships."[32]

Many daimyo who saw the country's situation as "in fact helpless," as one put it squarely, wanted to fight nevertheless. The indomitable Yamato spirit of courage and sacrifice—"Yamato" was what early Japanese had called themselves—would eventually win the day, whereas opening Japan to trade, even for a limited time, promised disaster; that "height of disgrace" would subject the discredited government to possible overthrow while humiliating the country before all others. All that being so, Ii believed the country should "make preparations in anticipation of an outbreak of war when the Americans return in the spring."[33]

Of all such voices, Tokugawa Nariaki's remained the most stirring. Trade with Americans, he contended in a letter to Abe titled "Maritime Defense: My Foolish Opinion" and a later "Memorial on the American Demand for a Treaty," would cost the country dearly in imports of consumer goods that gave the country "not the smallest benefit." But the *bakufu*'s first and most urgent task was to choose between war and peace, whose respective advantages and disadvantages he carefully considered. "If we put our trust in War, the whole country's morale will be increased, and even if we sustain an initial defeat, we will in the end expel the foreigner . . . [and] even be able to go out against foreign countries and spread our fame and prestige abroad . . . we must never choose the policy of peace . . ."[34]

More specifically, he predicted war would boost morale tenfold, whereas peace with the foreigners who had committed "abominable" actions would, for whatever temporary tranquility it might bring, lead to "complete collapse." The "arrogant and discourteous" Americans' knowing violation of the prohibition of entry constituted "the greatest disgrace we have suffered since the dawn of our history."

Japan's military prowess was great—as demonstrated, for example, by battles in Korea. (Nariaki didn't mention they'd come hundreds of years earlier.) To fail to expel the Americans would destroy national dignity and open the way to Christianity, the prohibition of which was "the first rule of the Tokugawa house." Although it was "widely stated" that foreigners had no designs apart from trade and that there would be no further difficulty if trade were permitted, "it is their practice to seek a foothold" that way, "and then go on to propagate Christianity":

> The *bakufu* can never ignore or overlook the evils of Christianity. Yet if the Americans are allowed to come again, that religion will inevitably raise its head once more, however strict the prohibition; and this, I fear, is something we could never justify to the spirits of our ancestors.[35]

It would also open the way to further foreign demands, the very misjudgment that had led to China's awful defeat in the Opium War. Yet despite all that, the *bakufu* was failing to strengthen the military. Once the ships that panicked everyone left and orders were given for returning life to normal, everyone relaxed, immediately dispersing the hurriedly assembled military equipment. "It is just as if, regardless of a fire burning beneath the floor of one's house, one neglected all fire-fighting precautions. Indeed, it shows a shameful spirit." But if the government would stop its temporizing and show itself resolute for expulsion, "now and henceforward," the laggard daimyo would be inspired to complete the necessary military preparations "without even the necessity of issuing orders. . . . Let not our generation be the first to see the disgrace of a barbarian army treading on the land where our fathers rest."

Further rousing the leaders who longed to repel or strike back at the Americans, Nariaki's rhetoric made him all but an object of worship by antiforeign patriots. It also pleased Emperor Komei, who, together with his supporters, was growing bolder, although the notion of abolishing the shogunate was still years in the future. When a high imperial advisor pointedly asked how the shogunate intended to calm Komei's unease about the Black Ships, Abe's response moved the balance of the two institutions further toward the throne. No decision had yet been made, the Chief Senior Councilor replied, but nothing would be done without considering the Emperor's peace of mind. He should freely communicate all his future wishes, and Abe would do whatever he was asked.[36]

The leaders who longed to repel composed a large majority. Of the eight hundred-odd replies to Abe's questionnaire, a mere handful favored an abrupt about-face, which would insult "the spirits of our ancestors." Any thought that the seclusion—essentially a Tokugawa policy, since that family had engineered and maintained it—could be abandoned without deforming the nation was shown to be unreal. Although most of the daimyo wanted to avoid war if possible, they agreed almost unanimously about a need to defend the country from foreign pressure. None offered a brilliant solution. Many responses were couched in vague and ambiguous or contradictory language—even more than usual, thanks to their daydreams about confronting Perry. (An even more optimistic subcommander of coastal defense, also a commissioner of finance, recommended taking no action because after a period of calm waiting, the foreigners would go away.) But the critical result was that roughly three-quarters of the lords of the domains had pronounced themselves ready to fight to preserve Japan's sacredness.

The closest approach to the consensus sought by Abe was in the wish to keep the foreigners out, even if no effort should be made until sufficient military strength was acquired, as the moderates recommended. "Whatever we do," a daimyo spelled out, "will be but a stratagem to last until the *bakufu* can complete its military arrangements." Takegawa Chikusai, a wealthy merchant with great interest in foreign affairs, reflected some of the contradictory attitudes toward Americans that were also expressed in block-print news sheets. While touting Japanese superiority, sometimes sarcastically, they depicted foreigners in exaggerated, sometimes witty drawings often accompanied by text that demeaned them. Similar ambivalence colored the great debate. Although Americans fit the image of greedy aggressors intent on making profits by subverting Japanese society and culture, their knowledge and power made them fascinating. If the opening was inevitable, American traders were probably preferable to all others. In any case, Takegawa warned in two treatises on coastal defense that a war for which the country was so ill-prepared must not be fought. Unless the barbarians who visited were blockheads or clay dummies, Japan couldn't win—not even by using dirty tricks, because Westerners no doubt knew more of them from their centuries of fighting among themselves. Futile war could be avoided by permitting peaceful foreign ships to enter some Japanese ports, which would help stabilize the domestic situation as well as being charitable and diplomatically wise.

But even Takegawa—whose opinion didn't count in any case—had no wish for their crews to come ashore or for Japan to join "the community of nations."[37] And the lord of the Toza *han*, whose opinion did count, was far more typical in his warning that Westerners, once admitted, would "subdue . . . our innocent people by giving the impression of brotherhood and good will."[38]

The confirmation of so much disunity was bad enough for Abe, but the expression of support for armed resistance was worse. He knew he had to be extremely careful, for the country's sake as well as his own. Convinced that war with America would be tragic, the question of how to accomplish the extremely unpopular opening without bloodshed became primary.

Months passed. The squeeze tightened as Perry's promised return grew closer and the lethargic pace of major decision making, with no mandate from the "referendum" or stroke of creative thinking, failed to quicken. The Chief Senior Councilor may have decided years before that the *kaikoku* was inevitable, but the prospect of American demand forcing it kept feeding the threat of revolt, perhaps even disintegration.

14

The China Crush and Russian Spur

The American Consulate in Shanghai

THE CHINA TO WHICH PERRY RETURNED in August after his second visit to Okinawa was deep in rebellion. A "state of agitation arguing some mighty revolution," as he'd describe it, had troubled him on his earlier visit, although not for what it was doing to the Chinese people, whom he liked even less than the Japanese. Years later, he'd find himself unable to "bring myself to believe" that they were "entirely devoid of generous impulses and honest convictions."[1] But in the presence of those "most inordinate feeders in the world,"* he scarcely concealed his contempt for

---

* "The Chinese servants employed in the Commodore's cabin ate, in miscellaneous food, including . . . leavings of the table, three times as much as the other attendants. In fact, the enormous quantities of rice they consumed, with whatever else they could seize upon, is almost incredible. As for

what he saw as their gluttony, dishonesty, and deceit. He hesitated to employ local workers to help refloat one of his ships run aground in 1853, fearing that they'd pick his pocket during the operation. So it wasn't surprising that his concern about the country's massive upheaval was almost entirely for its side effects on his mission.

In April and May, when he was preparing for his first thrust on Japan, the insurgent forces that occupied much of the country, including some of the ports used for foreign trade, diverted his attention because American businessmen in China, mostly in Shanghai, wanted protection from the East Asia Squadron. The American Commissioner who declared that nothing hoped for in Japan could equal the huge opportunities already existing in China believed Perry's duty lay where already settled Americans were being menaced. Those "defenseless" fellow citizens were "crying from all quarters for protection," the demanding man wailed—and was convinced their situation became worse during the squadron's fourteen weeks in Okinawa and Japan. Spreading into a virtual civil war, the rebellion made the claims on Perry's guns even more insistent. Shortly after his return to Hong Kong, a group of prominent American merchants wrote him that they could "scarcely magnify the importance of the present crisis in the affairs of this country or the influence . . . upon the prosperity of our commerce and the safety of our intercourse."

Actually, they much exaggerated the danger to themselves. The violent Taiping Rebellion, as the collection of essentially antiestablishment uprisings was known, did pose a huge threat to the Manchu dynasty—China's last, which would be toppled by Sun Yat-sen some sixty years later, in 1911. Support by the poor for the revolt that was killing tens of millions of Chinese understandably frightened foreigners with the threat of losing more than the trading privileges they'd secured from the government. Still, Perry had reason to resist their demands.

Not that he suddenly lost sympathy for business interests. On the contrary, he was, an American historian would state later in the century, the first official to see the Pacific's commercial and political problems as one and the same. "No American before his time, and few after it, ever had such an extensive ambition."[2] But the Commodore believed the rebellion

---

sugar and other sweets, there would have been no end to their pilfering, if they had not been carefully watched by the steward. This gross feeding exhibited its effects upon the Chinese servants, as it does upon dumb animals, for they soon became fat and lazy." *Narrative*, p. 200.

didn't menace those interests. "However the Chinese may have . . . cut each other's throats," no foreigner conducting himself properly "had been in the least degree molested," he asserted. Still seeing fatter fish for the traders to fry, he limited the squadron's use in China to showing the flag and making short voyages to bolster American groups who believed they were in special danger. He refused to allow his ships or the coal they'd need to be deflected from his primary goal of the opening of Japan that promised to boost the China trade. Remaining committed to "working upon the fears of the [Japanese] rulers," he knew the ships that did the frightening sorely needed repair. Summer heat and humidity had much weakened the canvas and cordage in particular, and protracted use of the steamers' engines with the minimum maintenance that could be performed at sea had done the same to pistons and valves. Finding fuel for the steamers made additional demands on his time and energy.

THAT ENERGY WAS DIMINISHED enough for the fifty-nine-year-old Commodore to ask to be relieved of command of the squadron. While his request for new orders took its considerable time to reach Washington and be acted upon there, the "wear and tear both of body and mind," as he put it, seemed as damaging as to his ships. The oppressive climate, "cares of command," and Washington's failure to provide the full squadron left him with "much to overcome." After a bad cold, probably worsened by exhaustion, his arthritis acted up again. "This cruise," he wrote his wife, "will use me pretty well up."[3] "The Commodore himself," he'd later elaborate, was "worn out by duties which were more than unusually heavy, in consequence of the supervision of the labors in connection with the accumulated results of the expedition, and large correspondence that became necessary" from the fears of the American merchants. "Finally prostrated," he "suffered from an attack of illness."[4]

Writing the Secretary of the Navy "from a sickroom," he permitted self-pity to tint his customary appreciation of himself, who'd "seen more service than any other Captain in the Navy." His cruises "on the deleterious coast of Africa and the Gulf of Mexico following so close upon each other and the still more trying climate of this [Asian] station have greatly impaired my health." Another year or more of service would probably be added "if [he] survived."

Apart from uncertainty about how Japan would receive him, the previous spring's visit to China had been less taxing. During the weeks he spent in Shanghai, he stayed on "the embankment": the already famous Bund of big banks, Western-style trading houses, and imposing mansions—the "numerous splendid dwellings," the Commodore observed, although he found the city, and others in China, "disgustingly filthy."[5] Many of the residences had been built after the recent Opium War. Little as it was known back home, the British victory of 1842 proved a boon for American merchants too, all the more because opium was replacing a declining supply of furs as a source of money for buying the Chinese silks, porcelains, and tea that were fetching fine prices in the States. Clippers also transported considerable quantities of opium itself to America, where it was still legal.

No one benefitted more than the principals of Russell and Company, later called the nineteenth century's largest American criminal organization because it was the world's leading dealer in the drug. Among its founders was William Huntington Russell, who cofounded Yale University's elite Skull and Bones society with Alphonso Taft, later the father of William Howard Taft, who would become the twenty-seventh U.S. president. Russell and Company's partners included future big benefactors of Princeton and Columbia Universities and a cofounder of the Council on Foreign Relations. The senior partner in China during the immensely profitable 1840s defended the trade as "fair, honorable, and legitimate," although morally unjustifiable. He was Warren Delano, Franklin Delano Roosevelt's grandfather.

(Townsend Harris, the soon-to-be first American consul in Japan, would delete mention of opium from his journal. Some who had made great fortunes from it eased their consciences in philanthropy, already characteristically American. Robert Bennet Forbes, who joined Russell and Company in 1830 and became one of the most prominent China traders, sent food to Ireland during the potato famine of 1845–1850.)

Perry's attitude was similar, for although he'd decry the "abominable traffic in opium," his Shanghai residence during that spring of 1853 was a magnificent mansion on the Bund that belonged to the same Russell and Company. The sumptuously quartered Commodore was also in much better health than now, on this second visit, when he had the additional bad luck of having picked a poor place for the bed to which his "attack of illness" drove him. This time he'd rented a house in Macao, chosen for its location near Hong Kong, Canton, and a little harbor that the squadron, reinforced by the additional ships arriving from the States, was using as a rendezvous.

Although much farther south than Shanghai, Macao was known as a "remarkably salubrious" summer residence of many Hong Kong and Canton rich. But that summer's uncommon heat worsened a collection of sicknesses. Perry's under-strength crews, already further reduced by punishments for crimes and disciplinary infractions, were further weakened by painful skin problems, a "low, nervous fever," as Samuel Wells Williams described his own, and debilitating infectious diseases, including malaria. "Scarcely an officer or man escaped an attack of fever of more or less severity." The deaths included the *Mississippi*'s bandmaster and Lieutenant Adams of the *Powhatan*, which had joined the squadron as Perry's new flagship. The Commodore knew so much about the workings of his ships, including the steam engines that needed overhaul, that many decisions would have gone to him even if he didn't sweat details so copiously. Fever tired him that much more.

When up to it, he attended some grand social events, including swish dinners and balls hosted by opium traders, which were reciprocated with entertainment by his officers and men, some on the *Powhatan* (named for the Indian chief who ruled coastal Virginia when Jamestown was settled in 1607). Otherwise, although he often remained bedridden, his work was crucial because so many of his talents were needed to prep the squadron, while fending off the ever-insistent, sometimes peremptory American Commissioner who believed himself entitled to decide its disposition and duty. Perry also encouraged the expedition's artists and sightseers to get on with their work of reporting and depicting what they were exploring. The most interesting pen belonged to twenty-nine-year-old Bayard Taylor, one of nineteenth-century America's best travel writers, who'd met Perry during his first China stay and won his reluctant consent to join the expedition.

Soon after Perry had settled in feverish Macao, the spirited Taylor embarked on a fourteen-week return voyage to New York, where he quickly published the first eyewitness account of the mission-in-progress in the influential *New York Tribune*. The expedition's other members had reason for wonder when they heard of Taylor's articles (which would be incorporated in his *A Visit to India, China, and Japan, in the Year 1853,* published two years later). Everyone under Perry's command had been prohibited "from making any communication to the newspapers and other public prints touching the movements of the squadron or the discipline and internal regulations of the vessels composing it." His permission would be required for publication of even private letters and notes, which in any case were to "avoid those topics" of the squadron's mood and movements.[6]

Although the Secretary of the Navy had imposed the censorship, Perry's approval, if not inspiration, was evident. Not surprisingly, he justified it in terms of terms of security needs and attributed it to his instructions, which added that

> All journals and private notes . . . were to be considered as belonging to the government until permission should be given from the Navy Department to publish them. The object of these regulations was to withhold information from other powers which, if communicated, might jeopard [*sic!*] the success of our mission.

A scattering of members risked ignoring the ban and later published chronicles they'd hid. They included translator Samuel Wells Williams, Lieutenant George Henry Preble, the future admiral who dryly noted that "to hear [Perry] was to obey," and an officer on one of the ships that would join the squadron for its second visit to Japan, John McIntosh Kell of the sloop *Vandalia,* who saw Perry as prepared to use force, although "from what I have heard of the Japanese, we will have no just cause to go to war with them." Some reflections of a fourth writer, a sailor named Thomas Dudley on the newly arrived *Powhatan,* might have been burned if they'd been found, for questioning whether foreign ships had "a right to ascend bays and rivers of another country and make surveys" over all objections. Dudley, a purser's clerk from Yonkers, New York, had no love for the Commodore. "If I ever despised a man, it is Perry and I question much if he is entitled to be called a man." He and his fellows had taken to calling him not "Old Bruin" but " 'old hog'—'beast' and such like." The crew of the *Powhatan,* now flying the Commodore's flag, felt differently about him than his own official account implied. For Dudley in particular, "who loathed Perry's vanity and penchant for autocratic rule," grumbling about him became "a blood sport."[7]

But despite eventual publication of those rare surreptitious letters and memoirs, the Commodore was largely successful in restricting media access, which helped shape his image with the American public. That was why he'd subjected Bayard Taylor to the same military gag by commissioning him into naval service before taking him aboard, as with the handful of other civilian specialists he hired under the same absolute authority.[8]

The new master's mate Taylor's initial impression of his commander was of "a blunt, honest old fellow and well-disposed towards me."[9] But what mattered were his *New York Tribune* contributions that praised Perry for his "firmness, dignity and fearlessness," his great skill and prudence. Having calculated that the dispatches would throw a flattering light on the squadron and himself, the Commodore made certain by reading every line before authorizing Taylor's departure for New York, with exemption from the forbiddance for his juniors to write or publish anything about the mission.

FROM THE MOMENT the Commodore returned to China, what the Russians called the nineteenth century's "dearest mineral" and Perry lauded as "that great mineral agent of civilization, *coal* [italics in the original],"[10] rarely left his thoughts. The snatching of a small supply from under his nose, as he saw it, prompted predictable anger, all the more because a Russian did it.

It was no surprise that Russia, with its relative proximity to Japan and with the Kuril Islands as stepping-stones, had been trying to open it long before young America began. Those efforts, initially by explorers, fishermen, and fur traders excited by tales of Japanese riches, were probably the first of any foreign power since the national closing had been fully enforced. Russian probings became more systematic and insistent under Peter the Great in the late seventeenth and early eighteenth centuries (although Catherine the Great would later pronounce Japanese goods not worth a sou). An early official venture was made in 1804, when a small delegation took advantage of a slight, temporary relaxation of *sakoku* rules to travel to Japan to request trade privileges. Refusal didn't deter St. Petersburg, the new capital of a great power whose economic surge and territorial expansion was second only to that of the United Sates. As Americans were pushing west to the Pacific, even more daring Russians were pushing east, across

Siberia's Amur River and into distant Kamchatka and Alaska. At the same time, the Tsarist government sought to prevent Britain and the United States from obtaining the same hold on Japan that they'd secured on China. Fearing the Russians wanted more than trade, Edo, in turn, tried to stop them by sending expeditions to Sakhalin Island and what would become their northern main island of Hokkaido, over which the despised Ainu still exercised some control. In 1811, their troops collared a little Russian force surveying the Kuril Islands. It was led by Vasili Golovnin, the naval captain who would develop fond feelings for his captors during his incarceration.[11]

The Deshima Dutch did nothing to diminish Edo's suspicion that the Russians' every move near and onto their land, sometimes in armed raids on villages, was in preparation for invasion. Although distant Washington had no reason for such anxiety, it too mistrusted St. Petersburg's intentions, especially the imputed one to "make the north Pacific a Russian lake." "There is no power in the other hemisphere to which the possession of Japan, or the control of its affairs, is as it is to Russia,"[12] an official paper warned.

That didn't stop Russian-American cooperation in some matters. After the British and French had wrested concessions from China, St. Petersburg and Washington would demand the same for themselves, getting their traders in on the profits but avoiding some of the imperialist stigma. But Perry in particular, with his all-American ambition and conviction the Almighty blessed it,[13] much disliked and distrusted the Russians, in whom he also saw a threat of its becoming "a great maritime power." If that autocracy came to dominate the Pacific, it would menace his Land of the Free, perhaps provoking a huge conflict, "Cossack struggling against Saxon . . . the antagonistic opponents of freedom and absolutism." Even after returning from the mission, the Commodore would predict absolutist Russia and free, rational America would one day join "a mighty battle . . . on which the world will look with breathless interest; for on its issue will depend the freedom or slavery of the world." Meanwhile, his focus was narrower. The Commodore's study of Japan had roused suspicion of Russia's long-standing designs on it, and he propagated the notion that St. Petersburg might somehow take possession of the closed country.

While he waited in Macao, discovery that a group of Russian ships was headed for Japan right then, just as his own were preparing to return, shook him considerably more. Four warships had been dispatched from the

Kronstadt naval base some six weeks before his *Mississippi* had departed from Norfolk in November 1852. The number was coincidental, but not the timing. News of Perry's preparations had disturbed the Russians, just as news of their preparations agitated him. "If Commodore Perry," he'd write of himself, "unfortunately should fail in his peaceful attempts," to open Japan and become involved in hostilities, "Russia was on the spot, not to mediate, but to tender to Japan her aid as an ally in the conflict."[14] Keeping intelligence about the mission "from the eyes and ears of the Russians and of any other people who might be planning a similar project" was an additional reason the Commodore offered for his strict censorship of others' writings during the voyage.[15]

The Russian force of late 1852 was commanded by Vice Admiral Efimii Vasilievich Putiatin, a distinguished officer whose imposing appearance and long experience in battle and statecraft—even his contribution to converting the Russian fleet to steam, although at first by purchase from England rather than domestic manufacture—roughly matched Perry's.[16] Delayed by hardships at sea and shipboard disorder, the squadron reached Canton in June 1853, shortly after the Commodore's had left for Japan via Okinawa. Putiatin told the American consul there he'd try to find Perry and propose cooperation in opening Japan, a suggestion much disliked by the suspicious Commodore, who was "unwilling to do anything that would give the Russians the slightest encouragement."[17] The Russian squadron, led by the flagship *Pallada*, actually arrived in Japan some three weeks after Perry had delivered the Fillmore letter and left for China again, via Okinawa.

Thus Putiatin came within those weeks of being first to deliver a letter, his addressed to the Governor of Nagasaki and the "Supreme Council" rather than to the Emperor. Even if he'd succeeded, however, the Vice Admiral was very unlikely to have beaten the Commodore to the punch because he never threatened to use force.

Russian admiration for the Japanese landscape matched that of the Americans. "What is this? Stage scenery or reality?" asked Ivan Goncharov, a talented novelist and essayist serving as Putiatin's secretary as well as the expedition's official chronicler. "Nothing frightening, everywhere nature was smiling: behind the hills . . . one greener than the other . . . the fields and meadows were smiling too."[18] But that was the beauty of Nagasaki, not Uraga Bay. Unlike Perry, Putiatin complied with the demand that he remove himself to where the Japanese relegated all intercourse with foreigners, at that great distance from Edo. And he did not bluster or brandish his big guns by "practice" firing them, let alone threaten bombardment—although the mere presence of his squadron almost contemporaneously with the American one helped convince the *bakufu* that the seclusion couldn't be sustained; surrender to Perry was their only realistic alternative. In an obvious analogy to foreigners, a Japanese historian would soon comment that "No matter how much you chase away flies on food, they'll gather in the same way."[19]

Putiatin waited three months in and around Nagasaki before departing for Okinawa with no conclusive answer to his government's request for trade. Whatever his personal ambition for Russia, his orders were to exercise restraint, and he obeyed them. Russia and Japan had border issues, most concerning Sakhalin and the Kuril Islands. Nicholas I had instructed Putiatin to "be as indulgent as possible (without compromising our interests)" about them, "bearing in mind that the achievement of the other goal—trade benefits—is of vital importance to us."

Although also greatly irritated by Edo's temporizing, deception, invention of excuses and discovery of new reasons for yet more delay, the Vice Admiral and his officers won the locals' respect by being less racist and more polite than the Americans. When visiting ashore, Putiatin made way for others to pass, sometimes even kneeling; and he publicly scolded a sailor of his who had cut down some trees. His men behaved better than Perry's, a few of whom would, during his second visit, get drunk and cause incidents, although some people might have expected that more of the Russians. Putiatin's officers in particular were more tolerant of cultural differences and more admiring of Japanese virtues than the Americans had been, and also less inclined to attribute *bakufu* deviousness to evil than to the bad luck of having to conform to a twisted system's rules. Their lesser arrogance was rewarded with permission to obtain firewood and potable water all along the coast (although Tokugawa Nariaki twice urged Abe to have the entire crew massacred).[20] Perhaps it also helped the Russians win slightly more favorable terms than the Americans when treaties with Edo would be signed in 1855.

Putiatin's Japanese ventures would nevertheless end unhappily. Playing hide-and-seek with British and French ships during that run-up to the Crimean War, he sailed in and out of Nagasaki three times from July 1853 to March 1854. He'd be in the town of Shimoda during the latter year when a devastating earthquake flattened it and the resulting tidal wave destroyed his flagship. With local help, the Vice Admiral and his crew managed to build a new ship[21] and to get home in time for Putiatin to participate importantly in the Crimean War that would distract Russia from its interest in Japan, as the Civil War would do to America six years later.

Now, in early 1854, Perry and Putiatin remained in acute competition, at least as the Commodore saw it. The Secretary of the Navy had been among those who had informed him of the dispatch of Putiatin's ships for, the Secretary assumed, "the laudable pursuit in which the squadron under your command is now engaged." But the Commodore whose every cell seemed to exude patriotism believed no European foray, Russian or any other, could be laudable. On this second visit to China, when his eagerness to block rather than encourage any possible venture by a rival fleet waxed still further, he'd been buying up all the coal he could—and he became furious when he learned that an American in charge of naval stores responded to Putiatin's pleas by lending him, in violation of the Commodore's orders, twenty tons of that carefully amassed supply.

Perry had intended to sail back to Japan in the spring if 1854, as he'd repeatedly warned officials at Uraga. Soon after returning to China, however, he began thinking of shortening his wait. Every hint of competition aroused him; every distraction and delay refurbishing his ships sparked anger. In Macao, he heard hints about French intentions too, and assumed the unknown destination for which a French squadron was buying supplies in Hong Kong, as he'd heard, was Edo. Now, in January, the much more infuriating news of Putiatin's acquisition of "his" coal prompted a decision to leave immediately. "The intelligence mentioned above induced me to alter my plans. . . . I determined—rather than allow either the French or the Russians to gain an advantage over me—to encounter all the inconveniences and exposures of a cruise to Japan with so large a force in mid winter, regardless of the terrible accounts given by writers, of the storms and fogs and other dangers to be met with on this inhospitable coast in the inclement season."[22]

It remained only to brush aside a last-minute Japanese attempt to stop him. In a letter sent through the Dutch colony, Edo told him that domestic difficulties rendered consideration of momentous changes in national policy temporarily impossible. The Emperor had died, requiring ceremonies for his replacement's accession, then three years of mourning.* (Edo informed Putiatin that the death rendered the government unable to transact important business for a year.) Perry should therefore inform his "king" of the reasons for a necessary delay.

The error about President Fillmore—despite the knowledge elsewhere in Japan that America was a republic—matched the Commodore's confusion, which Edo had been doing its best to protract, about who was governing Japan. Noting that nothing had been said about the illness "of the Emperor of Japan" during his first visit there, so relatively recently, Perry concluded that the statement notice of his death was "a mere *ruse* to obstruct the American negotiations." Even later, after accepting that "the Emperor" had indeed died, "there seemed to be no reason for the delay in public business" because it was never interrupted when Chinese Emperors died, and Perry inferred the same was true of Japan. "The Commodore was not . . . to be deterred from the prosecution of his plans by any unfavorable intelligence which those"—he didn't actually name the Dutch—"who might be disposed to obstruct them."[23]

Back in Japan, some *roju* members had opposed attempting to discourage Perry from returning, arguing the tactic would have a reverse effect.[24] However insightful that might have been, the Commodore needed no such additional spur. Although the winter sea indeed often threw up dangerous fogs and storms, the cause called. Rumors about the French designs were bad enough, but Putiatin, who might "interfere very seriously with my operations," was worse. Ignoring a Navy Department order to leave one of his three steamers in China, the incipient Russophobe sailed from Hong Kong to Edo Bay, via Naha, on January 14, 1854. "The Commodore . . . hoped the present rulers of Japan" would present no obstacles to "accomplishing friendly relations between the American nation and the Japanese."[25]

---

* It was Shogun Tokugawa Ieyoshi who had died, but the Japanese knew Perry remained unaware of the distinction, and they kept him so without lying outright by inventing a new word in their letter. Translated as "Crowned Head," it avoided using "Shogun" or "Emperor." Shiba Ryotaro, *The Last Shogun*, p. 28.

15

The Nonsolution

An illustration of an apocryphal report of harlots exchanging favors for squadron supplies from the Black Ship Scroll *painted in Shimoda, one of two treaty ports opened in 1854*

HEN PERRY HEADED BACK TOWARD OKINAWA, then Edo in mid-January, the Emperor was among the majority of politically active Japanese who remained staunchly opposed to establishing relations with America. Still convinced that preservation of Japan's unique culture depended on maintaining its isolation, the marginally reempowered monarch increasingly disparaged the government's dithering. What was taking it so long to end the clamor caused by the foreigners, those "unclean beasts?"[1] Abe and the *roju* continued assuring they'd be properly dealt with, but their clinging to the overriding nondecision to "evade any definite answer" to Perry in the hope he'd eventually become discouraged further diminished His Majesty's confidence in that body—and in the *bakufu*, that "nest of robbers," as a whole. Although not all criticism of the shogunate was so blunt, converts to the cause of restoring more authority to the throne continued growing.

At the same time, Abe kept trying to fortify defenses. With adherents of almost every argument for dealing with Perry stressing the need for a navy,[2] the Chief Senior Councilor had ordered some sixty ships from the Dutch in September.[3] The prohibition of constructing native warships was repealed the following month, and work began on a network of major gun emplacements closer to Edo than older ones in the bay. But those measures revealed evidence of daydreaming. Perry's frigates could have made mince-meat of the mere three of the sixty vessels that would be steam powered, and the new coastal defenses would take five years to complete. The full network, which lack of funds had already reduced from a proposed eleven batteries to three, would never be more than a chimera. The first phase of their construction, some five miles south of the capital (halfway to present-day Haneda airport), unnerved nearby residents. Realization that American shells aimed at the batteries might destroy their houses sent their Black Ship anxiety soaring again.

With antagonism to the government growing "to such a pitch that on any question, irrespective of its merits," powerful interests would oppose it,[4] Abe composed countless letters of explanation and advocacy, all with his characteristic tact and grace. He also met repeatedly with the key political figures, sometimes in Edo Castle and sometimes in their quarters, to render them honor. When he felt a letter or note delivered by messenger wouldn't do for Tokugawa Nariaki, he traveled to his residence in a village some three miles from the castle. The "ever placatory," never moralizing Chief Senior Councilor kept trying to appease one and all, including many whom his predecessors wouldn't have thought of consulting.

Abe's practice of talking to people of all opinions reinforced his reputation for inability to make up his mind. Seeking a hard-liner's support, the *roju shuseki* was pictured assuring him that although he really wanted to revive the samurai spirit, he doubted this was the time to argue about how. But to an official who leaned toward conciliation with the Americans, he was portrayed saying that although his real intention was also to arrange a limited opening to them, the Mito lord must first be won over in order to prevent revolt by the exclusionists. Trying to pin Abe down, a prominent daimyo asked whether it was then true that he, the Chief Senior Councilor, wouldn't go along with the Mito lord. Abe's elusive answer—that he'd follow the course that "benefits the nation"—was seen as demonstrating the fatal cost of indecision.

Domestic and foreign problems were inseparably entwined. While acceptance of Nariaki's stance threatened to provoke the unwinnable military conflict that might destroy the *bakufu*, the government might also be dealt a mortal blow if widespread resentment of willingness to make concessions, especially about trade, pushed Nariaki into open opposition. Everyone else's failure to propose a realistic policy didn't soften criticism of the *roju*'s lame decision to give Perry no real answer. Abe's "slippery as an eel" label seemed to enlarge as exhaustion diminished him physically.

Never more publicly criticized, the hesitant *bakufu* also seemed never less in control, and the truth was that Abe still didn't know what to do. Beyond his feeling that the *sakoku*'s end was inevitable and conviction that war with America would be disastrous, he had no positive policy to offer, even after casting his unprecedentedly wide net for advice. To people who wanted war, Abe seemed ready "to give Perry 'a firm reply' that would in all probability lead to war. To the daimyo Shimazu Nariakira, who wanted peace and trade, he also seemed to want peace and trade."[5]

Shimazu Nariakira was central to another major mare's nest that had recently opened amid multiple minor ones. His answer to the question of questions was that the Americans would be unlikely to accept a "no," and Japan would have no chance of rejecting them. Even if an attempt succeeded at first, he wrote Abe in September, "we know that they have ships that can traverse the seas at will . . . [and] they can at any time interrupt our sea communications."

The complication arising from that counsel derived from a convoluted relationship between the Shoguns and the Shimazu family, whose connection to the Ryukyus explained their anxiety about sea communications. Ever since the failure of those powerful lords of Satsuma province to support Tokugawa Ieyasu's sixteenth-century campaign to win control of a united Japan,[6] Edo Castle had kept those hereditary adversaries of theirs in the far south at a political as well as geographical distance. The alienation wasn't complete, however. After the Shimazus invaded Okinawa in 1609, the Tokugawas demanded a share of the profits squeezed from the island's foreign trade, and took it until the present time. Besides, the late Shogun Tokugawa Ieyoshi's widow was a Shimazu.

The Ryukyus also provided valued connections to the outside world. After a French squadron visited Okinawa in 1844, the then Shimazu daimyo sought permission to use the island kingdom as a conduit for trade with France. It was a measure of Abe's open-mindedness or concern about the increasing pressures from the West that instead of rejecting that astonishing request out of hand, he consulted with the daimyo's son, whose command of Dutch and insistent curiosity had given him rare knowledge of the outside world. Even then, nine years before Perry, the Chief Senior Councilor thought of using such trade to ease into cautious modification or even abandonment of the seclusion.

The learned, accomplished son he consulted was that Shimazu Nariakira, one of the daimyo who responded to the *roju*'s September "referendum" about how to respond to Perry. Abe's influence and intrigue had helped persuade his father to abdicate, so the youngish man whose hunger for knowledge made him attractive to the Chief Senior Councilor became the Satsuma lord. Like a substantial proportion of the few Japanese conversant with Western thoughts and ways, he wanted the *sakoku* to end and foreign trade to be resumed, but not for itself. With "temerity" but not "reserve," he now recommended an approach based on his regard for Western scholarship primarily as a means for acquiring enough military technology to repel European encroachment. Although approval of Perry's profoundly disturbing request would give him "the greatest fears for the future of our country," rejection might prompt the Americans to open hostilities when they returned. Therefore, time should be gained by sending them away with the explanation that the government had no other choice. After three or so years of great effort to complete military preparations, Japan's military spirit, which has "always been heroic," would help ensure victory.

But only if the right man was in overall command. Considering age, popular esteem, and knowledge of foreign affairs, Shimazu believed the most suitable man was the uncompromising Tokugawa Nariaki. "I therefore respectfully submit my request that the *bakufu* may entrust him with the duties of coastal defense."[7]

EVEN WITHOUT SHIMAZU NARIAKIRA'S ENDORSEMENT, Tokugawa Nariaki's stance appeared to be gaining popularity, in keeping with the virtually unanimous wish to keep the Americans out and the at least verbal commitment to the military buildup for which he'd long been calling. Together with increasingly assertive voices at the court in Kyoto, some of the most powerful daimyo and their leading subordinates supported the Mito lord. Their mood was suggested by a commander of a guard force who was more worried by the spiraling prices of weapons and armor than possible war. "We don't have to be afraid of the Americans and their guns," one of the block print news sheets quoted the defiant samurai. "If we decide to go to war, I'll kill them."[8]

But something unexpected happened as the Mito lord's advantage grew: he failed to press it. More than that, he partially retreated from his rejection of all things foreign except technology. Still distressed by military weakness, he admonished the lackadaisical *bakufu* to truly exhort the daimyo to complete the new installations. For now, people were "temporizing and half-hearted; and even though the Shogun exhort them day and night, he cannot make them resolute."[9] But performing what appeared to be a near about-face on other of his courses to save the country, he replaced his appeals for resoluteness with what he called "a temporizing and time-serving policy." Instead of decrying foreigners, he began warning of the danger of provoking their anger.

The essence of Nariaki's new brief was that "driving away the barbarians might not be such a good idea now." If attacked, the Americans might temporarily withdraw from Edo Bay, but only to prepare an attack of their own, maybe easily seizing a nearby island to do so, and also sinking the rice-bearing junks on which the capital depended. Therefore Edo should placate rather than fight them.

If the push for that turnaround was fear that the so-called dilatory policy's stalling might be used as a pretext for an American strike, its pivot was the Mito lord's view of Perry himself. Back in July, the Commodore's loud cannon "salutes" and goading white flags had registered deeply, but Nariaki kept his reaction to himself until well after the squadron's departure for Okinawa and China. A Japanese commentator would describe him as having climbed to the peak of a steep mountain, from where he could neither go higher nor back down. Stuck there, he sustained his rhetoric of thirty-odd years about expelling; but knowing Perry's guns had rendered it unreal, he privately said his actual purpose was to raise morale, not provoke Perry into starting hostilities. Previous Western visitors "never intended to start a war," he added; when fired upon, they departed. "But now they come spoiling for a fight," purposely waiting to be attacked—which would "just be playing into their hands" by providing an excuse to invade and exact even greater concessions.

The veteran hard-liner hadn't become a dove. The *bakufu*, he advocated, should only *show* itself as accommodating to Perry while the rest of the country, from which the strategy must be kept secret, should continue preparing for possibly unavoidable war. In other words, negotiate in secret while proclaiming a hard line in public, as "War at home, peace abroad," the name of his new policy, indicated. With the people inspired to fight, the government could afford to be cordial to the intruders. Asked for clarification, he said the idea wasn't to seek American friendship by granting their boundless demands but to prepare to smash them "without a second thought" if they started a war despite their civil reception.[10]

Still, that was a step back from outright hostility. In addition to greater reality on Nariaki's part, it showed the wisdom of Abe's determination to have the Mito lord on his side. Nevertheless, no hint of harmony relieved the tension in Edo. Still fearing Perry would attack, Nariaki pressed for a "great proclamation" that the entire country—samurai, peasants, artisans, and merchants; all four classes—should prepare for war. Moved by his threat to resign as defense advisor if it weren't issued, Abe asked him to prepare a draft. In it, Nariaki exhorted the people to recognize the great peril of continuing to live their peaceful lives, unresolved to cope with the encroaching foreign ships. Evidently judging the language too strong, Abe penned a revision while many government officials objected to issuing any such statement at all while the country was too weak to defend itself.

Nariaki, in turn, insisted nothing was more important to mounting an adequate defense than arousing united popular resolve, his key to victory. If it was double-talk to simultaneously inform foreigners that trade would be possible and to assure the country that no such thing would be permitted, that was what the national emergency demanded: military action had to be postponed until Japan was ready, while the people were assured the Americans would be expelled. Everything depended on delaying the conflict until a severe blow could be delivered.

When Nariaki submitted his supplementary arguments in mid-October, the responsible *bakufu* officials again objected, but he trumped them by asking to resign, and the government gave in. The final text of the great proclamation promulgated on December 1, 1853, was a kind of compromise between the Mito lord and his critics in that it didn't keep the real government plan secret, as he'd wanted, but did call on the country to prepare for war that the Americans might launch.[11]

Despite the defiant ring, the larger compromise came closer to calling for peace than for war. Meanwhile, the prospect of the Commodore's return, still expected in the spring, further energized the debates. Various new and revised slants were advanced, such as a notion that a treaty with America would prevent the European powers from imposing even harder terms, and that humane treatment of castaways and even the opening of some remote port for trade wouldn't threaten Japanese civilization. Still, nothing definite was decided. Months of fierce arguments had made the solution somewhat less vague than the *roju*'s "evade any definite answer" in hope a discouraged Perry would leave, but little more realistic. Both new plans were weak to the point of uselessness. The first, about granting the American requests but postponing their implementation, was based on the illusion that it might satisfy Perry. The second, about preparing for war should the Commodore react to the stalling by starting one, was an expression of the old wishful thinking.

16

The Hated Treaty

"The Great Bridge of Senju" from One Hundred Views of Edo, *woodcuts by Hiroshige Utagawa*

THE EAST ASIA SQUADRON'S RETURN to Japan sparked little of the previous summer's anguish. Huge foreign ships with mighty guns were no longer a revelation, and Edo Castle had expected the black ones, if not so soon and not with so many additions. Although Perry hadn't been sent *all* the firepower he'd wanted, the ten ships now under his command comprised roughly a quarter of the American navy, including many of its best. The latest American paddle frigate, the barely year-old *Powhatan* that had joined the steamers *Mississippi* and *Susquehanna*, stood out among the ships a Japanese observer saw filling "the whole bay." Four nine-inch and thirty-eight eight-inch guns, plus a large array of smaller ones, made the squadron the most powerful Washington had ever sent on a mission abroad.

The Commodore further fortified himself with the conviction that if he "receded in the least" from any position he'd taken, the Japanese would consider it a victory. "Finding that I could be induced to change a prede-termined intention in one instance, they might rely on prevailing on me by dint of perseverance to waver in most other cases."[1] At the same time, he saw himself as wanting to do everything possible "that might conciliate."

A winter storm blew icy spray on shivering sailors when the force en-tered the Uraga Channel on February 13, but the ships maintained their remarkable speed, "pennants flying, wheels turning, gun muzzles out, crews formed up amidships, and all approaching in faultless alignment."[2] Ignoring a small flotilla of guard boats as they pushed further into Edo Bay, "the strangers moved majestically on," their commander would re-cord, past the "harmless" native forts, the Kurihama hall where he'd pre-sented President Fillmore's letter, and the island the Americans had named "Perry." Not "altering their course a degree, or lingering a moment in their speed," the "train of formidable men-of-war"[3] approached demon-strative miles closer to the capital than in July before stopping at the "American Anchorage" in the early afternoon. Again commanding that no communication be made with the shore, Perry also ordered the squadron's boats to prepare for more surveying of the bay's upper reaches.

The Japanese guard boats rushed to the anchorage while land units took up positions along the shore. Also as before, cannon and military sup-plies jammed the highways to Edo and coastal residents were warned not to approach the foreigners. But as droves of them hurried to observe the great force, little sense of imminent disaster returned, and the rumors about the barbarians were markedly lower in pitch, as if the excitement had gone the way of the summer's vivid greens replaced by winter gray.[4] "Our country is a land of military prowess and a land of righteousness, beyond compare with the foreign red hairs," informed a news sheet in a story about a counterattack that would soon destroy American ships and 3,700 of their men in a single stroke.[5] Imagination aside, most people, although still kept ignorant of Perry's demands by the government, had already jettisoned some myths together with the better part of their panic. Great nuisance that foreign ships were, few Edo residents evacuated.

Nevertheless, the question of how to deal with the Black Ships remained unanswered. Abe had more or less decided to provision visiting American vessels at fair prices, to more generously minister to shipwrecked seamen, and, probably, to make arrangements for providing limited supplies of coal. But everything else remained fraught with the prospect of civil strife, on top of the threat, as most Japanese saw it, that Perry might strike even if full submission to him was made.

Meanwhile, the Commodore, still maintaining his ceremonial aloofness, refused to see a group of Japanese officials "of subordinate authority" who appeared by boat soon after the squadron had anchored. Told to talk to the *Powhatan*'s captain, they insisted that negotiations could be conducted only back at Uraga, some dozen miles farther south, where high officials were waiting. Through the captain, Perry countered—from his cabin, where he was suffering another arthritis attack—that he'd meet the Japanese negotiators on shore opposite the present anchorage. "But if the Japanese government would not consent to that, the Commodore would move his ships higher up the bay, even, if it should be deemed necessary, to Edo itself."[6]

Government representatives reappeared the following day to announce that if Uraga remained unsatisfactory, meetings could be held in a town some twenty miles south of it—farther from Edo, that is. Perry saw that as more evidence of Japanese "cunning and deceit," exhibited in "their usual imperturbable manner."[7] It was surely an early manifestation of the stalling on which Edo Castle, in its poverty of better means, was relying.

The tactic would work as well as could be expected: in the end, a site roughly midway between Uraga and Edo would be chosen for negotiations. The compromise would take ten days to achieve—including a Sunday, which Perry made an exception to his rule of conducting no business then because Japanese officials who'd come "a great distance in cold and boisterous weather on an errand of kindness" deserved a polite reception.[8] The kindness took the form of gifts, presented with smiles even though the question of where to negotiate remained strained on that day and succeeding ones. However, the ships were supplied with coal, water, and wood, and Japanese officials, much more hospitable than during the previous summer, favored their crews with fruits, vegetables, sake, chickens, and eggs. For Perry in particular, there were also oysters, sweet cakes, and a promise that unlike in July, no soldiers would confront him when he now came ashore.

That nourished something smacking of good fellowship on the surface, while the tension of the demands and counterdemands about an acceptable site, which more resembled a grunting wrestling match than a battle of wits, occasionally rose close to fracture. A riflelike crack sent a small American landing party's fingers jerking to triggers to return the fire until the sound was recognized as a snap of his fan by a Japanese official who may have been playing a practical joke.[9] On another day, a samurai planning to kill Perry, then himself, boarded a boat waiting to take officials to the anchored squadron. As it approached the flagship, an officer—the Commodore, the samurai wrongly believed—lunged to prevent an off-balance sailor from falling overboard. Reasoning that Japan need not fear a "great lord" who would save a humble sailor, the would-be assassin sheathed his sword.[10]

The most serious incident was caused by drunken sailors storming into a Yokohama shop and stabbing its owner, who was trying to stop them from swilling from a sake barrel and stealing. Goaded by what they saw as the lack of respect that behavior revealed, young Japanese soldiers prepared to attack the Americans, but were stopped by Sakuma Shozan, the passionately defense-minded Mito scholar.[11] Tipsy or not, the *Susquehanna*'s chaplain upset even the Commodore, who had great toleration for challenges to all Japanese restrictions. Strolling six or so miles north toward Edo one fine March day, the clergyman invited himself into houses and temples. He was courteously received, but not by a shopkeeper he insisted show him Japanese coins before pocketing some gold and silver ones in return for American currency of the same weight but baser metal. A boatman confronted with the chaplain's drawn sword when a bribe failed to get him ferried across a river also objected,[12] and complaint grew about Americans being "very despicable" barbarians.

Such episodes hinted at the simmering temperature beneath the diplomatic forms. During the negotiations themselves, a student of Western military methods who commanded the effort to upgrade Edo's coastal defenses would arrive with sixty followers who were "prepared to die" in the event that hostilities broke out. Although the "commissioners," as the Japanese negotiators would be called, rejected his offer to guard them because it might spark an American bombardment of Edo, the overture spoke of the sustained edginess.[13] For now, stubborn Japanese attempts to site the talks farther from Edo increased Perry's resentment and provided more evidence, as he saw it, that only his firmness could have overcome "the deceitful conduct of these people." "For the last ten days," he'd write after the matter had been settled, they "interposed all possible objections to the movement of the ships higher up the bay and endeavored by every means to persuade me to return to Uraga." But

> when they found that I could not be deceived by their cajolery, and had actually approached within eight miles of the capital, they suddenly abandoned the position from which they so often assured me they could not be moved, and proposed unconditionally to concede what I had with equal but more successful pertinacity contended for.[14]

At one point during those preliminary negotiations, the captain of one of his ships brought disturbing news. Despite the Commodore's veto of a retreat to Uraga as "quite evident[ly] . . . unsafe and inconvenient," a new building was being erected there to house the major talks. That irritating impertinence was topped by siting the new structure in a deep gorge and fencing it with palisades or stakes. Perry "at once declared that such obstructions would not have been tolerated." If he'd landed at Uraga, "my first act would have been to order the demolition of this barricade."[15]

He sometimes used a similar tone to the five commissioners, "intelligent-looking men richly dressed in gay silk[s]," as a squadron officer described them. Courteous when he wanted to be, sometimes even engaging, he turned curt when he suspected them of delaying. "I have the power of plenipotentiary to decide these matters in my own discretion, and I cannot believe that you, who are also here as plenipotentiary, are unable to give an immediate reply. . . . Please give me an answer at once." Direct opposition turned him sharper, enough for later reflection that he'd probably be charged with arrogance for "persisting as I did, and against the judgment of all about me." But he was "simply adhering to a course of policy determined on after mature reflection," which had worked so well before.[16] To improve its working now, he made repeated threats to use force and reminded the commissioners what it had accomplished for America in Mexico.[17]

As in July, however, his actions spoke louder than his words. On Washington's birthday, he flourished his might by inviting Japanese officials aboard the flagship to witnesses the entire squadron's smoky cannon salute. The following day, genial Kayama Eizaemon, the police magistrate whom the squadron had mistaken for Uraga's governor during its July visit,[18] suddenly reappeared. The Americans were doubly happy to see the man whom they'd taken to more than to any other Japanese official. His second-visit absence until now had led to speculation, despite the Japanese explanation that he was ill and would reappear after recovering, that he'd killed himself because his friendliness to the squadron had been condemned. If he'd indeed been ill, colleagues jealous of his relative success with the Americans in July had probably also conspired to keep him away. Now, however, the chief Japanese commissioner—an Abe appointee with some of the Chief Senior Councilor's people skills—recalled "Governor" Kayama in order to help prevent the Americans' cannon salutes becoming live salvos. Kayama, whose calm good manners continued to conceal his inner anguish at Japan's loss of face, joined the appeals to accept one of the sites proposed by the commissioners. Perry kept rejecting them, but not the presence of "the Governor," who would help inch the parties past this and future obstacles in the talks.[19]

A more urgent matter prompted Japanese pleading on February 24, two days after the show of strength on Washington's birthday. Ignoring the entreaties not to, Perry proudly "determined to put his threat into execution"[20] by ordering his ships to weigh anchor and move up the bay toward Edo. That was when he "actually approached within eight miles of the capital," as he wrote, from where it could be seen from the mastheads—"so near" that the striking of the city's bells "could be distinctly heard" during the night. His survey boats pushed to within four miles, where they found water deep enough for even closer penetration by his ships.

Now panic did return, and Tokugawa Nariaki, jolted back to his anti-barbarian fervor, pressed Abe to attack.[21] With the *roju* and the commissioners "on the verge of hysteria," the negotiating commissioners urged the opposite: make concessions. "There will be no choice but to trade with them," they advised Edo, elaborating that Perry's demands could be rejected only if the *bakufu* were prepared for the capital to be scorched.[22] Americans did not understand "the ethics of humanity, justice, loyalty, and filial piety at all," they despaired. Hotheaded, violent, and impervious to reason, the visitors tried to get their way "by all means and seem to overwhelm us by force."[23]

As the warships' appalling nearness to Edo tightened the noose, Tokugawa Nariaki urged striking them if they landed troops, although Ii Naosuke, the chief proponent of agreeing to trade (the better to build military might for restoring seclusion),[24] again warned that any conflict now would bring only defeat.

The commissioners' final try came in a rather feeble note on the twenty-fifth, almost two weeks after Perry's arrival. They wished it to be "well understood" that they wanted the negotiations to take place at Uraga, "and would gratefully acknowledge the friendly meeting of the Lord Admiral in complying with this order of the Emperor and our own wishes." Later that day, "Governor" Kayama appeared to announce that the ships, which had retreated slightly from their closest approach to Edo, would be "cheerfully furnished" with wood and water, but only back at Uraga—to which Perry replied that if water weren't given at the present anchorage, he'd send men ashore to procure it.[25] At that point, Kayama dropped all resistance and suggested the meetings be held roughly opposite to where the ships were then anchored—in Yokohama, now a city of some 3.5 million inhabitants but then a fishing village.

The Japanese had discovered, Perry would vaunt, that "the Commodore was immovable in purpose . . . and finding that the ships had already approached within eight miles of their capital, they thought it politic to stop them there, while it was practicable, by a conciliatory concession."[26] He didn't know for certain, but might have guessed, that his July declaration that he couldn't return to the States without succeeding in his mission—"even at the cost of unavoidable war," a Japanese document warned—still rang in their ears. Edo Castle gave its negotiators secret instructions to "handle the matter peaceably."[27]

After the site had been agreed on, a shipwrecked Japanese seaman who'd been renamed Sam Patch in America was brought up on deck for a second presentation to native officials—which mirrored an embarrassing first one in July. "No sooner did he behold those dignitaries," Perry would describe, "than he prostrated himself at once, apparently completely awe-stricken" and convinced, especially after his messmates' teasing predictions "of the danger to which his head would be exposed" on arrival back in Japan, that "his last hour had come":

> Captain Adams [of the *Powhatan*] ordered him to rise from his knees, upon which he was crouching with the most abject fear and trembling in every limb. He was reminded that he was on board an American man-of-war, perfectly safe as one of her crew . . . but it being found impossible to reassure him while in the presence of his countrymen, he was soon dismissed.[28]

Toward the end of the treaty negotiations some three months later, the Japanese participants would insist Patch come ashore and remain in Japan. The Commodore would counter that the decision must be his, and that if he did choose to stay, the commissioners must guarantee his safety. Brought up a third time, the castaway was again ordered to rise from his knees, to which he'd instantly fallen. In the end, he remained on board, preferring to brave any further anti-Asian taunting there and back in America than take his chances as a violator of the Japanese seclusion laws, which were still in effect—all the more because he'd converted to Christianity, which his homeland still hated and persecuted.

YOKOHAMA, THE SITE CHOSEN with such difficulty, was on the coast of a small district called Kanagawa, which faced Edo Bay. No doubt the *bakufu* ultimately accepted the hamlet of a hundred or so mostly thatched-roof dwellings housing some thousand people because it was still far enough from Edo—some fifteen miles south—to offer some buffer from the foreigners. Mixing with them and opening the possibility of making friends was "the last thing the *Bakufu* wanted," commented a recent Japanese history. As for Perry, he'd rejected the nearby town of Kanagawa, where the Japanese commissioners were temporarily living, because the squadron couldn't approach within gunshot range.* Yokohama's decisive attraction for him was sufficient room to anchor nine of his ships in line of battle directly facing the village, their guns "commanding an extent of shore equal to their entire range."[29]

---

* Although Perry knew the forthcoming treaty would be hammered out in "Yokuhama," as he wrote it, he'd attach the name Kanagawa to it, possibly because Japanese officials persuaded him that the hamlet was in that administrative district. Michael Auslin, *Negotiating with Imperialism*, pp. 43, 52. Japanese often call it the "Perry Treaty."

During his China stay, the Commodore's groundwork for this second visit had included determination to maintain his self-exaltation that had worked so well in July. Conducting business with "these very sagacious and deceitful people" had taught him it was necessary "either to set all ceremony aside, or to out-Herod Herod in assumed personal consequence and ostentation."[30] Whether or not he was actually capable of setting all ceremony aside, the earlier success of the latter approach, "far beyond my expectations," helped him choose the more showy alternative. For March 8, the day he'd picked for his second landing and the start of negotiations, the Commodore made "every preparation to distinguish the occasion . . . by all necessary parade, knowing, as he did, the importance and moral influence of such show upon so ceremonious and artificial people as the Japanese."[31]

Edo Castle still worried far less about ceremony than about its future. The imminent facing of the crucial decision had refired the debates, as if the arguments hadn't been made and remorselessly remade during the seven months since the East Asia Squadron's first appearance. Tokugawa Nariaki learned of an intended secret message from the *roju* to the commissioners whose purpose was to eliminate the need to confer with him during the forthcoming negotiations by directing the commissioners not to consult the *roju* about the various points as they came up. Nariaki's fury was all the greater because the larger instructions were to negotiate peacefully and accept Perry's proposals. But after demanding replacement of the leading commissioners, he performed what appeared to be another abrupt reversal, although it was probably intended to assert Japanese control of the trade he now saw as inevitable. He proposed enlarging some of the concessions that would have to be made, including making coal available at Nagasaki rather than a remote island. However, that would be three years hence, by which time Japan should have its own steamships for transporting coal.

The commissioners again fed Nariaki's disgust by protesting that the Americans, who couldn't possibly be made to wait that long, would use force if not given a more satisfactory answer. Still unwilling to risk the deep split and possible civil war that would follow any public opposition by Nariaki, Abe resorted to more guile. He persuaded the *roju* to instruct the commissioners not to grant trading privileges, although holding to earlier decisions to provision foreign ships and help shipwrecked sailors.

Then he countermanded that with new, secret instructions to promise trade in five years—three, if absolutely necessary—if the Americans were adamant. At that point, still before the opening of formal negotiations but not mutual soundings-out, Perry exhibited just such adamancy. He still talked about going to Edo if he'd consider that necessary; still warned of war, and embellishing his predictions about the result with gross exaggeration, announced he'd wage it with fifty ships that were in nearby waters, then fifty more that would come from California: a total of a hundred warships—far more than the U.S. Navy operated—within twenty days.[32] Edo shuddered. Although Abe refused permission to military commanders to warn Americans who'd landed to survey the coast that they'd be attacked, he told them to prepare for an American strike if the negotiations stalled, in which case small boats would attack the squadron.

MARCH 8 WAS COLD BUT "CHEERFUL" to Perry's eye. Drawn from the much-reinforced squadron, more Americans would participate in this landing ceremony than had in the one in July. The Commodore had "issued orders to the effect that all the marines who could be spared from duty should appear on the occasion in full accoutrement," together with all officers and sailors who could "possibly leave" their ships.[33] The resulting five hundred-odd seemed "more like an invading army" than the honor guard Perry had promised. Most of the thousands of natives who outnumbered them were civilian spectators; in marked contrast to July, the soldiers on view amounted to mere token guards for the commissioners and other dignitaries. That helped make the ambiance closer to festive than hostile, especially since few knew that hundreds of heavily armed men were hidden, with orders "to fight to the death if the Americans fired a shot."[34]

Half an hour before the meeting scheduled to take place at noon, a seventeen-gun salute was fired as the Commodore descended from the *Powhatan* into his barge. His choreography for his welcome had the twenty-seven boats that had delivered the American party ashore awaiting him there in two parallel lines. As the barge approached them, the officer in command ordered their sailors to "Stand up and off caps"—"a compliment he acknowledged by raising his own" before he stepped on shore to a salute of three drumrolls.[35]

The bayonets of the marines in their blue and white uniforms and "complete military appointment" glistened as bands from the three steam frigates played "The Star Spangled Banner." The men presented arms just before the Commodore passed between their twin ranks. The two huge black sailors who had borne President Fillmore's letter to the July reception hall now carried Perry's ensign and broad pennant. Accompanied by officers, the commander, in his full-dress uniform with a sword and gold-striped trousers, followed magisterially to a more spacious and elaborate hall, one of five buildings just constructed there. The ceremonies constituted "something less perhaps than a pageant," a witness recorded, "but they were effective, the escort on either side being more guards of honor and less guards of fear." Perry's sharp eye and tongue had seen to it that they were visible to all. From the *Powhatan* that morning, he'd spied a large cloth enclosing the reception hall "within a sort of prison yard . . . completely exclud[ing] it from the view of those without." The officer he instantly sent ashore to "demand what it meant" was given "some frivolous pretext about preventing intrusion and doing honor to the occasion." The Commodore "informed the Japanese that he would forego the honor," and that "he could not think of landing . . . until it was completely removed."[36] The cloth quickly disappeared.

That set the tone of the negotiations themselves, despite continued exchange of social invitations and Perry's displays of respect, including cannon salutes to the Emperor and Chief Commissioner and flying the Tokugawa crest from his flagship's masthead, the first such gesture in more than two centuries. (The Americans would evidently remain unaware that cranes, depictions of which were prominent in the hall's interior decoration, were a peace symbol.) The talks began the same day. After food and drink in the hall—from which the negotiating commissioners absented themselves in a demonstration of their superior status—Perry was handed a written reply to President Fillmore's letter. Its immediate concessions launched the *bakufu*'s effort to avoid making more of them, or at least to stall. Despite the distractions caused by the Shogun's recent death and his replacement's pledge to observe the ancient laws that positively forbade granting the American proposals, "we are governed now by imperative necessity"; therefore foreign ships would be provisioned and their shipwrecked seamen safeguarded.

With reason to suspect the lack of signature was intentional, Perry asked that a signed document be delivered to him the following day, then "entered at once upon the subject that was uppermost" in his mind. The subject was trade in the form, the Commodore explained, of negotiating a treaty "similar to the one between the United States and China."[37] That deepened never-quelled Japanese fears of suffering their neighbor's recent fate. The 1844 Treaty of Wanghia that governed Chinese-American relations was essentially a copy of the humiliating Treaty of Nanking the British had forced Peking to sign two years earlier, after crushing its defense in the Opium War.[38] It made China a virtual colony.

Perry saw it differently. In a letter to the commissioners sent "with the most profound respect," he said the thirty thousand-odd Chinese subjects who visited America had been "kindly received" and permitted to "engage in whatever occupation best suited them." That wasn't an outright lie, but came close in its failure to mention the fierce discrimination that caused wretched treatment of almost all those thousands. His claim that the Chinese government "has derived much benefit from its treaty with the United States"[39] came even closer, since the treaty added to the suffering the Taiping Rebellion was causing Peking and the rest of the China.

SO FAR, THE JAPANESE SPINS AND PREVARICATIONS, chiefly about why one or another potential meeting site had been impossible, were smaller than Perry's, but now Edo concocted larger ones. Opening a port in the Ryukyus couldn't be discussed because they were "a very distant country." The same applied to the port of Matsumae on Hokkaido, supposedly another very distant country, that one ruled by its own Prince. (Responding to Perry's pressure, the commissioners would soon consent to consult the Prince about the matter, but that, they said, would take a year. The Commodore answered that if the Prince were indeed an independent sovereign, he'd "go himself to Matsmai [sic] and negotiate with him.")[40] As for trade with America, it would violate ancestral laws. (That would have puzzled earlier Japanese ancestors because they'd traded happily; and some business was still being conducted with the Deshima Dutch.) Discussion of other matters had to be postponed because "our Emperor had but lately acceded to his throne" and "had no leisure for extraneous negotiations," since "all the numerous affairs of government" needed his attention In fact, the Emperor still had virtually nothing to do with the government, nor had he recently been crowned. It was the Shogun who was new, Tokugawa Iesada having succeeded his father in July; and he too, the mentally defective youth, was unable to exercise any real power. More than ever, Abe and the *roju* made the important decisions; with the other senior councilors increasingly deferring to him about those concerning Perry, he was also more than ever a prime minister, even as the discredited national government bled authority. More and more of its powers were slipping back to the stronger daimyo, which is why Abe still felt he mustn't alienate Tokugawa Nariaki, who might rally those other lords against the *bakufu*.

Nevertheless, the Commodore's dishonesty was probably greater than Edo Castle's. It was certainly more effective, notwithstanding his contempt for Japanese officials as liars (and for the interpreters too, "whose duty it is to lie").[41]

PERRY ANNOUNCED HE DARED not return from Japan until satisfactory answers to all his proposals were "placed in my possession." If necessary, he'd stay a year—or two years. Actually, it would take him twenty-three days, just over three weeks, to achieve most of his purpose. During their course, he and his party shared meals with the Japanese representatives and participated in other social exchange. Squadron crews made contact with "ordinary" locals during their exercise hours on shore—permission for which the commissioners had quickly if unhappily granted[42]—and when the ships received their daily water and provisions. Although the authorities remained "very jealous of any intercourse . . . with the people, and did all they could to prevent it, still there was necessarily a good deal of intermingling"[43]—also with gawking residents. Expressing an ancient Japanese passion for pictures, many "tourists" sketched and painted the odd foreigners with their long noses (while circulating rumors about their seemingly magical new daguerreotypes that brought death to their subjects within three years). Like Westerners before him, Perry saw "the common people" as much more disposed to fraternize than the officials were, but were kept from doing so by "fear of punishment":

> They were closely watched by their superiors, as in fact the latter were by their equals. . . . No one, even of the highest dignitaries, is entrusted with public business of importance, without having one or more associated with him, who is ever on the alert to detect and take note of the slightest suspicion of delinquency.[44]

Meanwhile, the old arguments were being made and remade during the diplomatic sessions and in to-and-fro letters. In the commissioners who were negotiating for Japan, Samuel Williams saw "none of that hauteur and supercilious conduct" suggested in books about the country. In comparison to other Asian officials he'd seen in operation—especially Chinese, with their "contemptuous treatment of foreigners"—"everyone must admit their superiority in point of courtesy, their decorum, their willingness to receive suggestions, and their general good sense in discussing the matters *brought forward for their acceptance* [italics added]." When he had time to sum up the expedition, Williams would see those qualities deriving from the national character, "since we have seen them among all classes to some extent. In no country could more agreeable and kind-hearted men be found."[45] Perry, by contrast—although he soon earned the commissioners' gratitude by dispensing with the American firearms—felt he must keep constant guard against their "deceitful diplomacy" and any compromise. "It struck me that it was better to have no treaty than one that would in the least compromise the dignity of the American character."

Not that Williams became fond of all Japanese ways. He found it "repulsive" to see their interpreter—not Kayama, although he too debased himself—"crouch down on hands and knees before [the commissioners], never rising, but shuffling from one to another and always addressing them in the lowest of whispers; what respect can a man have for himself in such a position?"★

(Some of the most important translation for the Japanese was being done not there but out of sight. The concealed expert was Manjiro—now Nakahama Manjiro—the former fisherman who, after being shipwrecked when he was fourteen and educated in America, risked returning to Japan in 1852.[46] Convinced that his loyalty was divided, Tokugawa Nariaki had seen to it that Manjiro was prohibited from communicating with any American during the negotiations, let alone from serving as an interpreter. Nevertheless, that

---

★ Samuel Wells Williams, *A Journal of the Perry Expedition to Japan*, p. 129. Perry was of similar mind about the Japanese, who were "never forgetful of the respect which they think due to rank." Not that he, who himself rarely forgot the respect due *him*, disapproved of that in itself; only its expression. "From the Emperor to the lowest subject in the realm there is a constant succession of prostrations. The former, in want of a human being superior to himself in rank, bows humbly to some Pagan idol, and every one of his subjects, from prince to peasant, has some person before whom he is bound to cringe and crouch in the dirt." *Narrative*, p. 348.

sole Japanese who could go directly from English to Japanese without using Dutch translated all the documents from Perry and every reply, working in a room to which the commissioners retired for discussion among themselves. That explained the mystery to the Americans of Japanese papers submitted not only in their own language and Dutch but also in English.[47])

But the Commodore's hubris also put a bad taste in the Reverend Williams's mouth. President Fillmore's letter had "asked for one port; now Perry wants five," he regretted after translating a reply to whom the Americans still believed was the Emperor. The same applied to that larger goal uppermost in the Commodore's mind. Whereas the President had wanted "simply an assurance of good treatment . . . now the Commodore demands a treaty, and suggests, in no obscure terms, 'a larger force and more stringent terms and instructions' if they don't comply."[48] In other words, Perry had taken it upon himself to up the ante, just as he'd done in July with his menacing supplements to Fillmore's letter.

He waxed most indignant about shipwrecked foreign sailors. Charging that the poor men were treated like slaves, he delivered a little sermon about exceedingly inhumane Japan's closed doors to its own castaways, which demonstrated that human life had little importance there. No, the commissioners protested, the Admiral's notions were based on mistaken reports and simply wrong. Japan, which excelled all other countries in the importance attached to human life, in fact provisioned needy foreign vessels with fuel and supplies. As for shipwrecked sailors, the law mandated kind treatment; only those who behaved unlawfully, like the violent *Lagoda* crew, were temporarily detained.[49]

The chief Japanese commissioner had begun his defense by assuring Perry it was "quite impossible to give satisfactory answers at once" to all the American proposals, as that was "most positively forbidden by the laws of our imperial ancestors." But as he gave ground, the dialogue switched to details. The Japanese wanted to limit shipwrecked seamen's freedom of movement because, they feebly explained, it was impossible "to ascertain who are pirates and who are not." Perry's objection was predictably categorical. All who "may resort to the ports of Japan . . . shall enjoy all the freedom granted to Japanese. It is altogether inconsistent with justice that persons thrown by the providence of God upon the shores of a friendly nation should be . . . treated as pirates, before any proof shall be given." Further mistreatment of strangers "will no longer be tolerated" by the American government,[50] nor would attempts to prevent them from meeting the Dutch and Chinese at Nagasaki. Americans would "never submit" to such restraints, and any further allusion to them "will be considered offensive."

More discussion followed Japanese submission to those points. Perry would report that the commissioners also agreed not to "confine" Americans or prevent them from moving about, but wanted to limit the distance they'd be permitted to walk:

COM. PERRY. I am prepared to settle the matter now, but they must not be confined to any house or street. Suppose we make the distance they may walk the same distance that a man can go and come in a day. Or, if you choose, the number of *lis* or *ris* may be agreed upon.

JAPANESE. We are willing that they shall walk as far as they can go and come in a day.

COM. PERRY. There is no probability that sailors would want to go on shore more than once from curiosity; beside, they will have their daily duties to attend to on board ship, and will not be able to go on shore.

JAPANESE. We do not want any women to come and remain at Simoda. [Shimoda, one of the ports soon to be opened to American vessels].[51]

After considerably more talk about the parameters of walks and Japanese insistence that no foreigner permanently reside anywhere on their land, attention turned to the question of consulates. The wary commissioners wanted to wait four or five years before authorizing them, in order to see how the new relationships in the opened ports would work. Perry argued that consuls, by reporting any difficulties between Japanese and Americans and assisting the former to carry out their laws and recover any debts owed by the latter, would prove advantageous to the Japanese. And "if no consuls are received, then a ship of war must remain in Japan constantly," its captain performing the necessary duties. That won the point, but Perry would grant a short deferment before the first consulate would open in the first port.

But most of the back-and-forth concerned trade, the ultimate Japanese taboo, about which the commissioners were prepared to make a stand, not least because the majority of the daimyo and other members of the political elite opposed it so vehemently, and bitterly suspected the *bakufu* was about to ignore them. "We certainly cannot yet bring it about," they replied to Perry's repeated proposal to open trade on the Chinese-American model. Japan's "feelings and manners," so different from those of other nations, would make it "exceedingly difficult, even if you wish it, to immediately change the old regulations for those of other countries."[52] Some trade might begin at Nagasaki, where American ships would be provisioned; but a second port couldn't be opened until after a five-year trial period.*

Thus the prospect of a proper commercial treaty remained in doubt, but much as he wanted one, Perry more wanted ports opened to America for other purposes, and their selection became the central issue for a time. Nagasaki wasn't among his choices—in fact, not even as the point of delivery for shipwrecked American seamen. Despite Japanese insistence that it was "the place set apart for strangers," whose "inhabitants and authorities . . . had been trained to enforce the laws with respect to foreigners"—which would take five years to replicate in another city— "the Commodore positively refused to accept Nagasaki." Perry vetoed the city precisely in order to avoid subjecting Americans to residents accustomed to demanding servility from foreigners, which might lead to "serious consequences." Besides—or first of all—it was "out of the route of American commerce."[53]

WHEN PERRY WASN'T ISSUING ultimatums or threats, he exuded concern for Japan's "peace and prosperity." He often combined the two, as if using quilt to cover his cudgel. If his purpose had been war, he asserted, his very small squadron (as noted, the largest Washington had ever sent abroad) would have been three or four times larger. Far from such intention, he declared in a typical letter to the commissioners, no other Western nation was "so intimately connected with the peace and welfare of Japan as the United States." Moved by "friendly intentions," desire "to pay the highest honor to his Imperial Majesty . . . [and to] evince, by every suitable act

---

* "This answer was not entirely unexpected, and put an end to all prospect of negotiating a 'commercial treaty,' in the European sense. It only remained, therefore, to secure, for the present, admission into the kingdom, and so much of trade as Japanese jealousy could be brought to concede." *Narrative*, p. 383.

of kindness, the cordial feelings entertained by him towards Japan," the President had sent the Commodore and his ships. Many others would follow.

Perhaps out of wishful thinking of his own, he apparently believed his eyewash worked. From time to time, especially after the Japanese had conceded a point and at social occasions, he saw them behaving "in the most amicable manner," with "the greatest good feeling" prevailing, and he wasn't alone in believing his genial hospitality was charming the commissioners. One of his clerks saw the isolated nation's "stern public sentiment . . . rapidly melting before our neighborly advances." The Japanese showed themselves "glad of our coming":

> They flocked on board and were received as friends. They admired our ships. They liked our dinners. As an impartial historian I must admit that they took kindly, sometimes convivially, to our brandies and wines. And on shore these courtesies were duly reciprocated. . . . Many meetings were held, and on most of these occasions an entertainment was served by the Japanese in native style. Sydney Smith [an English clergyman and wit] once said of his countrymen that "an Englishman is like an oyster—you must get into him with a knife and fork." That was one of the ways we got into Japan; many a treat went into that treaty.[54]

That was during the very days when the Black Ships remained anchored in the bay, not moving, as a Japanese novelist would put it, "until they got the answer they wanted from us, no matter what we might think about it. They just sat there, solid and threatening as boulders."[55] The country's greatest threat ever, as many Japanese remain convinced to this day, supposedly no longer alarmed its people. The tens of thousands of spectators who ignored the prohibition in order to crowd the beach and hillsides supposedly did so in order to enjoy the music of the Black Ships' bells, bands, and sentry calls. The truth was that the political frenzy about how to answer the threat was becoming ever sharper, and disturbances were breaking out across the land. Months earlier, when Tokugawa Nariaki had decried the men who, in "these feeble days," tended to "cling to peace"—men "not fond of defending their country by war"—he also protested their "slander [of] those of us who are determined to fight, calling us lovers of war, men who enjoy conflict." And "if things become desperate," Nariaki warned, the peace seekers

might, in their enormous folly, try to overthrow those of us who are determined to fight, offering excuses to the enemy and concluding a peace
agreement with him. They would thus in the end bring total destruction
upon us.[56]

Both dangers continued to swell. In Kyoto and Edo, anti-*bakufu* groupings were gaining confidence and allegiance from some of the strongest
daimyo. Despite the muting of Nariaki's expulsion rhetoric, rank-and-file
anti-Westerners, some forming nascent terrorist groups, were growing in
numbers and stridence. But the only glimmer of looming civil strife that
reached the Americans was an occasional fierce glance from a guard when a
party landed, easily lost amid a crush of curious looks.

In the negotiating sessions themselves, anger threatened to erupt into
violence more than once. By that time, ominous threats from Perry were
nothing new. If necessary, he'd go to war and, he said, "exhaust our resources" waging it. Americans had taken the Mexican capital, he reminded
from his anchorage two hours' steaming from the Japanese capital, and
"circumstances may lead your country into a similar plight." Losing control at one point, the chief commissioner said the Japanese were also ready
for war.[57]

It may be worth repeating that if Perry's threats, unsanctioned by Washington, had provoked a Japanese attack (which he perhaps wanted), he
might truly have opened fire. But while his ambition was still prompting
him to violate his orders now, in that March of 1854, he'd attained enough
of what he sought to further diminish the chances of military conflict. Nevertheless, it was still Abe more than the Commodore who ultimately avoided
war, and his chief commissioner—the man who, in exasperation, replied
that the Japanese were ready for it—saved Japan from "peaceful" capitulation on all points.

Hayashi Daigaku was neither a military officer nor the prince the Japanese presented him as, although Perry, much impressed by his "robes of
richly embroidered silk, his fine presence, his benevolent and intelligent
face, and his courtly manners,"[58] took him for the latter throughout, addressing his letters to him as "Your Highness." Hayashi wasn't a bureaucrat either, but an eminent scholar—an intellectual rival to Tokugawa
Nariaki, whose seclusionist and nationalist zeal he much disliked. Now
serving as Lord Rector of the *bakufu*'s institute of higher learning, he was

another illustration of Abe's inclination to make appointments from out-side the usual box—and to make allies wherever possible, for Hayashi was also the Shogun's foreign policy advisor. A decade earlier, Abe had asked him for advice on the delicate question of whether to permit the Shimazu family to trade with France, via Okinawa. His recommendation to approve that cautious, supposedly concealed opening to the West further angered Tokugawa Nariaki, all the more because Hayashi had promised the Mito lord that it would be "most difficult for Japan ever to permit this."[59] Now his generally nonconfrontational approach to the Americans earned him more of Nariaki's anger. The antagonists' deep distrust for each other ex-tended to mutual suspicion of sabotage, even treachery.

At Yokohama, the five commissioners had struggled hard, if sometimes clumsily. Saddled with their severe limitations of choice, with the awk-wardness inherent in the attempt to stall, and with Abe's orders to take no stance that might provoke hostilities, they could hardly have dealt rebuffs to the Americans. Still, Hayashi in particular had negotiated as well as anyone in his shaky position could have, Nariaki's censures to the con-trary notwithstanding. Having virtually nothing substantive with which to bargain, let alone hit back, he relied on his dignity and brains, which were most needed at the critical point in the talks.

It was critical because the *roju* that had decided to concede on the other issues nevertheless hoped against hope not to capitulate on trade, to which the deep emotional opposition had only grown. Perry had softened his ports demand. Although he expected five "to be opened to the Ameri-can flag . . . in the course of time," three would do for now. However, the full commercial relations he wanted in the three was the prospect most feared and hated by the great majority of the country's political elite, who visualized Japanese ways irretrievably undermined by barbarians moving about freely in the cities.

Without repeating his postulation that not to trade was a "crime against humanity," Perry argued that nations enriched themselves by selling what they had in order to buy what they didn't. The interests of commerce de-manded proper conditions for that natural practice, for which the honor of the United States also called. Hayashi made Japan's usual counterargument—that it was content with what it itself produced—but knew it wouldn't be enough to fend off the Commodore or to satisfy Abe. Under attack by Nar-iaki, who was fuming ever hotter about the concessions already made, the

Chief Senior Councilor had been promising antiforeign spokesmen he'd never allow trade to do its deeply repugnant corrupting.

But how not to allow anything? Maintaining his dignified manner with the Commodore, Hayashi decided to switch to the offensive for once by going deeper. Playing his weak hand more skillfully than ever and without specific direction from Abe, the starveling bargainer questioned the premise that commerce had a necessary role in Japanese-American relations. Hadn't Perry talked insistently about the greater value America placed on human life, and about Japan's obligation to provision needy ships and succor shipwrecked sailors? How were those matters connected to this other one on his agenda? "You have attained your purpose. Now, commerce has to do with profits, but has it anything to do with human life?"[60]

The adroit challenge forced a longer pause from Perry than military defiance would have. The Chief Commissioner had put his finger on the role of moneymaking in the mission's purpose without wagging it in Perry's face. The Commodore tried to think of the good answer he needed. Even if Hayashi's distinction was sound, the expedition's inspirers and supporters—big businessmen like Aaron Haight Palmer, the propagators of Manifest Destiny, the prominent Whigs closely connected to international merchant firms—wouldn't see it that way, trade being central to their vision of civilization's march to progress as well as to their personal prosperity.

When Perry recovered, he tried another tack. Still unaware of the Japanese fear prompted by the Treaty of Wanghia that opened Chinese ports wide to American trade, he gave Hayashi a copy and asked that he and the other commissioners review it. But that second attempt of his lacked conviction. The Commodore had already acknowledged that Hayashi's telling differentiation between profits and the professed American motivation had won the point. His Highness was right, the Commodore conceded. Commerce did benefit countries, but didn't concern human life. "I shall not insist upon it."

Perry's regret over that effective end of his campaign for a commercial treaty was softened by knowledge of what he'd won. The two ports to be opened, if not yet to trade, promised good things for American business. (The Commodore had decided to open the third, Okinawa's Naha, by applying direct pressure, which he'd soon do.[61]) Remote as it was, American whalers would be grateful to put into Hakodate, on the northernmost main island of Hokkaido—then called Ezo or Yezo—for repairs and replenishment, and tiny Shimoda on the main island of Honshu would be just as useful. The Japanese had proposed it because it was relatively isolated and distant from Edo: some hundred miles southeast, near the tip of the mountainous, sparsely populated Izu Peninsula. Perry thought it "could not be more desirable . . . as a stopping place for steamers and other vessels plying between California and China."[62] So even if commercial relations with Japan would have to be postponed, the China trade would get the desired boost. Shimoda would be opened immediately upon the signing of the treaty, and precious coal would be supplied.

THE TREATY OF PEACE AND AMITY between the United States and Japan, or Treaty of Kanagawa, as it would become known, was signed on March 31. Perry wrote Hayashi that he had "the greatest satisfaction" from learning Japan had "at last awakened to a conviction of the necessity of so altering its policy" as to agree to "an interchange of friendly intercourse with the United States." "Eureka! It is finished!" one of the Commodore's more admiring officers rejoiced less stiffly. "In vulgar parlance, the egg has hatched its chicken today. . . . Even Old Bruin would smile if only he knew how to smile."*

The Japanese tried to control the opposition emotion. Article I's promise appealed to a few of them. "There shall be a perfect, permanent, and universal peace, and a sincere and cordial amity between the United States of America on the one part, and the Empire of Japan on the other part, and between their people respectively, without exception of persons or places." However, virtually all saw the following eleven articles as codification of "desperate measure[s]" to appease a victor. "It was our object in these negotiations," the commissioners would conclude their report to the *bakufu*, "to win [Perry] away from any previous idea he had of opening hostilities . . . thus completing the whole affair in peace" without bringing "disgrace upon our country."[63] Although the vanquished indeed managed to avoid the worst, they gained no positive objective of their own, and Edo Castle was embarrassed enough to delay a full year before showing the text of the treaty to the daimyo at large and to the

---

* George Henry Preble, *The Opening of Japan*, p. 155. Preble wrote that the feat came at a good time because his ship's officers' mess was very depleted: no more coffee, no more milk or sugar for tea, "a few hams and some cans of pickled oyster, so salt we cannot eat them are all we have in our store room save a little strong batter and some flour." The officer would soon have to rely entirely on supplies from the crew's mess. p. 156.

court in Kyoto. On reading it, the crown issued its first national directive in centuries: an order to melt down temple bells for guns.

Perry was willing to compromise on matters of custom, as illustrated by omission of a Japanese signature on the English-language version. "It will be observed," he explained to the Secretary of the Navy, "that the practice usually pursued in affixing signatures to treaties was departed from" because "their laws forbade the subjects of the Empire from putting their names to any document written in a foreign language." (Or, in an historian's interpretation, the Japanese "succeeded in protecting the good names of the Emperor, the Shogun and the members of the council by omitting them from the humiliating document."[64]) Otherwise, the persistence of which he was so proud paid off handsomely in those eleven articles that delineated Japan's obligations to America, the most important of which was "the admission of vessels of the United States" to the two ports, "under certain rights and privileges never granted to the people of any foreign nation."[65]

Their right to buy supplies in those ports, even though the exchanges would have to be conducted through official agencies there, may have been a primitive form of trade, but Japanese sensibility to the word kept it from being named as such. (The negotiations had avoided "trade" by discussing exchange of mutual "gifts," the Americans using gold and silver rather than goods.) Subject to deliberation, however, available provisions might possibly be purchased and other business discussed. As for shipwrecked Americans, they'd be taken, unimprisoned, to one of those ports, where they would "not be subject to such restrictions and confinement as the Dutch and Chinese are at Nagasaki"; but American ships would enter no other port unless in distress. If Washington wanted, it could open a consulate in Shimoda eighteen months after the signing of the treaty. (Consular representation was one of the concessions the commissioners had taken upon themselves to make. Much worried about it, they downplayed the significance in their report to the *bakufu*: "when the time comes that we must accept the dispatch of officials to Japan, the treaty will have to be further expanded.")[66] Any other privileges and advantages not therein granted to the United States but later to other nations "shall be granted likewise to the United States and to the citizens thereof without any consultation or delay." That "most favored nation" article was a cornerstone of Western exploitation of Asia.

The victor's pleasure was further boosted by what he perceived as the commissioners' sharing of it. As soon as the treaty was signed, "the Commodore presented . . . Prince Hayashi with an American flag, remarking that he considered it the highest expression of national courtesy and friendship he could offer. The prince was evidently deeply impressed with this significant mark of amity, and returned his thanks for it with indications of great feeling."[67] Evidently no thanks came for Perry's offer to help Japan "in every way possible with warships and guns" in case it engaged in war with another country.[68] He didn't report that unauthorized overture to Washington, and nothing would come of it, as with his promise—which he'd made almost simultaneously with proposing to make the Ryukyus a protectorate—to help Okinawans.

Perry's satisfaction also enabled him to apologize to "the prince" for any trouble he might have caused, especially with his ignorance of Japanese law. Of course, he had no inkling that Tokugawa Nariaki had suggested to Abe that Hayashi kill himself to show the Americans no more "careless negotiating" would be tolerated.[69] In any case, an outfoxed Nariaki could now do nothing to invalidate the treaty, nor to stop Perry from touring Yokohama or making a last, panic-rekindling trip north.

That last sally was on April 10. The day before, the Commodore declared that "notwithstanding the urgent remonstrances of the commissioners," he'd "approach with the steamers as near to Edo as the depth of water would allow."[70] The remonstrances included passionate warnings that any such move toward the capital might easily provoke great riots there, and the grave dishonor to the commissioners might compel them to commit *seppuku*, ritual suicide. A personal plea from Hayashi that such an action would embarrass him before his government prompted Perry to counter with a quick answer made of whole cloth: that not to take it would do the same to him before *his* government. But further supplication persuaded him not to anchor the ships or disembark from them; merely view the capital from the *Powhatan*. To reassure Japanese officials, he offered to take some along, including their chief interpreter, who, made ill by the squadron's approach to the capital, resolved to leap in front of one of the cannon if he saw them being loaded. Another American account had the interpreter intent on killing himself in a more traditional way. Throwing his cloak and long sword to one of the officers, he said he had no more need of them. "My short sword will be all that I shall require."[71]

Japanese anxiety was extreme, but the cannon weren't fired; Perry abandoned his plan to salute Edo Castle with them. In his enduring misapprehension that it was the Emperor's residence, he called it "the palace." In his enduring use of prevarication to deceive the Japanese, he improved on his fabrication that not to make that little jaunt toward the capital would embarrass him. Now he insisted, even after the treaty had been agreed, that Washington had ordered it, and he had no choice but to obey.[72]

An ebb tide was too strong for the sailing ships but the steamers pushed on, with their Japanese passengers. Through a partially obscuring fog, their crews managed to make out half-completed forts in the channel, then houses in Edo's outskirts, while Perry confirmed to himself the ease with which his guns could have destroyed the city. His enjoyment was evident when its outline, including the castle's, appeared. Then he ordered his ships to come about and, as promised, return down the bay, he remaining convinced that the "very friendly position which we already had with these people"[73] remained intact.

A week later, as most of his squadron headed home, he'd depart with a few vessels for more than two months of surveying and otherwise preparing Shimoda and Hakodate for their new roles. His "no little feeling of regret" at leaving the "never-ending pleasure" of contemplating the beauties of upper Edo Bay was no doubt genuine, but his profuse thanks to the Japanese interpreters and regards to Hayashi Daigaku would prompt one of his officers to suggest the "humbug" was less appropriate on April 10 than it would have been on April 1.[74] Actually, a leave-taking spirit had entered earlier, at a dinner for some seventy leading officials and interpreters aboard the *Powhatan* for celebrating the conclusion of the treaty. Eager to show off the superiority of American hospitality to "their portions of fish soup," the Commodore "spared no pains in providing most bountifully," his "Paris cook labor[ing] for a week, night and day," to prepare dishes that "would have done credit to Delmonico of New York. Of course there was plenty of champagne and other wines with a good supply of punch for the upper table."[75] The attending Japanese seemed "greatly to relish" the drink, on which "Prince" Hayashi, "who always preserved his grave and dignified bearing," was one of the few who didn't get at least a little tipsy. The others "took the lead in proposing healths and toasts, and were by no means the most backward in drinking them. They kept shouting at the top of their voices, and were heard far above the music of the bands."[76]

Perry's assertion that his military might would "secure [Japanese] friendship" will baffle those who have suffered fear, if not those who cause it. While the Americans saw their guests' exuberant and occasionally boisterous behavior as an expression of great cheer and affection for their hosts, only the raucous celebrants knew the extent to which shame for their surrender mixed with relief that it avoided invasion boosted their copious consumption of wine and brandy and magnified their laughter at a minstrel show performed by the crew.

GIFTS HAD BEEN EXCHANGED BEFORE—including two illustrated chronicles of the Mexican War from Perry, whose exploits were described within—and more were added now. The quality of the Japanese offerings made Perry's determination that his would outshine them easier to fulfill. When it wanted to, Edo gave superb artifacts to foreign dignitaries, like those it formerly sent to the Chinese court. Whether because the Commodore wasn't a head of state or because another point was intended, the items presented to him were less than the country's best. Even with no means of making comparisons with past Japanese practice, some of his crews felt he got the worst of the April exchange. True or not, the respective offerings clearly reflected major differences in the two cultures, the Japanese ones consisting chiefly of bronze, brocades, silks, fans, lacquerware, and porcelains, plus a variety of seashells for the Commodore, who collected them. The Americans gave mostly goods of modern manufacture and technology (together with four volumes of Audubon's *Birds of America* and a hundred gallons of Kentucky bourbon).

The most substantial gifts were firefighting equipment, two telegraph sets with fifteen miles of wire, and a model train with tracks, tender, and car. Powered by steam raised in the locomotive's boiler, the latter was one-quarter full size, just large enough for "passengers" to ride it—which robed officials did, the whistle's shrill toot further increasing their amazement and delight.[77] The great appeal suggests Perry's abundant attention to what he'd give, and how profoundly they impressed the "innocent and childlike" recipients wasn't misplaced, but the long-term result would surely have stunned him had he lived to see it: a brass howitzer and hugely admired Colt revolvers—contributed by the manufacturer in a hope of future business—foreshadowed a great reordering of Japanese preoccupations. The former was mounted in a *Saratoga* launch that Perry was willing to give away because that ship was about to return to the States. Although he didn't want to part with others, he asked Washington to send more of the little craft to Japan, "equipped in the manner of those belonging to the Squadron," including the howitzers. He "most urgently" recommended that "Guns fully equipped with carriages" be sent to Japan for the sake of "a favorable influence on some future occasion."

No doubt some knowledge of the domestic turmoil on shore would have lessened his confidence that America would reap a "hundred fold" return from those "little acts of Courtesy."[78] On the other hand, a distinguished American scholar would speculate that even if Perry and his officers had had reliable information about Japan's real condition, they wouldn't have understood.[79] As the cheery toasts and gifts were being exchanged, block-print news sheets were depicting righteous samurai—and Japanese women too, to both of whom was attributed great farting power—driving away hairy barbarians. "Happiness in! Devils Out!" The sheets had begun parodying the treaty's blow to the *bakufu* for selling out to America, immediately after they showed the powerless government hiring foreigners and ordering them to respect Japanese regulations at their workplace—5,000 *ri* (some 12,000 miles) away. Perry was permitted to join the labors because he didn't worship the banned Christian God but, as a member of the "Rifle Sect," pure military force.[80]

Exuberance left the expedition members, who understandably saw their almost-finished job as very well done, even less likely to have made sense of such complications even if they'd known them. The satisfaction of the Commodore himself was ample enough to include generosity. The nations of the West to which Japan had been opened bore responsibility for showing that the ensuing intercourse would promote its interests, he'd soon declare. Future commercial treaties should be for the benefit "not of ourselves only, but of all the maritime powers of Europe, for the advancement of Japan, and for the upward progress of our common humanity."[81] As for the present, Edo Bay's "warm and genial" temperatures swelled that high-mindedness into a touch of affection for Japan, "the youngest sister in the circle of commercial nations" that needed only kind treatment in order to grow strong, healthy, and progressive.

That optimism was about to be conveyed to Americans eager to hear it, with no hint of the youngest sister's growing frenzy. While the squadron was still opposite Yokohama, the *Saratoga*, longest in commission among its ships, was given the honor of delivering the treaty to the thirty-one states, and the sloop of war "spread her white wings" for Washington on April 4, four days after the conclusion of the treaty. "To us who were at last home-ward bound, it was thrilling to hear the rousing cheers from each ship as we passed down the line, and from the Commodore's band the strains of 'Home, Sweet Home.' "[82]

Not yet able to enjoy that thrill, Perry departed on April 18 for two and a half months of exploration of the two soon-to-be-opened ports. One of his party would describe a "scrupulous coastal survey of [Shimoda's] harbor, the shoreline and contiguous areas . . ." As with the Deshima Dutch, the Americans were provided special "pleasure quarters" ashore, in order to curtail their contamination of the town's other women.* When local authorities tried to impose further restrictions, such as appointing guards for their real or supposed protection, the Commodore responded in character. "The prefect was . . . emphatically assured that the Americans could never submit with impunity to such treatment, as it was not only an infringement of the stipulations of the treaty [of Kanagawa], but a viola-tion of the laws of hospitality and an outrage."[83] But soon he reported "no further interruption to the friendly intercourse of the people of Simoda [*sic*] and their American visitors"; the authorities "seemed anxious to fa-cilitate the view of the Commodore." The reason apparently eluded him. The Americans "did what they wanted while they were here," a diarist wrote after the ships left Hakodate in June 1854. No resistance was mounted because "we are poor in army and navy [and] were obliged to greet them peacefully."[84]

The *Mississippi* was a special favorite of the Commodore because he'd supervised its construction fourteen years earlier, after which it served as his flagship in Mexico. Before he left Edo Bay for that survey tour, the frig-ate had sent a parting message: "We shall never feel greater confidence, or

---

* The use of prostitutes was a matter of some dispute among the Japanese. There is evidence that Abe sought to curtail it for fear that addiction to Japanese women might lead the Americans to pester non-prostitutes too. A native broadsheet satirized the fuss with drawings poking fun at the foreigners. "The Americans submitted a petition for permission to patronize the harlots in Shimoda," ran one of the captions. "The authorities agreed and notified the brothel-owners of Shimoda, who were delighted at the prospect and passed this news on to the harlots. Unexpectedly, however, the harlots unani-mously pleaded with their masters, saying, among other things: 'We are, to be sure, ill-fated, engaged thus in an ignoble profession. Nevertheless, we have never made any contract going so far as to sleep with foreigners.'" Peter Duus, *The Japanese Discovery of America*, p. 114.

stronger pride, than while under your command." (Three months after returning to New York, he'd pay a final visit to the ship, just berthed at the Brooklyn Naval Yard, to haul down his pennant.) On his own way home now, after his thorough inspection of the outlying ports, the Commodore again stopped in Canton, whose American merchants—the same who had derided him for leaving them too little protection when he sailed off to Japan—issued a collective declaration: "The name of Perry, which has so long adorned the naval profession, will henceforth be enrolled with the highest in diplomacy. Colombus, De Gamma, Cook . . ."

> You have conquered the obstinate will of man and, by overturning the cherished policy of an empire, have brought an estranged but culturated people into the family of nations. You have done this without violence, and the world has looked on with admiration to see the barriers of prejudice fall before the flag of our country without the firing of a shot.

Naval praise had greater meaning for the old sea dog, and in it flowed, specifically for "the most important success of the American Navy in the field of diplomacy." A letter from the Secretary of the Navy stated that "You have won additional fame for yourself, reflected new honor upon the very honorable service to which you belong, and, we all hope, have secured for your country, for commerce, and for civilization, a triumph the blessings of which may be enjoyed by generations yet unborn." Washington Irving would second the thanks for what America perceived as the painless victory soon after Perry was safely home. "You have gained yourself a lasting name, and have won it without shedding a drop of blood or inflicting misery on a human being. What naval commander has ever won laurels at such a rate?" The *New York Times*, which had warned that the poor, frightened Japanese would probably violate any treaty they'd been forced to sign,[85] now derided "the sneers, the ridicule, and the contempt of short-sighted European and American newspapers." The United States, it boasted, had upstaged Europe by using peaceful diplomacy to overcome obstacles "hitherto considered insurmountable."

This time, Perry himself would almost let his pride speak for itself, although not restrain himself from complaints about the mission's inadequate resources and the limitations on his freedom of action to surmount the giant hurdles. However, "exercise of force" had proved unnecessary because Edo, he wrote, "found that resistance would be useless." It "very wisely determined to adopt peaceful measures," although it tried "to evade by every possible means of falsehood and deceit the reasonable concessions demanded by my government." Whatever that contradiction signified, the Commodore claimed "the greater credit" . . . for winning more than Washington had anticipated, despite his inadequate force and "all the discouraging circumstances under which I labored."[86] Therefore, he respectfully submitted that "all, and indeed, more than all, that . . . could reasonably have been expected, has been accomplished."[87]

Samuel Wells Williams would wax joyful. The key that had been inserted into the Japanese lock was the beginning of the end of the long seclusion. American whalers would have protection from storms, Japanese coal would shorten the link between California and Asia, and he saw "a hundred-fold return" on the mission's costs "in the higher benefits likely to flow to the Japanese by their introduction to the family of civilized nations." And all that had been achieved peacefully. "Not a shot has been fired, not a man wounded, not a piece of property destroyed, not a boat sunk, nor a Japanese to be found who is the worse, so far as we know, for the visit of the American Expedition."[88] Williams felt utterly certain that God pointedly "prospered" the mission, which was "carried out with His blessing as a step in His plans for the extension of His kingdom in this land."[89] About the Commodore himself, the missionary translator—whom his son would call Japan's best friend in the squadron—became convinced that the Japanese "would suffer no evil from a man of Perry's principles." Williams would pronounce a final, approving assessment that served to negate his sometimes severe earlier reservations. "The appointment of a naval man as envoy was wise." Throughout the rest of his life, his son would add, the missionary-translator felt "profound gratitude that such a man had been providentially designed to perform this difficult mission."[90]

Later Americans would push on from that kind of praise of the expedition, which had succeeded "beyond the bravest hopes of its best wishers."[91] Almost all would stress that Perry "used no force whatsoever." Evoking naval commanders who "shaped the future in a single battle"— including Drake, Nelson, and Nimitz—a 1955 chronicler of the Black Ships would rejoice that Perry "did it without firing a shot."[92]

Underlining his disinclination to seek conquest, writers would draw a vital distinction between his mission and European ones. Occupation of others' lands smacked of colonialism, deeply repugnant to the sensibilities of Americans, who had liberated themselves from England only late in the previous century. Harvard's Samuel Eliot Morison, whose *Old Bruin* (1967) remains the standard biography of Perry, despite—or because of—its scarce mention of Japanese feelings except supposed indebtedness to him, claimed the Commodore "eschew[ed] forcible annexation, punitive expeditions, or forcing religion and trade on people who desired neither. . . . If this be imperialism, let us have more of it!"*

Apart from dissent by scholarly skeptics, a century and a half of similar congratulation remains at the heart of American memory of the mission, together with a vague belief that the Japanese were and remain essentially grateful to him.

---

* pp. 425, 429. Thomas Bailey, one of America's foremost diplomatic historians, echoed Morison's acclaim for Perry's restraint in the use of his cannon. In achieving his aims, Bailey affirmed, Perry "fired no shot, as he might well have done, and *left little or no rancor* [italics added]. His statesmanlike diplomacy not only won the respect of the Japanese but laid the foundations of the famous 'historic friendship.'" *A Diplomatic History of the American People*, p. 311.

17

The Departure of the Principals

"Commodore Perry Carrying the Gospel of God to the Heathen, 1853."

LTHOUGH MOST AMERICANS would surely have agreed that few choices of a mission commander "have been more brilliant . . . in terms of results achieved,"[1] Perry left East Asia doubting he would be suitably recognized. After his thorough exploration of Shimoda and Hakodate and final visit to Okinawa for compelling Shuri Castle to sign his onerous compact,[2] he took a long route home—from Hong Kong to Europe—on commercial vessels. Praise from the "very highest classes" in cities where he stopped on the way didn't relieve him of worry that no such honor would come where it really mattered. He feared the adage about no man being a prophet in his own country "may well apply."[3]

A final leg from England on a ship whose construction he'd supervised during his stint as General Superintendent of Mail Steamers brought him home at last in January 1855, after almost twenty-seven months abroad. Keeping his small Hudson River estate in Tarrytown, New York, he moved into a new house in Manhattan and indeed got less than the hero's cheers he believed he'd earned. The Treaty of Kanagawa had pleased Washington when news of it became public in July 1854, while the Commodore was still in Europe. (The text was to have been kept under wraps until signed by Franklin Pierce, the new President, but the *New York Times* obtained a copy. To defend against a charge of revealing official secrets, the paper claimed its invented correspondent in Japan—supposedly the Emperor's favorite, no less—had rushed it a translation of the Japanese version.) The *Times*'s Washington correspondent saw "the hand and blessing of God" in the "privileges and freedom" Perry had secured, and the *New York Herald* that had previously been contemptuous of Asians praised them as "enlightened, free, and tolerant."[4]

In local feting, New York's social elite supplemented a loving family's welcome by giving the Commodore a set of silver plates. Boston merchants, prominent in the China trade, struck a medal in his honor, and the governor of Rhode Island crowned a large ceremony in Perry's hometown of Newport by presenting him with a twenty-pound silver tray for services that included teaching the heathen "the observance of the Sabbath."[5] High notes in the national praise came from Millard Fillmore and members of his administration, the former President writing that the result "exceeded my most sanguine expectations . . . I congratulate you and the country upon the brilliant success of your mission." Still, the success prompted little interest in the nation as a whole. Even more than before, the burning issue of slavery smothered appreciation for the opening of Japan, to which President Pierce gave a mere two-sentence mention in his twenty-one-page annual message to Congress.

The relief secured by the Compromise of 1850 turned out to be as temporary as its opponents had predicted. Reaction to *Uncle Tom's Cabin*, published when the Commodore was leaving Norfolk, deepened the antagonism of both sides, but especially of abolitionists. Opposition to slavery's extension to the new Western territories was now so fierce that Southern senators whispered about secession. (The formerly unspeakable move would be taken six years hence.)

Perry's services to the mercantile community hadn't made him rich. During the expedition, he'd regretted how badly naval officers and crews fared after visiting "all climes for the protection of these very merchants. . . . Alas . . . we spend our lives in hard service to die in comparative penury."[6] Maybe that contributed to his anger at the business community's failure to sufficiently appreciate his contribution to their prosperity.[7] It was soothed by slightly belated fuller recognition and a handsome reward from a grateful Washington. Congress appropriated the then huge sum of $400,000 for him to write and publish his account of the expedition, plus $20,000 in compensation for his diplomatic expenditures during its course.[8]

The Commodore was happy at the prospect of "loudly trumpet[ing]" his feat, as a Japan specialist would later describe his rendition of the mission saga.[9] Unaccustomed to writing at length, he sought help. "I may claim to be a pretty good sailor . . . but I have no talent for authorship," he wrote Samuel Wells Williams in a vain effort to enlist his old translator's collaboration.[10] During his stay in England, he'd sought the same from Nathaniel Hawthorne, who'd published his masterpiece, *The Scarlet Letter*, in 1850, followed by *The House of the Seven Gables* the next year. Presently the American consul in Liverpool,[11] Hawthorne considered Japan a less hackneyed theme than virtually any other in the world; but the temptation wasn't strong enough for him to interrupt his own writing. One of the substitutes he suggested was Herman Melville, who regarded Moby-Dick's Pacific home as virtually a second country. However, Melville's antipathy to naval brass, a by-product of his affection for often exploited seamen, made him a bad choice. (If he had based the character of *White-Jacket*'s discipline-loving Captain Claret partly on Perry, the latter was apparently unaware of it.) In the end, the Commodore settled on the Reverend Francis Hawkes, rector of New York's (Episcopal) Calvary Church and an author of histories and biographies.

Diligent, compliant Hawkes got straight to work. Volume I of *Narrative of the Expedition to the China Seas and Japan, 1852–1854*, appeared in 1856, then two others the following year. A later chronicler of the expedition would find the "three fat volumes . . . solemn and humorless like the Commodore himself, but also vivid, well arranged and accurate."[12] They were also beautifully illustrated with paintings and drawings by the artists the Commodore had taken with him.[13] But the *Narrative*'s most salient attribute would lie in nearly all Americans taking its version of Perry's deeds as definitive. Unless familiar with the accounts of other eyewitnesses he tried to suppress, all published later, readers had no way of knowing what was misrepresented—such as the lot of the squadron's sailors, portrayed as having abundant and happy free time—and what was concealed, such as the white flags and the provenance of Okinawa's Gokokuji bell. "Time and again," Peter Wiley would point out, "the expedition was described as one in which violence was eschewed and no lives were lost" (clearly meaning by hostilities). Most misleading, the great confrontation was pictured as between "the representatives of a civilized nation and a semibarbaric people who were suspicious of foreigners, addicted to duplicity, obeisant in the face of authority, often brutish . . . and prone to lewd behavior."[14]

Hawkes's capable rendering of Perry's views and interests helped make the Commodore's take on the mission its more or less official record—the primary source of all subsequent accounts by third parties, including this one. His exceptional urge to appear faultless in everything further increases the danger of reliance on its unavoidable subjectivity. (When one of his ships ran aground and was nearly lost near Kanagawa in 1854, he ordered its captain to delete mention of circumstances that implicated the squadron commander. "Selfish man!" the captain noted in his diary.[15]) Even when Old Bruin's more obvious prejudices are discounted, his deeply self-justifying and often self-righteous view of the mission continues to greatly influence Western perception.

Personal problems were harder to solve. The fifteen-plus-year average life expectancy of Americans of Perry's social position who'd reached age sixty would have given him a considerable twilight if not for the damage to his health during his foreign assignments, including the demanding one from which he'd just returned. Despite that, he took command of the Brooklyn Naval Yard after completing the *Narrative*, and also served on boards supervising naval reforms. However, weakness on top of, or from, his old rheumatism kept him confined to his Manhattan house and even his bed during much of 1857. At the age of sixty-three, he was awarded command of the American fleet in the Mediterranean, the prestigious billet to which he'd aspired ever since serving there as a young officer. Although not entirely infirm, he was unable to report for duty. Shortly after publication of the final volumes of the *Narrative* in late 1857, he caught a severe cold and died unexpectedly on March 4, 1858.

The funeral would have satisfied his fondness for pomp. Among the carriage-born dignitaries, General Winfield Scott, the Commodore's army counterpart in the Mexican War, most resembled him, but his memory was no less honored by the crowds on foot. To the tolling of bells, fluttering of half-masted flags, saluting of naval guns from the harbor, and braving of freezing temperatures, five hundred men of a New York guard regiment and two hundred from the state militia accompanied Old Bruin's coffin from his house to St. Mark's Church, via Fifth Avenue.[16] The hundred-odd marines at the head of the column who'd served with the East Asia Squadron and used their own money to buy or rent uniforms for the occasion were even more moving. A Washington newspaper's extolling of the deceased as a model naval officer, "thoroughly American in all his views," and possessing a heart that beat "only to the measures of generosity and justice" served to further narrow the prism through which his countrymen viewed his accomplishment. Most Japanese of the time, together with residents of the expedition's Hong Kong and Okinawa staging points, perceived a remorselessly imperialist heart beating in the service of Yankee ambition and effrontery; and their memory would prove the stronger one. On the occasion of Perry's Yokohama landing in March, 1854, a young midshipman correctly predicted that the day, "if it be not hereafter remembered" by Americans, "will at least be kept long in mind by the people of [Japan]."

PERRY'S INTERESTS NATURALLY LAY far more in his cherished homeland. Like almost all outsiders, he clung to the notion that Japan was mired in its backward attitude and ways, whereas "rapid social transformation"[17] was actually taking place beneath the rigidity of many aspects of public and private life. "The old was being discarded," an eminent Japanese novelist would summarize, "even though the new things to replace them had not yet been created."[18] The literacy rate, which was among the world's highest, fed an impetus for basic changes that had been under way for years.

With rare exception, early Western visitors who expected to find a nation of Rip van Winkles utterly blank about the modern world were struck by how much more educated Japanese knew about them than the other way around. Some of Perry's Americans in particular were "astonished," one would exclaim, "at the vigor, intelligence and information of their unwilling hosts."[19] Another expressed surprise at his first meetings with visitors to the ships because "we found [them] so well informed. They questioned us about the Mexican War, then recent; about General Taylor and Santa Anna. . . . One of them asked if the monster gun on [the *Susquehanna's*] quarter-deck was a Paixhans gun. Yes, it was; but where and how could he ever have heard the name?"[20]

He had heard it through Western studies, which were otherwise called *rangaku*, "Dutch learning," because almost all its sources came from the Deshima colony. They included human sources: "Japanese thirsting for knowledge"[21] plied every learned man who resided on little Deshima, especially Engelbert Kaempfer in the late seventeenth century and Philipp Franz von Siebold in the early nineteenth, the two physicians whose books Perry read. Dutch learning's peephole on the West widened when a ban on European literature was rescinded in 1716 and a translation of an anatomy book was published in 1774. Twenty-nine years later, the shogunate created an office for translating more Dutch works, chiefly about astronomy and surveying. The subject scope assigned for translation was considerably broadened in 1811, from which point scientific works in particular were "regularly acquired and rendered into Japanese"—and Dutch became the channel for virtually all information and study about the West, although Chinese and Korean traders also continued to inform, especially about Western probes in Asia.

Soon ardent students were traveling to Nagasaki to study Western ways, especially medicine, chemistry, navigation, and astronomy as well as anatomy. When Perry arrived, some one hundred and forty Dutch interpreters were believed to be there, mixed with the students. Although they started no Industrial Revolution, their knowledge of it became one of the ways in which Western books "became more important than the copper [the ships] took back with them" to the Netherlands.[22]

Edo's attitude toward those quasi-official books was very mixed. A *roju* member who supervised their use later acknowledged that they "may serve to encourage idle curiosity" or "express harmful ideas." Alarmed by the great interest they prompted, Confucian scholars went much farther, denouncing European literature as subversive, especially as increasing numbers of readers advocated greater national openness or charged the *bakufu* with incompetence. Nevertheless, the *roju* official concluded the books were needed for their scientific and military insights. Advisable as banning might seem to some, that wouldn't have prevented people from reading them. (He didn't mention that banning might have provoked serious displeasure among a number of prominent daimyo who were eager to follow European developments.) The solution was to prevent "irresponsible people" from acquiring them "in large quantities" by depositing them in a government library.[23]

The history of Dutch learning was correspondingly checkered. Acquaintance with foreign cultures prompted a few to develop predictable affection for them, which then led to trouble. An artist much influenced by Western texts went so far as to speak out for equality, and if that didn't fly hard enough in the face of the Confucian-based Tokugawa hierarchy, he ventured that beggars were no less human beings than the Emperor. A year after some *rangakusha* (scholars of Dutch studies) protested the 1837 shelling of the *Morrison* that sought to return the three castaways,[24] a physician of Western medicine widely distributed a pamphlet that called for ending the seclusion. That audacity went too far for the *bakufu*. The rash progressive was imprisoned and committed suicide, while a crackdown on other critics of the alarmed government dealt a heavy blow to Western studies, especially after a group of intellectuals killed themselves in 1839 to atone for possibly embarrassing their daimyo in the eyes of the Shogun. Now another side of those who remained alive became more robust, if not paramount: the urge to know the enemy in general—and its technology in particular—in order to better defeat him and, paradoxically, maintain the *sakoku*. Fire had to be fought with fire.

But even those supporters of a hard-line antiforeign stance were evidence that the secluded country wasn't fully closed intellectually, culturally, or even technologically. And while time wouldn't *inevitably* move a substantial number of the intellectuals, scientists, and engineers toward spearheading a movement for greater openness in general, that was what commonly happened to curious people with knowledge denied to others. Actually, minds were already broadening, even among the "know-thine-enemy" *rangakusha* scholars. Many were contemptuous of foreigners, but not of foreign thought. Their urge to acquire more modern know-how drove them up against the social and governmental restrictions, and they pushed. Although it was often in the name of "western science, Japanese essence," no society has ever been able to quarantine one field of learning from another more than temporarily. Even as the seclusion was being held up as essential to Japanese identity, some scholars and inventors were convinced that transplantation of Western technology could fully succeed only in a more congenial soil of freer social rigidity.

That, in turn, prompted fear that importation of even foreign military skills would undermine Japanese society. But Western practicality and rationality couldn't be shut out. Francis Hall, the keenly observant American journalist from Elmira, New York, who made his way to Japan five years after Perry's second visit, found reason to believe that "light from the West streaming in a feeble ray through the pin point at old Deshima" was very slowly improving isolated Japan.[25] "Tangible evidence of the value of Western civilization" provided by books was being "adopted and adapted to Japan through a natural process of internal transformation, or what [Hall] saw as a form of gradual domestic evolution."[26] In addition, considerable "research and development" was being conducted in several important fields independent of Western inspiration. The modernization it drove was never smooth, nor directly Westernizing because it was taking place in its own manner, at its own speed. But it was no less critical for that, and far less traumatic.

Many merchants too—although the class was small in percentage of the total population—wanted the seclusion relaxed for the sake of trade, which motivated their brothers everywhere. Hall thought commerce, with its "leveling tendencies," would eventually diminish or eliminate "the aristocracy of caste and birth." (He saw the haughty samurai as "the idlest, most worthless man Nippon produces," and compared the ambitious merchants who were spearheading the great changes to the English dissenters who fled Puritan Massachusetts for market-oriented New York.) Additional pressure was coming from enterprising farmers who, being free of charters linking them to the feudal system, were also freer to make money, thereby fashioning significant changes of their own.

For roughly a century, samurai had been moving from the countryside to castle towns, much increasing demand for edibles and other products there. Formerly self-contained villages responded by selling more and more to markets, which required them to produce surpluses. The minority of successful farmers who did that and got rich sought to prevent hostility from the poor by undertaking social welfare improvements such as building local schools and refraining from gouging. While taking the edge off capitalist avarice in those ways, many became even more capitalist by using some their surpluses not only to specialize—175 varieties of rice at the beginning of the Tokugawa dynasty became some 2,000 by 1850[27]—but also to start proto-industrial manufacture of commodities like sake, soy sauces, textile dyes, and textiles themselves, most notably silk.

Samurai had status and authority but often no money. More and more merchants had money—especially after it began superceding the feudal economy of rice subsidies—but no power. Codes, rules, and a halfhearted *bakufu* attempts to restrict the accumulation of wealth and foster a "back to the soil" movement couldn't prevent the basic economic restructuring forged by capital accumulation and a virtually irrepressible urge to put the accumulations to use. While Edo Castle didn't fully grasp what was happening, some new manufacturers began collecting art and serving as patrons of its creators. A number who no longer considered themselves peasants stopped trying to bribe their daimyo to award them samurai rank. A few felt they had the power—because they had the money—to speak out for the freedom to pursue the activities that were giving them wealth and status. Those activities were anathema to most samurai, who wanted to keep running things as they had, with no foreigners to help promote changes. But the samurai of the "fixed, stolid and even reactionary qualities" were unable to prevent the dynamic new commercialism from turning the country haywire, as it seemed to them. Each new decade made the country's conditions less and less compatible with feudal structure.

Not that the intellectuals, much less the farmers, sought to introduce democracy, or even had a clear picture of it, or of civil rights. The handful who knew of George Washington may have delighted Perry, but had no real notion of republican government or its workings. (A reader of Western literature who, in 1861, asked journalist Hall for a picture of Washington was a very rare exception.) But if participatory government wasn't a goal of political thought, the economic and social changes may well have led to it, as in Europe. New entrepreneurs' plans to pursue, as well as economic interests to defend, often help develop democratic institutions.[28]

In any case, the growth of preindustrial manufacture, domestic trade, and popular education was altering the farming life that for centuries had locked the great majority of the people into the same habits and rhythms. Slowly but remorselessly, it was advancing the country from its agrarian-based feudalism.[29] Common interests of innovative farmers and wealthy merchants in the thriving urban centers, especially Osaka, increased the momentum. Recent investigation of farming villages' records has shown that their "hidden passions" were "a driving force behind the evolution of Japanese society and the creation of a new culture."[30] The opposition—and to any easing of the *sakoku*—was substantial, but nothing like it would become when foreigners would make their demands. Unless some stunning new event or development reversed the powerful economic course, *when* Japan would have ended its seclusion on its own terms was a more relevant question than *whether*.

MOST JAPANESE WERE NATURALLY aware of how impoverished and indebted to merchants many samurai had become, and how much economic life was otherwise diverging from its old patterns. But none—not even Abe Masahiro, Tokugawa Nariaki, or their most astute advisors—grasped the significance of the restructuring because the economic and sociological tools for measuring it and predicting its consequences hadn't been conceived. Only later did "generations of research . . . [make] clear how much things changed during the Edo years," and how much Japan's "backwardness compared to the West was overplayed."[31]

Perry couldn't have known the degree to which fundamental developments belied his belief that Japan required a Western model and invalidated his reasons for the mission's need. His impatience was characteristic of most systems' commercial pioneers and confederates, maybe capitalism's more than most. However, he also knew nothing about the political developments that took place after he departed from Japan—even while he was still there, inspecting Shimoda and Hakodate. The Treaty of Kanagawa was triggering "the most turbulent era in all of Japanese history,"[32] and he seemed hardly to care.

Maybe that was to be expected of someone so forceful. Since the qualities that propel people to bold action often diminish their desire to ruminate, few decisive commanders or statesmen engage in vigorous contemplation of their deeds' long-term consequences. For that matter, few elected officials spend much time pondering those consequences. Whatever the explanation, Perry all but lost interest in the land of his "mission accomplished." He also defaulted on his promise to free Okinawans of their burdens, as if it had been a passing fancy or useful deception. From his declaration that he could "conceive of no greater act of humanity than . . . to rescue, if possible, these miserable beings from the oppression of their tyrannical rulers"[33] he turned directly to his pursuit of more personally rewarding goals.

The old sailor did offer general advice about negotiating. Humanity as well as sound policy, he argued, required that all peaceful means should be exhausted before taking the last resort of hostile action. Even if force had to be applied, only "just and honorable means" should be used, and the goal must be "a more general and enlightened intercourse with the world. . . . We Christian people, claiming for ourselves greater advantages of civilization and moral cultivation, seek, unasked of [the peoples of the East] commercial and social intercourse . . . and if perchance difficulties arise . . . we immediately force upon them the alternative to our view of the case, or chastisement."[34] That was hardly the first or last expression of noble statements by a leader who might have had a double doing the opposite in the field, in Perry's case Edo Bay.

A Japanese scholar's recent suggestion that it is "an American characteristic, I think, not to be very sensitive toward a nation whose pride it has damaged"[35] may misrepresent by implying that Americans were domineering by nature. To the extent such generalization is valid, Americans may have been less bad-tempered and greedy than other imperial peoples. But their fervor and ignorance, especially of other cultures, sometimes caused grave damage. Settled on their own continent, the people of the new world power—excluding a small minority of scholars and diplomats—tended to know very little about the rest of the world. And although the charge of insensitivity may also mislead by intimating it was a United States monopoly, Perry helped draw the profile of the American soldier-explorer-adventurer-statesman who follows the heavy mark he makes on a foreign country with quick withdrawal and a move to something else, never recognizing *how* heavy the damage was and why.

The Japan he left was boiling in despairing confusion, fierce misunderstandings and arguments, bloody plots and counterplots. A post–Black Ship frenzy was "full of episodes that seem not to belong to waking life, but have the plausible inconsequence, the unearthly logic, of events in a dream."[36] No doubt the country's too-tight control before the treaty's signing was partly responsible for the eruptions of desperation afterward, as Ian Buruma recently suggested. In any case, young extremists seeking national salvation in ultraviolence now spiked "popular hysteria" and a "hellish struggle."

It was a time of violent intrigues and murderous plots, of rebellions and countercoups, of feudal lords from the southwest maneuvering against the Tokugawa loyalists. . . . Mobs gathered in the big cities . . . carrying Shinto images, visiting shrines, dancing half-naked in the streets, having sex in public, and raiding wealthy houses, while shouting in a state of quasi-religious ecstasy: "It's okay, it's okay, anything we do is okay!"[37]

Abe had long known that while war with Perry might invite the empire's destruction, exposed inability "to resist Occidental aggression would be to invite the ruin of the Tokugawa house."[38] That ruin had begun. The intrigues and murderous plots were mostly in pursuit of revenge—not yet against the barbarians who had caused the humiliation, but against those who'd allowed it to happen. Intense indignation about the capitulation washed over the court in Kyoto, raising the volume of "Revere the Emperor, Expel the Barbarian" ever higher. Elsewhere too, shock and anger at the *bakufu* that was "guilty" of failing to defend against the barbarians wobbled Tokugawa rule. "How empty your title, 'Queller of Barbarians'!" sneered a poem of the time. "You, whose ancestors in the mighty days/Roared at the skies and swept across the earth/Stand now helpless to drive off wrangling foreigners."[39] Decades of contempt for the weakness of the country's elite, with its imagined and real addiction to dissolute luxury, further fueled the orgies of violence. In the least bloody cases, only statues were decapitated.

ABE MASAHIRO SAW ONLY THE BEGINNING of the time of troubles. His long liking for sake had further weakened his health, and his fondness for women may have helped.

After the death of his young wife, Kinko, he remarried in the Black Ship year of 1853. Although he had no offspring with his second wife, his concubines gave him eleven.[40] The practice was widespread among the elite, especially when official wives produced no heir, and Kinko as well as his mother had urged him to take a certain Otoyo, whose allure he'd noticed in a sweet shop, as a lover. Soon Otoyo, a worker in that shop or its owner's daughter, would be a model for drawings of Edo beauties much favored in "The Floating World."

On the grounds that the Treaty of Kanagawa broke the law of the *sakoku*, Abe submitted his resignation shortly after its completion, but the

Shogun didn't accept it, so on he soldiered—and imbibed. Things are a little rough right now, he'd answer his doctors' urging to cut down on sake; please don't ask me to give up that little relaxation. The treaty's political liability made things yet more difficult for the *bakufu*. The depleted Chief Senior Councilor continued trying to achieve some kind of consensus in the very changed political circumstances—to keep furious factions from killing one another and to prop up Tokugawa rule. But his movements became unsteady and his sallow color greatly alarmed his friends. Still, his sense of responsibility, stiffened by worry about doom if he weren't there to mollify and try to mediate, kept him at the surely futile efforts until he finally did resign in October 1855, not long after Perry's return to New York.

Although there was little chance he'd have been able to prevent the forthcoming collapse if he'd remained longer in office, he'd surely have taken some further positive measures, such as sending students abroad, to advance the study of Western languages and science. As it was, he'd already founded several academic institutions for the purpose. Much more remarkably, he'd lasted a decade in the highest administrative office, almost all "in the teeth of the most intractable problems." None of his successors would manage to withstand "the enormous pressures of public life for nearly as long"—few, indeed, for more than two years.[41]

Friends and admirers, including Tokugawa Nariaki sent him their personal physicians, who predicted nothing good. Still able to enjoy his favorite pastime of horseback riding, he visited the then fairly tranquil Tama River (which, coincidentally, flows toward Kanagawa), until he badly injured himself in a fall when returning from there. That accident or another one was surely just a question of time. If the American mission had undermined *Perry's* health, the nervous strain of trying to save Japan from invasion and/or civil conflict all but destroyed Abe's, although he was not much more than half the Commodore's age. "There is now," he cited a growing belief, "a greater danger of internal rebellion than of foreign attack."[42]

His physical deterioration deeply worried his retainers. They needn't have read his private poems to know the stress he'd endured seeking a solution to the insoluble national problem; trying to prevent a break with Tokugawa Nariaki so the country wouldn't crack from within. (Far from supporting the Treaty of Kanagawa, Nariaki demanded its renegotiation on better terms for Japan. "Opposed when he should have expected support, blocked when possible, lobbied and intrigued against, Abe must surely have come to regret his policy of consultation."[43]) But the poems did add details of his physical and mental pain, exacerbated by great difficulty sleeping. Even when dozing, "I think of the foreigners, night and day. . . . I always see ships that come from abroad."[44]

Rather than rescue, however, the sake was probably his coup de grace, via cancer of the liver or kidneys. (Nariaki's gift of some special tonic wine of the Mito region didn't help.) He grew still paler. Knowing his days were limited, he summoned the Governor of Shimoda, where Townsend Harris had arrived the year before, and asked whether that first American consul had "the spirit of *jin*—benevolence, compassion, sympathy. Apparently willing to lie in order to comfort a dying man, the Governor said the menacing Harris indeed possessed such qualities. Abe's second wife, in character with their society, sought to ease the patient's suffering by bringing Otoyo to his side. Another love poem was almost certainly to her.

The spent thirty-eight-year-old died in August 1857, almost a year before Perry. His passing went unannounced for several days so that a nephew could be not-quite-legitimately adopted in order to prevent confiscation of Abe's *han*, the usual procedure when a daimyo left no legal heir. Officials trying to cope with Japan's ever more difficult problems lamented the additional loss "when Abe's knowledge and experience and skill at conciliation were so desperately needed."[45]

Leaving his mansion as if accompanying him to work in Edo Castle, the funeral procession made its way instead to a temple in the suburbs. His hope to bind the nation was in shreds, but respect and admiration for his person remained intact.

Without Abe, Tokugawa Nariaki's fading was quick. Within a month, he resigned as defense advisor, in which position he'd danced his curious jig of half-loyal opposition with Abe, and furthered the breakdown of Edo Castle's rule by moving to outright hostility to it. Just over a year later, he and other key daimyo who had trusted Abe were humiliated with public rebukes or forced into retirement or house arrest. (Confined forever to his Mito *han* for criticizing the signing of a new commercial treaty, or "Harris Treaty," without the Emperor's approval, Nariaki would die there in 1860.) The Kyoto court too, which Abe had managed to include in something resembling a working association, was "bullied . . . into mutinous silence"—to the ever greater fury of ever growing anti-Tokugawa militants. "Whatever magic Abe possessed" didn't survive him, a scholar of the period would summarize. "What had been during his lifetime an amicable series of relationships between *bakufu* and court, *bakufu* and daimyo, *bakufu* and people was irretrievably lost with his death."[46]

But if men with intimate knowledge of Abe's character and efforts honored that "last Bakufu leader" of true distinction, passionate antiforeigners, historians, and then the general public soon dismissed him for his failure to ward off the shock to Japan. He was criticized for lack of ability as well as of decisiveness. In 1936, after the country's shift to militarism had made it a threat to the world, one of Japan's leading historians would declare that Abe, "weak-kneed" and "no diplomat," had an ostrich's instinct and no consistent views. The "evading" and "procrastinating" lord was "a common politician, nothing special."[47]

More than a hundred years would pass before Japanese scholars would begin resurrecting the Chief Senior Councilor's memory not as a weakling, but as a knight of good sense who held as much of the country together as anyone could have, preventing worse damage and possibly the humiliation of full colonization, which Japan was among the few Asian countries to avoid.

18

The Pandora's Box

Trial runs of Yamato, *the world's best battleship, 1941*

PREDICTING THEY'D NEVER BE PERMITTED to land in Japan, American merchants in China scoffed that the Treaty of Kanagawa had secured no more than commitment to provide essentials to visiting ships. Their contention that the "wood and water" pact wasn't "worth a damn and the Japanese know it"[1] overstated the resistance, but not more than Americans at home overstated its promise. "Ere long," whooped a California newspaper, Perry's "entering wedge" would "open to us the interior wealth of these unknown lands, which shall pour their riches in our lap."[2]

American ships were eager to start the pouring, but the first to reach Edo Bay after the signing was a luxurious yacht that returned a Japanese castaway. The "very beautiful ship without any hostile weapons" was welcomed, but not the clipper that followed shortly and was directed to Shimoda soon after the Commodore had departed from there in July 1854. In its unwillingness to reveal how much the Treaty of Kanagawa had conceded, Edo Castle had published a summary that pretended American ships were entitled to enter Shimoda and Hadokate for supplies only. As if to set a pattern—especially for the next decade, when Japanese-American trade would be scant—local authorities refused to do business with the clipper.[3]

Most Japanese fists remained clenched against any foreign presence. Even if Westerners wouldn't start proselytizing for Christianity again, as many expected, they'd soil the sacred country with their ways and probably prepare for the American fleet to return and impose some form of colonial control on top of the pollution of commercialism. Still wanting no trade, much less an official American presence, Shimoda officials cold-shouldered Townsend Harris, the first Western consul, who arrived there in August 1856.

The qualifications of the prosperous merchant and former president of New York City's Board of Education included previous travel and trading in Asia. Earlier the same year, the devout Protestant had negotiated a new commercial treaty with Siam, the first Far Eastern country with which Washington had established relations, in 1833. In Shimoda, however, Harris was told no consul was needed because there were no difficulties to resolve; and if he stayed, he and others of his kind would "cause much trouble." Antipathy to his imperious presence burgeoned even before discovery that he was as resourceful and tenacious as Perry, although he'd become fonder of the Japanese people, perhaps because he'd have much more to do with them than the Commodore. But no admiration either way was now forthcoming. Appalled by the little port's opening to foreigners, a local poet lauded the cherry blossoms that "take not on the rank barbarian stench/But breathe to the morning sun the fragrance of a nation's soul."[4] (Nevertheless, Harvard historian Samuel Eliot Morison, whose praise of Perry would much influence Americans, would write that Shimoda "left a very favorable impression on the squadron, and the feeling was mutual."[5]) Ten years later, the perspicacious Francis Hall would find Japanese officials convinced the arrangements were only a five-year experiment, after which Japan would be "free to make such amendments as were necessary, or to do away with them altogether."[6]

Little Shimoda quaked about the foreigners who wanted to push their way in. Residents were warned to carefully secure their houses and shops against those who might come ashore "and stroll about here and there." "Naturally" women and children must never go outdoors and "the greatest caution must be taken" to prevent the intruders from looking at them.[7]

The brunt of the aversion fell on the pioneering Harris. The U.S.S. *Vincennes* had anchored off Kyushu, far to the south, the year before. The commander of the eighteen-gun sloop of war, Lieutenant John Rodgers, had neither knowledge of Japanese nor an interpreter, but thought he knew what had inspired his extensive survey of Japanese coastal waters: the Treaty of Kanagawa had prompted naval officers to speculate that the United States might annex Japan.[8] Although the rumors came to nothing, Lieutenant Rodgers, after investigating the Great Circle route, concluded that Asia's commercial possibilities were "so vast as to dazzle sober calculation."[9] Harris never made contact with him. He encountered great difficulty doing that even with Shimoda's authorities, who informed him it "wasn't customary" to reply to foreigners' letters.[10] Obstructed and shunned, the lonely man saw no American ship at all for fourteen months. He had no communication from Washington for four months longer, and—even worse, he thought—no warships supported him. Negotiations with the Japanese, he lamented, could be conducted only if "the plenipotentiary was backed by a fleet, and offered them cannon balls for arguments."[11] That was the "proper" way with the "false, base and cowardly people."[12]

But he bore his isolation manfully. "I have a perfect knowledge of the social banishment I must endure while in Japan," he'd written President Pierce before hoisting the first consular flag to fly in Japan from a former temple assigned him as a residence.[13] And he had the luck to be at his lonely post during what would become known as the Second Opium War, when England, now joined by France, was administering even more humiliation than during the First, in retaliation for Peking's failure to fulfill obligations of the treaty forced on it in 1844. (Burned Canton fell to British troops in 1857; Peking would soon follow.) Despite earlier indignation at European treatment of China, Harris staunchly applied the power of intimidation generated by Japanese fear that the British and French fleets would next turn to them, heightening Edo worries that if great care weren't taken, "in this country also . . . war may result from some trivial incident."[14] The hefty consul used his "rolling volley of words" to misrepresent and threaten in addition to melding supple persuasion, ample bluster, and creative cajolery to break down the opposition from local and Edo authorities.[15] Risking travel when it had been made perilous for foreigners (by samurai incensed about the concessions to the barbarians), he made his way to the capital in 1857, in an extravagant caravan designed to display American might. His claim to his journal that "the people were wild with curiosity to see my entry" and "would have rushed to Edo 'by millions'" if not prevented by the government was exaggerated, but not invented. Growing Japanese interest in foreigners prompted a spurt of publications by native scholars and translations of books and newspapers from the Dutch, Chinese, and English.

In the capital, Harris met with Shogun Tokugawa Iemochi, the retarded Tokugawa Iesada having shortly before died the early death that had been predicted for him. He achieved that exploit partly by convincing some whose ear he managed to reach that first trade arrangements with America would be Japan's best deal, much better than any with a European power—especially England, which wanted to import opium there.[16] At the same time, he continued using China as an example of what happened when Asian leaders refused to behave "sensibly." The first Opium War that destroyed so many Middle Kingdom fortifications and cities might have been avoided, he told the Shogun's new Chief Senior Councilor, Abe's replacement. China had become "as weak as she was when conquered by the Tartars," and although no one could know what England and France would do to it now, its prospects were grim, if only because it "must pay all the costs of the war."[17]

When hard-driving and -drinking Minister Harris, whom other visiting Americans disliked for those qualities, would shortly suffer a physical breakdown, Shogun Iemochi would order his best physician to attend to him. Now, in Edo, Iemochi approved the consul's proposal to conclude a commercial treaty for enabling the opening of trade. But it was a measure of how far the Edo–Kyoto balance had shifted that Harris had to seek imperial sanction too because Edo Castle feared submission to the Americans without it would lead to revolt. Emperor Komei, who was convinced that "to revolutionize the sound laws" handed down for centuries would disturb his people and "make it impossible to preserve lasting tranquillity," needed no encouragement to resist Harris, but got it nevertheless from some eighty nobles, most of them as antiforeign as he was, and all encouraged by waxing Shinto dedication to ancient pre-shogun principles. With very little knowledge or even interest in the outside world, most of that entourage was "poorly informed, impractical and xenophobic."[18] Despite that, or because of it, swelling imperial fervor in the country prompted samurai elsewhere to desert their domains and volunteer to serve those aides to the Emperor, who now urged him to consult the spirit of Tokugawa Ieyasu about the proposed commercial treaty. When a copy placed on the grave of the dynasty's founder prompted no response from within, Komei refused to give his consent, saying posterity would disgrace him if he did. "How could I apologize to [the sun goddess] Amaterasu?"[19]

The Emperor and his supporters were infuriated when the next Chief Senior Council—the replacement of Abe's replacement—dealt with the matter by ignoring him. The *bakufu*, still convinced that provoking the Western powers into military action was an even worse alternative than admitting Western representatives and trying to curtail their activities, thus won another day, giving Harris his treaty. But the shogunate's high-handedness further imperiled its authority.

SOME WOULD SAY THE 1858 Treaty of Amity and Commerce with the United States actually opened the door that Perry had merely unlocked. The four additional ports it permitted American ships to use—Nagasaki, Nigata, Hyogo (near the commercial center of Osaka), and Kanagawa (which would be joined with Yokohama)—were far more important for trade than Shimoda or Hakodate. Consul Harris was granted a right of residence in the sanctum sanctorum of Edo, and other Americans would be permitted do the same four years hence, in 1862, allowing Harris to celebrate having "forced this singular people to acknowledge the *rights of embassy*."[20]

But the American gains further insulted many Japanese. Six months earlier, Tokugawa Nariaki had proposed to the *roju* that he lead a group of *ronin* and other young samurai to America, where they'd supervise that end of Japan's infant trade with the New World. Aversion helped prompt his seemingly startling turnaround: even if his party were killed, Nariaki explained, that would be less dangerous than letting foreigners reside in Edo. When they were given permission to do so nevertheless, the Mito lord exploded that surrender to the American consul's demands was "leading the people of a sacred land to bow in front of a dog."[21]

Other samurai had reason to keep resisting foreigners. With the most to lose from major change, the higher reaches of the upper class looked aghast at the uncouth Americans who strode ashore to debase and defile "the people of our sacred land." A poet saw them as evil incarnate.

> Giants with hooked noses like mountain imp;
> Giants with rough hair, loose and red;
> They stole a promise from our sacred master
> And danced with joy as they sailed away
> To the distant land of darkness.[22]

Foreign traders—and by implication the *bakufu* that permitted them to enter—were blamed for all manner of disappointments and difficulties, including insufficient profit from sales of Japanese wares. Even countryside residents who had never seen the interlopers heard frequent denigration, especially from samurai parents and grandparents. One such young woman who had "nothing definite in my mind against America" nevertheless heard so much talk about "the disagreeable experiences of almost all persons who had dealings with foreigners that I had a vague feeling of distaste" for the unknown land.[23] While people who wanted to see new woollen cloth in country stores began asking for "animal-smelling goods," rumors that the foreigners' blankets had been dyed with the blood of stolen infants supplemented pre-Perry tales about their inhuman behavior. Although much of such talk would quite quickly disappear, many aristocratic families continued harboring regret and resentment of the "red barbarians who came uninvited to our sacred land [and] . . . cared nothing for beauty. . . . They talked like tradesmen and did not want to learn the hearts of the children of the gods."[24]

Responding in kind, some American visitors complained about local prices, obstacles to "normal" buying and selling, dogged "spying" on them, and immorality, the latter evidenced, as before, by mixed nude bathing and open display of sexual images. Although some Japanese developed a quick craze for business and took a liking to the informal strangers who conducted it with such panache, mutual disapproval persisted. Some Americans entered people's houses without removing their boots and took target practice oblivious to nearby picnickers. Their sailors were said to regularly get drunk, then brawl among themselves and with bystanders. And their officers were believed to remain determined to proselytize evil Christianity. (Although they'd been careful to do no such thing before the signing of the Treaty of Kanagawa, one of Perry's chaplains left missionary tracts in a temple directly thereafter.)

Americans were blamed for a major earthquake that rattled Edo in 1855: the "reckless decision" to change the old order had obviously displeased the gods too. "The peaceful world is now shaken up/those above quake, those below quiver." Still, the deprecation of foreigners wasn't universal. Accepting that they couldn't be vaporized from Japanese life, the more worldly, or would-be worldly, decided accommodation with them was necessary, and the sooner the better. Even a few formerly passionate antiforeigners had second thoughts. In 1862, a fervent anti-Westerner broke into a house to assassinate the resident *bakufu* official, who was trying to modernize the nascent Tokugawa navy on Western models. The intended victim convinced the would-be killer to put down his sword and listen to reason, then slowly persuaded him that learning from the West was in the national interest.[25] A prominent policy advisor named Shonan Yokoi embodied a more telling example. Four years before Perry's first arrival, Shonan had called for wiping out "the beast-like barbarians in the world." Four years *after*, he was on his way to a radical change of mind, advocating opening the country for the common good—and praising the United States extravagantly enough in 1862 to court arrest.[26] Two years later, Shonan, now leader of a political party and a devotee of Western science, supported the worldwide trend of all nations communicating with one another. If Japan alone clung to "the old custom of closing her door to foreigners and remaining in seclusion, this would instantly turn the multitude of nations into her enemies, inviting self-destruction right before our eyes."

Others began questioning the welter of social regulations, especially those that kept people in the ranks into which they'd been born. Still, the *bakufu* remained half paralyzed, and ignorance and fear of what the new order would be sharpened its birth pangs. But the conviction of virtually all concerned Americans that a backward, largely savage nation would be transformed into a modern, civilized one came close enough to gospel for the American magazine *Annual Cyclopedia* to report in 1871 that Japan deserved "universal admiration" for its "extremely rapid progress in the desired direction."[27] "Universal apprehension" would have been more accurate.

THE FIRST JAPANESE VESSEL to cross the Pacific was one of the little warships bought from the Dutch. Neither a boiler so small that steam propulsion was used only for entering and leaving ports nor advice from some American naval officers during the voyage diminished the great pride taken in the bold effort so soon after the country beheld its first steamships in the terrifying shape of the *Mississippi* and *Susquehanna*. It meant, a Dutch studies scholar among its passengers would crow, "that about seven years after the first sight of a steamship, after only about five years of practice [in navigation], the Japanese people made a trans-Pacific crossing without help from foreign experts."[28]

After a very rough month-plus at sea, the *Karin-maru* reached San Francisco in March 1860, two years after Perry's death. Its passengers were seventy-seven samurai braced for a long visit under instructions to learn all they could about the United States. The captain, himself a consummate samurai named Katsu Kaishu, provided clear guidance of what those patriots, all of whom had opposed the *kaikoku*, should examine. Being an historian and statesman as well as the founder of the brand-new Japanese navy for whose "glory" he'd accomplished the crossing, Katsu didn't point them exclusively to military matters, but that was his central focus: the same "mechanics, military science, gunnery, fortifications" he'd promoted when proposing the founding of a school for "the Study of Barbarian Books." One of the proposal's supporters, a fellow Tokugawa official who'd helped finalize Townsend Harris's Shimoda Treaty, made the point even more clearly by urging study of Western countries' "truly useful things": their armies and navies. The books he recommended for translation were "on bombardment, on the construction of batteries, on fortifications, books on building warships and maneuvering them, books on sailing and navigation, books on training soldiers and sailors, on machinery, books that set forth [those countries'] real strength and weakness."[29]

The American press adored the exotic visitors with their hemp sandals and double swords. San Francisco, Baltimore, Washington, and Philadelphia loudly lionized them, and their unprecedented procession in New York, accompanied by more than six thousand troops and thirty-two bands, inspired Walt Whitman's "A Broadway Pageant." "Over the Western sea, hither from Niphon Come/Courteous, the Princes of Asia. . . ." If the "swart-cheek'd . . . two-sworded" novelties were impassive, Whitman was opposite, declaring more about Americans than their guests in the same poem:

> I too, raising my voice. . . .
> I chant the World on my Western Sea. . . .
> I chant the new empire, grander than any before—As in a
>   vision it comes to me:
> I chant America, the Mistress—I chant a greater supremacy. . . .

Generous as many Americans were to the delegation, not all went as well as it might have, especially when rowdy crowds mobbed its members, whose intermittent laughs at what struck them as native absurdities were taken as evidence of their geniality. On the other hand, occasional racial slurs yelled at them prompted *Harper's Weekly* to lament they'd never know America had ladies and gentlemen too: "The barbarian and savage behavior has been entirely upon our part." Raucous Senate debate during their visit there prompted one of the seventy-seven to make a humorous comparison to Edo's boisterous fish market, and another to hope the barbarians would "turn their faces upward" to the glory of the Japanese empire. (The guests hated the meat and cheese they were served as much as shipwrecked American sailors had hated fish and soy sauce.) Nevertheless, many impressions undermined their assumptions about their own cultural and moral supremacy. Seven or eight of ten Japanese think of Europeans as "no different from dogs and horses," one of the members would write, adding—in a reference to Japan's substantial antiforeigner violence in 1860—that other Japanese attack Europeans with swords. "Well the Westerners do not do this. They show benevolence to foreigners, and they treat them like members of their own family." Most of the mission's members had been "angry and hateful" toward the Americans, but "all regretted their past error."[30]

Whatever was or wasn't learned or mislearned about civics, however, very little economic or military intelligence was acquired. Additionally disturbed by the presence of women at state affairs, the delegates were less concerned, as their diaries would show, with fulfilling their charge to investigate the "truly useful" soldierly things than with maintaining their dignity—which they did throughout, possibly aided by knowledge that they were being observed by informants in their number.[31] Their rigidity probably did more even than the distractions of social events and public relations to hinder the making of scientific discoveries and compiling of "militarily-useful" information during the long visit[32]—which, however, was entirely unrepresentative of Japan's otherwise brilliant success in absorbing and employing just such information. Back home, the country was already embarked on a frenzied campaign to beat the West at its own game.

Another purpose of the "Bakufu Mission of 1860" was to ratify Townsend Harris's commercial treaty. A few of the seventy-seven samurai spent as long as six months in America (which "seemed like six years to us," one would confess). No news from home, "not even a rumor" of it, reached them during that time. But when they returned and were told "something outrageous" had happened in their absence, one of their number immediately knew what it was: "something like an attack," he said, on the man who succeeded Abe Masahiro's successor and who was serving as a regent, or kind of chancellor, for the new Shogun, Tokugawa Iemochi. That guidance was needed because Iesada's replacement, although not similarly retarded or sickly, was only fourteen years old, and had no discernable leadership potential. The regent was Ii Naosuke, the influential daimyo who'd advocated resuming trade with the West back when Perry's demands were being debated.

A man who greeted the returning samurai at the port wondered how on earth he knew about the attack on Ii. "Who could have told you?"[33]

No longer quite so happy to be home now that his worry had been confirmed, the traveler said he didn't need to be told because he'd suspected throughout his absence that things were going badly. Back in San Francisco, the purchase of an umbrella by the *Karin-maru*'s Captain Katsu had prompted a discussion of what might happen to him in Edo if he appeared in public with the article of visibly non-Japanese manufacture. The conclusion was that he'd be quickly cut down, probably by lordless, often rootless samurai called *ronin*, some of whom were outright outlaws. The political disintegration prompted by the *bakufu*'s loss of authority after permitting the foreign entry helped create many more *ronin* now. Still, the prescient returnee didn't know *how* unfortunate things actually were until his interlocutor informed him that the attack was no mere raid on the regent's estate. Accompanied by Shinto priests, a gang of eighteen *ronin*, mostly from Tokugawa Nariaki's Mito *han*, had assassinated Ii. Although never devoted to change for itself, Ii continued championing it so that Japan would become strong enough to resist foreign force—which is why he signed the "Harris" treaty of Amity and Commerce on behalf of the Japanese government. As if that weren't enough to further infuriate ardent patriots, he'd also suppressed Nariaki and his supporters, who dreamed of bolting the country's doors again—although Ii's argument with Nariaki was also over the related issue of who would be appointed the next Shogun, the Mito lord campaigning for his son. Confined to his domain in 1858, Nariaki would remain there, virtually incommunicado, for his two remaining years of life.

Ii's hands were bloody even before assassins struck him down. The soon-to-be victim of anti-government frenzy had himself victimized his opponents, most notably by banishing that collection of Nariaki's followers, with orders that some be tortured. A few were compelled to commit suicide, after which Ii's own followers took to burning their corpses. Before he was done, Abe Masahiro's supplanter in the sense of essentially governing the country had purged over a hundred isolationists suspected of insufficient loyalty to the *bakufu*: men from that institution itself, from several domains, and from the imperial court, an ever-growing rallying center against the government responsible for the Western incursion. But now the regent who'd turned some of the shogunate's supporters into fierce enemies was himself dispatched in broad daylight near an Edo Castle gate. Many of the sixty or so samurai guarding Ii had sheathed their swords against a wet snow. Before they could wield them, four of their band were dead or dying, and an attacker had dragged Ii from his palanquin, lopped off his head, and rushed it to a mansion on the grounds, where he disemboweled himself. The killing or capturing of the attackers didn't diminish the day's further cost to the *bakufu*'s power. (Some *ronin* assassins were publicly beheaded; some arsonists were publicly burned. The corpses were occasionally left in place for days, as warnings.)

The number of deaths grew when pro- and anti-Ii advisors were compelled to commit *seppuku* after the other side gained ascendency or policies were otherwise switched. Village headmen and volatile lower samurai were becoming more and more involved in matters that hadn't concerned them before. As the acceleration of the tribulation and xenophobia that had been

well under way during Abe's last years took Japan closer and closer to anarchy, the massive violence of the "century of war" to which establishment
of Tokugawa rule had put an end in 1600 threatened to return. In 1862,
Francis Hall saw the "whole Japanese mind" troubled by a specter of
"imminent revolution" that would leave the *han* pursuing their individual
interests, with the fate of twenty-five million people "trembling in the
balance."

SWELLING CURIOSITY ABOUT FOREIGNERS and a minority's eagerness to contact them may have made haters even more furious. As late as
1860, many were determined, despite the Harris treaty, to prevent the actual opening of more ports, especially Edo. A Dutch-learning scholar turned
influential editor seethed that barbarian merchants' envoys go to the capital, "lodge in magnificent temples, possess escorts on the scale of a lord's
train, stand as equals of the [*roju*], and persist in their opinions without
deference to the powers of the Empire of Japan." In the newly opened ports,
they built mansions and staffed them with many servants, showed no respect to samurai, and criticized the country's hierarchy. "Foreign merchants conspire to impoverish our country by selling us baubles at high
prices, and purchasing raw silk tea and bronze—daily commodities—at
low prices. . . . Even their dogs refuse to lie down in submission."

As well as for the 1855 earthquake, Americans were held responsible
for causing floods and fires, and some continued behaving badly enough to
swell the hatred of them. Sailors threatened to seize the other open port
of Hakodate if they weren't supplied with women and rum. They were, as
a "health measure," but that didn't stop their brawling, sometimes with
locals.

Windfall profits provoked greater animosity among the educated because they harmed many while profiting few. Buying all the native gold
coins they could at three to one for silver instead of the world rate of sixteen to one, foreigners cleaned up by reselling the coins in China. Harris,
although he predicted more humiliation would leave "a sore feeling" in the
minds of the "proud Japanese,"[34] had nevertheless ensured that the trade,
in which he too profitably engaged, would be hugely advantageous to foreign traders. When Edo sought to stop the damaging traffic or discount

American coins by 25 percent, he again threatened force if his "reasonable expectations" (one of Perry's pet phrases) weren't met.

The country's gold supply plummeted. Unable to protect it, the government debased the currency by minting cheaper coins, which impoverished great numbers with rapid inflation. Some essential goods bought up by foreigners became scarce and expensive, driving up the cost of living. Tea doubled in price, raw silk tripled, and rice started its way toward a twelve-fold increase by 1867. "It will be a long time," predicted a *New York Times* reporter in 1864, before Japan's ignorant, superstitious millions, who "for generations looked upon the seclusion as their peculiar institution"—the American South's euphemism for slavery—stop blaming the West for such ills. New purchases of Western arms drained the always precarious national treasury at the same time, and soon more would be spent on reparations for assassinations of Westerners. Although the full economic effect wasn't yet apparent, "Japan's first extensive contact with the West was turning into a catastrophe."[35]

The reaction naturally increased Harris's concern about gangs that roamed the streets at night. "Patriots assassinate other patriots for views they have never held or professed, and statesmen declare intentions that everybody knows to be contrary to their real purpose. Feuds become alliances, friendships become hatreds, and the whole nation is in a state of uncertainty and doubt."[36] As the pitch of revenge became murderous, alien residents and visitors less redoubtable than Harris succumbed to occasional panic. Russian sailors were attacked in 1859, and assassinations of other foreigners began the following year, their killers hoping to save the nation by making an example of a few victims. "In a Japan coming apart,"[37] seven would be dispatched in eighteen months, most by *ronin*. By 1865, the number would be fourteen, with far many more wounded.[38]

Henry Heusken, Harris's Dutch interpreter, was among the first targets. By that time, extremism in defense of Japanese "purity" was increasingly regarded as a virtue; the Meiji government that had just replaced the Tokugawa shogunate (see below) would posthumously award imperial court rank to two of the men who participated in Heusken's murder. The British legation in Edo was also hit. After a first attack on it resulted in the killing of a European interpreter just outside the building, four were slain and nineteen wounded, mostly Japanese members of the staff, in a second that followed shortly. The British Minister had no doubt that the "compulsory treaties" with the Western powers helped provoke the assailants, or that the Japanese had "one object,"

> which is the expulsion of the foreigner and a return to their isolation. Their distrust of Foreign Powers is indiscriminate, and their hatred perfectly impartial. They slay the secretary of the United Sates legation [Heusken], and attempt the massacre of the inmates of the British legation with equal readiness and satisfaction.[39]

Succumbing to further foreign demands despite an imperial order not to, Ii had given permission for permanent legations to open in the capital. That was in 1858, five years after Perry's first visit, when Ii, having given up on Abe-like consultation, switched to a much more authoritative attempt to govern with a silenced opposition; but that was becoming ever more difficult. When, shortly before his own assassination, he notified the British Minister that the government could no longer guarantee his protection if he remained in Edo, British marines were installed. They failed to prevent a third attack on the legation building in February 1863. The raiders who burned it down carried papers proclaiming they were fully prepared to die while ridding the country of its internal and external enemies.[40]

ON WENT THE KILLINGS. An October 1863 *New York Times* dispatch from newly opened Yokohama spoke of assassins "prowling about in the vicinity of the [foreign] settlement, ready to pounce like wild beasts" on anyone who ventured outside it. A young English merchant visiting from Shanghai went somewhat farther when he made an outing to a nearby village with some friends. There they not merely failed to dismount for the palanquin of a prominent daimyo traveling the Tokaido highway, as required of all Japanese of lesser standing, but also rode into the procession, then tried to get clear by breaking through one of the rows of bodyguards. Incensed by the insolence, the lord's retainers drew their swords and virtually cut him in two. (Severing the ponytail of a young woman in the English group while doing her no further harm was a neater trick by one of the samurai swordsmen.) By that time, zealots had begun murdering not only cocky Englishmen but also Japanese who risked dealing with Westerners—or whom they felt admired them or even showed an interest in foreign affairs. The political thinker and policy advisor Shonan Yokoi, who'd gone from his call to "wipe out the beast-like barbarians" to advocating greater openness and tolerance for which he was suspected of harboring sympathy for republican ideas and Christianity, was assassinated in 1869.

Exhausted Townsend Harris had returned to the States in 1862. Although his replacement weakly insisted the fire that gutted the American legation in Edo the following year was accidental, the new Minister acknowledged he'd been repeatedly pressed to leave. By then, "the long-established authority of Edo was . . . being rapidly replaced by the long-lost authority of Kyoto."[41] At about the time of the fire, the crown summoned the Shogun to Kyoto to explain the government's behavior—and the Shogun obeyed! (He was accompanied by a force of some three thousand samurai, as opposed to more than three hundred thousand when a previous Shogan visited the palace, in 1634.) Not satisfied with the *bakufu*'s handling of foreigners, the Emperor declared all must be expelled on June 15, 1863. On that day, ships of a *han* in Honshu's far southwestern corner fired on French, Dutch, and American vessels, the latter a small steamer trying to transit the strait separating that island and Kyushu. (Not all Japanese were hostile. The previous year, local inhabitants and officials from Edo generously helped an American ship wrecked on a different coast.) Three weeks later in the same waters, the *han*'s shipboard cannon killed six crewmen of the *Wyoming*, a sloop of war that had been sent to Japan to protect American lives and property against the increasing anti-foreign agitation. That first such firing took place on July 11, 1863, almost exactly ten years after Perry's landing at Kurihama.

Secretary of State William Seward saw to it that America's retaliation for the attack in the strait went well beyond the *Wyoming*'s shells that sank the offending boats. Seward, whose involvement in the purchase of Alaska from Russia in 1865 would forever link his name to "folly," was no less interested in "the prize" of Asia, "chief theatre" of the world's future. (The association to "folly" is unfair. Among other domestic achievements, the extraordinary man, among the best in President Lincoln's cabinet, provided vital shelter for the Underground Railroad and helped Lincoln write the Emancipation Proclamation.) With the same kind of fervor that made him an ardent abolitionist, the Secretary also believed the "simple people of Japan" were obliged to stop interfering with God's will. In 1868, he would write Robert Pruyn,

Townsend Harris's replacement, that "Humanity . . . demands and expects a continually extending sway for the Christian religion" instead of suppressing it.[42] Focusing on the Asian commerce that would be the "chief fertilizer" of an even richer America, he proposed a joint British-American display of naval power to halt the violence against foreigners.

Harris vigorously opposed the plan; the sole foreign representative who'd remained in Edo rather than seek the protection of Western naval forces at Yokohama had become convinced Western governments didn't understand Japan.[43] Despite his own previous threats of war, he now hated the thought of its horrors being inflicted on "this peaceful people and happy land."[44] But Harris was now back in New York, and his successor, Pruyn, a good friend of Seward, agreed that chastising was needed. After all, errant Japan had been opened by the "utterances of bayonet and wide-mouthed cannon," not by any concern of its own for "the public good." It was "strike or be struck," as with "our Indian tribes." A "hand on the sword" would protect the American foothold.

The metaphor was inexact because ships would do the striking, and to secure Western interests as a whole, not just American. That was new. To help expand commerce and Christianity, Seward did "nothing less than reverse the decades-old principles" of America's Asia policy, especially determination to act alone in order to avoid association with European imperialism.[45] If the joint punishment would further advance Japan toward civil war, so be it; Japan *had* to accept relations with the world, and behave accordingly.

"Joint" meant first of all alliance with a Britain aggrieved by the fate of Charles Richardson, the young Englishman in the group of reckless riders who, in 1862, encountered the noble procession on the highway near Yokohama. The daimyo whose retainers slew him was a member of the powerful Shimazu house, rulers of the southern Satsuma *han* that dominated and exploited Okinawa. Despite some accommodation with the Tokugawas after failing to support them in the sixteenth century, the Shimazus remained their hereditary enemies, as did the lords of the Choshu *han* on Honshu. After the dynasty's founding, the Tokugawas made guarding against those two "outside" domains the chief focus of their military attention. They especially wanted to prevent them from advancing east to Kyoto, from where the Emperor might encourage them. Now Edo Castle still saw them as a threat, all the more because both remained proudly militaristic. Far as they were from the capital, the two domains together maintained almost forty thousand of the realm's best warriors.

Carrying the mutual antagonism into the 1860s, they were also home to the largest number of "men of high purpose," *shishi*, who menaced Edo Castle's now precarious rule. Although the *shishi*, mostly young samurai of lower status, originally professed loyalty to both the Emperor and the *bakufu*, the latter's inability to counter the foreigners turned them sharply toward the throne, making them among the most extreme proponents of "Revere the Emperor, Expel the Barbarians."

THE SHIMAZU LORD whose guards had murdered Richardson (and wounded two others in his party) refused to surrender his killers to the *bakufu*, and the "tent government," in its weakened state, lacked the means to compel him to. The requirement that the daimyo spend every other year in Edo had been abolished in the same 1862, after which the lords and their retainers fled "in the space of a week, 'like wild birds from an opened cage.' "[46] Seeking indemnity, Britain fumed and threatened. After almost two frustrating years, it sent a squadron of warships to Kagoshima, the seat of the Satsuma domain. Attempts to obtain satisfaction having failed there too, the squadron seized three ships in the harbor as hostages, then answered weak fire from Satsuma cannon with a proper bombardment. Making rubble of much of the city (although the Japanese guns and a typhoon caused sixty British casualties), it convinced the daimyo to pay the indemnity and punish the murders.

Satsuma's contribution to the *bakufu*'s collapse was hardly finished. Its powerful daimyo bore more grudge against Edo than against the British who had ruined his city. He was already assembling his own little navy because he'd begun to feel he owed no further loyalty to the tottering *bakufu*—nor obligation to respect its treaties with the Western powers because the Emperor, far from ratifying them, had ordered the foreigners expelled, and fumed when they weren't. For ignoring His Majesty in that, the shogunate paid with additional loss of respect and loyalty.

The Choshu *han* was also furious with Edo for having failed to heed the imperial edict to expel the loathsome foreigners. Its attacks on the Western ships in the strait had been a way of taking matters into its own hands.

Like Satsuma, it refused to make retribution for the damage to the vessels; and the *bakufu* was similarly powerless to compel it to. This time the British tolerated a year of useless negotiation and other evasion. Then, with the French and Dutch, they dispatched seventeen powerful warships, joined by their formerly standoffish latest American allies. (Russia, which had achieved its immediate territorial goals under its treaty with Edo and had few commercial ones, wasn't represented.) Washington's willingness to cooperate with London was strong evidence of Japan's importance to Secretary of State Seward. After all, cotton-hungry Britain continued to favor the Confederacy in America's Civil War.

The New World's politically important contribution to the chastisement turned out to be militarily insignificant. With so many ships fighting in that Civil War raging at home, Minister Pruyn, Harris's replacement, could add but a single, relatively piddling one to the punitive strike, and it failed to maintain the squadron's speed. Eager to secure American participation, the British offered to tow it, but it was stripped of its cannon instead, and "American honor" was upheld by installing the token firepower on a chartered ship, privately owned.

Pruyn's "sentinels in the outposts of civilization," as he saw Western officers in Japan, began bombarding in September 1864. After four days, troops were landed and Choshu's forts were seized. The straits were opened, the *bakufu* paid a large indemnity, and the Choshu lord, also deeply impressed by and covetous of Western military prowess, followed the Satsuma daimyo in reversing course. Like the latter in his smoldering Kagoshima, he quickly sought advice from the previously despised barbarians, who helped his force, like Satsuma's, become even stronger. "The Japanese had indeed been taught a lesson they would not forget, although it was not precisely the lesson Seward and Pruyn had hoped they would learn."[47]

SATSUMA'S AND CHOSHU'S visions of dislodging the foreigners had dimmed, but not their desire to destroy the shogunate. Their daimyo felt it was time for them to teach Edo a lesson with their forces that had been strengthened with Western weapons and tactics. Their attempts became a new tangle of shifting alliances.

For all his antiforeign feeling, the Emperor disapproved of the extremists, whom he ordered suppressed, together with a supporting Choshu contingent in Kyoto. Their daimyo responded with an attack to "rescue" His Majesty from his bad advisors and from *bakufu* treachery. More than half the ancient capital was burned before the extremists were defeated. The victorious force, sent from Edo, included Satsuma troops, but when the *bakufu* decided to punish Choshu itself, Satsuma switched sides and went to the besieged *han*'s aid. Unable to rally other daimyo to *its* side, Edo sent a second force in 1865.

Thus five armed conflicts, three with Western forces as well as these two internal ones, wracked the country in the 1860s. Although some earlier clashes had been fierce, the long-dreaded civil war's serious fighting began in 1866. Satsuma again joined the defenders against Edo's second strike. It admired the skill with which Choshu's already modernizing army fought, its troops using foreign firearms under the leadership of bright young men, a few of whom had secretly visited England. But the alliance had been cemented months earlier when Satsuma, fearing Edo would reimpose strict restrictions on all *han*, had made a secret pact with Choshu.

This time the lackluster *bakufu* force failed, suffering the worst defeat in Tokugawa history, although it was three times larger than the enemy. In addition to greater zeal and excellent arms bought from Western merchants, the "Sat-Cho" coalition had much better weapons of their own newly modern manufacture.

Inability to subdue its vassals dealt a fatal blow to Edo Castle's rule. It had been sorely weakened by independent-minded daimyo who resented Edo's monopoly on foreign trade and control of the open ports. Their opposition was reinforced by merchants who wanted the trade even more, craftsmen seeking escape from their guilds' restraints, and scholars eager to free themselves from many varieties of restrictions. However, the ultimate cause was the failure to prevent Perry's opening, and the coup de grace was delivered by domains emboldened and strengthened by the Western powers' military inspiration and weaponry.

THE LAW OF UNINTENDED CONSEQUENCES, an American writer recently suggested, is that peoples' and especially governments' actions "always have effects that are unanticipated or 'unintended.'" By the early twentieth century, the Perry mission's collection of them would include unforseen Japanese immigration to America. "Whin the gallant Commodore kicked opn th' door, we didn't go in," a satirist described the trouble. "They came out." Most of the early leavers, who would number some twenty-five thousand by 1900, joined the Chinese "coolie labor," preponderantly on Hawaii. But some pushed on to California, where their drive for education and advancement prompted resentment, especially among Irish immigrants eager to keep the newer arrivals down. The Hearst press and others soon portrayed them as a virulent "Yellow Peril." Months after they made large donations to the survivors of the San Francisco earthquake of 1906—no doubt in the hope of currying favor that might relieve the anti-Japanese paranoia as well as in memory of the damage caused by their own earthquakes—the city prohibited "Jap" children from attending school with "normal" ones. (Hurt as they and their countrymen back home were, few were prompted to consider how the assiduous Japanese avoidance of hairy, stinking barbarians might have offended Americans.)

Washington then bullied Tokyo into signing a Gentleman's Agreement—with nary a gentleman in sight, a British writer quipped—to stop almost all further immigration, including by Japanese laborers already in Hawaii. When America's Great White Fleet steamed into Tokyo Bay the following year, 1907, "visions of Commodore Perry danced in Japanese heads"—understandably because the so-called "friendly visit" was actually a "thinly veiled threat" sent by President Theodore Roosevelt. Some Japanese saw more menace in the concurrent development of the Pearl Harbor naval base—as if, wrote an angry newspaper, Japan had opened such a facility in Cuba.

All that was to come. Still in the nineteenth century, the unintended consequences might have been summarized the Aesop saying that "We often give our enemies the means of our own destruction."

The British squadron's overwhelming superiority that enabled it to raze much of Kagoshima in 1863 persuaded Satsuma's military-minded lord to use Britain as a model for his own little navy, and the soon-to-be formed Japanese national navy would shortly do the same. And after the Choshu lord too turned for military help to the formerly despised foreigners who had smashed his forts, quick improvement helped it become the backbone of the soon-to-be-formed, previously nonexistent Japanese national army, which would model itself on the Prussian one, after brief preference for the French. From then to Pearl Harbor, the pro-British navy and pro-German army would fashion a great Pacific rival to the United States, strongly influencing Tokyo's foreign policy along the way. "If it had been possible in 1853 to foresee Japan's future role," an American historian would suggest, "Perry's program might have been viewed in Washington in a far different light."[48]

Removal of "the battleship of seclusion," as a scholar would later call it, drawing attention to the real battleships under construction in the country's new yards, left the Japanese "feeling vulnerable and exposed. If national politics depends on national consciousness of self, then both were enormously heightened at this time."[49] Turning the inward-looking people outward, making them aware of the outside world as never before, the East Asia Squadron caused them to see themselves belonging to a political entity "rather than simply a way of life or style of civilization. Modern nationalism had begun."[50]

It surged partly because the Japanese people now saw themselves as subjects not of their *han*, one of the two hundred and sixty, but of an entire country, making it a true nation-state for the first time. Awareness of its existence as a political entity was hugely increased by fear that it might *cease* to exist. "The very process of dealing with the pushy barbarians *created* modern Japanese nationalism. Among shogunal officials, in daimyo castles, and in the private academies where politically concerned samurai debated history and policy, a new conception took hold of 'Japan' as a single nation, to be defended and governed as such."[51]

The change gathered momentum with the shogunate's final fall. While its troops were still attempting to regain control of Satsuma and Choshu, ineffectual Tokugawa Iemochi, the dynasty's fourteenth shogun, died. That event (which came only eight years after Iemochi had replaced retarded Iesada) was used as a reason or pretext to stop the fighting, but it continued, sometimes desultorily, until a second death in early 1867, this time of Emperor Komei.

In reaction or not, the country entered intervals of strange quiet followed by sometimes bizarre but blessedly nonviolent expressions that have never been satisfactorily explained, except, perhaps, as a release of tension. Cross-dressing was the least of an eruption of "ecstatic revelry—a combination of rioting, religious hysteria [and] sake-powered partying":

> Dancers—men and women, young and old—clogged the streets to clamoring bells, drums, gongs, chimes, and whistles. Drunken commoners tramped through the house of the privileged without—unforgivably—removing

their shoes. Popular lyrics celebrated food, sake and sex. People gave clothing away and threw money in the streets. The frenzy swept from Edo to
Hiroshima after thousand of amulets, paper charms with Shinto and Buddhist gods painted on them, began falling from the sky.[52]

THE NEW, FIFTEEN-YEAR-OLD Emperor would be the grandfather of
Hirohito. The new, twenty-nine-year-old Shogun was Yoshinobu, a son of
Tokugawa Nariaki, who'd long campaigned for him. Accepting the responsibility reluctantly, able Tokugawa Yoshinobu tried to reorganize the government while preserving the core of his leadership. Other lords, however,
fearing the growing power of Satsuma and Choshu, wanted still more authority shifted to the Emperor. Deferring to them, resigning his post but
not his power, foresighted Yoshinobu announced an "imperial restoration"
in late 1867. Not satisfied, the daimyo of Satsuma, Choshu, and other anti-
bakufu domains sent forces to seize the imperial palace, from where the
new Emperor, still under duress, announced his own, fuller restoration,
which Yoshinobu declared illegal.

The resulting Boshin War, or "War of the Year of the Dragon," spilled
more blood in 1868 and 1869. Again, the *bakufu* forces were badly defeated, although remnants held out six more months in northern Hokkaido. But by then, fourteen turbulent, sometimes frenzied years after
Perry's first arrival, Yoshinobu had been reduced to an ordinary daimyo
and Tokugawa lands had been confiscated because the *bakufu* no longer
existed. Although no one can say how long it would have taken for it to
follow the demise of its feudal counterparts elsewhere in the world if not
for the Commodore,[53] the Black Ships were the "single event" that marked
"the beginning of [its] end."[54]

The boy Emperor's reign was named Meiji, "enlightenment" or "age of
brightness." The Meiji Restoration of 1868, as it is also called because the
crown's putative ancient authority was supposedly restored, is taken as
the start of modern Japan. While revolts continued, the *bakufu* was abolished and the social classes dissolved except for the daimyo and certain
courtiers. All but a few daimyo were eased from political power and administrative positions before being given titles under a new peerage system established in 1884.

Closed screens now opened far wider than before. Although late

Tokugawa rule had tolerated "more freedom of movement and occupation than often suggested," it took the Meiji Restoration to do away with the restrictions of, among others, fixed classes, castle towns, and hereditary rights to land ownership.[55] Some liberation from the "bowings and prostrations" up and down the hierarchy that had disgusted Perry followed. ("Every Japanese is . . . by turns master and slave, now submissively with his neck beneath the foot of one, and again haughtily with his foot upon the neck of another."[56]) Although mental and emotional change of that kind was slow to penetrate the countryside, the official end of the class system left many people feeling freer. Some underlings even managed to gain the upper hand over their social superiors.

The two hundred and sixty domains became seventy-two prefectures and three metropolitan districts—including Edo, renamed Tokyo in 1868[57] as it was becoming the commercial as well as the political center. The Tokugawa administrative structure that had grown in response to parochial needs and as supplementary to an ineffective hierarchy that continued operating in Kyoto was largely a jumble.[58] The new one was streamlined, systematized, and highly centralized.

Japan was on the way to its stunning emergence from obscurity. Selling girls as geishas or prostitutes was banned (although it would continue until at least the early 1950s). The patchwork of widely different educational attitudes and facilities was rapidly regenerated and expanded into one of the world's best school systems. In 1889, Japan became the first non-Western country to adopt a constitutional political system. A parliament was installed, together with national representation and a measure of dedication to genuine democracy.[59] A truly modern spirit found its way into some government institutions, or portions of them; and some in civil society enjoyed the fruits of Europe's Enlightenment, above all in scientific inquiry. Modern communications and transportation opened the country to people who'd never thought of leaving their villages, let alone their *han*. International travel was permitted; foreign literature became widely available, other makings of a tolerant, liberal society were conceived or imported. In 1873, signs outlawing Christianity were quietly taken down, indicating official toleration. (Missionaries would not fulfill their hope of saving millions of Japanese souls.) As the visual arts recovered from a certain staleness that had begun dulling it during the later decades of isolation, eagerly devoured translations of Western literature helped writers climb from the shallowness into which many had descended. In a wide range of fields—architecture, interior and stage design, the decorative arts, music, dancing, even fashion—creativity was unleashed that would dazzle the world.

In terms of basic rule, however, Meiji was less a real revolution than a switch of people in power and their direction. Despite the structural and institutional changes, despite the democratic forms and admirable administrators who sought to make them work, the government remained largely feudalistic and society remained hierarchical, or "vertical"—but now controlled by western *han* that had long felt uneasy with the Tokugawas: the former "outside" domains, which had pushed their way to the inside. And the younger, more entrepreneurial leaders with their more modern cast of mind than that of the older generation of often xenophobic samurai trusted in something quite different to protect the country: *development.* The new national goal, pursued with an ardor few peoples could match, was expressed in the mantra that was displayed and shouted everywhere: "Enrich the Nation, Strengthen the Military."

Although that urge had gripped a scattering of Japanese earlier, nothing remotely like Japan's new purpose emerged until the Commodore had sired an overriding desire for military prowess that accompanied the growing conception of Japan as a unified nation. No country in the world would learn the military lessons of the Industrial Revolution better than Japan, whose history from Perry's arrival to the conclusion of World War II can be summarized by its leaders' determination to "Modernize! Industrialize! Build Big Guns!" The country could be saved from Western domination only by acquiring all the means for producing Western weapons, which the gritty Japanese spirit would put to better use.

The new priority meant modernizing that spirit too. A 1872 National Edict of Education, soon to be a cornerstone of the imperial way of life, instituted "moral" training in primary and middle schools. Its two great principles were filial piety and absolute loyalty to the Emperor. With some exceptions, all twenty-one-year-old males—not just samurai but peasants too—were conscripted for service in the infant national army the following year. (Several years later, the military's loyalty would be attached to the Emperor exclusively and civilians would be excluded, practically speaking, from all decisions involving war or peace.) And the newly centralized government's preaching and supervision of profound changes in the conception of life's purpose had even greater effect.

Although everyone knew his or her place, or was supposed to, in the late Tokugawa period, villages, guilds, and artistic and intellectual circles enjoyed considerable autonomy so long as they didn't break the larger rules. Edo Castle intervened when it felt threatened, but otherwise left the civic and social groupings more or less to their own devices—whereas the Meiji state quickly became much more invasive, pervasive, and authoritarian. In some ways, especially its practice of relentless indoctrination, it also came closer to being overtly dictatorial. The people had to be remade into citizens of a modern state, *modern* meaning not democratic or even individually prosperous but above all strong. "Enrich the Nation, Strengthen the Military."

The Meiji state's unified power, centralized administration, and far greater intent and ability to control life was a sizeable step in roughly the opposite direction of the decentralization some political thinkers believe is essential for democratic development. Much heavier censorship was part of it, including far stricter application to the arts. Partly in an effort to make Japan look better in Western eyes, the sexual explicitness that so disturbed early American visitors was repressed. Together with other distractions, the vivid and playful representations gradually came to be regarded as subversive to the new nationalist morality of building strength through hard work and abstinence.

If popular attitudes would never become fully puritan, it wasn't for lack of trying to make them so. The first Meiji prime minister was a former samurai—the class having been eliminated in 1869—who had prepared to fight Perry in 1853, when he was a teenager. "The major task facing us today," he told his colleagues, "is inculcating the entire populace with the spirit of loyalty, devotion, and heroism that was formerly associated with the samurai class, and making those values their values":

> Thus we must teach the common people to work and study hard for the sake of their neighborhoods and villages, and never to waver in matters that would lead to the destruction of their families. Moreover, they must develop a peaceful and obedient character, show respect for the law, and demonstrate an understanding of our noble moral ideas and highly refined national sentiments.[60]

Similar values had always been key; but never so impelled. In the remaking that began shortly after Perry, serve-thy-country ideology became paramount. It appeared "as a conscious enterprise, a perpetual civic concern, an affair, indeed, of state," and its exhortation was delivered at every local level, as never before. Even while leaders tackled many crises prompted by a need to transform the country's institutions, they

> expressed their sense that institutions alone were insufficient to secure the nation. It was not enough that the policy be centralized, the economy developed, social classes rearranged, international recognition striven for— the people must also be "influenced," their minds and hearts made one.[61]

A year into the era of the new imperial state, it sent missionaries to the countryside to proselytize for it, like models for Soviet agitators fifty years hence. The most urgent national business, declared a high bureaucrat in 1881, wasn't the government ordinances the prime minister drafted but "inspiration." It succeeded in making millions of newly "modern" civilians proud to be ferociously toiling in grim factories because they were contributing to the insulted country's resurgence. But the consequences would include oceans of pain and mountains of death, to paraphrase one of the endlessly repeated World War II slogans.

Centralizing, moralizing, and nation exalting were all but certain to take place in one or another form, as they did in Europe when dukedoms and principalities coalesced into nation-states; but here military strength remained the holy grail. Oversimplifying only slightly, Japan's modernizing and westernizing was a huge crash program for mobilization.[62]

Men who had sided with the Emperor—a few from the court in Kyoto, but mostly from Satsuma and Choshu—dominated the new government. Many were young samurai-bureaucrats with much greater knowledge of the outside world and a near bursting new nationalism that promised restoration of Japan's honor, which Tokugawa spinelessness had soiled. Understanding the country would continue to "be at the mercy of the West if it could not match its technology base," the new leaders and their even more eager subordinates committed themselves to the "speedy acquisition of national strength,"[63] in pursuit of which they began sending quickly educated scientists to Europe. There had already been six larger and several smaller missions to the West under the shogunate, including one in 1867 to buy warships and weapons in the United States.

At home, the feverish modernization devoted only to "hardware"[64]—the intense concentration on building industrial and military strength—may have been greater than any in world history, including even Stalin's five-year plans. Meiji Japan's real, if unofficial, strategy rested, as Ian Buruma put it, in conviction that "the best way to fight the barbarians . . . was to learn all their tricks first." Other old slogans became official and virtually ubiquitous: "Japanese Spirit, Western Things" and "Eastern Ethics, Western Science." "It was precisely because Japanese saw the urgency of keeping their culture uncontaminated and hence preserving its essence against the threatened external pollution that many felt justified using militant forms of political and cultural action."[65]

Very little of the wealth won by the single-minded devotion to "Rich Country, Strong Military" trickled down to the farms on which the vast majority of the population still toiled. Although they were deep in depression by the 1880s, Tokyo scarcely noticed while sustaining the campaign, especially for a navy, considered the most urgent need. Great keels were laid and completed—amazing feats of dedication on the infant industrial base, but at more huge cost. It was almost entirely Japan's warship tonnage that put the country among the Great Powers by 1910; in manufacturing as a whole, its output was a quarter of Britain's and less than a tenth of America's. While huge battleships were being superbly engineered and constructed, the majority of the population was bent over rice paddies, panting to feed itself and sometimes surviving by ignoring the new laws prohibiting the sale of daughters into prostitution.

Nine years later, at the Versailles Conference that wrangled over the peace terms of World War I, Tokyo's delegation proposed gentle condemnation of the racial prejudice suffered by Japanese businessmen and other world travelers. After a majority vote to support the amendment, President Woodrow Wilson, fearing California senators would abandon support for the League of Nations, announced that it could not carry; and it didn't.[66] Partly as a bone thrown to Japan the following year, it was awarded a League mandate over the formerly German-owned or -run Marshall, Mariana, and Caroline islands—the Pacific outposts whose capture by American forces in World War II would cost thousands of lives. Three years later, at the London Naval Conference of 1922 that formulated "five-five-three" for British, American, and Japanese tonnage, anger at having failed to win equality would prompt further Japanese determination to rely on strength because, Tokyo was convinced, Japan would never be treated fairly. Congress would seem to confirm that in 1924 when it would single out Japan by excluding all immigration whatever from there, even though there was virtually none by then.

AS SO OFTEN, to have arms was to use them. Pre-1853 Japan had no desire to expand or conquer; the *bakufu*'s hoary promise of military improvement had been for defense. But with an old saying that "the weak are meat, the strong are eaters" back in vogue, the Meiji state conducted a massive campaign to reject peace-oriented Buddhism, and the new national army felt itself ready to test its wings. The year 1873, when Christian missionaries were again officially permitted to proselytize, was also important because a punitive force was then sent to Taiwan. (*American Cyclopedia*'s call for universal admiration for the newly opened nation's race toward modern civilization had come two years earlier, and many Westerners who had considered the country barbarous when it was at peace with its neighbors believed it was now becoming civilized.) The following year, Japan felt itself militarily strong enough to began expanding into neighboring islands, including the Kurils and Bonins. In 1876, its forces opened Korea more painfully than it itself had been opened forty-two years earlier, the general in charge attributing his success to use of the Commodore's methods.

Three years later, the quick study in imperialism caused another tragedy by formally taking the Ryukyus, then subjecting its residents to ruthless Japanization and exploitation in the name of "reform." A native professor's regret that that "buried" Okinawa's identity is not entirely hyperbole.[67] Following its victory in the Sino-Japanese War of 1894–1895, Japan annexed Taiwan too, then abused it as thoroughly, but more systematically, than any Western colonial power presumably would have. After a full invasion of Korea during the same war, it brutally colonized and exploited the humbled peninsula, bleeding its "brother" of agricultural and mineral riches before annexing the "protectorate" in 1910 and closing it again for its greater profit.

Any explanation of such expansion as more or less natural because the targets were so near would have run up against the phenomenon of Japan's emergence as a major naval power. Hardly a white man in the world had thought the upstart had the slightest chance to defeat a great European power until it did so in the Russo–Japanese War of 1904–1905, a stunning triumph. Virtually every ship of a mighty Russian fleet was sunk or captured by a navy that hadn't existed when a few Japanese copied a vessel Admiral Putiatin built to take his men home after the 1854 tidal wave destroyed his flagship.[68] The West was "amazed to see this island empire, so weak in Perry's day, shoot up like Jack's beanstalk to the size and strength of a modern giant."[69]

The new Pacific rival perturbed the United States from that moment on. Washington's quick dispatch of the Great White Fleet to Tokyo in 1907 and development of Pearl Harbor as a naval base was for keeping yesterday's squirt in its place. Of course, subsequent relations with Tokyo would warm as well as cool, the countries enjoying periods of the proverbial "mutual understanding" and even cooperation. But while the war-and-peace prospects would be in various grays rather than a sharp contrast of black and white, "the hue of fluctuating Japanese-American affairs rarely assumed a very light shade,"[70] especially after Japan's 1905 victory further encouraged it to copy the world powers, including some of their most repugnant attitudes. Now Japan became America's most important potential enemy, as shown by the army-navy "Orange" war plans. The Japanese fleet, its challenge seen as all the greater for having seemingly materialized from thin air, became the leading opponent in the American navy's war games, while eager Japanese militarists, whose political power grew during the 1920s and 1930s, continued to see the intimidating American fleet, long perceived as an instrument of imperialism, as potential oppressor number one. The technically demanding Pearl Harbor strike was decades away, but one country was furiously acquiring the means of launching it against the other.

The Perry mission that alone didn't ignite the explosion of Japanese aggression in the 1930s was nevertheless the core of the fuse. That was obvious to General Ishiwara Kanji, who masterminded the 1931 invasion of Manchuria that started World War II in Asia. After Japan's defeat, intellectually accomplished Ishiwara told the International War Crimes Tribunal that Perry's sabotage of the national integrity and exposure of the country to pitiless international grabbing were responsible for the attack on America. The General's opposition to extending the war to there from the Asian continent added weight to his assessment of the Commodore's influence.

Memory of Perry also stirred Admiral Yamamoto Isoruku, the "Japanese Nelson" who devised and directed the tactically brilliant Pearl Harbor raid. A grandson of a young feudal lord who had fought on the losing side in the civil turmoil that followed in the Black Ships' wake, Yamamoto grew up imbibing anger at the barbarian intruders. The lord was killed, his highly conservative domain was abolished in punishment,[71] and the boy—his name changed to Yamamoto because he'd been adopted—seethed against America for what he considered its responsibility for his ancestor's loss and the family's impoverishment by touching off that civil strife in particular and humiliating Japan in general. If his reasoning seems stretched to Americans, it's logical to many Japanese, with their take on Perry's contribution to the collapse of the old system and their country's plunge into bloody chaos. In any case, the angry youth would go on to fame and notoriety as that planner of the "sneak attack" (although he was evidently distressed by the government's failure to declare war at least a few hours before his planes struck).[72]

The conventional wisdom, nourished by the Japanese naval establishment's postwar efforts to restore its reputation, is that Yamamoto opposed war with the United States until ordered to initiate it. Although that may be true, the implication that the "reluctant admiral," who studied at Harvard in 1919–1920 and served as the naval attaché in Washington shortly afterward, harbored good feelings toward America is challenged by evidence that he, viewing Perry as a national *and* family enemy, actually nursed deep resentment. "I wanted to return Commodore Perry's visit," he replied to a question about why he originally enlisted in the navy, his "frostbitten" smile seeming to diminish his ambiguity."[73] Well before he made admiral, an acquaintance sensed the "bitter-hearted" officer nurtured icy hate toward Perry's homeland. And when Yamamoto foresaw war with the United States, he confided to a friend that he looked forward to visiting the White House "in order to dictate peace."

But people didn't have to have won military medals to "remember Perry" in December 1941. Millions saw a prominent Tokyo newspaper's cartoon of a dismayed Uncle Sam uncorking a giant samurai from a bottle, much like block-print papers distributed days after Perry's arrival had depicted righteous warriors driving away foreign devils. It expressed more than celebration of the destruction of those American battlewagons; it was retaliation for, among other things, Perry's squadron that had had its way with Japan and initiated its exploitation. Some took an extra measure of satisfaction in the sinking of four battleships, the number that composed the East Asia Squadron in 1853.

Can the two phenomena really be likened? Doesn't the difference between visits by ships that never fired in anger and a massive strike that killed and wounded some four thousand people those eighty-eight years later render the analogy outrageous? But Perry's big guns did fire to display their might, slashing Japanese pride and sense of self, "practically turn[ing] the country upside down, and . . . everything into confusion."[74] July 14, 1853, would live in shame and humiliation, if not quite in infamy, especially among the army officers who would essentially govern Japan in 1941.

During the near century between that day and the discharge of Japanese rage in World War II, the grievances were well remembered, although invariably hidden. The introduction along the way of what Laurens van der Post would call the West's "great Roman virtues" like law was forgotten, but never Perry. "All that mattered" was the memory of what followed his trespass: the detested hypnotizing by European power and forced submission to European laws; the chagrin and anger of that century of not living their own lives. "But now the spell was broken," the revenge was out in the open at last, and its messengers seemed drunk on it.

Obviously, the Black Ships alone didn't spawn that savagery. The horrendous slashing and killing, the hideous sadism by an army that had been remarkably chivalrous earlier in the twentieth century, began a decade before Pearl Harbor—in the same Manchuria, where fellow Asians were regularly tormented even more than Westerners would be, when their time would come to suffer Japanese occupation. A study published in 2005 rightly calls the scale of Japanese atrocities in Asia "colossal": prisoners worked and starved to death, civilians and soldiers systematically executed, incomparably worse exploitation than that of the British and French.[75] The Chinese people in particular endured vast cruelty after the Japanese invasion in 1937. But many Japanese didn't applaud in the brutal campaigns on the Asian continent, despite their massive glorification by the government. Tacit confirmation that they weren't sufficiently popular came in Tokyo's post–Pearl Harbor reinterpretation of them as having always been against the Anglo-American enslavers there. A sprinkling of courageous intellectuals even criticized the treatment of fellow Asians—but not the blow to Uncle Sam. Would the rampages into which fervent militarists drew Japan have happened without the instant passion for military mastery aroused by the Commodore's wallop to Japanese self-esteem? Surely the plots, strikes, and sadism would have been less likely to develop, at least with such ardor, without him.

19

The Legacy

The model train given by Perry

MEASURING A NATION'S HISTORICAL consciousness must be harder than trying to snare a slippery fish in murky waters. The hypothetical net would make the latter tricky enough even if the fish—images of a past age, with its expectations and morality—weren't so difficult to see through the lens of changed attitudes. Still, it's safe to say trauma is better remembered than progress. Asked about the formation of their nation-states, some Europeans would attribute it to Prince Metternich, but more are able to recollect their reading about the fourteenth-century bubonic plague called the Black Death. A question about Protestant-Catholic relations would no doubt jog handed-down memories of the calamitous Thirty Years' War that took place more than two centuries before Perry's mission.

Many benefits entered through Perry's opening, and Japan accepted, as China rarely did, that it could learn useful things from the West. Still, the rush of challenges to ways and thoughts that seemed to have existed unchanged for centuries was great enough to prompt a distinguished scholar's recent conclusion that they wrought "the most turbulent era" in the country's history.[1] "People in late Tokugawa Japan . . . were correct to feel threatened. Their way of life, from the material to the political, was about to change irrevocably."[2]

Fourteen years after the Commodore's departure, a nearly eight-hundred-year-old system of feudal rule was replaced with "a modern state ruled by the army, wealthy businessmen, and government officials."[3] That possibly greatest transformation in world history seemed to put everything up for grabs, including people's sense of themselves. Nor could the majority guess that the new goals and practices would deliver massively greater material wealth. Another way of saying "Enrich the Nation, Strengthen the Military" might have been "Strong State, Poor People," including poor in visual comforts: much of the land of distinctive scenes and feudal protocol began to vanish.

As machined merchandise replaced handmade artifacts, an elderly samurai, stripped of many privileges like the rest of his class and forced to sell his family heirlooms one by one, tried to comfort his heartsick family about the industrialization that was erasing many traditions: "Useless beauty had a place in the old life, but the new asks for only ugly usefulness." A son had changed enough to declare that now the country "must fight on the battlefield of commerce . . . in this new world, wealth is the only power." People were told that adoption of foreign methods, especially business methods, was "the new way of making Japan strong, so the high-nosed barbarian could no longer beat the children of Japan in trade."[4]

A few seized the opportunity. Although it was mostly opportunity to make money, an activity the former social elite disdained (even though some had been happy to engage in it covertly), a certain number expanded intellectually and culturally. However, most of the "old" families were appalled, and saw Tokyo "overflowing with wild enthusiasm for everything new and supreme contempt for everything old."[5] A poet bewailed the "disgusting" new pursuit of commerce:

people's hearts
awesome though they are
are being pulled apart
and consumed by rage[6]

The government's determined limiting of contact with Westerners may have helped keep the consequences less dire than their detractors had predicted, but it didn't stop nostalgia from spurting as picturesque villages and towns began growing into strident cities. Those who believe Japan is "arguably the world's ugliest country," as longtime resident Alex Kerr recently wrote, tend to ignore its mountains, rural landscapes and gardens, temples and shrines. Outside such preserves, however, much of the country, whose beauty had struck even Perry's preoccupied men, was on its way to becoming a "groaning, shrieking, roaring, clashing, squealing and thundering"[7] sprawl of concrete and neon. Striking as some buildings are, the jumble of them overwhelms the senses, and urban clutter obscures much of the work of superb architects and designers.

What did Perry have do with that? Some people's quiet ache for the old life of supposedly purer ways—for the nightingales that once sang and ancestral harmony that supposedly reigned—includes misplaced reproach of him. Yearning for an idealized golden age existed as early as the turn of the nineteenth century, more than fifty years before the Commodore arrived. Besides, Japanese pining for the past is the kind that usually grows from relative plenty after satisfaction of more basic needs. It also usually "wears a distinctly utopian face," as a student of the phenomenon recently put it. The "longing for an impossibly pure context of lived experience" is "hostile to history."[8]

Even if Perry *were* responsible for the eyesores, fairness requires some gratitude to him for the affluence, which most people do feel in the part of them that recognizes his sparking of the industrial and technological leaps that made it possible. Of course, great pride is taken in the progress. When the Commodore's model train given at the conclusion of his second visit began moving, the recipients, eyeing it "fearfully from a safe distance," uttered "cries of astonishment."[9] Their progeny export bullet-train technology to America.

Like everyone else who started a country moving in a new direction,

Perry prompts ambivalence, and his homeland is both admired and resented, depending on people's mood. Tokyo's aptly named Rainbow Bridge spanning the harbor soars above fortifications that were hurriedly constructed in defense against the Black Ships that some of Abe Masahiro's advisors were convinced would destroy the capital. But nothing less contradictory than a scaled-down replica of the Statue of Liberty stands near the guns, almost peering at them, and few Japanese can offer an explanation of the juxtaposition other than that the perception of America is complicated. The interpretations of symbols shift with the current events that prompt approval or disapproval of Washington's policies.

Other considerations appear to invalidate the occasional attribution to Perry of the loss of supposedly eternal Japanese ways and values. One is that the great transformation from feudal to modern can, despite the contradiction, be understood as more a continuum than a surge in response to a single event. As noted, change was gaining momentum as the economy made many feudal arrangements obsolete, and even if no Black Ship had arrived, the old serenity—which was rarely perceived as such at the time, nor much appreciated by millions eking out their living—was surely doomed. It has been lost everywhere in the industrialized world, even if less glaringly in countries with more territory to spare for the blemishes that maturate near factories. (Japan's capitalism is unfortunately crammed into an area one-twenty-fifth America's size.)

The nostalgia for pre-Perry Japan—which is to say the invariably romanticized impressions of it—derives as much from human vagaries as anything real in the past. Even when the great majority of Japanese enjoy amenities and abundance undreamed of by their forefathers and when virtually every social measurement refutes the notion that life has worsened, an assumed greater sense of belonging and purpose often makes visions of the old times appear brighter. Modern society's social fragmentation and scramble to prosper nourish a longing for what was perceived as the past's greater "meaning."

Perry is hardly responsible for that phenomenon either, nor for the *kaikoku* as such. Barring some marvel, the West couldn't be held off much longer; if not America, if not in 1853, one country or another would have penetrated, and the great changes would have begun. To blame the Commodore for corrupting and polluting traditional society's supposed purity is a long stretch of the imagination about the possibility of keeping bolted the ever-weakening door.

However, nostalgia's place in the Japanese psyche is more complicated than that, and so is the Commodore's role. Although seemingly better old times are hankered for throughout the world, the Land of the Gods is a special case.

JAPAN WASN'T THE ONLY COUNTRY that made vast, sudden changes in an effort to catch up with perceived threats from the West. Russia did the same under Peter the Great, who reigned from 1682 to 1725 with radical policies known to a few Japanese scholars even during the seclusion. One or two who championed urgent modernization to face the Western menace saw the great Tsar as a role model for forging power from a weak state little blessed by geography. What they didn't know in their impatience for strength was the pain inflicted by Peter's often brutal campaign to adopt Western ways, which many of his subjects considered perverse. Whipping—sometimes literally—his backward country to adopt them, especially those that increased military strength, the Tsar-Reformer broke old patterns and insulted old beliefs, which many of his people included in their concept of Nature. Russia never recovered from the trauma. The wounds persist, especially a fracture between "Westernizers" who still want further movement in that direction and the Slavophiles who yearn to return to Russia's "superior" old self, fed by its "special" roots.

But Russia's sense of identity was less undermined than Japan's because the man who coerced the transformation was in *national* uniform (never mind that the Tsar Westernized the country's uniforms too). As "one of us," Peter was a hero to most, at least some of the time. Shaken as they were, people take patriotic pride in his Russianness—even a little pleasure, perverse or not—while Japan betrays greater evidence of "cultural ambivalence, the chronic sense of contingency on values and behaviors external to native tradition."[10] Its cries—"They've robbed us of our culture. We hardly know who we are anymore"[11]—have an added edge of insult, the foreign "robbers" being easier to deplore and harder to forgive, all the more because the West has dominated many Japanese opinions of themselves since Perry.[12]

No doubt the persistent puzzlement of the robbed about who they are helps explain the ceaseless spate of literature promising readers a solution to the mystery of what constitutes a "real" Japanese soul. Another clue is what an American student of Japanese culture calls "the compulsion to assert uniqueness." Although every society views itself as unique, few "are compelled to affirm its own as loudly and insistently as the Japanese"—a condition caused by "deep uncertainty about who they were, about what it meant to be Japanese in the modern world."[13]

In that way, Perry still represents invasion in part of the national psyche. Acknowledged for his help, the Commodore is nevertheless disliked for having imposed even more unnatural ways than Peter did on Russia: more unnatural because the changes in Japan, whose contact with the West had been far more limited, constituted a sharper break in continuity. Donald Keene, another gifted interpreter of Japanese culture, called the transformation "miraculous. . . . The nation changed in an unbelievably short period of time." Japanese artists of the time rendered the vessels of the East Asia Squadron as truly alien things of evil mein, staring at implied victims with malevolent eyes (in contrast to admiring American canvases of the same ships painted more or less simultaneously). Although that is but one of many images in the inner mind's eye of today's Japanese, it hasn't been erased. In Tokyo Disneyland, a painting of the Black Ships helps illustrate a potted film history of Japanese foreign relations. As the screen fades to a picture of a cannon and the sound track delivers a startling bang, the theater's switch to a moment of darkness surely prompts predictable thoughts about what happened to powerless Japan when it was forced to discard its traditional styles and patterns. Although basing a judgment on The Walt Disney Company's commercial creations would be silly, that one hints at the stronger feelings prompted by Perry.

TWENTIETH-CENTURY JAPAN'S WRITING of one of history's most remarkable success stories—its rise to second or third place in industrial power and first as a creditor to the world it had shunned—didn't expunge the impulses generated by the Black Ships. No mere achievement is likely to because all are largely beside the emotional point. Before there was time to recover from the pain of surrender, additional shocks were administered. In-rushing American and European standards, which were based on concepts such as individualism, had little in common with the invited, limited infusions of Chinese culture during the seventh and eighth centuries. A great novelist named Natsume Soseki would call the doses of profoundly foreign culture a tidal wave. It made the post-Perry years "traumatic and disruptive to a degree . . . rarely found in the history of cultural intercourse."[14] Defensive nationalism surged back, not only in the country's thin layer of leaders and fervent patriots, but also among a bewildered people at all levels of society. One way and another—including via school lessons about the momentous turning point—the reaction was passed from generation to generation.

The national turmoil was too relatively recent for the process to be anywhere near complete in the early twenty-first century, especially since America did nothing to dim its memory. On the contrary, it began ruling the defeated World War II aggressors by reminding them about the firepower that had given Perry his way. Preparing for the surrender ceremony in September 1945, the battleship *Missouri* dropped anchor in Uraga Bay, almost precisely where the Black Ships had before the Commodore introduced himself to the Japanese with his thunderous cannon salutes.

As the flagship's band played "The Star-Spangled Banner" rather than the "Hail Columbia" that had reverberated across the same waters eight years short of a century earlier, good America was even more resolved to reform bad Japan. The battleship *Mississippi*, which had helped complete Okinawa's destruction by leveling lovely Shuri Castle two months earlier, was anchored nearby. No wonder the defeated people would begin speaking of Japan's "second opening." Perry's frigate of the same name—in honor of which old American charts identified Uraga Bay as "Mississippi Bay"—had steamed toward the heart of Lord Abe's Japan.

General Douglas MacArthur, who presided over the formal surrender proceedings, bore a striking resemblance to the Commodore, especially in his proud self-assurance, talent for self-dramatization, and advocacy of a permanent American military presence in Asia. "Firmly convinced of the rectitude of American purpose, and fully persuaded of the universal applicability of the American ideal,"[15] both brought a sense of mission to Japan. For the few who might have missed the point, the General ordered Perry's original thirty-one-star flag, the very one that had flown over the first *Mississippi*, prominently displayed on the strapping new *Missouri*, just above the table where the surrender documents waited. Far from "ironic," as American accounts called the flying of the old flag, it had been rushed there by plane from Annapolis. John Dower, the leading historian of the American occupation, would call its "flaunting" a deliberate reprimand calculated to hammer home the point about the durability of American power. One thousand five hundred fighter planes and four hundred B-29 Superfortresses roaring over the battleship's sixteen-inch guns drove home the symbolism of the far greater might now backing up the Commodore's assertion of it those ninety-two years earlier.[16]

Imperious MacArthur began his occupation by underlining the obvious implications. "We stand in Tokyo today reminiscent of our countryman, Commodore Perry," he declared at the profoundly satisfying—to the victors—ceremony that began his "shogun's" reign. Warming American hearts, he informed that Perry's purpose had been to "bring to Japan an era of enlightenment and progress, by lifting the veil of isolation" to the world's "friendship, trade and commerce."

The Japanese made no reply during their six years of dancing to the General's tune—and with every reason, Americans felt certain, in their fury at Japanese savagery during the war. Not even after the occupation ended and the occupying troops went home—apart from the thousands that continued serving on the sprawling U.S. bases—did native voices express criticism of Perry, and not only for fear of reprisal from an America that remained overwhelmingly dominant in the "fundamentally asymmetrical" relationship, to use Washington's current euphemism for the mighty lopsidedness. By that time, the Japanese had had a long history of concealing their real feelings about the Commodore.

REGULAR MENTION OF the Japanese tendency to conceal emotion tends to obscure its role in their foreign policy. Cloaking and camouflaging are of course real enough, both having struck European visitors when they first arrived. One of the earliest Portuguese Jesuits concluded in the mid-sixteenth century that the Japanese had three hearts: "a false one in their mouths for all the world to see, another within their breasts only for their friends, and the third in the depths of their hearts, reserved for themselves alone and never manifested to anyone."[17] Later observers, including some in the twentieth century, seconded that judgment—which of course applies to almost every people, except that Japanese values and codes require that faces be kept composed and words be carefully watched, generating what foreigners tend to see as Asian "inscrutability." Asia as a whole is relevant because the West annexed or exploited most of it by political or economic means, if not military. Its people learned to hide their feelings about the imperialism that affected almost all of them, one way and another.

In Japan's case, the considerable divide between the "inner" and "outer" selves common to all humankind may be reinforced by the country having remained "profoundly traditional" beneath what Ian Buruma calls its "concrete and glass facade." "In many ways, the Japanese continue to be a nation of farmers not quite sure what to make of their new affluence."[18] They're even less sure about how to behave in the presence of Westerners, first of all Americans. People have some liking for the American culture, most conspicuous in the local Disneyland, McDonald's restaurants, and movie advertisements, and they're also largely content with the skewd Japan-U.S. relationship. Washington's military protection—especially against resurgent China, which is increasingly perceived as a potential threat—enables Japan to pursue other interests, chiefly economic. Vaguely fearing impoverishment if they lose that protection, many value their relatively free ride, whose chief cost is conformity in foreign policy. But resentment festers in the inner self, all the more because it's still, or again, suppressed.

Applying psychoanalytic speculation to a country of a hundred million-odd is of course fraught with danger. Still, Nakahama Manjiro, the first Japanese to establish personal relations with Americans after the New Bedford whaler rescued the fourteen-year-old fisherman, may be worth another look.[19] Although a grateful President Coolidge would say about Manjiro's explanations of Perry's land that it was "as if America had sent its first ambassador,"[20] a Japanese scholar who later straddled both cultures would call the young man something more relevant to Japan's subsequent development: the prototype of its "identity crisis after the pins were knocked from so many certainties grounded in history." "In one sense, the 150 years since Perry has been a journey in search of identity for *all* Japanese."[21]

The resulting "recurrent seasons of bewilderment and despair akin to a national identity crisis,"[22] to the extent that it indeed applies to the country as a whole, may reinforce the inner-self–outer-self pattern of some critical Japanese feelings. In any case, the two nations assumed a big-brother–little-brother relationship from the moment Perry was accommodated. Never mind for now that the errant little one remained somewhere convinced of his own ultimate superiority, especially in taste and wisdom; at the same time, he was eager to learn from his bigger, stronger sibling. At the same time too animus and even hatred still lurked underneath—often in the unconscious, except among a relatively small rightist minority that openly denounced American dominance.

Does that make the Japanese people strange? Is the dichotomy even particularly Japanese, and is Freudian insight needed to register it? "Psychological reactance," a clinical tool used after the theory was advanced in 1966, proposes that people who believe their freedom is under threat often behave in ways opposite to what they've been told or ordered. Specifically, they do what they think will restore their freedom, and the effort puts them under stress. In addition to anger, they experience anxiety, resistance to pressure, and desire to escape from those feelings. That happens even when they wouldn't have resented doing the things asked if a different manner had been used; if the things hadn't been *demanded*.

A Japanese scholar and essayist who is indeed a Freudian is more specific. He believes the powerlessness to oppose the Black Ships pushed "a sense of humiliation . . . somewhere deep" into the Japanese psyche. That scholar, Kishida Shu, likes to portray his country not as the miffed-but-grateful little brother but as a raped woman: "The forcible opening of Japan's ports can be thought of symbolically as the forcible opening of a woman's loins,"[23] the acts are "psychologically equivalent." Ian Buruma, with his acute perception of the feelings beneath composed Japanese faces, agrees in his fashion. "The Americans had guns, the Japanese lifted their skirts." But the first to bring the vivid image of sexual violation out of the closet may have been a hugely popular native novelist who died in 1996. Shiba Ryotaro, the author of *Drunk as a Lord* and *The Last Shogun* among other novels set in the Perry and immediate post-Perry periods, also spoke of "groveling in the dirt," which would have been as painful to Japanese lords as rape is to women.

People often conceal the suffering of submission to force; many rape victims in particular say nothing, chiefly out of shame. In Japan's case, a prolonged, collective Stockholm syndrome of associating with the powerful could conceivably have caused the silence, but in the absence of clinical evidence, some answers might come from a simpler "How would *you* feel?" What people wouldn't rage "inside" after being subdued by Perry-like dictates? Who wouldn't feel hurt and humiliated—unless one magically perceived the surrender as a boon, as most Americans do? A painting of the time titled *Commodore Perry Carrying the Gospel of God to the Heathen, 1853* was another metaphor, that one for the American assumption of superiority. Conveying the gospel well fit their view of themselves as introducing an advanced civilization to a backward one.

The corollary, which continues to shape the American perspective, was that any bad feelings between the two peoples was caused by Japan, specifically its unnatural seclusion. That moral and practical evil so perverted Japanese attitudes that the backlash to Perry eventually suppurated into the causes of World War II. A sprinkling of despairing Japanese shared that unlikely view. As defeat neared in World War II, a philosopher and cultural historian named Watsuji Tetsuro blamed the tragedy on the centuries of isolation, which he believed necessitated the forced, rushed modernization, the "drive to compete and excel, with its disastrous end of the Pacific War."[24]

Without taking that analysis further back to Western behavior that helped prompt the *sakoku*, Professor Kishida, the Freudian, believes the Commodore's rape, an "extremely unfortunate" start of the national relationship, continues to exert a "decisive influence" on Japanese perceptions.

A decisive influence *still*? Certainly none perceptible to twenty-first-century Americans. On the contrary, mention of the notion invariably prompts skepticism or derision. Why do Japanese, apart from some right-fringe extremists, almost never raise the supposedly vital matter? If the fear at first sight *is* still decisive—if the "Black Ships Trauma," the title of one of Kishida's books, is so important—why do virtually all indications of popular attitudes suggest the opposite?

Doesn't Japan much more honor than condemn Perry? Aren't his wedding ring and coat button kept in Tokyo's Imperial Museum together with a lock of his hair and snippet of his gold braid? In support of his view that Perry was no "boorish and bullying imperialist," Roger Pineau, who edited his journal, proudly pointed to written-in-stone evidence on a scrupulously maintained bust of the Commodore at the tip of the Izu Peninsula, which the Black Ships passed on their first passage toward Uraga Bay.[25] Doesn't that and a thirty-three-foot shaft of marble in Kurihama's "Perry Park" prove Japanese admiration of him? ("This monument commemorates the first arrival of Commodore Perry, Ambassador from the United States of America, who landed at this place July 14, 1853.") According to that view, the militant patriots who pulled down the shaft in 1944 belong to the dark war years that represent an aberration from the rule of Japanese respect and affection for the Land of the Free.

In addition to the Perry marble that would seem to indicate that he's a hero in Japan too, the mission's anniversaries are celebrated with public observances like parades, and schools paint the Commodore as a benefactor of Japan. As Arthur Walworth put it, the authorities appear to have "canonized the man whom in 1853 they would have liked to cannonade."[26] They also laud him to visiting Americans, some of whom repeat the praise in their books. Claiming that Perry "took great care to respect the sovereignty of Japan and the dignity of individual Japanese,"[27] Harvard's Samuel Eliot Morison, who has been called "the greatest American historian of the twentieth century," concluded his biography of the Commodore with acclaim for the "cordial relations" he supposedly initiated with the country. As illustration, Morison quoted a Japanese woman who'd won a Ph.D. from New York's Columbia University. The one-in-ten-million exception who proved the rule, although the professor didn't mention that, was "'all for Perry, of course. But for him, I would be doing nothing but pouring tea and arranging flowers!' So let us leave the subject there."[28]

ALTHOUGH SOME JAPANESE indeed hail Perry some of the time for "start[ing] their country on the road . . . to dazzling progress," in the words of Ferdinand Kuhn,[29] homage to him may reveal less about their emotions than how they've dealt with them. A much more knowledgeable American suggests that Japanese feelings of envy and bitterness—which are "by definition *ura*, hidden"—are "so completely internalized" that discussing them is difficult.[30] Other observers see the respect for the Commodore largely as camouflage thrown up by the outer self. Whether the well-documented reaction to trauma is called repression, denial of reality, or adjusting to reality, enough is known to require no explanation here, except to comment that Japanese inner and outer selves appear to be so compartmentalized that they're hardly on speaking terms with each other.[31] However, more detail about Japan's post-Perry history may help explain the relative silence about the disgrace of 1853–1854.

Japanese negotiating skill and determination to protect the country's territorial sovereignty kept the treaty Townsend Harris forced on Edo in

1858 less onerous than the one Britain had wrenched from China after the First Opium War.* Still, its terms were abhorrent to the Japanese.

They relinquished the right to establish tariffs on incoming and outgoing goods, which the treaty set and Edo was powerless to change. Legal jurisdiction over the ports themselves was surrendered in the sense that Americans accused of crimes—like nationals of the Europeans powers, in accordance with *their* forthcoming treaties with Edo—would be tried not in Japanese courts but consular ones staffed by foreign judges using foreign law: the demeaning practice known as extraterritoriality ("Americans committing offenses against Japanese shall be tried in American Consular courts, and, when guilty, shall be punished according to American law").† Samuel Wells Williams, who in 1855 was appointed Secretary to the U.S. Legation in China, made fervent attempts to exclude extraterritoriality, whose severely deleterious effects he'd seen there—but in vain. Another tenet carried over from Perry's Kanagawa Treaty was a Most Favored Nation clause that automatically gave the United States any privilege Japan might grant to any other country. That feature of so-called "hitch-hiking imperialism" delivered further profit by sharing advantages secured by other countries—advantages that put a straightjacket on Edo's foreign policy by depriving it of the ability to maneuver among nations. Japan was given no matching rights or privileges in the United States.

Within months of the signing of the "Harris" treaty, Britain, Russia, France, and Holland—the first of seventeen countries—secured almost identical ones, which were renegotiated in 1866, after Western naval guns had demonstrated their power during the expeditions against Satsuma and Choshu. Despite acceding to Japanese insistence on outlawing the opium trade, the new American one was "one of the most thoroughly un-American

---

* "The bakufu did not allow the importation of opium, did not cede any land outright, did not allow Christianity outside the ports, prohibited travel in the interior, and paid no indemnity to the West. In short, Japan escaped some of the harsh conditions of an imposed treaty. Moreover, by refusing Western ships access to the interior . . . the bakufu denied the imperial powers the key means by which they had expanded their control over colonized areas." Michael Auslin, *Negotiating with Imperialism*, pp. 21–22.

† Japanese authorities could arrest foreigners for breaking native laws, but they would be turned over to their consuls for trial, at which the consuls would be both judge and jury. While the treaty ports as a whole remained Japanese, all aliens in their Foreign Settlements, as they were officially designated, were thus protected. Unhappy at the prospect of dealing with unruly seamen and merchants who spoke no Japanese, the *bakufu* had first approved of extraterritoriality, but it and the succeeding Meiji government resented it more and more as Westerners began demanding protection for their businesses, children, servants, Japanese mistresses, and even, after Christian missionaries were readmitted in 1873, Japanese converts.

treaties ever ratified" by Washington.[32] Placing many goods on a tariff-free list and setting a maximum of 5 percent on the value of all others—as opposed to the 15 to 20 percent Western nations imposed for themselves—it prevented Japan from protecting its infant industry and from obtaining more than a modicum of revenue from the increasing foreign trade, which it was also unable to regulate. To raise the capital required for continued industrializing, the government turned to oppressive domestic taxes.

"I have seen things that made my blood boil in the way the European powers attempt to degrade the Asiatic nations," ex-president Ulysses Grant told the Meiji Emperor when he visited Japan on a diplomatic mission in 1879.[33] Harris had died the previous year, but not before regretting the "unequal treaties," as they were called. He'd expected them to be revised "long since,"[34] but they paid too handsomely for that, although they outraged Japanese public opinion. Front-page stories in the new national press about Westerners punished lightly or not at all for rapes and other crimes inflamed the new national consciousness. In 1886, a consular court in Kobe exonerated the captain and crew of an English ship who, after it had sunk off a nearby coast, rowed the lifeboats to safety, leaving all the Japanese passengers to drown. Newspaper articles and editorials heightened the grief and righteous indication that overwhelmed "all people, whether in or out of government."[35] The outrage would continue for decades, even after Japan had imposed its own unequal treaties on Korea and China.

It also prompted more killing of foreigners. Although high officials sent apologies to the Russian legation after a policeman attacked a visiting Russian prince with his sword in 1891, a wide range of Japanese continued to roil at the "shameful" treaty concessions. No person "high or low" viewed them as "anything but the greatest obstacle" to the nation's effort to establish itself as Asia's sole "modern" country.[36]

If the Japanese view sounds exaggerated, one of the period's most distinguished American scholars recently summarized that the treaty "clearly placed Japan in a semi-colonial position."[37] While few Americans thought of the relatively recent Boston Tea Party in that context, nor questioned the conviction that the revolutionary republic would never impose similar injustice on others, the treaty terms acted as another slow poison that rendered the *bakufu* unable to take independent action. No longer fully sovereign Japan was politically as well as economically subordinate to the Western powers.

More than shame of capitulation sealed Japanese lips. They had to swallow their feelings in order to free themselves of the unequal treaties, a "matter of life and death" for each successive cabinet. "Every powerful political figure threw himself into the undertaking, heedless of the cost."[38] The lengths to which the Japanese were willing to go in order to conceal their feelings while trying to placate would be reflected in much later homage to General Curtis LeMay, who, as commander of the 21st Bomber Command's B-29s in 1945, switched from so-called "precision" raids in daylight to massive, low-level runs over crowded urban centers using incendiary bombs at night. One after another, Japanese cities—Kobe, Nagoya, Osaka, Yokohama, Toyama, Kawasaki—were consumed by firestorms so blistering that glass melted and people trying to flee burst into flames, as in the Tokyo raid that killed more than a hundred thousand civilians. Twenty years later, the Japanese government awarded LeMay its highest civilian medal, the First Class of the Order of the Rising Sun, for helping rebuild the country.

Although the unequal treaties imposed nothing so deadly, they too prompted bootlicking. To curry favor with its "betters," Japan imported dozens of foreign judges and prosecutors, and allowed English to be used in its courtrooms. Foreigners' run of the country included the right to vote, even when they misbehaved. The remarkable concessions were made because the yoke would be lifted only if and when its installers signaled that the yoked had become civilized. (The first great day of that kind would come in 1911, when Tokyo would regain control of its tariffs.) Their efforts to demonstrate how enlightened they'd made themselves went well beyond introducing a Western-style legal system and trying to maintain strict observance of the international laws forced on them.

Some bordered on the grotesque. Six years after the Meiji Restoration, earnest couples in fastidiously formal Western dress and dancing to Western music were packing a Tokyo hall named Rokumeikan (Deer Cry Pavilion) opened in a British architect's expensive Renaissance structure. (The limping Foreign Minister's variant of the male costume, topped by a frock coat and silk hat, when he'd sign the 1945 surrender agreement aboard the *Missouri* would look more pathetic than silly.) Even geishas scrapped their lovely kimonos in favor of distant continents' wardrobe, and the Emperor's Western dress was visible to all because he was driven in an open carriage. The government financed Rokumeikan's elaborate amusement[39] because it believed, with reason, that the humbled nation had to teach aristocrats the skills that would enable them to mingle comfortably with Western diplomats. Approval as "civilized" could be won only by demonstrated mastery of Western ways.

Copying manners and fashion wasn't new, as the sixteenth-century fancy for Portuguese clothing showed,[40] but now others were in control, and they wanted much native culture abandoned. Diligent Japan was good enough at that too for a British afficionado to declare, half a century after the first sighting of the Black Ships, that it was no longer the hermit of the East, but "the most Western of the nations of the West."[41]

Some samurai, giddily embracing the formerly forbidden that often elevates fads to the top, genuinely relished beef, short hair, and dancing in public with women. Attraction and its opposite, which can stimulate the psyche concurrently, probably helped turn a few sophisticated circles "from fear and hatred of foreigners to an excessive admiration."[42] Dissidents and reformers who wanted to democratize the centralized, single-minded Meiji state began idealizing the United States and painting the likes of George Washington and Patrick Henry as magnificent models. A political novel of 1885 by a journalist who'd studied in the States opened with the wisdom that the American way was to "side with the weak and crush the strong." Fukuzawa Yukichi, one of modern Japan's first and most respected experts on the West, instructed that the gap between the U.S. and Japan was "as vast as the gap between heaven and earth" because the people of the "rich, strong and civilized" former "produced schools instead of arms," enjoying liberty and singing "the praises of peace"[43] while Japan had "not one thing in which we excel."

Japan's thrusts into Korea and Taiwan during the Sino-Japanese War of 1894–95 were in some measure imitations of American imperialism and European colonialism. Shortly afterward, a Chinese man of letters observed that the Japanese relentlessly devoted themselves to Western studies despite their heavy hearts and detestation of Westerners.[44] They did that, feigning humility, in order to achieve domination later—or, to quote novelist Natsume Soseki again, in order to survive, "and this is what makes us so pitiful." Writing at the time, Natsume, who was compared to Charles Dickens, believed that slavish imitation of the West and worship of white people had to leave his people empty, dissatisfied, and anxious.[45] Since the burdens of the unequal treaties could be shed only with American acquiescence, it was no wonder that Japanese statesmen and opinion makers often repeated the assurance that "we want to be just like you."

But convincing the inner selves of a people raised in an ancient culture very different from the European—people who weren't at all "just like you" and couldn't be—was harder. Many Japanese believed exposing the abasement would have been unwise while the country remained in thrall to the Western powers. It was better to keep the truths unspoken, all the more because thought about them would have been difficult and painful.

The turmoil still burdens the subconscious. Accepting the 1994 Nobel Prize in Literature, the novelist Oe Kenzaburo said that Japan's postopening modernization was "oriented toward learning from and imitating the West," despite the Asian country's "deep-rooted culture." "Even in the West, to which our culture was supposedly quite open, we have long remained inscrutable or only partially understood."[46] Oe believes Japan remains split "between two opposite poles of ambiguity" that are "so powerful and penetrating that it divides the state and the people."

ALTHOUGH THE ARGUMENT that the outer self still "fawns on and acquiesces to the West" while the inner one "detests the West and clings to a megalomaniacal pride to salve intense feelings of humiliation"[47] can't be tested, some behavior appears to support it. Apart from a slice of delightful exceptions who feel comfortable with Westerners, most Japanese would prefer to avoid them. As if to confirm the 1852 *New York Times* prediction that the Japanese would "feel at perfect liberty" to violate any treaty they were forced to sign, Japan remains the most anti-immigrant of all industrialized nations, ranking near the bottom of major economies in percentage of foreign investment and foreign residents. A third of the respondents in a twenty-first-century poll said they wanted no more tourists from abroad; many regard "No Foreigners" signs as a practical way to save themselves unpleasantness. Although overt evidence of that is rare in Tokyo, the capital is a telling example in another way because so few foreigners live in other cities and the native–foreigner gulf remains remarkably wide even there. Partly because many real estate agents shun clients from abroad, more than three-quarters of the European-American population live in just three of Tokyo's twenty wards.

With "the image of the predatory West" remaining strong throughout modern Japanese history,[48] a so-called "vulnerability complex" lies deep in the bones. For all their worldwide dealings, major Japanese companies continue to exclude their relatively few foreign employees from the councils of trust and power and do the same even with native employees who have lived abroad.[49] Some foreigner scholars and researchers find even prestigious Tokyo University an "intellectually closed shop" that also excludes them socially.[50] Thus the spirit of Dejima Island's quarantine lives on. Virtually every *gaijin*—"foreigner" with a trace or more of distrust and aversion—can tell his or her own stories about the enduring condition.

Maybe many of those who avoid *gaijin*, tactfully or not, merely want to save themselves the "anxiety" they cause (which can be anonymously reported to a Justice Ministry web site opened in 2003). Or to avert the kind of trouble suggested when the Governor of one of the forty-seven prefectures—Kanagawa, coincidentally or not—recently called foreigners "sneaky thieves" or "petty crooks." (Protest from some of the Governor's audience prompted a grudging apology.) On a larger scale, the wonderfully internationalist creativity in design and manufacture hasn't erased the stubborn sense of separateness that leaves hearts much less open to Americans than minds, even though most physical barriers against outsiders are down.

Is that surprising when the national relationship remains entirely "asymmetrical"? Several years after Washington, practically speaking, dictated the 1946 Constitution's famous words of permanent demilitarization—the Japanese people "forever renounce war as a sovereign right of the nation" and vow never to maintain "land, sea and air forces, as well as other war potential"—fear of communism supplanted wounded memory of the Pacific War as impetus for American policy. Japan was then given some old American uniforms and instructed to arm 75,000 "police officers" with machine guns and—even less suitable for police work—tanks and bazookas. Again the winner's word was essentially the subservient loser's command, and when Washington demanded more troops—no fewer than three hundred fifty thousand of them, well equipped—the prime minister's attempted resistance was in vain, and the unwilling people were soon directed to rearm more or less fully. The forbidden battalions, flotillas, and air squadrons are still weakly disguised as a "Self-Defense Force," even though the country is now among the world's largest military powers.

There the relationship is stalled, its military aspect closer to a boss and employee than to big and little brother, and the Cold War's end has changed little. The distress of the great majority of Japanese at Washington's strong pressure on Tokyo to contribute to its subsequent occupation of Iraq was ignored, as usual. The traumas of a century and a half ago still fill a reservoir of anger and antipathy, unemptied "even in periods of success and apparent self-confidence."[51] Virtually nothing continues to be heard about it because almost everyone keeps his or her share cloaked in the inner self.

All goes back to the Black Ships that affected Japan–U.S. relations, some students of the matter are convinced, more than the dropping of two atomic bombs. Samuel Wells Williams saw the 1858 commercial treaty as completion of Perry's work and confirmation of the mission's success: a "triumph" of intercourse with a Japan "reopened by Christian nations without injury to a single individual in the empire, without browbeating or threatening its government, and . . . with the general consent of the people."[52] The missionary was gratified to learn that "the Japanese officials remember [the Commodore] with respect." But the sadder truth is that Japan's hidden enmity is unlikely to disappear unless acknowledged and released, which is in turn unlikely while both countries continue to dissemble. Meanwhile, "Man's struggle against humiliation," as André Malraux called it, persists, together with American pride in the Commodore's feat that catastrophically primed Japan for aggression.

Afterword

A statue of Perry in Newport, Rhode Island, and a statue of Abe in the garden of the Fukuyama Castle Museum

T HE MANSION THAT housed the U.S. Naval Academy during its Civil War evacuation from Annapolis borders Touro Park in Perry's hometown of Newport, Rhode Island, a fitting site in light of the Commodore's work to found the academy's predecessor, the Naval School.[1] The same little park, up a hill from the port's tourist attractions, provides a lovely setting for a statue of Perry himself. Erected in 1868, ten years after his death, it was restored in 1993, with the help of the city of Shimoda.

Perhaps because the statue makes the Commodore less huffy-puffy than most photographs, if fails to suggest his military accomplishments, which nothing during the past century and a half has dimmed. Old Bruin surely belongs where his most recent biographer placed him, in "the first rank of 19th-century American naval heroes."[2] Nor could he have conducted the Japan expedition with anything but the values and concerns of the time, including the voracious European appetite for overseas territories, which he felt America had to match. Blaming the patriot for not being guided by later morality would violate a cardinal rule for examining history.

But the mission's long-term results are another matter. Not to measure them with today's values would violate a major purpose of such examination.

Years of asking Americans about Perry confirmed for me that the vast majority more or less agree with an admirer who called him "the surgeon who operated successfully on the suppurating sore of Japanese isolationism." But many more of the world's people, including those he affected most profoundly, see him differently.

Although Japan's opening in the second half of the nineteenth century comes as close to inevitable as anything in history, that doesn't diminish the importance of the opener's qualities. Only absolute determinists who believe great movements leave no room for human influence, that free will stops operating when grand designs unfold, would challenge that assertion. Even in the context of that day's conviction of Western superiority in general and American exceptionalism in particular—the notion that the new republic had a kind of divine right of instruction and expansion— the Commodore stood out for his arrogance toward Asians. While most Americans were nationalists in their ways, he was a super-nationalist. While virtually all believed in using force for protection, the eager imperialist who took liberty with his orders to do Japan no wrong used it to dictate, risking hostilities with, as a recent American writer put it, "a country that sought to be left alone and bothered nobody unless bothered by somebody."[3]

The positive consequences included the speedy victory that saved lives and immediate pain on both sides, as some Japanese acknowledged. *Sama*, one of the language's stronger honorifics, is addressed to people of much higher rank. Hearing of the Commodore's death, a Yokohama resident asked if Americans worshipped "Perry-sama."[4] "Perry the Great," as the translation there might be, was implicit acknowledgment of his skill in conceiving and executing his possibly cleverest tactic of convincing Edo he was a very important person. In the end, it doesn't matter how much he was acting a role or expressing his real feelings about his person, mission, and country. Even if Lord Abe deserved the greater credit for avoiding war, it's hard to imagine another American commander who could have matched Perry's achievement of winning without firing a shot in anger.

But surely his drive also increased the attendant pain. Some Japanese commentators are convinced that a more patient, tolerant officer would have made a great difference. One of the country's most accomplished novelists felt certain that if Westerners had taught the "true mutual responsibilities of nations," the "shock and deceit and confusion" generated by "world conquerors" would have been avoided. If only, mused Toson Shimazaki, the Black Ships hadn't come with men who used force and white flags to demand the country's opening, the Japanese might not have looked at them "with such revulsion."[5]

Only *might*, but an East Asia Squadron lieutenant, the future admiral George Preble, tacitly agreed by citing Japanese regret that "we Americans were in too much of a hurry and wanted everything now." It wasn't easy for them to "put bye in a moment [to] the customs and laws of three centuries." Preble quoted a Japanese of Perry's day who acknowledged the time had come for his country to open but insisted that "the innovations must be gradual" and appear to the people "to be conceded and not forced from them—all very reasonable, I think."[6] A Japanese translator put it similarly to Perry himself. "You must give us more time. It is all very plain to you, but we are like people coming out of a dark room into the glare of sunshine, and we do not yet see the bearing of things clearly."[7]

Perry gave neither time nor respite from brandishing guns in a way that had much the same emotional effect as firing them. The claim of his admirers—rarely scholars—that he behaved as an American gentleman, using only astute diplomacy,[8] seems to me specious, especially since many who make it also commend his deft application of force. The pillar of goodness made of his disinclination to seek traditional conquest also rings hollow. At bottom, the vague but great American admiration for Perry's mission rests largely on the fact, often seen as surprising, that he restrained himself from not making use of its superior force to acquire land or colonies. Repeated declarations that he was no imperialist are another way of saying the same, but the evidence points the other way. Only presidential restraint kept the Commodore from establishing protectorates on Okinawa, Formosa, and elsewhere in Asia. "Colonies," he declared after returning from the mission, "are almost as necessary to a commercial nation, as are the ships" that transport commodities.[9]

As for his intentions for Japan, much depends on the definition of *imperialism*. The full-throated chorus that continues to exult that America never engaged in any such thing rests largely on the half-truth that it never grabbed other people's land, as the European empires did so egregiously.[10]

"It's worth remembering that the United States did not occupy Japan," the Commodore's latest booster, the author of a highly regarded book, asserted in 2003. "Perry came in search of treaties, not territory."[11] But territorial acquisition is irrelevant to imperialism, which most scholars of international relations now define as a state's attempt to dominate or impose its will on a foreign area. That area need not be an entire country, and the goal, whose attainment is also irrelevant, needn't be permanent rule. The essential ingredient is an effort to "dominate, control, or impose [that state's] views," and if that's not what Perry did in 1853–1854, another of the writer's conclusions might apply: "If we allow emotion to intrude, it is possible to excuse every American action as harmless or altruistic."[12]

THE HISTORY OF THE PACIFIC—a name that should have rung with irony during the near century of preparing for and making war after 1853—would surely have been very different if not for the Black Ships shock. I feel as certain of that as of any historical "What if . . . ?" even knowing others disagree. While virtually everyone accepts that twentieth-century Japan became "a fierce and dangerous enemy of the United States," some historians believe other circumstances made it so.

One argues that the country "took a wrong turning about fifty years after Perry's visit."[13] The wrong turn was modeling itself on warlike Prussia, including a requirement that the ministers of war and the navy must be a general and an admiral on active service. But while the generals and admirals who exercised political power in the 1930s and 1940s indeed created great trouble, that was a secondary cause—one of many, of course—of Japan's belligerence before and during World War II. It's as clear as almost anything in the record that the striving to be a major military power—the switch from feeble defensive efforts of 1853–1854—started in reaction to Perry. A few people saw that even then, including the East Asia Squadron sailor who noted that it couldn't be said Japan, "any more than an oyster," ever yearned to be opened. "The Japanese did not seek—they abjured our company," a lonely Briton reminded. "It was only the *terror* [italics added] of our fleets which thrust our society upon them against their will." And the excited Japanese reaction to Perry's gift of the howitzer prompted translator Williams to suppose that the recipients "will soon begin to cast others like it" and "think themselves able to resist foreign aggression as soon as they have made guns."[14]

Sure enough, the vengence of history, as Laurens van der Post called it, began later the same year, when Abe's order of Dutch warships harbored the embryo of a "higher" purpose for the country that had lacked a national army and navy. The flag the new vessels would fly was chosen the following year: the red sun on the white background that would also flutter—remarkably soon, relatively speaking—on great battleships and aircraft carriers, and glint from dive-bombers as well. The Imperial Naval Academy's genesis occurred the year after that, when a Nagasaki school began training cadets in modern sea warfare. Soon a Western-style military school near Edo, sire of the passionately nationalistic Imperial Military Academy, was doing the same for army cadets, while the previously rare interest in Western manufacture, especially everything promising military advantage, began to soar. Would the painful, pernicious, and ultimately disastrous campaign to militarize have happened, at least with such speed and ferocity, without foreign intrusion?

Modern Japan acquired features Perry never imagined, partly because he knew so little about the feudal land he tackled. On top of his unavoidable ignorance of the country, his makeup made him unlikely to ponder the matters that most need consideration before confronting other peoples. Maybe a more reflective person wouldn't have undertaken the mission, or at least might have entertained some doubt that the opening would greatly benefit Japan too. Perry had none, and the Japanese people—together with most others in and around the Pacific, including Americans—actually lost terribly.

The "hundred-year war" to militarize was more a likely reaction than a paradoxical one to the military officer who humbled Japan. Use of force like his rarely pays in the long run, and even less often without prompting anger and denial, the latter being my guess about what moved Shimoda to help restore Perry's Newport statue. Self-motivated decisions often take longer to put in place, but almost always bring greater, longer-lasting benefits, with far less danger of backlash.

No one knows what would have happened if Japan had been left to open on its own, or whether the other Western power that would have demanded it if the Commodore hadn't would have been worse. But it's now apparent that the American mission failed on most important counts after its fleeting victories in Uraga and Kanagawa. Some of the most telling evidence of that was provided by Francis Hall, the astute American reporter who lived in the country more or less continuously for seven years not long after the *kaikoku*. Exploring the districts open to foreigners, keen-eyed Hall registered good and bad with admirable openness and understanding. Recording closed Japan's appreciation of other countries he noted that the intelligentsia had "books of sterling value . . . a hundred imported articles . . . improved ways of the healing art, tangible evidences of the value of Western civilization." His conclusion was extraordinary enough to put in italics: *"Thus I am often led to think that had Perry never opened Japan to the West . . . [it] would have improved in civilization steadily if not rapidly."*

That judgment was all the more persuasive because Hall, for all his appreciation of the country (although he arrived full of foreboding, expecting "little pleasure"), saw its faults clearly and criticized them sharply. His devout faith hardly inclined him to approve the determined Tokugawa persecution of his fellow Christians. Nevertheless, he went farther with his conjecture about the "fundamental question" for the Japanese people:

> Nay more, I sometimes think—considering the character of the people that had been left to *ask in* [his italics] Western influences through the Dutch . . . and not felt them, as it were, *forced* upon them as now—taken their own way, without compulsion or restraint, the gain to this people would have been greater and more permanent than now.[15]

That notion is gaining acceptance among Western observers with knowledge of grassroots Japan. New evidence of Tokugawa trends and greater understanding of human psychology support the argument that using force was pernicious. That the Japanese people would have been happier and richer without it of course remains speculative, but speculation can add value to history's raw material. A less hurt Japan would surely have profited the rest of the world too.

The lingering Japanese resentment might be eased by acknowledging the bullying of the naval chauvinist who considered Abe's people mankind's enemy, although they'd been harming no foreigners (apart from Okinawans). That's surely too much to hope for while Washington still bends Tokyo to its bidding (making many Japanese feel their country remains abnormal), but there's no reason to keep honoring Perry for wrong as well as the right reasons. Of course, the nineteenth century can't be changed, but contemporary Americans might benefit from mulling a U.S. senator's protest, as Perry departed from Norfolk, that the republic was about to pose a threat to a nation with which it had no quarrel. Casting off the destructive myth of the Commodore's wise and benevolent mission would be a blessing.

LORD ABE MAY BE EVEN LESS known in Japan than Perry in America. "Abe Masahiro?" replied an obviously educated officer of New York's Japan Tourist Office when I asked about monuments to him. "Who's that?" Busy helping other visitors, she had no interest in finding out.

There *is* a statue of the *roju shuseki* on the grounds of Fukuyama Castle in Fukuyama City, near the old family *han*, some five hundred miles southwest of Tokyo. The bronze has him in a kimono rather than military dress, and his left hand is holding a Western book. Strollers occasionally glance at the doll-like face, but the site, which goes unmentioned in the city's tourist materials, has few visitors. As for Tokyo, his octogenarian great-great-grandson lives in a comfortable little house in one of its relatively quiet quarters. Modest by American standards, it occupies part of the grounds of several old Abe mansions in and near Edo. Surely the high courtesy with which the great-great-grandson received me there wasn't for myself but for American interest in his largely forgotten ancestor. In the absence of an official memorial or library, his study is a kind of mini-museum dedicated to him. Elderly Abe Masahichi's softness of manner, elegant speech and tailoring, and exceptional eagerness to please made him, I guessed, much like young Masahiro when he led the *roju*. Although an American historian's conclusion that the Chief Senior Councilor's "attempt to compromise with all . . . succeeded in pleasing none"[16] is probably correct, the conciliator who couldn't possibly have pleased many merits a bow. A very recent Japanese opinion that he had "a strength of judgment rarely seen in history"[17] may be deserved.

ENDNOTES

PREFACE

1.   However, a Black Ships Festival imposed by the post–World War II American occupation has been dropped.

2.   Laurens van der Post, *The Prisoner and the Bomb*, p. 20.

3.   *New York Times*, August 11, 2003, p. 4.

4.   Shu Kishida, *A Place for Apology*, pp. 14–15.

5.   Osamu Dazai, quoted in Ian Buruma, "The Ghosts of Pearl Harbor" in *The New York Review of Books*, December 19, 1991, p. 9. "It is remarkable how hostile one can feel towards people whose eyes and hair are of a different color," Osamu continued. "I want to beat them to death. . . . Oh, beautiful Japanese soldiers, please go ahead and smash them!"

6.   A distinguished literary critic quoted in Buruma's *Inventing Japan*, p. 111. "A hundred years of fitful Westernizing, following Commodore Matthew Perry's famous 'opening' of Japan to the West in 1853," a reviewer commented, "had come to this, a suicidal attack in more ways than one." Christopher Benfey, "The Emperor's New Clothes," in *The New York Times Book Review*, February 9, 2003, p. 15.

CHAPTER I

1.   *New York Times*, February 24, 1852, quoted in Alfred Tamarin, *Japan and the United States*, p. 64.

2.   To his wife, Perry would allow that his visit to Japan was "one of the most important events" of *all* modern history. James Thomson et al., *Sentimental Imperialists*, p. 66.

3.   Ueda Shizuteru, "Nishida, Nationalism, and the War in Question," in James W. Heisig and John C. Maraldo (eds.), *Rude Awakenings*, p. 77.

4.   The clash's far greater effect on Japan than America is suggested by the great imbalance of writing about it in the two countries. For example, Woodrow Wilson's expansive *History of the American People*, published in 1902, made no mention of the Perry expedition.

5.   Quoted in Francis Hall, *Japan Through American Eyes*, p. 393.

6. The government would soon ask a former fisherman named Manjiro to provide information about America, where strange circumstance had taken him (see p. 135). About the amazing propulsion, Manjiro would explain that "A fire is kindled in the hold of a steamship. When the smoke rises, it turns gears, and the momentum of the wheels on both sides moves the ship as though it were flying." Peter Duus, *The Japanese Discovery of America*, p. 82.

7. Oliver Statler, *The Black Ships Scroll*, p. 8. Some eighty years later, a grandson of Perry would seek to comfort Tokyo's ambassador to Paris by pointing out that the steam vessels that dumbfounded and terrified the Japanese "had not long before been novelties in our own harbors." Since the great ships with their new locomotion represented fearsome intrusion, not welcome progress, in isolated Japan, that took the matter well out of context, a common practice among Perry's admirers.

8. M. William Steele, *Alternative Narratives in Modern Japanese History*, p. 6.

9. The sign had been supplied by a tiny Dutch colony. See p. 38. "At sea of Japan, the foreigner may not fish," an old manual instructed guard boat officials how to challenge potential visitors. "You must go way with first speedy wind. . . . It is a great prohibition of Japan to negotiate with strangers."

10. The song continues:

> Down in her hold there labor men
>
> Of jet-black visage dread;
>
> While, fair of face, stand by her guns
>
> Grim hundreds clad in red.

11. An earlier Venetian explorer is thought to have disappeared at sea trying to reach the islands.

12. Quoted in William L. Neumann, *America Encounters Japan*, pp. 5–6.

13. From "Dutch Ships" (1818) by Rai Sanyo, published in Donald Keene (ed.), *Anthology of Japanese Literature from the Earliest Era to the Mid-Nineteenth Century*, p. 437.

14. The persistence of that inclination is suggested by recent headlines such as "The Hermit Nuclear Kingdom" in *The New York Review of Books* in 2005 and "North Korea: The Hermit Kingdom" by CBS News in 2006.

15. John Sewall, "With Perry in Japan," p. 352.

16. Wilhelm Heine, *With Perry to Japan*, p. 33.

17. Matthew Perry, *Narrative of the Expedition to the China Seas and Japan, 1852–1854* (henceforth *Narrative*), p. 262.

18. Proposing an expedition in January 1851, he advised that its "real objective . . . should be concealed from public view."

19. Herman Melville observed in 1850 that a ship was "a state in itself," with the captain "its king."

20. Cited in John H. Schroeder, *Matthew Calbraith Perry*, p. 182.

21. The first article of a "constitution" of the year 604 CE stated that *wa* should be valued above everything else (Walter LaFeber, *The Clash*, p. 6). Before and after the interval of civil disorder largely caused by reaction to the Black Ships, "the Japanese fervently assumed that society and their own happiness advanced on the wheels of consensus and harmony, much as Americans credited their success to openness and acquisition for ascent" (p. 7).

22. Francisco Cabral, chief of the Jesuit mission in Japan from 1570 to 1581. Quoted in John Dower, *War Without Mercy*, p. 95.

23. Senator Stephen A. Douglas of Illinois, speaking in the same 1853.

24. "Ode to Japan," 1902.

25. J. W. Spalding, cited in Peter Booth Wiley, *Yankees in the Land of the Gods*, p. 282.

26. Wilhelm Heine, *With Perry to Japan*, pp. 67–68.

27. *Narrative*, p. 232.

28. *The Selected Writings of Lafcadio Hearn*, p. 429.

CHAPTER 2

1. In other versions, pirates had damaged the junk or the passengers landed intentionally because they wanted to trade.

2. John Roberson, *Japan from Shogun to Sony, 1543–1984*, p. 7.

3. Shunsuke Tsurumi, *An Intellectual History of Wartime Japan, 1931–1945*, p. 14. "The elite culture of Japan has invariably been an imported one, and the mass culture, indigenous," p. 15.

4. In *The Tale of Genji*, the masterpiece of Japanese classical literature, Prince Genji insists his son study Chinese classics because "without a solid foundation" in them "this Japanese spirit about which we hear so much is of no great use in this world."

5. Samuel Wells Williams, *A Journal of the Perry Expedition to Japan (1853–1854)*, p. 227.

6. Quoted in Donald Keene (ed.), *Anthology of Japanese Literature*, p. 436.

7. Charles Boxer, *The Christian Century in Japan, 1549–1650*, pp. 314–316.

8. Lewis William Bush, *77 Samurai*, p. 12.

9. Boxer, *The Christian Century*, p. 317.

10. See p. 38.

11. The map was probably a copy rather than an official one itself. Rumor or mockery had it that before the beheading, the corpse was pickled in salt so that the criminal investigation could continue. The Deshima resident to whom he gave it was a physician named Philipp Franz von Siebold. Although von Siebold was expelled from the country and forbidden to return, he did so in 1859, six years after Perry's first visit, and stayed several years, long enough to be saddened by the Western powers' treatment of opened Japan.

12. Although that figure has long been cited, recent investigation suggests the actual number may have been smaller.

13. Some aspects of Western history, such as the Inquisition, were probably as cruel. And although nothing could excuse the Japanese savagery, it spilled less blood than the Thirty Years' War that took millions of European lives at the same time, partly because Catholics, Lutherans, and Calvinists were convinced the heretic "others" deserved to die. If a method existed of measuring the scope of cruelty and violence in societies as a whole, Japan of Perry's day would surely have scored lower than America.

14. Peter Duus, *The Japanese Discovery*, p. 47.

CHAPTER 3

1. Peter Booth Wiley, *Yankees in the Land of the Gods*, p. 287.

2. Ronald Spector, "The American Image of Southeast Asia, 1790–1865," p. 301.

3. Centuries earlier, Japan too was barbarian, like the other East Asian tributaries of China, considered *the* civilized land.

4.   John Dower, *War Without Mercy*, p. 238.

5.   Jack Seward, *The Japanese*, p. 144. Some may have heard echoes in the 2004–2005 campaign by the White House and Department of Agriculture to reopen Japan to American beef. Pre-Perry Japan also killed no birds for sport or food.

6.   Louis G. Perez, *The History of Japan*, p. 83.

7.   Extending from the west coast of the Boshu Peninsula toward the then tiny fishing village of Yokohama, that bank formed a natural barrier to the entrance of the bay.

8.   "A Doctor's Memorandum" (from the diary of an Edo physician), p. 4. Identified, but not with full certainty, as "Dr. Ito," he may have been a former student of Philipp Franz von Siebold, the German physician and scientist who had served the tiny Dutch colony in Nagasaki. See pp. 60 and 337 (end note 11, Chapter 2).

9.   Nitobe Inazo, cited in Pat Barr, *The Coming of the Barbarians*, pp. 221.

10.   Cited in Toson Shimazaki, *Before the Dawn*, p. 79.

11.   Ibid., p. 78.

12.   "Memorandum of Kayama Eizaemon, *yoriki* (police magistrate) in [*sic*] the staff of the Uraga Governor," p. 13.

13.   Toson Shimazaki, *Before the Dawn*, p. 21.

14.   Nitobe Inazo, cited in Foster Rhea Dulles, *Yankees and Samurai*, p. 53.

15.   John Sewall, *The Logbook of the Captain's Clerk*, p. 352.

16.   Edward Barrington de Fonblanque, *Niphon and Pe-che-li, or Two Years in Japan and Northern China*, p. 18.

17.   James L. McClain, John M. Merriman and Kaoru Ugawa (eds.), *Edo and Paris*, p. 14. The Tokugawas' policy of granting residence sites to merchants in order to stimulate the city's growth succeeded admirably.

18.   Oliver Statler, *The Black Ships Scroll*, p. 10

19.   Donald Keene, *Emperor of Japan*, pp. 15–16.

20.   Bayard Taylor, *Perry's Bay*, p. 7.

21.   The explanation was in a note written in a hybrid Sino-Japanese used in official documents.

22.   Prior to the Industrial Revolution, factory activity was often trading.

23.   See p. 24. A minor contribution to suppressing the rebellion helped win the Protestant Dutch their permission to remain.

24.   Alfred Tamarin, *Japan and the United States*, pp. 6–7. Perry wrote of "the most degrading conditions," *Narrative*, p. 272.

25.   Henry Franklin Graff (ed.), *Bluejackets with Perry in Japan*, p. 34.

26.   Ibid., p. 7.

27.   Toson Shimazaki, *Before the Dawn*, p. 94. Shimazaki believes the Dutch traders "set the precedents" and gave Japanese officials their ideas about foreigners.

28.   Marius B. Jansen, *The Making of Modern Japan*, p. 92.

29.   Ibid., p. 93.

30.   Although King William II may have intentionally addressed his "friendly advice" to the "All powerful Emperor" knowing it would go to Shogun Tokugawa Ieyoshi, it's more likely that not even the knowledge of Japan absorbed though Deshima had enabled the Dutch to sort out who ruled Japan.

31.   The Commodore would write disparagingly of Dutch "avarice and cruelty," and

fume at them for giving Edo advice not to his liking, then claiming *they*, not he, had really opened Japan. In some of that he was neither alone nor badly mistaken. Russians too spoke, as a naval captain imprisoned in Japan put it, of "the misrepresentations of the selfish Dutch."

32. See p. 237.

33. "A Doctor's Memorandum," p. 3.

34. Harold Bolitho, "Abe Masahiro and the New Japan," in Jeffrey P. Mass and William B. Hauser (eds.), *The Bakufu in Japanese History*, p. 174.

35. Ian Buruma, *Inventing Japan*, p. 24.

36. Ibid., p. 25.

37. That disdain, and the virtually inevitable corruption in a self-perpetuating regime, were probably the principal causes, but the *bakufu* added to them by cancelling its debts to merchants more than once. Or they restructured them, further discouraging commercial interest and development by giving themselves two interest-free centuries to repay.

38. William Beasley, *Japan Encounters the Barbarian*, p. 9.

39. Malcolm D. Kennedy, *A History of Japan*, p. 117. Japanese peasants were "faced with a constant struggle with Nature to wring a living from their scanty soil. In Tokugawa times they were faced with the further handicap of being battened on by rapacious landlords, samurai, and money-lenders alike. Then, as now, earthquakes, typhoons, floods, tidal waves, volcanic eruptions, and fires were of frequent occurrence and took a heavy annual toll of lives and property" (p. 116).

40. Frederick Wells Williams, *The Life and Letters of Samuel Wells Williams*, p. ii.

41. Fred Notehelfer in the Introduction to Shimazaki Toson, *Before the Dawn*, p. xvi.

42. When the Continental Congress met in Philadelphia, letters between it and Savannah traveled far more slowly than between Edo and Kagoshima, which, although they were roughly the same distance apart, were on different islands, Honshu and Kyushu.

43. Donald Keene, *Toshimasa*, p. 6.

44. George B. Sansom, *The Western World and Japan*, pp. 216–17.

45. "Floating World" of course suggests water, a common symbol for sex, which was also referred to as "clouds and rain."

46. Walter LaFeber, *The Clash*, pp. 24–25.

47. Samuel Wells Williams, *A Journal of the Perry Expedition to Japan (1853–1854)*, p. 183.

48. *Japan: An Interpretation*, p. 16.

49. Noel Perrin, *Giving Up the Gun*, pp. 90–91.

50. Cited in Shunzo Sakamaki, "Western Concepts of Japan and the Japanese 1800–1854."

51. See p. 278.

52. The story was also told in a 1958 Hollywood film, *The Barbarian and the Geisha*.

53. Lafcadio Hearn, *Japan: An Interpretation*, pp. 385–86.

54. Susan Hanley, *Everyday Things*, pp. 1, 190, and 197.

CHAPTER 4

1. Japanese dictionaries still give *Tanegashima*, the island of the first Portuguese landing, as a word meaning "gun."

2. Noel Perrin pointed that out in *Giving Up the Gun* (1979), which threw new strong light on Japan's cooled romance with firearms. A. B. Mitford, otherwise known as Lord

Redesdale, wrote even in 1893 that "no opportunity was lost of throwing dust in the eyes of westerners, whom even in the most trifling details, it was the official policy to lead astray." *Tales of Old Japan*, p. 1.

3.   Williams, whose translating for Perry would give him opportunity for close observation, was actually in charge of the missionary press in Canton.

4.   Neil Postman, "Deus Machina," in *Technos: Quarterly for Education and Technology* 10 (Spring 2001), p. 1.

5.   Wilhelm Heine, *With Perry to Japan*, p. 68.

6.   Herbert Gowen, *Five Foreigners in Japan*, p. 228.

7.   Biddle's flagship, the *Columbus*, was a seventy-four-gun ship of the line. Three French warships that arrived in Nagasaki during the same month were given fresh provisions and departed the following day (Shunzo Sakamaki, "Japan and the United States," in *Transactions of the Asiatic Society of Japan* 18, Second Series, p. 187).

8.   *Narrative*, p. 235.

9.   John H. Schroeder, *Matthew Calbraith Perry*, p. 168.

10.   Marius B. Jansen, *The Making of Modern Japan*, p. 91.

CHAPTER 5

1.   John Glendy Sproston, *A Private Journal of John Glendy Sproston*, p. ix.

2.   Cited in John H. Schroeder, *Matthew Calbraith Perry*, p. 152.

3.   The first *Fulton*, designed by Robert Fulton himself, was never fitted out.

4.   Wilhelm Heine, *With Perry to Japan*, p. 7.

5.   Frederic Troutman, translator of *With Perry to Japan*, p. 6.

6.   Samuel Wells Williams, *A Journal of the Perry Expedition to Japan*, p. 222.

7.   Ibid., p. 193.

8.   Ibid., pp. 129–30.

9.   Ibid., pp. 199–200.

10.   Quoted in Ferdinand Kuhn, *Commodore Perry and the Opening of Japan*, p. 11.

11.   William Harlan Hale, "When Perry Unlocked the Gate of the Sun," p. 114.

12.   William L. Neumann, *America Encounters Japan*, p. 29.

13.   John H. Schroeder, *Matthew Calbraith Perry*, p. 19.

14.   Ibid. p. 50. Nevertheless, that senior midshipman developed strong respect for Perry, his direct superior.

15.   George Preble, *The Opening of Japan*, p. 145.

16.   Perry's great-great-grandfather had settled in the Commodore's cherished America in 1639.

17.   Arthur Orrmont, *The Indestructible Commodore Matthew Perry*, p. 12.

CHAPTER 6

1.   See p. 268.

2.   Cited in Henry Franklin Graff (ed.), *Bluejackets with Perry in Japan*, p. 46.

3.   Katherine Plummer, *The Shogun's Reluctant Ambassadors*, p. 68.

4.   Sakuma Shozan, "A Plan for Coastal Defense" (1842), cited in Peter Duus, *The Japanese Discovery of America*, pp. 58–59.

5.   Donald Keene, *Travelers of a Hundred Ages*, p. 384.

6.   Peter Duus, *The Japanese Discovery of America*, pp. 58–59.

7.   Ibid., p. 56.

8.   Among other evidence, Indian sculpture found on islands off the coast of British Columbia is virtually identical with Japanese works.

9.   Subjugating the mostly hunting and gathering Ainu, then called "Northern Barbarians" and numbering 25,000 or so, contributed to the Shoguns' appellation of "barbarian-subduing." However, they were generally considered not fully barbarian, if not fully civilized either.

10.   Peter B. Wiley, *Yankees in the Land of the Gods*, p. 28.

11.   The decree was called "Order for the Provision of Fuel and Water." See p. 95.

12.   Shunzo Sakamaki, "Japan and the United States, 1790–1853," pp. 48–49.

13.   George A. Lensen, *Russia's Japan Expedition of 1852 to 1855*, p. 58.

14.   In 1771, a Baron von Benyowsky, who'd been exiled to the Kamchatka peninsula in far eastern Siberia, took control of a small ship with other convicts and sailed south to Shikoku, where he, pretending to be Dutch, frightened the inhabitants by stating that Russia was planning to invade Hokkaido (Mikiso Hane, *Modern Japan*, p. 65).

15.   Vasili M. Golovnin, *Memoirs of a Captivity in Japan During the Years 1811, 1812, and 1813*, Vol. II, pp. 49–50. See p. 219.

16.   Peter B. Wiley, *Yankees in the Land of the Gods*, p. 109.

17.   Herbert H. Gowen, *Five Foreigners in Japan*, p. 220.

18.   Cited in Shunzo Sakamaki, "Western Concepts of Japan and the Japanese 1800–1854," pp. 8–9.

19.   Shunzo Sakamaki, "Japan and the United States, 1790–1853," p. 20.

20.   Cited in ibid., p. 186.

21.   Katherine Plummer, *The Shogun's Reluctant Ambassadors*, p. 185. The whaler's captain also told Perry he thought that Japanese ports, access to which clearly interested him more than the treatment of American castaways, could be opened only by force.

CHAPTER 7

1.   The invention of the potato chip was among the vast number of less grim events to which slavery was linked in the summer of 1853. A black man born free in Minerva, New York, and working as a carpenter, violinist, and cabbie in Saratoga Springs, some sixty miles away, was abducted in 1841 and sold into slavery in Louisiana. Citizens of Saratoga Springs helped arrange his release twelve years later. Returning there, he made his invention while working as an elegant restaurant's chef.

2.   John H. Schroeder, *Matthew Calbraith Perry*, pp. 9, 40. Few whites anywhere objected to minstrel shows, which the squadron performed to entertain the Japanese.

3.   Peter B. Wiley, *Yankees in the Land of the Gods*, p. 269.

4.   See p. 94.

5.   Peter B. Wiley, *Yankees in the Land of the Gods*, p. 271.

6.   Oliver Statler, *Shimoda Story*, p. 440.

7. Like graphic depictions of sexuality would be, the nakedness was much disapproved. This expression of it was by the Reverend Samuel Wells Williams (Frederick Wells Willaims, *The Life and Letters of Samuel Wells Williams*, p. 194)

8. Matthew Perry, *The Japan Expedition, 1852–1854: The Personal Journal of Commodore Matthew C. Perry* [henceforth *Journal*], p. 68.

9. John H. Schroeder, *Matthew Calbraith Perry*, p.183.

10. Ibid., p. 105.

11. Ibid., p. 170.

12. Ibid., p. 183.

13. *Narrative*, p. 235.

14. *Journal*, p. 95.

15. Toson Shimazaki, *Before the Dawn*, pp. 81–82.

16. *Narrative*, p. 269.

17. Squadron officers had asserted they'd "never *endure the disgrace* [italics added] of having failed to fulfill their state mission." Memorandum of Kayama Eizaemon," p. 2.

18. *Narrative*, p. 328.

19. Ibid., p. 244.

20. Memorandum of Kayama Eizaemon, p. 2.

21. Ibid., p. 3.

22. Sofue Ichiro, *Abe Masahiro*, pp. 310–18.

23. Peter B. Wiley, *Yankees in the Land of the Gods*, p. 327. Coincidentally, the Shogun's sister also died on July 27. She was the mother of the lord of the Mito *han*, who would severely criticize Abe for doing too little to improve military defenses but would also collaborate with him in a fashion.

CHAPTER 8

1. John Sewall, "With Perry in Japan," p. 354.

2. The negotiations with Perry should have been conducted by Kayama's colleague, the magistrate in the imposing black cloak and red helmet who, on July 8, had been first to board the *Susquehanna*, since that official had the duty that month. The Uraga governor's appointment of Kayama instead—on the grounds that he'd previously been given confidential instructions about the matter—provoked loud complaints from jealous fellow bureaucrats.

3. Making similar use of that much-used indirect language in his August 1945 call for surrender, Emperor Hirohito would explain it was because the war had not "turned in Japan's favor, and trends of the world were not advantageous to us."

4. Quoted in Peter B. Wiley, *Yankees in the Land of the Gods*, p. 310. Determination to avoid armed conflict had moved the *roju* to accept the "temporary expedient." Mitani Hiroshi, *Escape from Impasse*, p. 130.

5. Bayard Taylor, *Perry's Bay*, p. 20.

6. Frederick Wells Williams, *The Life and Letters of Samuel Wells Williams*, p. 60.

7. Ibid., p. 20.

8. Edward Barrows, *The Great Commodore*, p. 360.

9. Wilhelm Heine, *With Perry to Japan*, p. 73.

10. *Narrative*, p. 254.

11. Ibid., p. 261.

12. Bayard Taylor, *Perry's Bay*, p. 22.

13. *Narrative*, p. 255.

14. *Narrative*, p. 256.

15. Fillmore was an "accidental" president in the sense that he, as vice president, acceded to the office after Zachary Taylor died in 1850.

16. William Neumann, *America Encounters Japan*, p. 39.

17. *A Journal of the Perry Expedition to Japan*, p. 51.

18. *Meiji Japan Through Contemporary Sources* 2, pp. 15–16.

19. See Kanichi Asakawa, *Letters of Kanichi Asakawa*, p. 154, and Kimitada Miwa, "Perry's Fourth Letter and Nitobe Inazo" in *Japan and China*, pp. 43–44. Professor Miwa believes Nitobe, the author of *Bushido* (subtitled both *The Warrior's Code* and *Soul of a Nation*), shares with Perry responsibility for hiding knowledge of the fourth letter. The pro-American Nitobe did that with intention to strengthen Japanese-American friendship.

20. *Narrative*, p. 261.

CHAPTER 9

1. That reasoning was presented to Abe in, among other places, a memorandum to him from three magistrates shortly after Perry's arrival (William G. Beasley, *Select Documents on Japanese Foreign Policy*, pp. 107–8).

2. *Journal*, p. 98.

3. Ibid., p. 100.

4. *Narrative*, p. 273.

5. John Sewall, "With Perry in Japan," p. 356.

6. Cited in William Beasley, *Select Documents on Japanese Foreign Policy*, p. 109.

7. *Narrative*, p. 267.

8. Another feature on the American charts was "Saratoga Spit," a shoal so named after the *Saratoga* briefly grounded on it during the squadron's reconaissance.

9. *Narrative*, p. 273.

10. Ibid., p. 273.

11. His comments about the Japanese would include full appreciation of their liking for every variety of alcohol the squadron served them and its effect. At a later reception, they "became quite uproarious," sang "a succession of brisk and cheerful tunes," and "kept shouting at the tops of their voices." All American observers agreed, including Dr. James Morrow, who reported them as "free drinkers . . . many of them became very merry."

12. *Narrative*, p. 273.

13. Ibid., p. 270.

14. Toson Shimazaki, *Before the Dawn*, p. 22.

15. Ibid., p. 96.

16. See p. 112.

17. "A Doctor's Memorandum," p. 9.

18. Lafcadio Hearn, *Japan: An Interpretation*, p. 407.

19. Shiba Ryotaro, *The Last Shogun*, p. 28.

20. "Early Japanese Encounters with Americans," in *Inside/Outside Japan* 6, no. 4, May 1997. Manjiro "knew the American people, the magnitude of their country, their wealth and commerce, their prestige and power," a sailor who'd joined the navy to pay off his college debts would write. "He was the channel through which, by a kind of preordination, American ideas filtered into Japan" (John Sewall, *The Logbook of the Captain's Clerk*, p. 214).

21. Conrad Totman, *Politics in the Tokugawa Bakufu*, pp. 89–90.

22. Ibid., pp. 109, 232, 233.

23. Sofue Ichiro, *Abe Masahiro*, p. 12.

24. Walter LaFeber, *The Clash*, p. 14.

25. Sofue Ichiro, *Abe Masahiro*, p. 289. The book then has Abe suggesting contrivance of a "limited" breach, a "middle position" between keeping Japan closed and opening it. That was wishful thinking, but Abe surely knew it. He made the Nagasaki official privy to the secret as a tactical move—to win his confidence and use him as a "seawall" against other passionate exclusionists.

26. Ibid., p. 13.

27. Peter B. Wiley, *Yankees in the Land of the Gods*, p. 258.

28. Shiba Ryotaro, *The Last Shogun*, p. 13; *Drunk as a Lord*, p. 27.

29. Harold Bolitho, "Abe Masahiro and the New Japan," p. 178.

30. Ibid., p. 173.

31. Conrad Totman, *Early Modern Japan*, p. 464.

32. Lafcadio Hearn, *Japan: An Interpretation*, pp. 3 and 21.

33. Francis Hall in the *New York Tribune*, cited in Fred G. Notehelfer, *Japan Through American Eyes*, p. 53.

34. "There was practically no way a ruling senior councillor could interfere in the Great Interior. Guards there, in theory at least, were exceptionally subject to the shogun's wishes, and . . . there was little a councillor could do to ensure that guard personnel did not connive against him" (Conrad Totman, *Politics in the Tokugawa Bakufu*, p. 107).

35. *Inventing Japan*, p. 20.

36. Marius B. Jansen, *The Making of Modern Japan*, p. 33.

37. Malcolm D. Kennedy views the "spies," as some foreign writers call them, as part of an "extensive, elaborate, and extremely efficient intelligence organization, the spiritual forebear of the secret police of modern times" (*A History of Japan*, p. 124).

38. Harold Bolitho, "Tokugawa Shogunate" in *Kodansha Encyclopedia of Japan*, vol. 8, p. 56. *Bakuhan*, a term used by Japanese historians to capture the balance between the tent government in Edo and the lords' rule of their domains, suggests a blend of authority.

39. Peter Duus, *Feudalism in Japan*, p. 94.

40. Marius B. Jansen, *The Making of Modern Japan*, p. 33.

41. *Kodansha Encyclopedia of Japan*, vol. 8, p. 54.

42. The Tokugawas were also daimyo, in their case of an enormous *han* comprising about a quarter of the country's registered arable land and controlling about the same percentage of the production of rice, the official currency.

43. Shiba Ryotaro, *Drunk as a Lord*, p. 20.

44. The most powerful of the Outside Lords would soon deal a deathblow to the shogunate, just as Edo Castle had long feared. See Chapter 18.

45. See pp. 96, 102, 115, 149.

46. Sofue Ichiro, *Abe Masahiro*, p. 283. Nariaki also considered Shogun Tokugawa Ieyoshi, the father of dimwitted Iesada, "an idiot." Mitani Hiroshi, *Escape from Impasse*, p. 144.

47. Cited in Peter B. Wiley, *Yankees in the Land of the Gods*, p. 326.

CHAPTER 10

1. *Journal*, p. 103.

2. *Narrative*, p. 263.

3. *Journal*, p. 96.

4. Ibid., p. 103.

5. In international parlance, "Loo-choo" would change to "Ryukyu" in 1875, four years before Japan formally annexed the islands.

6. Most Okinawans were darker and shorter than most Japanese, and their mixed ancestry also showed in their rounder faces. The earliest Ryukyuans probably crossed a prehistoric land bridge from the Asian mainland, and were joined by Malayans and Micronesians carried north by the Black Current, as well as by some Japanese who ventured down from *their* far larger islands to the north.

7. See pp. 18, 19, 51, and 61.

8. See pp. 19–21, 59.

9. Apart from those towns, almost all the population lived in scattered villages and hamlets, and worked as farmers.

10. See p. 308.

11. Ivan Goncharov, *The Frigate Pallada*, p. 433. One of Perry's translators, a Chinese, believed Okinawan manners resembled "those of the golden age of high antiquity" (cited in Peter B. Wiley, *Yankees in the Land of the Gods*, p. 379).

12. Samuel Wells Williams, *A Journal of the Perry Expedition to Japan (1853–1854)*, p. 98. "Few prospects could delight the eye more, but how great an increase of interest would be given . . . if one could feel that these villages and towns were the abode of a Christian people!" A visit to a Buddhist temple prompted Williams to hope: "May God in his mercy soon change the sullen superstition of the inmates to a joyful faith in His son." p. 39.

13. Taylor rhapsodized about "green and beautiful" shores whose "groves and fields of the freshest verdure" reminded him of "the richest English scenery"—and in other districts, of Sicily. Swelling hills "rose immediately from the water's edge . . . picturesquely broken by abrupt rocks and crags." Their slopes were covered with gardens and fields of grain, their crests by woods of cedar or pine. Perry added that the composite's "very inviting" first appearance "looked, if possible, more brilliantly green and beautiful" the following day. The interior, when he visited it, appeared "exceedingly beautiful . . . in no part of the world have I seen a greater richness or variety" of vegetation.

14. *Journal*, p. 62.

15. The news would be rushed from there to Edo. See pp. 43, 102.

16. *Journal*, p. 115. Perry's determination to demand respect for his adolescent country wasn't unique. Perhaps he knew about George Washington's abiding aim to do the same among older nations, which caused the first President to maintain a calculated stiffness in the presence of foreign representatives, although Washington was never a bully.

17. *Journal*, p. 61.

18. *Narrative*, p. 280.

19. Ibid., p. 279.

20. November 2, 2003, interview with Dr. Kurayoshi Takara, professor of history, University of the Ryukyus, and editor of *Perry to Dai Ryyukyu Perry and Great Okinawa* (Naha: The Ryukyu Broadcasting Company, 1997).

21. In a letter to Perry, Shuri elaborated, in typically self-deprecating language, that it sent "whatever we could prepare for tribute" to China in return for such favors as investiture of the Okinawan kings (*Narrative*, p. 222).

22. Six or seven years before Perry arrived, several Protestant and Catholic missionaries whose activities Shuri had hampered departed without having obtained a single conversion.

23. George Kerr, *Okinawa: The History of an Island People*, p. 285. This is the best English-language history of the island.

24. Ibid., p. 287.

25. "Commodore Perry at Okinawa: From the Unpublished Diary of a British Missionary" in *The American Historical Review* 51, no. 2 (January 1946), pp. 264–65. The quote is from Bettelheim's diary, partially reproduced by William Leonard Schwartz, a British missionary who served on Okinawa after World War II.

26. *Journal*, p. 134.

27. *Narrative*, p. 225.

28. "The man does not seem to know his own mind for a day." Samuel Wells Williams, *A Journal of the Perry Expedition to Japan (1853–1854)*, p. 11.

29. *Narrative*, p. 153.

CHAPTER 11

1. Basil Hall Chamberlain, "The Luchu Islands and Their Inhabitants," in *The Geographical Journal*, April 1895, p. 319.

2. "Not to have written a book about Japan is fast becoming a title to distinction," Chamberlain spoofed in 1890.

3. *Narrative*, p. 187.

4. William Leonard Schwartz, "Commodore Perry at Okinawa," p. 268.

5. *Narrative*, p. 188.

6. Samuel Wells Williams, *A Journal of the Perry Expedition to Japan*, p. 92.

7. *Journal*, p. 65.

8. *Narrative*, p. 190.

9. Ibid., p. 190.

10. Ibid., p. 192.

11. Exertion of "all possible patience," he'd explain, could not enable him to "hold out to the end of the feast" (*Journal*, p. 109).

12. *Journal*, p. 86.

13. To Okinawan objections to that new abuse, as they saw it, of the temple property, Bettelheim reported Perry as saying they had "gods enough to worship in other places." Cited in George Kerr, *Okinawa*, p. 320.

14. Ibid., p. 314.

15. *Narrative*, p. 229.

16. Marie Hansen-Taylor and Horace Scudder, *Life and Letters of Bayard Taylor*, p. 256.

17. *Narrative*, p. 277.

18. Ibid., p. 278.

19. Ibid., p. 279.

20. Ibid., p. 282.

21. Samuel Wells Williams, *A Journal of the Perry Expedition to Japan*, p. 71.

22. *Narrative*, p. 282.

23. Tragedy would strike the *Plymouth* in the Bonins. A typhoon killed thirteen men when it sank a boat that had been dispatched to fish and hunt.

24. Leonard Gordon, "Early American Relations with Formosa 1849–1870," p. 270.

25. *Narrative*, vol. 2, pp. 173, 179.

26. A biographer of Commodore James Biddle would call Perry "an anomaly" in that respect (David Long, book review of Peter B. Wiley's *Yankees in the Land of the Gods* in *Journal of American History*, December 1991, p. 1084).

27. "When we look at the possessions in the east of our great maritime rival, England, and of the constant and rapid increase of their fortified ports, we should be admonished of the necessity of prompt measures on our part." Happily, that "unconscionable" country hadn't yet moved in on Japan; which lay on "a route of commerce which is destined to become of great importance to the United States"; therefore no time should be lost securing "a sufficient number of ports of refuge there and in other Pacific islands."

28. *Narrative*, p. 496.

CHAPTER 12

1. *Facing West*, p. 8.

2. Cited in Ibid., p. 80.

3. *Yankees in the Land of the Gods*, p. 456.

4. "To the Americans, raised on the myth of their own fight for freedom from British oppression, formal rule over subject peoples was unpalatable" (Niall Ferguson, *Colossus: The Price of American Empire*, p. 343).

5. Cited in Ronald Spector, "The American Image of Southeast Asia," p. 303.

6. Henry Franklin Graff, *Bluejackets with Perry in Japan*, p. 54.

7. Cited in Peter Duus, *The Japanese Discovery of America*, p. 70.

8. Allan Cole, *The Dynamics of American Expansion Toward Japan, 1791–1860*, p. 2.

9. Until the inauguration of the Pony Express in 1860 and of transcontinental telegraph service a year later, it still took weeks for a message sent from the West Coast to reach the East.

10. See p. 74.

11. *Narrative*, p. 60. See p. 60 of this book.

12. Walter LaFeber, *The Clash*, p. 12. A century later, prominent right-wing Americans would use the same reasoning to stake American claims to Middle Eastern oil.

13. Edward Barrows, *The Great Commodore*, p. 84.

14. Refreshing himself in the company of magnates who were making wads of money in

China, he'd also make a little for himself on the high prices fetched by Mexican silver dollars.

15.   John H. Schroeder, *Matthew Calbraith Perry*, p. 250. Angered by a temporary failure to acknowledge his help to New York and Boston merchants, he'd propose publishing letters that would "bear witness to the services of a naval man." Peter B. Wiley, *Yankees in the Land of the Gods*, pp. 457, 460.

CHAPTER 13

1.   Some of his goldfish, for which his childhood affection remained strong, died at roughly the same time as the third child. That was after their transfer to a new pond in Edo Castle's compound, to which the family moved when he was appointed to the *roju* in 1843.

2.   Interview of Masamichi Abe (great-grandson of Masahiro Abe), November 9, 2003.

3.   Marius B. Jansen, *The Making of Modern Japan*, p. 271. All educated Japanese could read Chinese.

4.   www.wsu.edu/~dee/CHING/CHING.HTM.

5.   *Narrative*, vol. 2, p. 176.

6.   Some historians believe Japan's inferiority complex vis-à-vis the China from which it had borrowed so much of its culture began losing its grip when China's military forces fared so poorly against the British.

7.   Francis Hall, *Japan Through American Eyes*, p. 393. To those who heard it, the warning sounded all the clearer because Japan was so near to China and Britain was believed to be constantly seeking new conquests.

8.   Quoted in Marius B. Jansen, *The Making of Modern Japan*, p. 270. Exiled, practically speaking, to Turkestan, the incorruptible former Canton commissioner valiantly tried to persuade the imperial government to adopt Western technology, especially for military arms and methods. But while he was virtually ignored, Japan would heed that lesson and spend much of the following century preparing for war.

9.   Cited in ibid., p. 272.

10.   Marius B. Jansen et al., *The Cambridge History of Japan*, pp. 263–64.

11.   Malcolm D. Kennedy, *A History of Japan*, p. 111.

12.   Francis Hall, the astute American journalist who would long reside in Japan shortly after its opening, found samurai "the idlest, most worthless man Nippon produces, but he has the privilege of caste, and uses it to make all sorts of exactions upon those more humble than himself." Fred G. Notehelfer (ed.), *Japan Through American Eyes*, p. 40. Some critics during the late Tokugawa period itself—themselves samurai, as was true of virtually everyone with a public voice—suggested the source of the problem lay in the considerable migration to the cities. Samurai virtues would be restored if the men returned to their villages.

13.   David J. Lu, *Japan: A Documentary History*, p. 275.

14.   Cited in Peter B. Wiley, *Yankees in the Land of the Gods*, p. 269.

15.   Shozan's study of Dutch books had convinced him that the science that underlay Western military technology was the only valid science; the theories based on Confucianism and Buddhism were invalid. See p. 87. A political opponent would assassinate him in 1864, during the country's post-Perry turmoil.

16.   Jacqueline Houtved in www.columbia.edu/~wtd1/w4030/syllabus.html

17.   Shiba Ryotaro, *The Last Shogun*, p. 4. That was especially wise in light of Nariaki's reputation as a huge womanizer.

18. For target practice, Nariaki ordered his samurai to fire at whales. For gunpowder, he tried to produce artificial nitrates. Of the 291 (old-fashioned) guns he cast from 1830 to 1853, he donated 74 to the *bakufu*. Among other efforts to manufacture modern weapons, he secretly experimented with a torpedo in 1837, some seventeen years before it was first perfected, in France. Richard T. Chang, *From Prejudice to Tolerance*, pp. 74–75.

19. Shiba Ryotaro, *Drunk as a Lord*, p. 108.

20. George B. Sansom, *The Western World and Japan*, p. 287. Many coastal defense officers, most of whom were appointed by the Bureau of Finance, wanted to avoid conflict with the West more than they wanted to build defenses.

21. "By one of those strange contradictions in which Japanese dynastic history is so rich, the Mito branch of the Tokugawa had from the seventeenth century developed an attitude of independence, if not hostility, towards the ruling Tokugawa house." George Sansom, Ibid., p. 284.

22. See p. 41.

23. Conrad Totman, "Political Reconciliation in the Tokugawa Bakufu: Abe Masahiro and Tokugawa Nariaki, 1844–1852," p. 186.

"After Abe freed Nariaki from house arrest, the relationship began to improve. Thereafter Abe became kinder and kinder—allowing Nariaki to be consulted on the conduct of Mito affairs in 1848, giving him control of Mito government the following year," and making him a government consultant now, in 1853 (Harold Bolitho, "Abe Masahiro and the New Japan," p. 178). Nariaki's full rehabilitation—presided over by Abe, with some steps back mixed with the forward ones—was marked by his invitation to visit the Shogun in Edo Castle in 1852.

24. George Sansom, *The Western World and Japan*, p. 278.

25. Conrad Totman, "Political Reconciliation," p. 183. Totman elsewhere calls Abe's approach to politics "superlatively cautious."

26. Jerrold Packard, *Sons of Heaven*, p. 192.

27. The Emperor also ordered the major Shinto shrines and Buddhist temples to offer prayers for the parrying of the Westerners.

28. Richard von Doenhoff, "Biddle, Perry and Japan," pp. 85–86.

29. Cited in Marius B. Jansen, *The Making of Modern Japan*, pp. 281–82.

30. Ibid, p. 282. Other leaders shared Ii's confidence that Japan could quickly master Western military technology.

31. Peter Duus, *The Japanese Discovery of America*, pp. 101, 118–119.

32. Cited in William Beasley (ed. and trans.) *Select Documents on Japanese Foreign Policy*, p. 114.

33. Ibid., p. 116.

34. David J. Lu, *Japan: A Documentary History*, pp. 281–86.

35. Ibid., p. 283.

36. Donald Keene, *Emperor of Japan: Meiji and His World*, p. 24.

37. Jacqueline Houtved in www.hum.au.dk/cek/kontur/docs/kontur_02/pdf_filer/jh_japanese.pdf.

38. Cited in Foster Rhea Dulles, *Yankees and Samurai*, p. 59.

CHAPTER 14

1. *Narrative*, vol. 2, p. 175.

2. Tyler Dennett, cited in Foster Rhea Dulles, *America in the Pacific*, p. 66.

3. Cited in Peter B. Wiley, *Yankees in the Land of the Gods*, p. 364.

4. *Narrative*, p. 289.

5. *Journal*, p. 59.

6. *Narrative*, p. 79.

7. www.clements.umich.edu/Webguides/D/Dudley.html.

8. Taylor would later turn over his journal to the commanding officer, who would use it when composing his own narrative and apparently never return it.

9. Marie Hansen-Taylor and Horace Scudder, *Life and Letters of Bayard Taylor*, p. 251.

10. *Narrative*, p. 75.

11. See p. 92.

12. A navy report of the time worried that Russia might become "the controlling maritime power of the world," without specifying how it would overtake Britain. As for Russia taking possession of Japan, "there is no evidence" that it then considered it. George Alexander Lensen, *Russia's Japan Expedition of 1852 to 1855*, p. 128.

13. Nations' history and fate "are doubtless directed by an overruling Providence, and probably we could not, if we would, change their course, or avert our ultimate destiny" *Narrative*, vol. 2, p. 178.

14. *Narrative*, p. 62.

15. Cited in Lensen, *Russia's Japan Expedition*, p. 128.

16. Admiral Putiatin was to have led a mission ten years earlier, prompted by Britain's great gains in the 1842 Opium War, but it was abandoned on the grounds that Russia's commercial interests in the Far East didn't justify its cost.

17. William L. Neumann, *America Encounters Japan*, p. 42.

18. Ivan Goncharov, *The Frigate Pallada*, p. 270. Despite its vivid detail, Goncharov's account may be less than fully accurate. He may have concealed unhappiness and even possible attempts at mutiny among the crew, which was kept uninformed of the mission's purpose. And he portrayed Japanese men as "ludicrous and effeminate."

19. Cited in Lensen, *Russia's Japan Expedition*, p. xxiii.

20. Harold Bolitho, "Abe Masahiro and the New Japan," p. 184.

21. The Japanese prohibition of building oceangoing ships had been lifted by that time. While helping, local carpenters watched the construction intently, and built an exact copy soon afterward—a mere fifty years before the Japanese fleet would stun the world by demolishing the Russian one at the Straits of Tsushima. Now, in 1854, Tokugawa Nariaki suggested executing the entire crew of Putiatin's flagship.

22. *Journal*, pp. 136–38.

23. *Narrative*, p. 323.

24. Richard Chang, *From Prejudice to Tolerance*, pp. 81–82.

25. *Narrative*, p. 322.

CHAPTER 15

1.   Malcolm D. Kennedy, *A History of Japan*, p. 100.

2.   The lack of a navy had hit hard from the first. The Edo physician who recorded the city's panic in July noted that many people considered "real defense" "unthinkable" without one. "Whether they be daimyo or government [*bakufu*] officials, I heard them complain that we were powerless because of the absence of warships. They appear to have for the first time opened their eyes to reality and are all in great surprise and consternation." "A Doctor's Memorandum," p. 9.

3.   Soon convinced so important a matter shouldn't be left to foreigners, Abe decided Japanese officials should be sent to Holland to supervise the construction. His *bakufu* subordinates wanted them to observe other countries as well, and Nariaki advised starting with America and Russia. Although nothing would come of those proposals, they revealed a new willingness, even desire, to amend the seclusion. Richard Chang, *From Prejudice to Tolerance*, p. 74.

4.   George Sansom, *The Western World and Japan*, p. 284.

5.   Harold Bolitho, "Abe Masahiro and the New Japan," p. 181.

6.   See p. 59.

7.   Cited in William Beasley (ed. and trans.), *Select Documents on Japanese Foreign Policy*, pp. 112–13.

8.   Toson Shimazaki, *Before the Dawn*, p. 110.

9.   Peter Duus, *The Japanese Discovery of America*, p. 105.

10.   Richard Chang, *From Prejudice to Tolerance*, p. 82. Because Nariaki and his scholars "considered war as a means of awakening the Japanese from their two-century-long lethargy, they welcomed the risk of war. But they did *not* court it; they acted on the belief that an unwanted war was being thrust upon Japan by the West in general, and in 1853 by Perry in particular" (p. 89).

11.   Ibid., pp. 85–86.

CHAPTER 16

1.   *Journal*, p. 159.

2.   William Harlan Hale, "When Perry Unlocked the Gate of the Sun," p. 100. The *Southampton*, which had arrived earlier, was waiting in a predesignated anchorage.

3.   *Narrative*, p. 327.

4.   But Mount Fuji remained visible, providing "one of the most glorious scenes ever beheld," in the estimation of the Reverend Samuel Wells Williams.

5.   Peter Duus, *The Japanese Discovery of America*, p. 108.

6.   *Narrative*, p. 328. Perry's spelling was the then customary "Yedo."

7.   Ibid., p. 329.

8.   *Journal*, p. 160.

9.   A Japanese account makes no mention of a joke. One of the commissioners "folded his fan with a sharp report. The foreigners were much alarmed, and their expressions changed; they placed their hands on the pistols which they wore at their waist and assumed a resolute attitude; but when [the commissioner] leisurely drew out his spectacles and began slowly to examine the [Americans' calling] cards one by one, they noticed his lack of concern and appeared to be relieved of their anxiety." *Diary of an Official of the Bakufu*, p. 99.

10. Ferdinand Kuhn, *Commodore Perry and the Opening of Japan*, pp. 79–80.

11. See pp. 87 and 198. Although still upset by the grave problems foreigners posed to Japan, Shozan knew rash action by angry soldiers wouldn't solve them, and wanted to prevent it from undoing the arrangements the *bakufu* was in the process of making with Perry. Donald Keene, *Travelers of a Hundred Ages*, p. 385.

12. *Narrative*, p. 360. An historian would comment that the Japanese, by protesting but mildly because they supposed no harm was intended with the sword, which the chaplain had drawn "for his own amusement," showed far more Christian charity than the chaplain's conduct. Arthur Walworth, *Black Ships Off Japan*, p. 182.

13. *Diary of an Official of the Bakufu*, pp. 110–11.

14. *Journal*, p. 163.

15. Ibid., p. 161.

16. *Narrative*, p. 339.

17. William Neumann, *America Encounters Japan*, p. 43.

18. See p. 106.

19. However, more jealousy would descend on Kayama, and he'd be relieved from his duties a second time, on the grounds, among others, that he leaked national security information to the Americans. www.japan-society.org/commodoreperrry_p3.html.

20. *Narrative*, p. 337.

21. Richard Chang, *From Prejudice to Tolerance*, p. 87.

22. Ibid., p. 88.

23. Peter B. Wiley, *Yankees in the Land of the Gods*, p. 394.

24. See p. 207.

25. *Narrative*, p. 338.

26. Ibid., p. 338.

27. William Beasley, *Select Documents on Japanese Foreign Policy*, p. 123.

28. *Narrative*, p. 342.

29. *Narrative*, p. 344.

30. *Journal*, p. 159. It's unclear whether Perry knew that in addition to loving ostentation, King Herod the Great, of the pro-Roman dynasty that ruled Palestine during the birth of Christianity, resorted to wholesale executions, including the killing of his own sons and the ordering of the massacre of the Innocents.

31. *Narrative*, p. 345. Anticipating a good meal during that landing, Perry's officers brought along their knives and forks to enable them to attack it better than with chopsticks; but the meal much disappointed them.

32. www.navyandmarine.org/ondeck/1800perryjapan.htm. Perry also misinformed the commissioners that the Americans had "many thousands" of steamships. *Narrative*, p. 352.

33. *Narrative*, p. 345.

34. Ferdinand Kuhn, *Commodore Perry and the Opening of Japan*, p. 82. The *bakufu* had rejected a plan by Sakuma Shozan—see pp. 87, 198, and 234—then Commissioner of War, to surround the site with enough troops to defeat the Americans if they resorted to showing force during the talks, as many suspected they would. Richard T. Chang, *From Prejudice to Tolerance*, p. 112.

35. George H. Preble, *The Opening of Japan*, p. 145.

36. *Narrative*, p. 344.

37. *Narrative*, p. 350.

38. In a letter to the commissioners, Perry described it as "identical . . . in all its essential features . . . with that at present subsisting between the United States and China." *Narrative*, p. 351.

39. *Narrative*, p. 352.

40. Ibid., p. 364.

41. *Journal*, p. 180.

42. Permission to buy a burial plot for a marine who'd died and others who might also perish during the squadron's stay was less readily granted, but when it was—and the commissioners agreed to the grounds of a Yokohama temple rather than those of a Uraga lighthouse—Perry was very grateful.

43. *Narrative*, p. 358.

44. *Journal*, p. 180.

45. Samuel Wells Williams, *A Journal of the Perry Expedition to Japan*, p. 206.

46. See p. 136.

47. Years after the treaty's signing, Nakahama Manjiro himself solved the mystery for the Americans. Now a Japanese naval officer, he told the story to a former sailor on one of Perry's ships. John Sewall, *The Logbook of the Captain's Clerk*, p. 214.

48. Samuel Wells Williams, *A Journal of the Perry Expedition to Japan*, p. 129. Perry's milder dissembling to the commissioners included that "he had been sent . . . by his government to make a treaty, and if he did not succeed"—he sometimes said "succeed *now*"—the United States would probably send more ships to make one." *Narrative*, pp. 350, 356, 383.

49. See p. 73.

50. *Narrative*, pp. 362–63.

51. Ibid., p. 385.

52. Ibid., p. 361.

53. Ibid., p. 362. A Japanese account confirms that Perry's interest was in facilitating the passage of American vessels to Canton, for which ports in southeastern Japan were wanted. "I therefore reject Nagasaki." *Diary of an Official of the Bakufu*, p. 108.

54. John Sewall, "With Perry in Japan: Personal Recollections of the Expedition of 1853–54," p. 358.

55. Toson Shimazaki, *Before the Dawn*, p. 92.

56. Peter Duus, *The Japanese Discovery of America*, p. 106.

57. Peter B. Wiley, *Yankees in the Land of the Gods*, p. 403.

58. *Narrative*, p. 335.

59. Conrad Totman, "Political Reconciliation in the Tokugawa Bakufu: Abe Masahiro and Tokugawa Nariaki, 1844–1852," p. 190.

60. Cited in Peter B. Wiley, *Yankees in the Land of the Gods*, p. 404. The commissioners would report to Edo Castle that they pointed out to Perry, or dissembled, that the Japanese "had little experience in trade and could not lightly permit it." Besides, "the main theme of his present request was kind treatment for the citizens of his country and we had, after full consideration, given an undertaking to provide wood, water, and so on; that trade was conducted entirely with a view to profit on both sides, having no relevance to considerations of humanity, and that we were therefore unable to discuss this question at the present time." William Beasley, *Select Documents on Japanese Foreign Policy*, p. 126.

61. See p. 179.

62. *Journal*, p. 171.

63. William Beasley, *Select Documents on Japanese Foreign Policy*, p. 127. The commissioners emphasized their first priority was avoiding war and their second was holding concessions to a minimum.

64. Arthur Walworth, *Black Ships Off Japan*, p. 191. That clearly made it much more than "a mere shipwreck convention," as Richard van Alstyne, an historian of American expansionism, called it.

65. *Journal*, p. 201.

66. William Beasley, *Select Documents on Japanese Foreign Policy*, p. 127. On top of the commissioners' reluctance to reveal their concessions about consulates, translation difficulties would cause two differing versions of the treaty to be written.

67. *Narrative*, p. 379.

68. Arthur Walworth, *Black Ships Off Japan*, p. 192.

69. Peter B. Wiley, *Yankees in the Land of the Gods*, p. 416.

70. *Journal*, p. 198.

71. John Sproston, *A Private Journal of John Glendy Sproston*, p. 18.

72. *Diary of an Official of the Bakufu*, p. 119.

73. *Journal*, p. 200.

74. Samuel Wells Williams, *A Journal of the Perry Expedition to Japan*, p. 162.

75. *Journal*, p. 188. The exchange of last banquets at Yokohama gave Perry another opportunity to scorn Japanese food in comparison with American. "While full of hospitality, [the Japanese] left but an unfavorable impression of their skill in cookery," especially since "appetites [were] but scantily gratified by the unusual fare. . . . The dinner given to the commissioners on board the *Powhatan* would have made, in quantity, at least a score of such as that offered by the Japanese on this occasion." *Narrative*, p. 380.

John R. C. Lewis, a 20-year-old grandnephew of George Washington, found many dishes at a native banquet "indescribable and partaken of only as a matter of etiquettrey, deriving their charm probably from the dishes which were of the most magnificent description and pattern." But Lewis saw the Japanese themselves as quiet and inoffensive, noting that children happily greeted members of the crew.

76. *Narrative*, p. 375.

77. "There stood the locomotive and car, exquisite specimens of American workmanship, the engine already hissing and fuming, impatient to show itself off, the car as sumptuous as the richest woods and finest art could make it. . . . The telegraph seemed to be more of a puzzle to [the Japanese] than the steam-engine. . . . They would go to one end, deliver a message, and then trot mystified to the other end, only to find their message safely arrived." John Sewall, *The Logbook of the Captain's Clerk*, pp. 359–60.

78. Cited in Richard A. von Doenhoff, "Biddle, Perry and Japan," p. 87.

79. George Sansom, *The Western World and Japan*, p. 281.

80. William Steele, *Alternative Narratives in Modern Japanese History*, pp. 14–15.

81. "It would be a foul reproach to Christendom now to force Japan to relapse into her cheerless and unprogressive state of unnatural isolation. . . . Cautious and kindly treatment now will soon lead to commercial treaties as liberal as can be desired." *Narrative*, pp. 388–90.

82. John Sewall, "With Perry in Japan," p. 360. Another officer mused that he'd be willing to break an arm if that would "ensure a speedy return home." In fact, the *Sarato-*

ga's return voyage of some eleven weeks would be the fastest to date between Japan and America.

83.　*Narrative*, p. 426.

84.　Kojima Matajiro, *Commodore Perry's Expedition to Hakodate*, p. 17. An official who informed the Hakodate daimyo that the Americans were coming reported inaccurately that they'd been forbidden to land at Shimoda but did so anyway. "They did no violence but went to farm houses asking for food and other things, for which they are asserted to have expressed thanks." The official recommended that all wine be concealed so the Americans—who are "short-tempered" and even grow angry quickly when opposed—could not see it. "Therefore anything they ask for must be given and things of value better be hidden." "They are said to like children and to give them candy," he continued, "but if they should kidnap them, it would be terrible." And: "they notice women especially, so do not let them be seen while the ships are in port." Ibid., p. 2.

85.　See pp. 2–3.

86.　*Journal*, pp. 182–83.

87.　*Narrative*, p. 388.

88.　Samuel Wells Williams, *A Journal of the Perry Expedition to Japan*, p. 224.

89.　Ibid., pp. 224, 222.

90.　Ibid., p. v.

91.　Frederick Wells Williams, *The Life and Letters of Samuel Wells Williams*, p. 223.

92.　Ferdinand Kuhn, *Commodore Perry and the Opening of Japan*, p. 156.

CHAPTER 17

1.　William Harlan Hale, "When Perry Unlocked the 'Gate of the Sun'." In *American Heritage*, April 1958.

2.　See p. 179.

3.　John H. Schroeder, *Matthew Calbraith Perry*, p. 250.

4.　William L. Neumann, *America Encounters Japan*, p. 46.

5.　Arthur Walworth, *Black Ships Off Japan*, p. 231.

6.　*Journal*, p. 60.

7.　See Chapter 12.

8.　"The government of the United States," Perry had complained, "is the only one in the world" that instructs its naval officers to reciprocate "the civilities of foreign officers without making the slightest provision" for the necessary expense. *Journal*, p. 196. Perry would also be given a thousand copies of the *Narrative*. Two thousand would go to the Navy Department, and almost that number to Congressmen and high Washington officials.

9.　Ian Buruma, *Inventing Japan*, p. 14

10.　Arthur Walworth, *Black Ships Off Japan*, p. 232. The Reverend Williams was back in China. Endorsed by Perry, he'd soon be appointed Secretary to the United States Legation there, and remain twenty-two years in that post.

11.　Hawthorne, who'd written a campaign biography of Pierce, could have been an ambassador but his present position paid him much more for less work: in addition to his salary, he got a substantial fee for every ship that left Liverpool, Britain's chief port to America, for the U.S. After Perry's visit, on Christmas Day 1854, Hawthorne described the

Commodore as "a brisk, gentlemanly, offhand, but not rough, unaffected and sensible man, looking not so elderly as he ought, on account of a very well made wig."

12. Ferdinand Kuhn, *Commodore Perry and the Opening of Japan*, p. 166.

13. Agriculturalist James Morrow refused to have his drawings included, including of plants unknown in America, on the grounds that he'd been sent to Japan by the Secretary of State, not Perry; Dr. Morrow was probably the single expedition member whose inclusion wasn't personally approved by the Commodore. A fire destroyed most of Eliphalet Brown's two hundred-odd daguerreotypes while they were awaiting transfer to lithographic plates; the five that survived included one of Sam Patch. See p. 237. Outraged reaction to a Wilhelm Heine drawing in the very first small edition, of naked Japanese bathers of both sexes, caused its removal from later editions, including the very large one for, essentially, government distribution.

14. Peter B. Wiley, *Yankees in the Land of the Gods*, p. 465.

15. Ibid., p. 398.

16. The Commodore would be buried in his hometown of Newport, Rhode Island, which would later honor him with a statue and a monument. Paintings of the Black Ships—some by an anonymous Japanese artist whose works were collected in what would be called the Black Ships Scroll, a source of insight and amusement about the 1853 visit—are displayed in Newport's Naval War College Museum. In 1953, the U.S. Post Office issued a five-cent stamp to mark the hundredth anniversary of the 1853 visit.

17. Fred Notehelfer, "What If Perry Had Not Come to Japan?" Paper delivered at the University of Maryland, March 9, 2004, p.12. SEE http://www.inform.umd.edu/umcp_Today/Important_Notices/FYI/archive/2004.03.09.html

18. Toson Shimazaki, *Before the Dawn*, p. x.

19. "Not only could certain of the Japanese locate Washington and New York, but they also knew the whereabouts of a few prairie and Rocky Mountain towns." Edward Yorke McCauley (Allan B. Cole, ed.), *With Perry in Japan*, p. 27.

20. John Sewall, *The Logbook of the Captain's Clerk*, p. 353.

21. George Sansom, *A History of Japan*, p. 230. Von Siebold introduced Western medicine to Japan. Virtually every Western visitor to newly opened Japan would say that eagerness to learn matched the uncommonly high literacy rate.

22. Marius B. Jansen, *The Making of Modern Japan*, p. 92.

23. Conrad Totman, *Early Modern Japan*, p. 473.

24. See p. 85.

25. Francis Hall, *Japan Through American Eyes*, p. 400.

26. Fred Notehelfer, "What If Perry Had Not Come to Japan?" p. 3.

27. Noel Perrin, *Giving Up the Gun*, p. 86.

28. Professor Fred Notehelfer, director of UCLA's Center for Japanese Studies, provided information and insight for this interpretation in a note to the author on February 23, 2004.

29. See Dr. Fred Notehelfer's introduction to Francis Hall, *Japan Through American Eyes*, p. 22.

30. Irokawa Daikichi, *The Culture of the Meiji Period*, p. 47.

31. Marius B. Jansen, *The Making of Modern Japan*, p. 94.

32. Irokawa Daikichi, *The Culture of the Meiji Period*, p. 6.

33. *Narrative*, p. 220.

34. *Narrative* vol. 2, p. 175

35. Kishida Shyu, *A Place for Apology*, p. 5.

36. George B. Sansom, *The Western World and Japan*, p. 281.

37. Ian Buruma, *Inventing Japan*, p. 26.

38. *Japan: An Interpretation*, p. 407.

39. Donald Keene, *Anthology of Japanese Literature*, p. 439.

40. Abe Masamichi, letter to the author, January 22, 2006. After almost all of the eleven died very young, Abe adopted the son of his elder brother.

41. Harold Bolitho, "Abe Masahiro and the New Japan," p. 173.

42. Ibid., p. 185

43. Ibid., p. 184.

44. Interview of Abe Masamichi, November 15, 2003.

45. Oliver Statler, *Shimoda Story*, p. 428.

46. Harold Bolitho, "Abe Masahiro and the New Japan," p. 174.

47. Tokutomi Iichiro in *Kinsei Nihon Kokumin Shi—Peri raiko oyobi sono toji* ("Modern Japanese History—Perry's Arrival and the Times"), pp. 138, 218, 230–258.

CHAPTER 18

1. Oliver Statler, *Shimoda Story*, p. 33. When Perry stopped in England on his return in 1854, the *Times* commented that Englishmen had had greater privileges in sixteenth-century Japan than the treaty won for the Americans. Arthur Walworth, *Black Ships Off Japan*, p. 230.

2. Quoted in William L. Neumann, *America Encounters Japan*, p. 46.

3. Keishi Ohara (comp. ed.), *Japanese Trade and Industry in the Meiji-Taisho Era*, p. 7. One of the frustrated early American traders "put the Japanese against the world" in diplomacy. John Curtis Perry, *Facing West*, p. 87. By the turn of the century, however, American trade with Japan would surpass its trade with China.

4. Donald Keene, *Anthology of Japanese Literature*, p. 439.

5. Morison's Introduction to Perry's *Journal*, p. xix.

6. Francis Hall, *Japan Through American Eyes*, p. 544. Japanese hope nourished by their translation of what they called the "Perry Treaty" that consulates could be rejected if one side opposed, increased their antipathy to Harris.

7. Herbert H. Gowen, *Five Foreigners in Japan*, p. 231.

8. Arthur Walworth, *Black Ships Off Japan*, p.233.

9. Walter LaFeber, *The Clash*, p. 25.

10. George B. Sansom, *The Western World and Japan*, p. 289.

11. Marius B. Jansen, *The Making of Modern Japan*, p. 283.

12. Cited in William L. Neumann, *America Encounters Japan*, p. 53.

13. Walter LaFeber, *The Clash*, p.19. In the end, Harris would come to appreciate many qualities of the Japanese, whom he'd pronounce a "*clean* people. Everyone bathes every day." But like most Americans who would soon follow him to the country, he was shocked by what seemed to him terrible indecency. All ages and both sexes of the poor used the same bathroom "in a state of perfect nudity. I cannot account for so indelicate a proceeding on the part of a people so generally correct." P. 21.

14. George B. Sansom, *The Western World and Japan*, p. 286.

15. "Well I remember," a Japanese baron who had served Harris as an office boy would recite some seventy years later, "The old man with ruddy face,/Stroking his white beard/ Who argued vehemently,/Such was his sincerity." Herbert H. Gowen, *Five Foreigners in Japan*, p. 227.

16. American confusion about how Japan was ruled hadn't ended. Harris presented the Shogun with a letter that was addressed to "His Majesty the Emperor of Japan."

17. http://web.jjay.cuny.edu/~jobrien/reference/ob76.html

18. Marius B. Jansen, *The Western World and Japan*, p. 298.

19. Jerrold Packard, *Sons of Heaven*, pp. 104–5.

20. Walter LaFeber, *The Clash*, p. 21.

21. Ibid., p. 475.

22. Sugimoto Etsu Inagaki, *A Daughter of the Samurai*, p. 313.

23. Ibid, p. 62.

24. Ibid. pp. 312–13. Some wondered whether America was a land "where only tradesmen live." pp. 62–63.

25. That episode became material for historical dramas still staged in the twenty-first century.

26. Shonan, who would become a key figure in Japan's modernization, sent two nephews to be educated in America: the first Japanese to study at the U.S. Naval Academy. Shonan listed America's major policies as stopping wars "in accordance with divine intentions," "broaden[ing] enlightened government" by learning from all countries, and working "with complete devotion" for the people's welfare by entrusting power to the wisest instead of to the president's son. "All methods of administrative laws and practices and all men who are known as good and wise throughout the world are put into [America's] service and a very beneficial administration—one not completely in the interest of the rulers—is developed." Peter Duus, *The Japanese Discovery of America*, p. 139.

27. Cited in William Neumann, *America Encounters Japan*, p. 66.

28. Peter Duus, *The Japanese Discovery of America*, p. 146.

29. Marius B. Jansen, *The Western World and Japan*, p. 318.

30. Peter Duus, *The Japanese Discovery of America*, p. 25.

31. Marius B. Jansen, *The Western World and Japan*, p. 318. But they also developed a distaste for Americans' inexplicable lack of manners. "With regard to decorum," one observed, "there was hardly any observance. A sailor might remove his cap, but did not bow to his captain . . . there is really no distinction between the captain and his first mate. The high and low alike work closely together. . . . As to the captain, he is not arrogant, and treats his men like his colleagues. They are personally close to each other. In an emergency, they do their best to help one another, and if there is a moment of sorrow, it is shared by everyone with tears." David J. Lu, *Japan: A Documentary History*, p. 294.

32. "As for scientific inventions and industrial machinery," the Dutch studies scholar would write, "there was no great novelty in them for me. It was rather in matters of life and social custom and ways of thinking that I found myself at a loss in America." Cited in Peter Duus, *The Japanese Discovery of America*, pp. 149–50.

33. Fukuzawa, Yukichi, *The Autobiography of Yukichi Fukuzawa*, p. 130. Actually, the attack on Ii was reported in the American press, so the samurai might have been told about it by one of the mission's coordinators.

34. William L. Neumann, *America Encounters Japan*, p. 54.

35. Walter LaFeber, *The Clash*, p. 26.

36. George Sansom, *The Western World and Japan*, p. 281.

37. Walter LaFeber, *The Clash*, p. 25.

38. Francis Hall, *Japan Through American Eyes*, p. 585.

39. Cited in Arthur Walworth, *Black Ships Off Japan*, p. 236.

40. Malcolm D. Kennedy, *A History of Japan*, p. 142.

41. Ibid.

42. Cited in Walter LaFeber, *The Clash*, p. 27.

43. Shortly after the arrival in Yokohama of British and French forces, *ronin* killed two British officers who were visiting a thirteenth-century bronze figure of the Buddha near the ancient capital of Kamakura, some twenty miles south. The British and French forces would withdraw from Yokohama only in 1875.

44. William L. Neumann, *America Encounters Japan*, p. 58.

45. Walter LaFeber, *The Clash*, pp. 27–29.

46. William Lockwood, *The Economic Development of Japan*, p. 8.

47. Walter LaFeber, *The Clash*, p. 29.

48. Foster Rhea Dulles, *America in the Pacific*, p. 74.

49. Albert M. Craig and Donald H. Shively (eds.), *Personality in Japanese History*, p. 39.

50. Peter Duus, *The Rise of Modern Japan*, p. 60.

51. Andrew Gordon, *A Modern History of Japan*, p. 52.

52. Patrick Smith, *Japan: a Reinterpretation*, p. 58.

53. Although the relatively quick crash of the *bakufu* soon to take place would speak of its weakness, many factors promised stability and "the vitality it possessed even during its last years." Albert M. Craig and Donald H. Shively, *Personality in Japanese History*, p. 3. Putting it another way, an historian of the period concluded that "no [pre-Perry] internal crisis or development could muster sufficient shock force to seriously endanger the regime." Jeffrey Mass in *The Bakufu in Japanese History*, p. 9.

54. Ryotaro Shiba, *Drunk as a Lord*, p. 108. The historian William Lockwood used another metaphor, that of a winter of discontent's snow that spring would have melted in due course. "The presence of Perry in the Bay of Yedo [*sic*] was like an untimely thaw . . . in February. The snow melted, the streams gathered . . . the shogunate and the feudal system were washed away." *The Economic Development of Japan*, p. 8.

55. Marius B. Jansen and Gilbert Rozman, *Japan in Transition*, p. 279.

56. *Narrative*, p. 349.

57. Tokyo means "East Capital," which distinguished it from the West Capital of Kyoto.

58. Marius B. Jansen and Gilbert Rozman, *Japan in Transition*, p. 16.

59. A Council of Local Officials was convened in 1875 and assemblies of the prefectures, usually composed of at least several of the old *han*, were in formal session fifteen years later. The first Imperial Diet, or national parliament, opened in 1890.

60. Patrick Smith, *Japan: A Reinterpretation*, pp. 62–63.

61. Carol Gluck, *Japan's Modern Myths*, p. 3.

62. Some aspects of the twenty-first-century Japanese economy still seem faintly military, especially in the Tokyo bureaucracies that have much to do with giving it direction. One observer recently called it "a wartime economy operating in peacetime."

63. Cyril Black (ed.), *The Modernization of Japan and Russia*, p. 130.

64. Patrick Smith, *Japan: A Reinterpretation*, p. 56.

65. Shmuel N. Eisenstadt, *Japanese Civilization*, p. 429.

66. Margaret MacMillan, *Paris 1919*, p. 320.

67. Interview with Dr. Yamaguchi Eitetsu, November 3, 2003.

68. At that point, in 1905, most of the Japanese battleships had been bought from England, but native yards were learning to build superior ones of their own.

69. Ferdinand Kuhn, *Commodore Perry and the Opening of Japan*, p. 157.

70. Edwin Falk, *From Perry to Pearl Harbor*, p. 186.

71. The abolished *han* was called Nagaoka. Lord Takano Tadamichi was, of course, a high-ranking samurai.

72. "We were accustomed to congratulating ourselves on how Commodore Perry, less than one hundred years earlier, had 'opened' Japan with a naval show of force. The benighted Japanese had been urged to learn from and emulate the civilized West. They did." John Paton Davies, *Dragon by the Tail*, p. 217.

73. Willard Price, "America's Enemy No. 2: Yamamoto," *Harper's Magazine*, April 1942, p. 451.

74. Shiba, Ryotaro, *Drunk as a Lord*, p. 163.

75. Christopher Bayly and Tim Harper, *Forgotten Armies: The Fall of British Asia, 1941–1945*.

CHAPTER 19

1. Irokawa Daikichi, *The Culture of the Meiji Period*, p. 6.

2. Andrew Gordon, *A Modern History of Japan*, p. 49.

3. Alex Kerr, *Dogs and Demons*, p. 359.

4. Sugimoto Etsu Inagaki, *A Daughter of the Samurai*, pp. 7, 95.

5. Ibid., p. 31.

6. Quoted in Andrew Gordon, *The Modern History of Japan*, p. 51. Toson Shimazaki put it a little differently: "What they [the foreigners] wanted from us was not the culture that Japan had built up over the centuries, but sulfur, camphor, silk, and the gold and silver produced in these islands. . . . Formerly we had despised money, now it was worshiped and it was all the same thing." *Before the Dawn*, p. 723.

7. Hal Porter, *The Actors: An Image of the New Japan*, p. 14.

8. Susan Stewart makes a strong argument for that in *On Longing* (1984). The past sought by nostalgia, the lack felt, "has never existed except as narrative."

9. Irokawa Daikichi, *The Culture of the Meiji Period*, p. 7.

10. John Nathan, *Japan Unbound*, pp. 8–9.

11. Ian Buruma, *The Wages of Guilt*, p. 36.

12. John Whitney Hall, "Changing Conceptions" in Marius B. Jansen (ed.), *Changing Japanese Attitudes Toward Modernization*, p. 11.

13. John Nathan, *Japan Unbound*, p. 5.

14. Ibid., p. 51. Irokawa notes that the early Meiji period is therefore said to be "the most dramatic in Japanese history."

15. James Thomson et al., *Sentimental Imperialists*, p. 207. Deep suspicion of Russian motives was another trait MacArthur shared with the Commodore. See p. 219.

16. Kishida Shu, *A Place for Apology*, p. 8. People might still have wanted to protest against Perry, but that was now a "wild dream," professor Kishida added.

17. Cited in Patrick Smith, *Japan, A Reinterpretation*, p. 42.

18. Ian Buruma, *Behind the Mask*, pp. 16–17.

19. See pp. 135 and 244.

20. Partially accurate as that was, the thirtieth president revealed that his understanding of Perry's effect was as weak as that of almost all other Americans by writing that thanks to Manjiro, "Perry could enjoy so cordial a reception."

21. Historian, journalist, and translator Junji Kitadai, "The United States & Japan: 150 Years of Transpacific History," February 19, 2004, speaking at the Japan Society, New York.

22. John Nathan, *Japan Unbound*, p. 9.

23. Kenneth Butler and Kishida Shu, *The Black Ships Trauma*, p. 2. A devoted Freudian approach probably *is* required to fit Perry's view of the Japanese as effeminate to the interpretation of his mission as rape. But the logic of humiliation and resentment should be obvious to non-Freudians. Many students of China, among other Asian countries, emphasize that was what its people felt for having been forced to open to Western traders and missionaries, and to relinquish sovereignty over parts of their country by granting extraterritoriality to foreign enclaves.

24. Marius B. Jansen, *The Making of Modern Japan*, p. 94. Crackpot or not, some Japanese continue to insist on roughly the opposite: that a wrongful desire for, or identification with, nonindigenous thoughts and things is ruining the country. Their solution is to make the Japanese people confident and proud again by returning to pre-Perry ideals, specifically the samurai spirit.

25. See Pineau's Introduction to his *The Japan Expedition, 1852–1854: The Personal Journal of Commodore Matthew C. Perry*. Another little statue stands in the shadow of the capital's Tokyo Tower, in a little park between it and beautiful Zojoji Temple's ample grounds. In 1927, the Japanese erected a monument to Townsend Harris too, near the Shimoda where he began his service as the U.S. minister.

26. *Black Ships Off Japan*, p. 234.

27. *Journal*, p. xviii.

28. Samuel Eliot Morison, "*Old Bruin*," p. 443.

29. *Commodore Perry and the Opening of Japan*, p. 158.

30. Patrick Smith, *Japan: A Reinterpretation*, pp. 42, 45.

31. Japanese acceptance and denial of their geographic and temperamental place in the world may be linked to that, partly through Perry's blow to national pride. Ever since his arrival, Richard McGregor contends, the country "has swung, almost schizophrenically" between "insisting on not being Asian at all, and declaring itself the epitome of Asianness." *Japan Swings*, p. 40.

Jack Seward attributes the instant-switch facility to a profound attachment to bedrock values. "As quickly and easily as the Japanese can adapt what they want from foreign cultures, they can with equal quickness and ease turn their backs on those cultures." That probably reveals "that underneath the changing surface of the Japanese national character lies a constant, hard-to-change base, at the core of which is their devotion to their own culture and its values." *The Japanese*, p. 70.

32. William L. Neumann, *America Encounters Japan*, p. 61.

33. Ibid., p. 51.

34. Oliver Statler, *Shimoda Story*, p. 574.

35. Hall, John W. [et al] ed., *Cambridge History of Japan*, p. 488.

36. Toson Shimazaki, *Before the Dawn*, p. 722.

37. Interview with Professor Fred C. Notehelfer, November 15, 2003.

38. Toson Shimazaki, *Before the Dawn*, pp. 722–23.

39. See Karatsu Rie "Cultural Absorption of Ballroom Dancing in Japan."

40. See p. 17.

41. Douglas Sladen, *Queer Things about Japan*, p. vii.

42. George B. Sansom, *The Western World and Japan*, p. 282.

43. Peter Duus, *The Japanese Discovery of America*, pp. 36–37.

44. Alain Peyrefitte, *The Collision of Two Civilizations*, p. 549.

45. Cited in John Nathan, *Japan Unbound*, p. 11.

46. Ibid, p. 12.

47. Kishida Shu, "Curing Japan's Schizophrenia," in *Hokubei Mainichi* (a San Francisco daily newspaper), November 29, 1986: a translation of the original article in *Tomiuri Shimbun*.

48. James Thomson et al., *Sentimental Imperialists*, p. 295.

49. Andrew Horvat's *Open Up, Japan!* pp. 31–63, offers many persuasive accounts of such ostracizing together with a strong summary of the enduring self-isolation in general.

50. Hal Porter provides startling examples in *The Actors: An Image of the New Japan*.

51. William Beasley, *Japanese Imperialism*, p. 27.

52. Frederick Wells Williams, Prefatory Note to Samuel Wells Williams, *A Journal of the Perry Expedition to Japan*, p. ix.

AFTERWORD

1. Newport also hosts a Black Ships Festival every July.

2. John H. Schroeder, *Matthew Calbraith Perry*, p. xiii.

3. Frederic Trautmann's Introduction to Wilhelm Heine, *With Perry to Japan*, p. 4.

4. Francis Hall, *Japan Though American Eyes*, p. 378.

5. Toson Shimazaki, *Before the Dawn*, p. 93.

6. George Henry Preble, *The Opening of Japan*, p. 138.

7. Samuel Wells Williams, *A Journal of the Perry Expedition to Japan*, p. vi.

8. Ferdinand Kuhn makes a typical argument for that view in his *Commodore Perry and the Opening of Japan*, p. 160. When the Commodore, he maintains, "came knocking at the closed door of Japan," he "had a chance to do the same" as the Dutch and British, who had already seized Asian colonies, or the French, who were bombarding towns and killing civilians in their conquest of Indo-China. "He could have pushed [the closed door] by force, but he and his government in Washington were wise enough not to do so."

9. A paper by Perry read before the American Geographical and Statistical Society on March 6, 1856.

10. To take just a few of countless recent examples, President Richard Nixon's description of the United States as the only great power in history "without imperialist claims" was seconded by an assertion of Sandy Berger, President Bill Clinton's National Security Advisor, that the U.S. was the "first global power in history" not to be an imperial power, and by an unequivocal statement of President George W. Bush in 2003: "America has never been an empire. It was the only great power in history that had a chance to be and refused" because it preferred "greatness to power, justice to glory." *New York Times*, February 26, 2003.

11. Christopher Benfey, "Tom Cruise, Bob Dylan, Commodore Perry," *The Great Wave*, also in *the New York Times*, December 6, 2003, p. A15. Benfey's book was published in 2003.

12. See James Gould, "American Imperialism in Southeast Asia Before 1898."

13. Ferdinand Kuhn, *Commodore Perry and the Opening of Japan*, p. 161.

14. Samuel Wells Williams, *A Journal of the Perry Expedition to Japan*, p. 158.

15. Francis Hall, *Japan Through American Eyes*, p. 401.

16. William Beasley, *Select Documents on Japanese Foreign Policy*, p. 25.

17. Mitani Hiroshi, *Escape from Impasse*, p. 294.

BIBLIOGRAPHY

___

BOOKS

Arakawa, Yuko, and Yamaguchi, Eitetsu. *The Demise of the Ryukyu Kingdom: Western Accounts and Controversy*. Ginowan City, Okinawa: Yojushorin, 2002.

Asakawa, Kanichi. *Letters of Kanichi Asakawa*. Tokyo: Waseda University Press, 1990.

Auslin, Michael R. *Negotiating with Imperialism: The Unequal Treaties and the Culture of Japanese Diplomacy*. Cambridge: Harvard University Press, 2004.

Bailey, Thomas. *A Diplomatic History of the American People*. Englewood Cliffs, NJ: Prentice-Hall, 1980.

Barr, Pat. *The Coming of the Barbarians: A Story of Western Settlement in Japan, 1853–1871*. London: Macmillan, 1967.

Barrows, Edward M. *The Great Commodore: The Exploits of Matthew Calbraith Perry*. Indianapolis and New York: Bobbs-Merrill, 1935.

Bayly, Christopher, and Tim Harper. *Forgotten Armies: The Fall of British Asia, 1941–1945*. Cambridge, MA: Belknap Press, 2005.

Beasley, William. *Japan Encounters the Barbarian: Japanese Travelers in America and Europe*. New Haven: Yale University Press, 1995.

———. *Japanese Imperialism, 1894–1945*. Oxford: Clarendon Press, 1987.

——— (ed.). *Select Documents on Japanese Foreign Policy, 1853–1868*. London: Oxford University Press, 1955.

Benfey, Christopher. *The Great Wave: Gilded Age Misfits, Japanese Eccentrics, and the Opening of Old Japan*. New York: Random House, 2003.

Black, Cyril E. (ed.). *The Modernization of Japan and Russia: A Comparative Study*. New York: Free Press, 1975.

Boxer, Charles. *The Christian Century in Japan, 1549–1650*. Berkeley: University of California Press, 1951.

Buruma, Ian. *Behind the Mask: On Sexual Demons, Sacred Mothers, Transvestites, Gangsters, Drifters and Other Japanese Cultural Heroes*. New York: Pantheon, 1984.

————. *Inventing Japan: 1853–1964*. New York: Modern Library, 2003.

————. *The Wages of Guilt: Memories of War in Germany and Japan*. London: Jonathan Cape, 1994.

Bush, Lewis William. *77 Samurai: Japan's First Embassy to America*. Tokyo: Kodansha International, 1968.

Busk, M. M. (ed.). *Manners and Customs of the Japanese in the Nineteenth Century*. New York: Harper, 1841.

Butler, Kenneth, with Shu Kishida. *Kurofune genso* (The Black Ships Trauma). Tokyo: Treville, 1986.

Butow, Robert. *Japan's Decision to Surrender*. Stanford, CA: Stanford University Press, 1954.

Chang, Richard T. *From Prejudice to Tolerance: A Study of the Japanese Image of the West 1826–1864*. Tokyo: Sophia University Press, 1970.

Cole, Allan Burnett. *The Dynamics of American Expansion toward Japan, 1791–1860*. Chicago: University of Chicago, 1943.

————. *Japanese Society and Politics: The Impact of Social Stratification and Mobility on Politics*. Boston: Boston University, 1956.

————. *A Scientist with Perry in Japan: The Journal of Dr. James Morrow*. Chapel Hill: University of North Carolina Press, 1947.

———— (ed.). *With Perry in Japan: The Diary of Edward Yorke McCauley*. Princeton: Princeton University Press, 1942.

Costello, John. *The Pacific War: 1941–1945*. New York: Rawson, Wade, 1981.

Craig, Albert M., and Donald H. Shively (eds.). *Personality in Japanese History*. Berkeley: University of California Press, 1970.

Daikichi, Irokawa. *The Culture of the Meiji Period*. Edited by Marius B. Jansen. Princeton, NJ: Princeton University Press, 1985.

Davies, John Paton. *Dragon by the Tail: American, British, Japanese, and Russian Encounters with China and One Another*. New York: Norton, 1972.

De Fonblanque, Edward B. *Niphon and Pe-che-li, or Two Years in Japan and Northern China*. London: Saunders, Otley & Co., 1862.

Diamond, Jared. *Guns, Germs, and Steel: The Fates of Human Societies*. New York: Norton, 1999.

Dower, John W. *War Without Mercy: Race and Power in the Pacific War*. New York: Pantheon, 1986.

Dulles, Foster Rhea. *America in the Pacific: A Century of Expansion*. Boston: Houghton Mifflin, 1932.

————. *Yankees and Samurai: America's Role in the Emergence of Modern Japan, 1791–1900*. New York: Harper & Row, 1965.

Duus, Peter. *Feudalism in Japan*. New York: Knopf, 1969.

————. *The Japanese Discovery of America: A Brief History with Documents*. Boston: Bedford Books, 1997.

————. *The Rise of Modern Japan*. Boston: Houghton Mifflin, 1976.

The editors of Time-Life Books. *The U.S. Overseas*. New York: Time-Life Books, 1969.

Edwardes. Michael. *East-West Passage: The Travel of Ideas, Arts and Inventions between Asia and the Western World*. New York: Taplinger Publishing, 1971.

Eisenstadt, Shmuel N. *Japanese Civilization: A Comparative View*. Chicago: University of Chicago Press, 1996.

Falk, Edwin. *From Perry to Pearl Harbor: The Struggle for Supremacy in the Pacific.* New York: Doubleday, 1943.

Ferguson, Niall. *Colossus: The Price of American Empire.* New York: Penguin, 2004.

————. *Empire: The Rise and Demise of the British World Order and the Lessons for Global Power.* New York: Basic Books, 2003.

Fewster, Stuart, and Tony Gorton. *Japan: From Shogun to Superstate.* New York: St. Martin's Press, 1987.

Fukuzawa, Yukichi. *The Autobiography of Yukichi Fukuzawa.* Tokyo: The Hokuseido Press, 1948.

Gaddis, John Lewis. *Surprise, Security, and the American Experience.* Cambridge, MA: Harvard University Press, 2004.

Gerster, Robin. *Legless in Ginza: Orientating Japan.* Melbourne: Melbourne University Press, 1999.

Gluck, Carol. *Japan's Modern Myths: Ideology in the Late Meiji Period.* Princeton: Princeton University Press, 1985.

Golovnin, Vasili M. *Memoirs of a Captivity in Japan During the Years 1811, 1812, and 1813.* London: Henry Colburn, 1924.

Goncharov, Ivan A. *The Frigate* Pallada. New York: St. Martin's Press, 1987.

Gordon, Andrew. *A Modern History of Japan: From Tokugawa Times to the Present.* Oxford: Oxford University Press, 2003.

Gowen, Herbert H. *Five Foreigners in Japan.* New York: Fleming H. Revell, 1936.

Graff, Henry F. (ed.). *Bluejackets with Perry in Japan: A Day-by-Day Account Kept by Master's Mate John R.C. Lewis and Cabin Boy William B. Allen.* New York: New York Public Library, 1952.

Grew, Joseph. *Ten Years in Japan: A Contemporary Record Drawn from the Diaries and Private and Official Papers of Joseph G. Grew, United States Ambassador to Japan.* New York: Simon & Schuster, 1944.

Griffis, William Eliot. *Matthew Calbraith Perry: A Typical American Naval Officer.* Boston: Cupples and Hurd, 1887.

Gubbins, John Harriton. *The Making of Modern Japan.* London: Seeley, Service, 1922.

Hall, Francis. *Japan Through American Eyes: The Journal of Francis Hall, Kanagawa and Yokohama, 1859–1866.* Edited by Fred G. Notehelfer. Princeton, NJ: Princeton University Press, 1992.

Hall, John, and Jansen, Marius B. (eds). *Studies in the Institutional History of Tokugawa Japan.* Princeton, NJ: Princeton University Press, 1968.

Hane, Mikiso. *Modern Japan: A Historical Survey.* Boulder, CO: Westview Press, 1986.

————. *Premodern Japan: A Historical Survey.* Boulder, CO: Westview Press, 1991.

Hanley, Susan. *Everyday Things in Premodern Japan: The Hidden Legacy of Material Culture.* Berkeley: University of California Press, 1997.

Hansen-Taylor, Marie, and Horace Scudder. *Life and Letters of Bayard Taylor* (two vols.). Boston: Houghton, Mifflin, 1884.

Hearn, Lafcadio. *Japan: An Interpretation.* New York: Macmillan, 1904.

————. *The Selected Writings of Lafcadio Hearn.* New York: Citadel Press, 1949.

Heine, Wilhelm. *With Perry to Japan.* Honolulu: University of Hawaii Press, 1990.

Horvat, Andrew. *Open Up, Japan!* Tokyo: Kodansha, 1998.

Houchins, Chang-su. *Artifacts of Diplomacy: Smithsonian Collections from Commodore Matthew Perry's Japan Expedition, 1853–1854.* Washington, DC: Smithsonian Institution Press, 1995.

Huffman, James L. *Creating a Public: People and Press in Meiji Japan.* Honolulu: University of Hawaii Press, 1997.

Icenhower, Joseph B. *Perry and the Open Door to Japan.* New York: Franklin Watts, 1973.

Irye, Akira. *Power and Culture.* Cambridge: Harvard University Press, 1981.

Jansen, Marius B. (ed.). *Changing Japanese Attitudes Toward Modernization.* Princeton: Princeton University Press, 1965.

———. *The Making of Modern Japan.* Cambridge, MA: Harvard University Press, 2000.

———, and Gilbert Rozman (eds.). *Japan in Transition: From Tokugawa to Meiji.* Princeton, NJ: Princeton University Press, 1986.

Jansen, Marius B., et al. (ed.). *The Cambridge History of Japan* (6 vols.). Cambridge: Cambridge University Press, 1988–1999.

Kamikawa, Hikamatsu. *Japan-American Diplomatic Relations in the Meiji-Taisho Era.* Tokyo: Pan-Pacific Press, 1956.

Katsu, Kokichi. *Musui's Story: The Autobiography of a Tokugawa Samurai.* Tucson: University of Arizona Press, 1988.

Keene, Donald (ed.). *Anthology of Japanese Literature.* Tokyo: Tuttle, 1956.

——— (ed.). *Anthology of Japanese Literature from the Earliest Era to the Mid-Nineteenth Century.* New York: Grove Press, 1955.

———. *Emperor of Japan: Meiji and His World, 1852–1912.* New York: Columbia University Press, 2002.

———. *The Japanese Discovery of Europe, 1720–1830.* Stanford: Stanford University Press, 1969.

———. *Travelers of a Hundred Ages: The Japanese as Revealed Through 1,000 Years of Diaries.* New York: Henry Holt, 1989.

———. *Yoshimasa and the Silver Pavilion: The Creation of the Soul of Japan.* New York: Columbia University Press, 2003.

Kendall, George Wilkins. *Dispatches From the Mexican War.* Norman, OK: University of Oklahoma Press, 1999.

———. *The War Between the United States and Mexico.* New York: Appleton, 1851.

Kennedy, Malcolm D. *A History of Japan.* London: Weidenfeld & Nicolson, 1963.

Kerr, Alex. *Dogs and Demons: Tales from the Dark Side of Japan.* New York: Hill and Wang, 2001.

Kerr, George H. *Okinawa: The Story of an Island People.* Tokyo: Charles E. Tuttle, 1958.

Kimura, Ki. *Japanese Literature: Manners and Customs in the Meiji-Taisho Era.* Tokyo: Obunsha, 1957.

Kishida, Shu. *A Place for Apology: War, Guilt and U.S.–Japan Relations.* Dallas, TX: Hamilton Books, 2004.

Kodansha Encyclopedia of Japan. Tokyo: Kodansha International, 1983.

Kojima, Matajiro. *Commodore Perry's Expedition to Hakodate.* Tokyo: Hakodate Kyodo Bunkakai, 1953.

Komori, Tatsukuni. *Ningen Abe Masahiro to sono seiji.* Tokyo: Akashi Shoten, 1985.

Koschmann, J. Victor. *The Mito Ideology: Discourse, Reform and Insurrection in Late Tokugawa Japan, 1790–1864.* Berkeley: University of California Press, 1987.

Kuhn, Ferdinand. *Commodore Perry and the Opening of Japan*. New York: Random House, 1955.

LaFeber, Walter. *The Clash: A History of U.S.–Japan Relations*. New York: Norton, 1997.

Lehmann, Jean-Pierre. *The Image of Japan: From Feudal Isolation to World Power*. London: Allen & Unwin, 1978.

———. *The Roots of Modern Japan*. New York: St. Martin's Press, 1982.

Lensen, George Alexander. *Russia's Japan Expedition of 1852 to 1855*. Gainesville: University of Florida Press, 1955.

Lockwood, William. *The Economic Development of Japan: Growth and Structural Change, 1868–1938*. Princeton, NJ: Princeton University Press, 1954.

Lu, David J. *Japan: A Documentary History*. Armonk, NY: M.E. Sharpe, 1997.

MacMillan, Margaret. *Paris 1919: Six Months That Changed the World*. New York: Random House, 2003.

Mason, R.H.P., and J.G. Caiger. *A History of Japan*. Rutland, VT: Charles Tuttle, 1997.

Mass, Jeffrey P., and William B. Hauser (eds.). *The Bakufu in Japanese History*. Stanford, CA: Stanford University Press, 1985.

Matsumoto, Kenichi. *Daisan no Kaikoku to Nichibei Kankei* (The Third Opening of the Country and U.S.–Japan Relations). Tokyo: Daisan Bunmei Sah, 2004.

Mattice, Harold A. *Perry and Japan: An Account of the Empire and an Unpublished Record of the Perry Expedition*. New York: The New York Public Library, 1942.

McClain, James L., John M. Merriman, and Kaoru Ugawa (eds). *Edo and Paris: Urban Life and the State in the Early Modern Era*. Ithaca, NY: Cornell University Press, 1994.

McGregor, Richard. *Japan Swings: Politics, Culture and Sex in the New Japan*. London: Allen & Unwin, 1996.

Mehri, Darius. *Notes from Toyota-Land: An American Engineer in Japan*. Ithaca, NY: Cornell University Press, 2005.

Meiji Japan Through Contemporary Sources, volume 2: *1844–1882*. Tokyo: Centre for East Asian Cultural Studies, 1969.

Mitford, A. B. *Tales of Old Japan*. London: Macmillan, 1871.

Miwa, Kamitada. *Kakusareta Perry no shiro hara: Nichibei Kankei no Image ron teki, seishin shi teki kenkyu [Perry's Hidden White Flags: A Study in the Images and Intellectual History of the US-Japan Relationship]* Tokyo: Sophia University Press, 1999.

Miyoshi, Masao. *As We Saw Them: The First Japanese Embassy to the United States (1860)*.

Morison, Samuel Eliot. *"Old Bruin": Commodore Matthew Calbraith Perry: 1794–1858*. Boston: Atlantic Monthly Little, Brown, 1967.

Morrow, James. *A Scientist with Perry in Japan*. Chapel Hill: University of North Carolina Press, 1947.

Munroe, Kirk. *A Son of Satsuma, or With Perry in Japan*. New York: Scribner, 1922.

Nakahama, Akira. *Nakahama Manjiro no shogai* (The Life of Manjiro Nakahama). Tokyo: Toyama-bo, 1970.

Nathan, John. *Japan Unbound: A Volatile Nation's Quest for Pride and Purpose*. Boston: Houghton Mifflin, 2004.

Najita, Tetsuo. *Visions of Virtue in Tokugawa Japan: The Kaitokudo. Merchant Academy of Osaka*. Chicago: University of Chicago Press, 1987.

Neumann, William L. *America Encounters Japan: From Perry to MacArthur*. Baltimore, MD: Johns Hopkins University Press, 1963.

Nihon Hakugaku Club (eds.). *Rekishi no Igai na "Ura Jijo"* (Interesting Untold Historical Facts). Tokyo:PHP Research Institute, 2001.

Nihon no Kindai 1 [A History of Modern Japan], Kakoku Ishin [Opening the Country: Restoration, 1853–1971]. Tokyo: Chou Koran Sah, 1998.

Notehelfer, Fred. "What If Perry Had Not Come to Japan?: Reflections on 19th-Century Japan and the Idea of Alternatives."

Oblas, Peter. *Japan for the Asking*. Tokyo: Obunsha, 1984

Ooe, Shinoo. *Perry Kantai Dai Kokai Ki* (The Log of Perry's Big Fleet). Tokyo: Rippu Shobo, 1994.

Orrmont, Arthur. *The Indestructible Commodore Matthew Perry*. New York: Julian Messner, 1962.

Packard, Jerrold. *Sons of Heaven: A Portrait of the Japanese Monarchy*. New York: Scribner, 1987.

Palmer, Aaron Haight. *Documents and Facts Illustrating the Origin of the Mission to Japan*. Washington: H. Polkinhorn, 1857.

Passin, Herbert (ed). *The United States and Japan*. Englewood Cliffs, NJ: Prentice-Hall, 1966.

Perrin, Noel. *Giving Up the Gun: Japan's Reversion to the Sword, 1543–1879*. Boston: David R. Godine, 1979.

Perry, John Curtis. *Facing West: Americans and the Opening of the Pacific*. Westport, CT: Praeger, 1994.

Perry, Commodore M.C. *Narrative of the Expedition to the China Seas and Japan, 1852–1854*. Mineola, NY: Dover Publications, 2000.

Perry, Matthew Calbraith. *The Japan Expedition, 1852–1854: The Personal Journal of Commodore Matthew C. Perry*. Edited by Roger Pineau. Washington, DC: Smithsonian Institution Press, 1968.

Perez, Louis G. *The History of Japan*. Westport, CT: Greenwood Press, 1998.

Peyrefitte, Alain. *The Collision of Two Civilizations: The British Expedition to China 1792–4*. London: Harvill, 1993.

Plummer, Katherine. *The Shogun's Reluctant Ambassadors: Japanese Sea Drifters in the North Pacific*. Portland, OR: The Oregon Historical Society, 1991.

Porter, Hal. *The Actors: An Image of the New Japan*. Sydney: Angus and Robertson, 1968.

Preble, George Henry. *The Opening of Japan: A Diary of Discovery in the Far East, 1853–1856*. Norman, OK: University of Oklahoma Press, 1962.

Reischauer, Edwin O., and Albert M. Craig. *Japan: Tradition and Transformation*. Boston: Houghton Mifflin, 1978.

Roberson, John R. *Japan: From Shogun to Sony 1543–1984*. New York: Atheneum, 1985

Rodrigues, Jo"o. *This Island of Japan*. Tokyo: Kodansha International, 1973.

Sansom, George B. *Japan: A Short Cultural History*. New York: Appleton-Century-Crofts, 1962.

———. *A History of Japan*. Stanford, CA: Stanford University Press, 1958–1963.

———. *The Western World and Japan: A Study in the Interaction of Eastern and Asiatic Cultures*. New York: Random House, 1949.

Sato, Kazuhiko. *Tanoshiku Shiraberu Zukai Nihon Rekishi Bakumatsu Meiji Ishin Ni Kaksuyaku Shita Hitobito* (The Illustrated Book of People in Japanese History: People Who Played an Important Role at the End of the Edo Period and During the Meiji Restoration). Tokyo: Tokyo University of Arts and Sciences, 2000.

Schroeder, John H. *Matthew Calbraith Perry: Antebellum Sailor and Diplomat*. Annapolis: Naval Institute Press, 2001.

Schwantes, Robert S. *Japanese and Americans: A Century of Cultural Relations*. Westport, CT: Greenwood Press, 1955.

Sewall, John. *The Logbook of the Captain's Clerk: Adventures in the China Seas*. Chicago: Lakeside Press, 1995.

Seward, Jack. *The Americans and the Japanese*. Tokyo: New Currents International, 1990

———. *The Japanese*. New York: William Morrow, 1972.

Shiba, Ryotaro. *Drunk as a Lord: Samurai Stories*. Tokyo: Kodansha International, 2001.

———. *The Last Shogun: The Life of Tokugawa Yoshinobu*. Tokyo: Kodansha International, 1998.

Shin Jinbutsu Oraisha hen. *Abe Masahiro no subete*. Tokyo: Shin Jinbutsu Oraisha, 1997.

Sladen, Douglas B. W. *Queer Things about Japan*. Detroit: Singing Tree Press, 1968.

Smith, George. *Lewchew and the Lewchewans: Being a Narrative of a Visit to Lewchew or Loo Choo in October, 1850*. London: T. Hatchard, 1853.

Smith, Justin Harvey. *The War with Mexico*. Gloucester, MA: Peter Smith, 1963.

Smith, Patrick. *Japan: A Reinterpretation*. New York: Pantheon, 1997.

Sofue, Ichiro. *Abe Masahiro*. Tokyo: PHP Kenkyujo, 2002.

Spalding, J. Willett. *The Japan Expedition: Japan and around the world; an account of three visits to the Japanese empire with sketches of Madeira, St. Helena, cape of Good Hope, Mauritius, Ceylon, Singapore, China, and Loo-Choo*. Boston: Adamant Media, 2005. (Reprint of 1855 edition by Redfield in New York.)

Sproston, John Glendy. *A Private Journal of John Glendy Sproston*. Tokyo: Sophia University, 1940.

Statler, Oliver. *The Black Ships Scroll: An Account of the Perry Expedition at Shimoda in 1854*. Rutland, VT: C. E. Tuttle, 1964.

———. *Shimoda Story*. Tokyo: Charles Tuttle, 1971.

Steele, M. William. *Alternative Narratives in Modern Japanese History*. London: Routledge Curzon, 2003.

Stewart, Susan. *On Longing: Narratives of the Miniature, the Gigantic, the Souvenir, the Collection*. Durham, NC: Duke University Press, 1993.

Sugimoto, Etsu Inagaki. *A Daughter of the Samurai*. New York: Doubleday, 1930.

Tamarin, Alfred H. *Japan and the United States: Early Encounters 1791–1860*. New York: Macmillan, 1970.

Taylor, Bayard. *A Visit to India, China, and Japan, in the Year 1853*. New York: G. P. Putnam, 1859.

———. *Perry's Bay: Being an Eye-Witness Accounting Aboard the Flagship* Susquehanna. Hollywood, CA: W. M. Hawley, 1995.

Toson, Shimazaki. *Before the Dawn*. Honolulu: University of Hawaii Press, 1987.

Thomson Jr., James C., Peter W. Stanley, and John Curtis Perry. *Sentimental Imperialists: The American Experience in East Asia*. New York: Harper, 1981.

Tokunaga, Shin'ichiro. *Bakumatsu kakuryoden*. Tokyo: PHP Kenkyujo, 1989.

Totman, Conrad D. *A History of Japan*. Malden, MA: Blackwell, 2000.

———. *Early Modern Japan*. Berkeley: University of California Press, 1993.

————— *Japan Before Perry: A Short History*. Berkeley: University of California Press, 1981.

—————. *Politics in the Tokugawa Bakufu, 1600–1843*. Cambridge: Harvard University Press, 1967.

————— *Tokugawa Ieyasu, Shogun: A Biography*. San Francisco: Heian International, 1983.

Tsurumi, Shunsuke. *An Intellectual History of Wartime Japan, 1931–1945*. London: KPI, Ltd., 1986.

Van der Post, Laurens. *The Prisoner and the Bomb*. New York: Morrow, 1971.

Varley, H. Paul. *Japanese Culture: A Short History*. New York: Praeger, 1977.

————— *The Onin War: History of its Origins and Background with a Selective Translation of The Chronicle of Onin*. New York: Columbia University Press, 1967.

Wakabayashi, Bob Tadashi. *Anti-Foreignism and Western Learning in Early-Modern Japan: The "New Theses" of 1825*. Cambridge, MA: Harvard University Press, 1986.

Walworth, Arthur. *Black Ships Off Japan: The Story of Commodore Perry's Expedition*. Hamden, CT: Archon Books, 1966.

Watanabe, Shujiro. *Abe Masahiro jiseki* (2 vols.). Tokyo: Tokyo Daigaku Shuppankai, 1978.

Wiley, Peter Booth. *Yankees in the Land of the Gods: Commodore Perry and the Opening of Japan*. New York: Penguin, 1991.

Williams, Frederick Wells. *The Life and Letters of Samuel Wells Williams*. Wilmington, DE: Scholarly Resources, 1972.

Williams, Samuel Wells. *A Journal of the Perry Expedition to Japan (1853–1854)*. Yokohama: Kelly & Walsh, Ltd., 1910.

Wray, Harry, and Hilary Conroy. *Japan Examined: Perspectives on Modern Japanese History*. Honolulu: University of Hawaii Press, 1983.

Yamamoto, Tsunetomo. *Hagakure: The Book of the Samurai*. Tokyo: Kodansha International, 1979.

Yanaga, Chitoshi. *Japan Since Perry*. New York: McGraw-Hill, 1949.

Zakaria, Fareed. *From Wealth to Power: The Unusual Origins of America's World Role*. Princeton, NJ: Princeton University Press, 1998.

ARTICLES AND MEMORANDA

"A Doctor's Memorandum," unsigned diary entries by an Edo physician in Roger Pineau Papers, 1966–1985, number 89–010, Box 1, Location A08/11/12, Smithsonian Institution Libraries.

Bolitho, Harold. "Abe Masahiro and the New Japan." In Mass, Jeffrey P., and William B. Hauser. *The Bakufu in Japanese History*. Stanford, CA: Stanford University Press, 1985.

—————. "Tokugawa Shogunate." In *Kodansha Encyclopedia of Japan*. Tokyo: Kodansha International, 1983.

"Diary of an Official of the Bakufu" in *Transactions of the Asiatic Society of Japan*, second series, 7 (December 1930), pp. 98–119.

Gallacher, Robert. "Castaways on Forbidden Shores." In *American Heritage* 19, no. 4, June 1968.

Gordon, Leonard. "Early American Relations with Formosa 1849–1870." In *The Historian* 19, no. 3 (May 1957).

Gould, James W. "American Imperialism in Southeast Asia Before 1898." In *Journal of Southeast Asian Studies* 3, no. 2. September, 1972.

Hale, William Harlan. "When Perry Unlocked the 'Gate of the Sun.' " In *American Heritage* 9, no. 3 (April 1958).

Hall, Basil Chamberlain. "The Luchu Islands and Their Inhabitants." In *The Geographical Journal* 5, no. 4 (April 1895).

Kayama, Eizaemon. "Memorandum of Kayama Eizaemon, *yoriki* (police magistrate) in the staff of the Uraga Governor." In Roger Pineau Papers, Smithsonian Institution archive, accession 89-010, box 1.

Karatsu, Rie. "Cultural Absorption of Ballroom Dancing in Japan." In *Journal of Popular Culture*, January 2003.

Miwa, Kimitada. "Perry's Fourth Letter and Nitobe Inazo." In *Japan and China: Miscellaneous Papers*. London: London School of Economics, 1993.

Sakamaki, Shunzo. "Japan and the United States." Reprinted in *Transactions of the Asiatic Society of Japan* 18 (1939).

———. "Western Concepts of Japan and the Japanese 1800–1854." In *Pacific Historical Review* 6 (1937), pp. 1–14.

Sewall, John. "With Perry in Japan: Personal Recollections of the Expedition of 1853–54" in *The Century Illustrated Monthly Magazine* 70, no. 3 (July 1905).

Shizuteru, Ueda. "Nishida, Nationalism, and the War in Question." In Heisig, James W., and John C. Maraldo (eds.). *Rude Awakenings: Zen, the Kyoto School, and the Question of Nationalism*. Honolulu: University of Hawaii Press, 1995.

Spector, Ronald. "The American Image of Southeast Asia, 1790–1865." In *Journal of Southeast Asia Studies* 3, no. 2. September, 1972.

Toby, Ronald. "Reopening the Question of Sakoku. Diplomacy in the Legitimization of the Tokugawa Bakufu." In *Journal of Japanese Studies* 3, no. 2 (Summer 1977), 323–363.

Totman, Conrad. "Political Reconciliation in the Tokugawa Bakufu: Abe Masahiro and Tokugawa Nariaki, 1844–1852." In Craig, Albert M., and Donald H. Shively (eds.). *Personality in Japanese History*. Berkeley: University of California Press, 1970.

Von Doenhoff, Richard A. "Biddle, Perry and Japan." In *United States Naval Institute Proceedings* 92, no. 11 (November 1966).

Williams, Samuel Wells. "Narrative of a Voyage of the Ship *Morrison*, Captain Ingersoll, to Lewchew and Japan, in the Months of July and August, 1837." In *The Chinese Repository* 6, no. 8 (December 1837).

INDEX